VOICES FROM CAPTIVITY

of related interest

The Forgiveness Project
Stories for a Vengeful Age
Marina Cantacuzino
Forewords by Archbishop Emeritus Desmond
Tutu and Alexander McCall Smith
ISBN 978 1 78592 000 4 (Paperback)
ISBN 978 1 84905 566 6 (Hardback)
eISBN 978 1 78450 006 1

Voices of Modern Islam
What It Means to Be Muslim Today
Declan Henry
ISBN 978 1 78592 401 9
eISBN 978 1 78450 763 3

Peace Inside
A Prisoner's Guide to Meditation
Edited by Sam Settle
Foreword by Benjamin Zephaniah
Illustrated by Pollyanna Morgan
ISBN 978 1 78592 235 0
eISBN 978 1 78450 528 8

Violence, Restorative Justice, and Forgiveness
Dyadic Forgiveness and Energy Shifts
in Restorative Justice Dialogue
Marilyn Armour and Mark Umbreit
ISBN 978 1 78592 795 9
eISBN 978 1 78450 795 4

Psychiatry in Prisons
A Comprehensive Handbook
Edited by Simon Wilson and Ian Cumming
ISBN 978 1 84310 223 6
eISBN 978 0 85700 206 8
Part of the *Forensic Focus* series

VOICES FROM CAPTIVITY

Incarceration from Siberia to Guantánamo Bay

J E THOMAS

Jessica Kingsley *Publishers*
London and Philadelphia

First published in 2018
by Jessica Kingsley Publishers
73 Collier Street
London N1 9BE, UK
and
400 Market Street, Suite 400
Philadelphia, PA 19106, USA

www.jkp.com

Library of Congress Cataloging in Publication Data
Names: Thomas, James Edward, 1933- author.
Title: Voices from captivity : personal experiences of incarceration / James
    Edward Thomas.
Description: Philadelphia : Jessica Kingsley Publishers, [2018] | Includes
    bibliographical references.
Identifiers: LCCN 2018002446 | ISBN 9781785924989
Subjects: LCSH: Imprisonment. | Prisoners' writings, English.
Classification: LCC HV8705 .T46 2018 | DDC 365/.60922--
dc23 LC record available at https://lccn.loc.gov/2018002446

British Library Cataloguing in Publication Data
A CIP catalogue record for this book is available from the British Library

ISBN 978 1 78592 498 9
eISBN 978 1 78450 884 5

Printed and bound in Great Britain

MIX
Paper from
responsible sources
FSC   FSC® C013056
www.fsc.org

What is it you would see?
If aught of woe or wonder cease your search.

Horatio in *Hamlet* Act V Scene 11

This book is for our daughters-in-law, Colleen and Carol, and
for our grandchildren, Joseph, Henry, Emily and Matilda.
May they remember those whose freedom has been lost.

Acknowledgements

I have to thank Hazel Mills for the amount of work she has put in to making this script presentable. My debt to her for her work here and in previous books is more than I can say. Olwen Thomas has worked very hard indeed at checking the manuscript, especially the notes. She was also of critical help in arriving at a title, and I thank her. I am indebted, too, to Tilda Yolland for reading the script so carefully and for correcting errors, as well as pointing out sentences which were unintelligible. Thanks go to Philip Thomas for discussion about possible illustrations, and to Simon Thomas for advice on legal matters.

I want to thank Professor Emeritus Malcolm Jones and Special Professor James Muckle, both of the University of Nottingham, for their help in trying to understand communications with Russian sources.

There are many people who help those seeking information. They are an undersung group. I want to thank the archivists in Australia, Carol Smith and Helen Ouf of The State Library of Western Australia; in Germany, Stefan Grote of the Bundesarchiv; in the USA, Scott Jacobs of the Clark Library, University College of Los Angeles; and, in England, Sarah Moore, Librarian at HM Prison Service College.

Contents

Introduction

This is a book about the experience of being locked up. I draw upon the reflections of hundreds of captives. These include rich and poor, people of all colours, men and women, old and young. They range from people who have stolen money to those who have tried to overthrow the state, or who have been accused of doing so. There are those who are guilty of heinous crimes and those who have committed no offence at all, or have engaged in behaviour which no civilised mature society would define as criminal. Some have had a chance to hear the evidence against them, and an opportunity to refute it, many have not.

I make no judgement on the reasons why people find themselves in captivity, or on the accuracy of what they say. The fact is that this is what they believe they experienced, and no one is in any position to say that they are mistaken.

Most of the evidence I have set out is first hand from the experience of captives. Occasionally it is second hand from those who have been in contact with captives. Sometimes I quote from purely academic or theoretical writing. I also sometimes draw on similarities between prisons and what Erving Goffman (1961) calls 'total institutions'. These include monastic establishments and the military. But the central fact about captivity remains: a person is locked up and has to cope with this horror. This horror is to be found across all cultures and traditions, and is timeless and universal.

I trace the career of the captive from the moment of being first locked up. I examine the shock of having to adjust to the loss of freedom, and having to live in a society of people thrown together at random. Next, I explore the strange relationship of the captor and captive, and then the ways of compensating for the key deprivation of sexual relations. The various forms of punishment and cruelties inflicted on captives, over and above the fact of imprisonment itself, are set out and then I deal with the especial plight of the political prisoner. Finally, I draw upon the problems captives face when the ostensibly happy day of release arrives. Although I have divided their experience into 'chapters', there is much overlapping: for example, sexual attacks on women are both a matter of sexual deprivation and the imposition of torture.

Many captives have written about their grief, their woe and their determination to overcome their quite extraordinary experience. It is impossible to do justice to all of their suffering or to their recovery from that suffering, and so, because of the sheer volume of reflection, I have had to be selective about the lives I have quoted. Nothing can adequately embrace the total misery of life in captivity which has been shared by millions.

— 1 —

On Being Locked Up

The overwhelming impression made upon new captives is that they are entombed. And yet they are alive, frightened, miserable and confused. Apart from the dire events which have led to their incarceration, there is the prospect, for the majority, of being propelled into a world which is beyond their imagining, but which they may be certain has no redeeming features.

Rupert Croft-Cooke was convicted of homosexual behaviour in 1953, at that time defined as a criminal offence, and sentenced to six months imprisonment, which he served in Wormwood Scrubs and Brixton prisons in London. Always denying his guilt, he wrote a moving account of how a prisoner feels when they wake up on their first morning of captivity:

> Whatever his crime or failure or bungling or bad luck may have been, he is consciously or unconsciously in a state of raw sensitivity. At Wormwood Scrubs, a prison for first offenders, he is probably spending the first hours of his life in captivity, separated from those he loves, and fearful of the future. Yesterday was the most cruel and critical day of his life. He stood in the dock and was sentenced, locked in a cell below the courts with others similarly treated, handcuffed, put through the long and painful business of Reception, and finally left in a cell. He has

risen this morning without having slept and has been brought before the man responsible for his immediate future.[1]

This statement sums up the universal experience of the newly arrived captive, even if this is not the first time they are being locked up. And more shocks are to follow.

One of these, and surely the most feared, is the expectation that they are likely to be physically hurt. Another English prisoner, Erwin James, serving a life sentence for murder, has a lesson in the endemic violence present in all kinds of captive institutions even before he has spent a night in prison:

> A stream of denim-clad men in identical blue-and-white-striped shirts are shuffling past my door. I step out and join the flux. Down two flights of metal stairs to the ground floor, we head towards a set of trestle tables.
>
> A row of prisoners in white are serving food. Before I get there I am stopped in my tracks by a scream.
>
> 'He's fuckin' dead meat!'
>
> '*Nonce*! He's fuckin' dead meat!'
>
> I turn and see two men: one wields a mop handle, the other a metal bucket. They are using the metal instruments to beat a third prisoner, who cowers in a cell doorway.
>
> 'He's fuckin' dead meat!'
>
> Suddenly I am aware that no one else is stopping. Nobody is intervening. Few even look in the direction of the violence. I fall back in line, pick up a tray and return to my cell. As I sit on the chair and spoon down the food, all thought and feelings about why I am in prison are relegated. My first priority, I now understand, is to learn to survive.[2]

Very soon after arrival, the deadening process of 'reception' – the euphemism used to describe the next stage – is set in motion. Watching the reaction of new arrivals tends to make any observer wonder if there cannot be an alternative to imprisonment.

The women's prison at Holloway, London, is one of the best known prisons in the world. And it was there that Jenny Hicks started a five-year sentence for fraud. Despite her considerable experience of being locked up, this time even she was surprised at what she met:

> The reception at Holloway was quite horrific. There were women there who had been in police cells for days and had not had a proper wash. There were women at various stages of shock or trauma – some withdrawing from drugs or drink – and all of us had our clothes taken from us and were wrapped in those horrible towelling dressing-gowns. I was put in this small box like a horse box and I sat there eating the piece of white bread and butter and cold sausage which had been given to me.[3]

Another prisoner, Amanda, also had experience of Holloway. When she arrived in 1997, what struck her, as it has for generations of captives, was the grime:

> I just couldn't believe it when I opened the door that I was going to be put in a room like this, with graffiti all over the wall. The room was filthy, the mattresses were filthy. Two of us got moved together, and we literally scrubbed our room from top to bottom. I scrubbed my loo, and it was sparkling in the end.[4]

In many other countries the atmosphere was at least as bad, and often worse. The Nigerian writer and political activist Ken Saro-Wiwa was shocked to learn about conditions in the cells of the Central Police Station in Port Harcourt. These were a good deal worse than Holloway:

> If you had no money, you were subjected to brutality and condemned to stand up all night to fan the guardroom bosses with old newspapers. If you had money, you might be allowed to stay outside the toilet room in which some of the inmates were forced to sleep so cramped was the available space.

Of course, there was no food. Inmates had to depend on food sent in by their families. And whenever such food was sent, it had to be shared with the inmates, the bosses having the greatest share thereof.[5]

When he was imprisoned himself, the system was so chaotic and corrupt that as a well-off political prisoner, he was able to engineer better conditions, as such prisoners often can:

> I took a look at the food which was being served and almost puked. It was fit neither for man nor beast. Thereafter, for me, it was a matter of receiving visitors, having read the newspapers which arrived with my breakfast. There was a bit of time to read, and I followed the news on my radio very keenly. The day ended at about seven o'clock when the warders locked us in. Quite dreary, I would think. And not meant to keep one in good health.[6]

This is an incidental comment on another phenomenon of captivity: that in many situations, mostly in developing countries, money buys privilege.

The first task of an institution, whether penal, allegedly therapeutic or functional – or whether the inmates are captive or volunteers – is to isolate the inmates and to break any links they have, social or emotional, with the world of freedom. This is often facilitated by using islands, which not only are potent symbols of that break, but have the advantage of making escape very difficult. The examples are legion: Alcatraz off California, Devil's Island off South America, Rottnest off Western Australia, Robben Island off Cape Town, Sakhalin Island off Siberia and two prisons on the British Isle of Wight. All of these island prisons feature in this book. Indeed, so obviously suitable are such locations that when Lord Mountbatten, in the wake of spectacular escapes from English prisons in the 1960s, recommended the creation of a super high security prison, he suggested islands, including the Isle of Wight as suitable sites. This despite the fact that it already had three prisons.

When institutions are not located on islands, they can be inland many miles from centres of population; the Russian Gulag is a notorious case. When the famous English prison, Dartmoor, was established to house Napoleonic prisoners of war (POWs), that part of Devon was very remote. In the United States, Rose Giallombardo points out, Alderson Prison in West Virginia is in a remote rural area well away from urban conurbations: 'At all times, the mountains form a remarkably compact wall around the prison and in many ways present a more formidable obstacle to freedom than a man-built fortress.'[7] A major grievance of Palestinians imprisoned by the Israeli authorities is that they are removed from the Occupied Territories and locked up in Israel, a situation which one critic defines as very like being consigned to Devil's Island.

But as well as effectively removing captives from the rest of society and making escape difficult, such locations have, from the point of view of the captives, predictable disadvantages. Visits from family and friends are problematic, and often impossible, but for the authorities, there is the advantage that 'contamination' by undesirable outside influences is made difficult. Not only penal establishments are built in near inaccessible places. So are other kinds of institutions which seek to remove people from their community. This is a common denominator of many such institutions, such as monasteries: 'most commonly monasteries have been founded in lonely, retired spots, at a distance from large centres of population...this has made easier a complete separation from the world'.[8]

The first stages of the experience of imprisonment are, of course, arrest, trial (if any), conviction and, finally, being locked up. Frank Norman, a thief who had experience of English prisons, was phlegmatic. He takes us from the moment of his sentence in the 1950s:

As I came along the passage leading from the court to the peters a twirl shouted, 'One lagging C.T.'

The princeable officer, who was sitting at his desk at the end of the passage noded his head and recorded the sentence in his book. That is how it started.[9]

For any captive, under restraint for the first time, the fear begins with that moment when the loss of freedom is certain, and here the common denomination of the captive experience begins, regardless of any particular situation. This fear must be especially pronounced when the captive is young.

Stuart Wood was sent to Reading Gaol in England in 1901 to await trial for theft. He was subsequently sentenced to a month in prison, but it was the beginning of a long career of imprisonment. He was 16:

We drove up to the massive iron-studded gates, a bell clanged harshly, they swung open and swallowed us up, shutting out our freedom and sunshine just as they shut out all individuality and freedom of action. There one ceased to be a human being with a brain to think and a heart to feel, and became merely a body to be duly signed for, photographed, measured, filed away in records, and arrayed in the 'grotesque garb of sorrow'.[10]

Quite often the gate displays a slogan. On the entrance to one of the Kolyma *lagpunkts* there was a banner which read: 'Labour in the USSR is a Matter of Honesty, Glory, Valour and Heroism!' And the chilling sign above the gate of the notorious Robben Island Prison in South Africa read: 'Ons Dien Met Trots' – 'We Serve with Pride'. Most infamous is the sign above Auschwitz Concentration Camp: 'Arbeit macht frei': 'Work Leads to Freedom'.

Whether or not there is a sign, the shock is considerable. Prisoners of war, for example, find it difficult to believe the wild change in their situation, as A.J. Barker explains:

At the moment of capture the transformation from fighting man to prisoner of war is bound to be abrupt and difficult...right up to the moment of capture captors and their prisoners are trying to kill each other. Then, without any change in their loyalties the relationship between the self-same people undergoes a radical metamorphosis. Past hatreds still exist but both sides are expected to show forbearance with each other.[11]

For the troops of the seemingly all powerful British Empire at the beginning of the Second World War, their position seemed unbelievable. Ian Watt's reaction was typical, and is a constant theme in the reminiscences of British prisoners in the Second World War:

> All the allied troops were crowded into the barrack areas of the Changi peninsula in the north of Singapore Island. For most of us prisoners the immediate reaction was one of numb and bewildered fear; we thought, 'This *can't* have happened to me because I know I can't face it.'[12]

The shock does eventually recede, and the questions facing a person are: What is going to happen? What should I do? Is anyone going to tell me? Captives soon learn what lies ahead, as did Peter Wildeblood in his English prison when he reflects on his time:

> The purpose, or at least the effect of sentencing a man to prison is to strip him of everything he has – of the possessions, the habits, the attitudes of mind that go to make up a distinguishable human personality.[13]

The famous Russian writer, Alexander Solzhenitsyn, sentenced in 1945, served eight years in the Russian Gulag for 'anti-Soviet propaganda' and 'founding a hostile organisation'. Despite the disparity between his background and that of Wildeblood, he shares something of the same feeling. He writes of:

> That glimmering light which, in time, the soul of the prisoner begins to emit, like the halo of a saint. Torn from the hustle-

bustle of everyday life in so absolute a degree that even counting the passing minutes puts him in touch with the Universe, the lonely prisoner has to have been purged of every imperfection.[14]

An English prisoner, Brian Stratton, served nine years for robbery in the early 1960s. He reaches the same conclusion as Solzhenitsyn, but expresses himself in more basic terms:

One thing screws really hate is for any con to retain his personality in prison. The screws want everyone to become vegetables.[15]

A woman in Soviet Russia felt the same shock. Even people as far apart as she and Stratton note the same devastation of any individuality:

Here in Lubyanka, you are already not a person. And around you there are no people. They lead you down the corridor, photograph you, undress you, search you mechanically. Everything is done completely impersonally. You look for a human glance – I don't speak of a human voice, just a human glance – but you don't find it.[16]

Another male Russian prisoner, Gustav Herling, agrees with what is an especially ubiquitous experience:

A prisoner is considered to have been sufficiently prepared for the final achievement of the signature only when his personality has been thoroughly dismantled into its component parts.[17]

Life in a prison camp is bearable only when all criteria, all standards of comparison which apply at liberty, have been completely obliterated from the prisoner's mind and memory. A new arrival in the camp was encouraged by older prisoners with the traditional saying: 'It's nothing, you'll get used to it.' 'Getting used to it' meant forgetting how he had once thought, how felt, whom and why he had loved, what he had disliked and to what he had been attached.[18]

Reception can range from the shocking to the horrific, especially for those who are undergoing it for the first time, and most especially for those whose life style is far removed from any such experience. Sometimes this first experience is mild, at least compared with some. An American, Thomas Green, who had been in and out of penal establishments since he was 13, was sent to a 'Home for Juveniles', which he describes as: '(a prison for children and) nothing more'. There he:

> Was turned over to an old man with one arm. 'One Arm Joe' as he is known to the inmates. One Arm Joe took my clothes, after slapping me in the mouth for asking why, and threw me in a shower, turning scolding hot water on me.[19]

Krishna Nehru Hutheesing faced another shock. She recounts how she and a group of young women were received into prison because they had taken part in a political protest in pre-independence India. They were put into a dark cell, and from the corner emerged three women much disfigured by leprosy who began to try to touch them. Their screams brought the superintendent, who was horrified, and gave the wardress a dressing down. The girls were released after six hours in the prison:

> But the experience had shattered our nerves and somewhat dampened our patriotism for a short while. Though our first term in prison had ended rather suddenly it gave us an inkling of what to expect in future if we got arrested.[20]

The change from a previous life is dramatic and traumatic, beginning with the forced contact with other captives. For someone as socially elevated as Hutheesing, this was more than simple inconvenience:

We were crowded together, our beds about four feet from each other, and everyone wanted to do different things such as reading aloud, humming a song or chanting verses from the Gita or Ramayana. The utter lack of privacy became unendurable as the time went by...no means of escaping to a quiet corner by oneself. We had to bathe in public – wash our clothes in public and put up with taunts from the matron as well as the wardresses if we showed any signs of being finicky regarding cleanliness or food. The nervous strain kept us tense and we often got involved in petty quarrels with each other.[21]

As always, it was as bad as it could possibly be in Russian prisons. Fyodor Dostoevsky was a Russian nobleman, sentenced to death in 1850, later committed to four years of penal servitude and five years of military service, for his part in the Petrashevist conspiracy. This conspiracy, allegedly, set out to overthrow the government and the Tsar. He wrote a novel, *The House of the Dead*, which is largely autobiographical, and it is from this novel that the extracts in this book are drawn.

His introduction to the prison was a forecast of what was to come. The Major (the head of the prison) came in:

His crimson, pimply and aggressively unpleasant face made us feel decidedly unwell: 'What's your name?' the Major asked my companion. The Major spoke rapidly, abruptly and jerkily, and was obviously trying to impress us...

'Sergeant! Take them to the prison immediately, see that they have their heads shaved, civilian style, half the head only; get fetters on them tomorrow.

'Mind now, you'd better behave yourselves! I don't even want to know you exist! Or else...it's cor-poral pu-nishment! Put one foot wrong and it's the r-r-rods.'[22]

Dostoevsky, after this, records profound shock: 'I spent all those first three days in a state of the most painful emotion. "This is the end of my travelling: I am in prison!"'[23]

The process of forced adaptation begins with reception. This is a carefully calculated matter. There are well-tried ways of forcing adjustment to this new world. It begins with some of the most enduring and universal of rituals. As we have seen already from captives' experiences, all are designed to strip the individual of all traces of a previous personality. The usual collective procedure is to make the captive undress, wash, issue a uniform, remove hair – sometimes *all* the body hair – and give the individual a number. The order in which these actions take place varies, but the total effect is the same.

The first step usually is to take off the captive's clothes. The purpose of this is not just to prepare the individual for washing and to inspect for vermin, but is intended as studied humiliation. Then follows bathing while at the same time there might be the issuing of uniforms: an important stage in the process of removing any traces of a person's individuality. This is the first step in the process of what is called 'institutionalisation', that ultimate goal, which is designed to make prisoners realise that they must forget any previous routines and identities.

Derek Williams, a first-time 'white-collar' offender, describes going through reception in Wormwood Scrubs prison in London: 'Then had come the most humiliating instruction of all: "Strip." He climbed out of his professional man uniform, and then, when he had hesitated: "Yes, undies as well."'[24]

'Zeno', who never gives his real name, was given a life sentence for murder in England in the late 1950s when he was 38. He seems to be from the same sort of background as Derek Williams, and recognises the significance of the procedure:

The clothes I take off will be out of date when I come out, and I watch a trusty gather them carelessly into his arms and disappear with them. I feel as if part of myself has been taken away.[25]

Solzhenitsyn describes the next humiliation which was inflicted on the prisoners:

> What awaits you in the bath? You can never be sure. They begin suddenly to shave all the women's hair off…or a line of naked men is clipped by women barbers only. [In one prison] it's more natural for the entire service staff in the bath to be male and for a man to smear on the medicinal tar ointment between the women's legs.[26]

The Gulag seems to have been especially indifferent to the embarrassment of captives, and can be likened to the Nazi Concentration Camp in that respect. Anne Applebaum writes of one female captive's description of how:

> We undressed and handed over our clothes for treatment and were about to go upstairs to the washroom when we realised that the staircase was lined from top to bottom with guards. Blushing, we hung our heads and huddled together. Then I looked up, and my eyes met those of the officer in charge. He gave me a sullen look. 'Come on, come on,' he shouted. 'Get a move on!'[27]

The persistent, relentless systems of humiliation might lead to a conclusion that there is some kind of a universally agreed method of demeaning the new captive, even though the cultures and traditions in which prisons are set are very different from each other. And remarkably this seems to be so.

Nathan Leopold, and his accomplice Richard Loeb, were convicted of the especially brutal and senseless murder of a young boy in Chicago in 1924. Leopold was 19 and both were sentenced to life imprisonment. Leopold later expressed his regret for what he had done. They arrived at Joliet State Prison in Illinois:

> Hairless, we were escorted back down the sidewalk to a low wooden building, set back from the walk. This proved to be the

clothing room, which contained also the shower stalls, where each inmate had his three-minute weekly shower. In the shower room we were ordered to strip and lay our clothes on a bench in front of the showers. A second inmate arrived with barber's clippers stepped up and removed all the hair from our bodies. Then we were handed a piece of laundry soap and told to step into the shower. While we were under the showers another inmate brought us a bundle of prison clothes for each of us, and when we had finished bathing, gave each of us a stick with a huge gob of blue ointment which he instructed us to rub into the skin under our arms and in our groins.[28]

The shock for these two rich and privileged men would have been profound, and was to be experienced by many. And here was the climax: they then dressed into clothes 'several sizes too large' and the two men looked at each other. 'I don't know whether the humor or the pathos of the sight was greater.'[29]

Some forty years later, the Illinois state system did not appear to have changed much. Thomas Green earlier told us about 'One Arm Joe'. In 1966, Green, by now an 18-year-old, and so qualifying as an 'adult', went to a 'Diagnostic Unit' of the Illinois State Penitentiary:

The first barber clipped all of the hair from each man's head, the second barber clipped all of the hair from under each man's arms, and the third barber clipped all the hair from above the penis of each man. After the shock and humiliation of this clipping process we again formed a line, looking self-consciously at each other and wondering 'Dear God, do I look that funny?'[30]

Women in most systems were treated with the same coarseness as men. A woman in the Gulag considered that in some way, the clothes were the culmination of a process of studied humiliation: 'They had deprived us of everything, they deprive us of our names, of everything that is part of a person's personality, and dressed us, I can't even describe it, in a shapeless dress.'[31]

The procedures in Ravensbrück, the only German Concentration Camp solely for women, were as humiliating as those of the Gulag:

> And everything comes off, to be thrown into large brown paper bags, along with all clothes and all possessions. The prisoners give everything up: last letters, photographs of children, embroidered handkerchiefs, knitted hats, little baskets, poems, combs. 'Until nothing is left.' Wedding rings too.
>
> Stark naked the women are staring at their feet again, but some look up and shriek to see that male SS [Schutzstaffel] officers have been present all along, standing and staring. They laugh and shout when they see the women's humiliation.
>
> Then the shavers come, and some of the women are pushed aside. 'Get a move on' – and the selected women's hair is shaved off close to the scalp. Then another woman comes through. She makes the same women stand with their legs apart and shaves their pubic hair.[32]

Several captives with experience of both compare the Nazi Concentration Camp with the Soviet Gulag. The conclusion seems to be that apart from those Concentration Camps devoted to extermination, life in the Gulag was worse. A doctor who had experience of both explained:

> I was in Dachau…there I had a clean bed. I had soap to wash with, a toothbrush, clean underwear, warm clothes for the winter. All the time I was confined I had contact with my family. I was sent letters and parcels. I was not hungry…a terrible thought sometimes comes into my head… At times I think that if I had to choose between *Pechor-Lag* and the Dachau concentration camp, I would choose Dachau.[33]

In Auschwitz, Jewish women were treated with quite exceptional coarseness, even allowing for the intrinsic humiliation of the procedure of reception. This treatment was, of course, in accord with the overall doctrine of the Nazis about the sub-human nature of Jews:

> The gynaecological examination, brutal enough at Ravensbrück, was performed here by the coarsest of Ravensbrück's prostitute asocials, who were told to probe not for disease but for hidden jewellery. Some of the Jewish women were as young as fourteen and many were virgins, a fact that delighted the watching SS, who looked on, yelling obscenities. An SS doctor arrived on the scene and said he didn't believe these young Jews were all virgins and he would find out for himself.[34]

Another victim of the Concentration Camps was Pierre d'Harcourt. He was imprisoned by the Germans because of his involvement in the French Resistance in the Second World War. He recalls the same kind of procedure: 'We entered the delousing block. Here an orderly ran an electric shaver all over our bodies as if we were sheep, removing every single hair. Next we were sprayed with fine powder.'[35] Frank Norman's reintroduction to the English experience was not as humiliating: 'I got into the bath which had about six inches of water in the bottom.'[36]

Mohamedou Ould Slahi was, on his own admission, a member of Al Qaeda, the extreme Islamic organisation, but, he insists, only during the period when they were fighting against the Russians in Afghanistan. He was forcibly removed from his home and ended up in Guantánamo Bay, the American establishment in Cuba used to detain people suspected of involvement in terrorist activity.

Prisoners at Guantánamo Bay had a rougher experience of reception than Frank Norman's relatively civilised English treatment. This is Mohamedou Ould Slahi's own account of his wash:

> Finally two escorting guards dragged me into the clinic. They stripped me naked and pushed me into an open shower. I took a shower in my chains under the eyes of everybody, my brethren, the medics, and the Army. The other brothers who proceeded

[*sic*] me were still stark naked. It was ugly, and although the shower was soothing, I couldn't enjoy it. I was ashamed and I did the old ostrich trick: I looked down to my feet.[37]

In recent times, foreigners, notably Europeans, have made the serious mistake of trying to smuggle drugs into countries where the penalties are well known to be severe. A French woman, Beatrice Saubin, sentenced to life, but who served ten years in a Malaysian prison for drug offences, describes her bathing ritual:

> I stood naked before a woman in uniform. She ordered me to turn around and inspected all my clothes… As my clothes were being examined, I shivered in embarrassment and grief. Beyond a barred door and brown cloth curtain, my humiliation continued. I had to stand up in front of the tank, pouring water over myself with the coloured plastic bowls resting on the edge.[38]

There was an added humiliation for Saubin, since she was in a foreign country with alien companions: 'As soon as the guard left, the prisoners degenerated into bold-faced voyeurs. They swarmed around me and stared, jabbering away and pointing at my thighs, stomach, hips and breasts.'[39]

Concomitant with the bath is the haircut. If it does not take place at the same time as the bath, it will happen soon after, and the effect is long lasting. People, not only prisoners, are usually very particular about their hair, since it is an important expression of their personality. Brian Stratton indulges in that sense of humour often found in British prison writing, even about haircuts:

> For anyone who has never been in the nick, heed my advice. Beware of nick barbers! They couldn't cut a hedge, most of them, never mind hair.
>
> The Parkhurst ones were definitely to be avoided. Geronimo used to do a better job than that lot.[40]

The arguments about haircuts are a source of much anger, and later Stratton did not joke about it. Just three months before his release, he was ordered to have his hair cut. This became the reason for another explosive row with the authorities, since he hoped upon discharge that 'a hairdresser would be able to do something with it'.[41] On this occasion Stratton won.

The procedure is the same even in the non-penal institution, which, nevertheless, demands uniformity. T.E. Lawrence (Lawrence of Arabia), a hero of the First World War, joined the Royal Air Force (RAF) in the ranks after the war, an action which puzzled people then, and still does. He wrote a book about his experiences in the RAF under the pseudonym 352087 A/c Ross. This was his personal number; every serviceman or woman in every armed force has one. Here he describes his first days:

'And put the man down for a regimental haircut,' he went on. That meant the clippers all over his head, and him a disfigured convict for weeks.[42]

Recruit-heads were clipped to the blood and pale as the scalp's pink. [43]

Concomitant with this comes the abolition of names. Captives in their memoirs naturally never forget their new imposed identity, in the case of all those locked up, political, criminal or others, this is spelled out in numbers. Frank Norman writes of that seminal moment: 'Another twirl called our names again, when he got to my'n – "Norman?" "Yes sir." "Your number is 1797."'[44] All captives have numbers: d'Harcourt's number was 21,521. Brendan Behan's was 537, W.F.R. Macartney's was 620 and Colonel MacKenzie's was 128 then 7 then 676. Solzhenitsyn tells us that at the Schüsselburg fortress near St. Petersburg: 'The prisoner had a number and no one called him by his family name.'[45] In some systems numbers are only used for administrative purposes, England being a case in point. In Holloway, a famous English prison for women, Jane Buxton's number was 11557, but her fellow prisoner, Margaret Turner, explains that the number was not so significant or humiliating: 'Contrary to my expectations we are not addressed as Convict Number So-and-So; surnames only are used so it's not much worse than being in the WRNS [Women's Royal Naval Service] again in that respect.'[46]

Other systems maintain the impersonal address associated with numbers. A Chinese prisoner felt the shame very strongly:

> When ordered to pin a paper strip with his number, 273, to his chest, Cong Weixi feels as though he were 'a death row inmate awaiting the executioner's bullet, and had already bid mankind a final farewell'.[47]

In addition, to add to the certainty of identification, in the Nazi Concentration Camps prisoners were given differently coloured triangular patches to wear which showed clearly to what category a person belonged: whether political, homosexual, 'asocial' or Jew. This means of identification also served the purpose of encouraging hostility between the several categories.

Next comes the issue of uniform. Many of these rituals are applied to those who join religious orders, with the shaving of heads, the issue of uniforms and the adoption of a new name; although in this case humiliation is not necessarily an intention. This is how St. Benedict orders the new monk should be treated: 'Then forthwith he shall there in the oratory, be divested of his own garments with which he is clothed and be clad in those of the monastery.'[48]

The processes are intrinsically humiliating, but in addition there are likely to be feelings of being abused. Frank Norman relates what happens after his bath:

> By the time he got back with the coarse grey clothes I was out of the bath with a towel about two ft. long wrapped around my middle.
>
> 'Here you are.' He said, 'I hope they fit but I doubt it and here's the best pair of shoes I could find.' I put this gear on and it

fitted where it touched, and was as coarse as sack cloth. When I dressed I came out of the bath cubicle feeling like a right tramp and most probably looked like one, too.[49]

Prince Peter Kropotkin was a Russian nobleman and Anarchist. His first contact with prisons was in 1862 when, as a 19-year-old Cossack officer, he was appointed secretary to a committee on prison reform. Appalled by what he saw of prison conditions, he made recommendations for improvement which were ignored. This led him to despair of any government's capacity to change things and led him to embrace extreme politics. The result was that he was imprisoned in the infamous St. Peter and St. Paul Fortress in 1874, but after two years he escaped from a military hospital to which he had been transferred. In 1882, he was imprisoned in France for being a member of the outlawed International Working Men's Association. He was released in 1886 and became an articulate and unremitting critic of the prison as a part of society's mechanism of oppression.

Although the conditions of his imprisonment in France were fairly liberal for the time – he was allowed to write, for example – he drew attention to the much less congenial circumstances of his fellow 'criminal' prisoners. Like so many others he deplores the humiliation of the prisoners' uniform. In Lyon Prison:

> When they had, however, put on the uniform of the prison – the brown jacket, all covered with multi-coloured rags roughly sewn to cover the holes, and the patched-up trousers six inches too short to reach the immense wooden shoes – they came out quite abashed with the ridiculous dress they had assumed. The very first step of the prisoner within the prison walls was thus to be wrapped up in a dress which is in itself a story of degradation.[50]

W.F.R. (Wilfred) Macartney served a sentence for espionage in the late 1920s and 1930s. His uniform was a classic English prison dress since his jacket had the broad arrows, beloved of cartoonists, but very real at the time:

> I undressed and put on the prison clothes, which were on a chair: dirty-looking trousers sprinkled with broad arrows, thick socks, a cotton shirt, a brown jersey, and a drab coat with hundreds, as it seemed to me, of broad arrows all over it.[51]

In the very variable environment of the American women's prisons, there seems to be the universal phenomenon of uniform, which women seem to find even more demeaning than men:

> The inmate is hard-pressed indeed not to view the issue of clothing as a punishment and as a deliberate attack on her self-image...the clothing issued to the new inmate is often faded, certain to have been worn by generations of prisoners, and either sizes too large or too small... The mortifying process in connection with clothing perhaps reaches its apex for the inmates in the issue of the shapeless cotton petticoats and the brown or white cotton panties that resemble men's boxer-type shorts far more than they do ladies' underwear. Yet the inmate cannot keep her own underwear.[52]

Beatrice Saubin, in the very alien environment of a Malaysian prison, was duly issued with her uniform:

> Zuraida gave me a set of prison whites and explained that I was going to share her cell. As I put on the ill-cut costume-drawstring waist, pants too short, top too big – the women bombarded her with questions about me. In fright I withdrew into our cell.[53]

For the patient in some psychiatric hospitals, there is a potential further humiliation about dress. If patients are incontinent, or are self-harming or behave in other ways which require constraint, it may be necessary to dress them in restrictive clothing for their own comfort or safety. In an extension of this intention to protect patients from themselves, and causing great distress, Goffman alleges that at some times: 'Some mental hospitals have found it useful to extract the teeth of "biters", give hysterectomies to promiscuous female patients, and perform lobotomies on chronic fighters.'[54]

Something of the same humiliation, but not as extreme, is found in the armed services. T.E. Lawrence, upon joining the Royal Air Force, describes the classic experience of the recruit being fitted out with uniform:

> 'Quick!' cried Corporal Abner. 'Into your khaki: yes it'll fit, of course: all khaki fits – where it touches. You're to get rid of your civvy duds before dinner'... We wanted to weep while we pulled on the harsh trousers as high as our knees and wound the drab puttees from boot-top upwards, till it gripped the trouser-helm above the calf. When we had finished dressing we were silenced by our new slovenliness. The hut of normal men had gone, and barbarous drab troops now filled it.[55]

During the Second World War, people of German birth, even though they had escaped from the Nazi regime, were regarded as suspect. They were interned, not as criminals, but because they were aliens and therefore could be potentially dangerous. They were sent, *inter alia*, to Canada, and somewhat to their surprise had to wear uniform:

> Few of us had expected to find ourselves dressed up as harlequins. A bright red stripe along one of the trouser legs, another red stripe across a cap modelled on those worn by engine drivers in America, and a bright red circle between the shoulder blades on shirts, jackets and coats – these were to make us clearly visible targets...thus at one stroke the last outward and visible signs of individuality were removed and replaced by an outfit which made most of us feel quite depressed because it was so ludicrous.[56]

In England in the post-war period there was extensive protest about nuclear arms, and British government policy about them, a protest which is still very much alive. Phoebe Willetts was sentenced to six months in 1960 for protests on behalf of the Campaign for Nuclear Disarmament. She served her sentence in an open prison, which she points out in her book *Invisible Bars* by no means reduced the quintessential pains of captivity. This included wearing a uniform, which she contrasts with the pleasure of briefly wearing her own clothes when she was transferred from the closed prison:

> That brief momentary reminder that once we had been human beings, wearing clothes of our own choice as symbols of our one-time personalities. The taste of honey was brief but sweet as we took off the light slippy feeling of nylon undies to put on once more the heavy white cotton vest and bloomer-like knickers referred to as 'bangers'... Only the pathetic attempts of the 'young prisoners' (the under twenty-ones) to tie the bits of cotton belt attached to the side, the wrong way round in order to look different. As I put on my faded sack, and the heavy black shoes which I had learnt from experience must always be chosen a size larger than my usual, I stepped once more into the category of second-class beings, to have to seek a deeper differentiation than the superficiality of clothes which I had once relied upon.[57]

But there was to be: 'a considerable joy and privilege in store for me'. Because it was impossible to find a brassiere to fit her, the officer said: '"Well, you had better wear your own." How great was my joy.'[58]

From here the next move is to a cell. In all the reminiscences about prison, this is the one which seems to be one of the most traumatic: the moment when the captive sees the cell for the first time. Nawal el Sa'adawi is a distinguished Egyptian doctor, writer and activist who was made subject to a 'Precautionary Detention Order' in September 1981. There was no hearing and no appeal against arrest. She found herself in the Barrages Prison:

> If the most difficult moment in the life of one sentenced to execution comes just before the guillotine falls on his neck, then

the hardest moment I'd ever known came just before I entered the cell.

My eyes follow the movement of the chain clutched in the cracked fingers of a blotchy brown hand, around which the massive keys swing. The one key resembles a huge mallet with the head of a hammer and a long steel arm indented by jagged teeth.

In the dark, the shadows of the steel-barred doors are reflected on the high walls like legendary phantoms. Steel clanging against steel, the sound colliding with the walls and the echo reverberating over the inner walls, as if hundreds of steel doors are being closed and locked.[59]

I remained open-eyed, contemplating my surroundings: the scabby black ceiling, cracked walls, steel bars, a small window high in the wall, next to the ceiling, blocked with a steel grille. Women's and girls' bodies lying on the ground or on the black metal bunk beds.[60]

Prisons often have a very distinctive smell. Like other captives, in Illinois Nathan Leopold was overcome by the singular smell of the cell block:

The building was pervaded by an odour hard to classify but one that is indelibly associated in my mind with prison. It seemed to consist mainly of the odour of worn metal, but it contained components also of disinfectant, of sour wet mops, and of unwashed humanity. It was an odour unique in my experience and impossible to describe: those who have had experience of it will recognise it instantly.[61]

Arthur Koestler was condemned to death by the Fascists in the Spanish Civil War. When he was released, his escort explained that: 'You have engaged in a perifidious [*sic*] campaign against National Spain, Señor.' His offence was that he had reported in the British press the manifest involvement of Germany and Italy on the Fascist side in the war. Like other captives, the locking of his door was traumatic:

> For the first time I heard the sound of a cell door being slammed from the outside. It was a unique sound. A cell door has no handle, either outside or inside; it cannot be shut except by being slammed to. It is made of massive steel and concrete, about four inches thick, and every time it falls to there is a resounding crash as though a shot had been fired. But this report dies away without an echo. Prison sounds are echoless and bleak.[62]

Peter Wildeblood, coming from a stable background, and like many others, completely unprepared for what was ahead, not surprisingly felt the same. It is a signal that whatever power a person has had over movement, that power has gone:

> There was something peculiarly final about the shutting of that door. Throughout the next year, whenever I was told to go to my cell and lock myself in, I hesitated a moment before doing so, as a man hesitates before closing his own front door, making sure that his Yale key is in his trouser pocket. But here there were no keys. It was like being locked in a safe.[63]

Another English middle-class prisoner had similar feelings, but he suffered an extra trauma:

> The full impact of what had happened to him did not come to Derek Williams until the door crashed into place. He had always been slightly claustrophobic, and the walls and ceiling seemed to come crashing in on him, making it difficult for him to breathe easily. He wanted to shout for the warder to come back and open the door, just an inch so that he could breathe.[64]

Then, for the British middle-class prisoner, came his first call for violent adjustment to his new circumstances. Such prisoners have, seemingly, never met the usual run of people found in prison. One of his new cell-mates spoke:

> 'This your first fucking time, mate?
>   Williams nodded.
>   'I thought so. You can always tell, you know,' now addressing the smaller man on the other bed. 'It's their look when they close the fucking door that gives them away.'[65]

Other middle-class English prisoners have the same feeling:

> For most of them though, the real horror is being locked away or as they say in prison slang 'banged up' for the first time in their lives. As one man put it: The real impression is hearing that door bang behind you and the key in the lock and realising that until somebody out there puts the key back in again, you are there and there is nothing you can do about it.[66]

John Hoskison was another English middle-class prisoner. A professional golfer, he was sentenced to three years in 1995, after he had knocked down and killed a cyclist. He too reflects on that first horror:

> Never had I imagined that hearing a cell door slam shut could be so devastating. I stood transfixed, literally shocked by the sound and the dreadful feeling of finality it gave me. The last bolt slid into place and I realised my punishment had only just begun. I took a deep breath, turned my back on the solid steel door and surveyed my new home.[67]

Peter Elstob was a prisoner in the cruel Spanish Civil War, and he wrote a vivid account of his first experience. This was especially unnerving for him, not only because the situation was so volatile, but because he was in a foreign country:

They put me in number twelve. The door swung protestingly open and the stench that escaped nearly knocked me down. Don't worry, they told me grimly, you will get used to that.[68]

Prisoners are often told that they will 'get used to that'. He goes on:

We picked our way over the collection of debris that occupied the cell and I was graciously given permission to sit on the bed, a folding plank with greasy blanket. The jailer went out and locked me in the dark. But he returned in a minute pushing another prisoner along in front of him. This one carried a broom and a vacuous expression.

The kind jailer kicked him a few times and he went to work sweeping out my cell. The jailer caught him behind the neck and flung him out. I wondered if all this was for the purpose of making me understand discipline.

The keeper paused at the door and bowed.

'*Buenas noches, señor,*' he said with what he probably thought was a smile.[69]

The parallels between secure psychiatric hospitals and prisons are obvious, as is demonstrated by this personal experience:

Audibly a door is unlocked from within. It opens and a male nurse receives you from those who have delivered you. He closes the door behind you – and locks it again.

Not ostentatiously, but he locks it nevertheless.

Then, dispassionately, neither hostile nor friendly, he invites you to change out of your suit into the ward uniform of ill-cut clothes or pyjamas – because on these there will be no belts or braces or shoe-laces with which you may strangle either yourself or others: hidden in them are no knives or razor blades with which to cut a throat.[70]

Menachem Begin, sometime Prime Minister of Israel, was born in Brest-Litovsk, which was, at the time of his birth, in Poland. In 1941, he was sentenced by the Soviet government to eight years under Section 58, for being an 'element dangerous to society' and sent to a Soviet camp. He is one of many who are transfixed by the small opening in the door which enables staff to keep watch on captives:

> The peep-hole in the door which enabled the guard to spy on the prisoner's movements unobserved – I was acquainted with that too. The Polish *Urki* used to call it 'Judas', after Judas Iscariot, symbol of treachery in the eyes of all mankind. It was called that in Lukishi, too, though not particularly by the criminal prisoners. The attitude of the prisoners to the 'watching eye' can be gleaned from the name they gave it.[71]

Years before, in England, an English suffragette prisoner, Constance Lytton, was equally drawn to the 'Judas': 'I was fascinated in a grim sort of way by the "eye" in the door of which I had heard so much.'[72] The 'Judas Eye' seems to be a mixture of horror and awfulness to captives. Rupert Croft-Cooke quotes from another prisoner's memoir:

> He was worried by the peep-hole in his door. 'From time to time I could see an eye applied there to watching me closely [*sic*]. All that night, as I lay awake, turning restlessly on my narrow plank bed, it seemed to me that the unpleasant sense of being watched would prevent me ever sleeping at all in prison.'[73]

The reception procedure is designed to regiment, to crush individuality and to induce obedience. Captives recognise this and reflect upon it. The experiences of T.E. Lawrence are very like those reported by others who are propelled into a society, the membership of which is not of their choosing, or at least is not quite what they expected:

So get it into your head right away that you're not wanted to understand anything before you're told. Got it? [74]

Our time weighs the same whether we work or waste it. Then we will present to our instructors a blank grey sheet, on which to draw up, by drill and instant obedience, an airman.[75]

The whole reception procedure, then, is designed to disorientate the prisoner and to divorce them from their previous existence. Any system of captivity requires obedience. From the beginning, if there is any sign of independence or refusal to conform, the system has solutions. These range from mild insistence, to the induction of absolute fear, to physical punishment. There will be an insistence on deference to staff.

Frank Norman, as an experienced prisoner, knew what to expect. For Pierre d'Harcourt, it was an entirely different matter, as it always has been for those locked up by totalitarian regimes. In his case, as a member of the French Resistance in the Second World War, he was consigned to a Gestapo prison. As well as the usual apprehension experienced by prisoners, there was the distinct likelihood that he would be beaten or even killed. We shall go on to see that he soon experienced the capricious violence of the staff.

Do these elaborate rituals actually work? Were these procedures, designed to disorientate the prisoner and to divorce them from their previous existence, effective? D'Harcourt tells us just how effective. Through most of the reception, he tells us, they were surprised at how unapprehensive they were. But when it was all over: 'I remember so well how I felt: dazed, lost, directionless and above all completely anonymous. The number in my hand was the only token of my identity, my very existence.'[76]

For some, such as Margaret Turner, a protestor against nuclear weapons, the regime in Holloway is familiar, in this case reminiscent of her time in the Royal Navy:

I am often reminded, quite forcibly of my life in the W.R.N.S. sixteen years ago. Instead of calling the officers 'Ma'am' we are expected to call them 'Miss', and there is no squad drill out on the square but there are the same petty restrictions and the loss of all individuality and initiative.[77]

It is remarkable how quickly the process of institutionalisation begins. After a relatively short time, when the new routine of everyday life is disrupted, the newcomers are ill at ease, as T.E. Lawrence reports:

> We had been so obedient to Corporal Abner that we had forgot the habit of decision. No other corporal has been assigned us and we feel neglected at not being overseen. It will be curious if service experience takes altogether our power of free navigation.[78]

The resilience of captives is a constant in their reflections, and is remarkable. Dostoevsky expresses this perfectly:

> But time went by, and little by little I began to settle down. With every day that passed, the ordinary scenes and events of my new life had a less and less disturbing effect on me. Incidents, surroundings, people all became familiar.[79]

Lawrence realised that the deep experience of initiation would never quite be erased: that the changes which the captive has to make are going to be a problem later, in his case even changing to a freer life within the RAF:

> Just for twelve weeks, we say: and beyond is the warm thoughts of our sheltering trades, after we are posted to some ordinary station; a return to the natures that were ours before enlistment. Yet we deceive ourselves, so colouring the future: for the lessons here are biting deep, and we shall never be the old selves again.[80]

At the opening of this chapter I quoted Erwin James. Towards the end of his life sentence he was moved to an open prison and his reception there was in stark contrast to his first:

> The reception process was informal. Just two prison officers, disarmingly friendly and helpful; and I noticed there was no 'reception orderly'. My kit was checked speedily and then confusingly, the prison officers picked up a bag of my kit each. The one with the moustache noted my look of puzzlement and smiled, first at me then at his colleague. 'Follow us,' he said. 'We'll show you to your room.'
>
> This helpful attitude was totally alien to any other reception process I'd ever encountered before. And then there was a bigger surprise. Just as I picked up my last bag of kit to follow the officers, a man with a clipped moustache and a military bearing, dressed in jersey and slacks, stepped forward and introduced himself as the prison's probation officer. He offered me his hand and I shook it as he delivered his thunderbolt. 'Welcome,' he said. And then he said it again, 'Welcome.' The warmth and conviction in his voice was overwhelming.
>
> 'Thank you,' I replied, trying for the second time that day to check the constriction swelling in my throat. My pals were right after all. There really was more to this 'open conditions' situation than I had bargained for.[81]

This small act of decency, though, was not the end of James's punishment. He served a total of 20 years before being released.

Most captives (but not all) adjust to this alien world, as Barker describes in his account of prisoners of war: 'At the same time his responsibilities diminish; everything is found, the routine worries of earning a living are removed, and the POW moves slower and slower with the stream.'[82]

The most concise, and pitiable, account of the total horror of reception into captivity is from one of the most cruel confinements of all – Auschwitz, a Nazi Concentration Camp. Primo Levi, later to become a renowned writer, was an Italian Jew, captured in December 1943 and sent to Monowitz Camp, part of the Auschwitz complex, in early 1944. Only 3 out of 125 returned to Italy at the end of the war:

> At the sound of the bell, we can hear the still dark camp waking up. Unexpectedly the water gushes out boiling from the showers – five minutes of bliss; but immediately after, four men (perhaps they were the barbers) burst in yelling and shoving and drive us out, wet and steaming into the adjoining room which is freezing; here other shouting people throw at us unrecognisable rags and thrust into our hands a pair of broken-down boots with wooden soles; we have no time to understand and we already find ourselves in the open, in the blue and icy snow of dawn, barefoot and naked, with all our clothing in our hands, with a hundred yards to run to the next hut. There we are finally allowed to get dressed… Then for the first time we became aware that our language lacks words to express this offence, the demolition of a man. In a moment, with almost prophetic intuition, the reality was revealed to us: we had reached the bottom. It is not possible to sink lower than this; no human condition is more miserable than this, nor could it conceivably be so. Nothing belongs to us anymore.[83]

After the trauma of reception, most captives marshal an astonishing reserve of strength to face the fact that there is little they can do except to face the reality and search for ways to survive. There are similarities in the methods adopted throughout the captive world, and these are the methods which I will now describe.

Notes

1. Croft-Cooke, Rupert. *The Verdict of You All.* p.61.
2. James, Erwin. *A Life Inside: A Prisoner's Notebook.* p.74.
3. Carlen, Pat (ed.). *Criminal Women: Autobiographical Accounts.* p.130.
4. Carlen, Pat. *Sledgehammer: Women's Imprisonment at the Millenium.* p.82.
5. Saro-Wiwa, Ken. *A Month and a Day: A Detention Diary.* p.40.

6. *Ibid.* p.231.
7. Giallombardo, Rose. *A Society of Women: A Study of a Women's Prison.* p.21.
8. Rutledge, Dom Denys. *The Complete Monk: Vocation of the Monastic Order.* pp.155–156.
9. Norman, Frank. *Bang to Rights.* p.9. The publisher kept Norman's mis-spellings and punctuation and so have I wherever I quote from his work throughout this book.
10. Wood, Stuart. *Shades of the Prison House: A Personal Memoir.* p.23.
11. Barker, A.J. *Behind Barbed Wire.* p.128.
12. Watt, Ian. 'The Liberty of the Prison' in Moir. p.140.
13. Wildeblood, Peter. *Against the Law.* p.116.
14. Solzhenitsyn, Alexander. *The Gulag Archipelago 1918–1956: An Experiment in Literary Investigation.* p.483.
15. Stratton, Brian. *Who Guards the Guards?* p.14.
16. Applebaum, Anne. *Gulag: A History of the Soviet Camps.* p.136.
17. Herling, Gustav. *A World Apart.* p.71.
18. *Ibid.* pp.100–101.
19. Chang, Dae and Armstrong, Warren B. *The Prison: Voices from the Inside.* p.46.
20. Hutheesing, Krishna Nehru. 'In British Hands' in George Mikes (ed.) *Prison: A Symposium.* p.106.
21. *Ibid.* p.111.
22. Dostoevsky, Fyodor. *The House of the Dead.* p.330.
23. *Ibid.* pp.95–96.
24. Breed, Brian. *White Collar Bird: The White Collar Man in Prison and His Problems.* p.16.
25. Zeno. *Life.* p.13.
26. Solzhenitsyn *op. cit.* p.542.
27. Applebaum *op. cit.* p.173.
28. Leopold, Nathan. *Life + 99 Years.* p.75.
29. *Ibid.*
30. Chang and Armstrong *op. cit.* p.51.
31. Applebaum *op. cit.* p.174.
32. Helm, Sarah. *If this is a Woman: Inside Ravensbrück.* p.24.
33. Begin, Menachem. *White Nights: The Story of a Prisoner in Russia.* p.204.
34. Helm *op. cit.* p.184.
35. d'Harcourt, Pierre. *The Real Enemy.* p.106.
36. Norman *op. cit.* p.15.
37. Slahi, Mohamedou Ould. *Guantánamo Diary.* p.34.
38. Scheffler, Judith A. *Wall Tappings: An International Anthology of Women's Prison Writings 200 to the Present Day.* p.153.
39. *Ibid.*
40. Stratton *op. cit.* p.123.
41. *Ibid.*
42. Lawrence, T.E. *The Mint.* p.94.

43. *Ibid*. p.76.
44. Norman *op. cit.* p.17.
45. Solzhenitsyn *op. cit.* p.457.
46. Buxton, Jane and Turner, Margaret. *Gate Fever*. p.12.
47. Williams, Philip F. and Wu, Yenna. *The Great Wall of Confinement: The Chinese Prison Camp through Contemporary Fiction and Reportage*. p.107.
48. Rule of St. Benedict Ch. 58 quoted in Goffman *op. cit.* p.20.
49. Norman *op. cit.* pp.15–16.
50. Kropotkin, Peter. *In Russian and French Prisons*. p.266.
51. Macartney, Wilfred F.R. *Walls Have Mouths*. p.66.
52. Giallombardo *op. cit.* pp.96–97.
53. Scheffler *op. cit.* p.154.
54. Goffman, Erving. *Asylums*. p.79.
55. Lawrence *op. cit.* pp.49–50.
56. Burmeister, Werner. 'Enemy Alien' in Moir. p.99.
57. Willetts, Phoebe. *Invisible Bars*. p.4.
58. *Ibid*. pp.3–4.
59. El Sa'adawi, Nawal. *Memoirs from the Women's Prison*. p.27.
60. *Ibid*. p.30.
61. Leopold *op. cit.* pp.78–79.
62. Koestler, Arthur. 'A Personal Affair' in Mikes. pp.76–77.
63. Wildeblood *op. cit.* p.98.
64. Breed *op. cit.* p.12.
65. *Ibid*. pp.13–14.
66. *Ibid*. p.54.
67. Hoskison, John. *Inside: One Man's Experience of Prison*. p.7.
68. Elstob, Peter. *Spanish Prisoner*. p.64.
69. *Ibid*. pp.64–65.
70. Bryan, Jeremy. 'True Madness' in Mikes. p.195.
71. Begin *op. cit.* pp.40–41.
72. Lytton, Constance. *Prisons and Prisoners: The Stirring Testimony of a Suffragette*. p.69.
73. Croft-Cooke *op. cit.* p.53.
74. Lawrence *op. cit.* p.44.
75. *Ibid*. p.58.
76. d'Harcourt *op.cit.* p.107.
77. Buxton *et al. op. cit.* p.29.
78. Lawrence *op. cit.* p.109.
79. Dostoevsky *op. cit.* p.126.
80. Lawrence *op. cit.* p.117.
81. James. *A Life Inside op.cit.* pp.130–131.
82. Barker *op. cit.* p.187.
83. Levi, Primo. *If This is a Man*, and *The Truce*. pp.32–33.

— *2* —

Settling Down

Once the receiving procedure is over, captives have to come to terms with their future. 'Reception' will have introduced them, often very effectively, to institutional life: from the abolition of choice, separation from the opposite sex, obeying orders without question, wearing uncomfortable, often dirty, clothes and to eating food which is generally poor or vile, but which, nevertheless, they learn to welcome. The worst situation with regard to food is when all that is available is that which can be scrounged.

The required adjustment will depend on the country in which the prison is located, the purposes of the prison, the traditions inherent in the treatment of prisoners, the personality of the individual and even their gender. This seems to be important and Giallombardo is not the only one to suggest that women find adjusting to being locked up more difficult than men.[1]

Because of these factors, there are intensely personal reactions to particular circumstances. But as always there are generic experiences. And dominating the thoughts of the new arrival is a determination to live. The Russian Varlam Shalamov had good reason to write about this, albeit in the form of fiction. In 1929 he was sentenced to three years hard labor for being involved in 'crime'. Then, in 1937, he was sentenced again, this time for five years for 'counter-revolutionary Trotskyite activities'. He was tried yet again in 1943 because he praised a Nobel Prize winner and the effectiveness of the

German army, and he was sentenced to ten years. He stayed in the camps until the end of the war. He was 'rehabilitated' in 1956. Of the character in his short story, he writes:

> He had to take some action, think of something with his weakened mind. Either that or die. Potashnikov had no fear of death, but he couldn't rid himself of a passionate secret desire, a last stubbornness to live. He didn't want to die here in the frost under the boots of the guards, in the barracks with its swearing, dirt, and total indifference written on every face. He bore no grudge for people's indifference, for he had long since comprehended the source of that spiritual dullness. The same frost that had transformed a man's spit into ice in mid-air also penetrated the soul. If bones could freeze, then the brain could also be dulled and the soul could freeze over. And the soul shuddered and froze – perhaps to remain frozen forever. Potashnikov had lost everything, except the desire to survive, to endure the cold and remain alive.[2]

However, typically, whatever their fears and feelings, many decide that they will not show the effect their first taste of prison is having on them. This middle-class English prisoner did not face the prospect of death as Shalamov did, but he felt something of the same determination: 'It was a cold harsh environment, but I was determined not to let it get me down or rather to show that it was getting me down. Survival depended on your state of mind and I was determined not to let it deteriorate.'[3]

Stuart Wood, an English prisoner at the beginning of the twentieth century, was reprimanded and threatened on an occasion when, feeling happy on a bright day – 'one's natural buoyancy conquers the spiritual blight of whitewashed walls and servitude' – he whistled a tune in his cell. The Chief Warder opened his cell and said: 'We've got some nice little cages for song birds like you. Some of you fellers take prison for a convalescent 'ome. You don't come 'ere to whistle.'[4]

After this reprimand, in a thoughtful passage, Wood reflects on what captivity means:

> To people living in a normal world such a matter sounds very trifling; but in a prison nothing is trifling. A harsh word or a threat swamps one's courage and routs cheerfulness. Waves of bitterness and depression sweep over one's soul, blotting out the sunshine and quenching the wavering joy of life.[5]

Of course, the damage that can be done to the personality is relative. Paramount is the nature of the physical environment. In this respect some prisoners are lucky. Notable amongst these are prisoners of war of the British and some of those prisoners of the Germans in the Second World War. A.J. Barker describes the situation of one group of British prisoners of war in Germany:

> Living quarters were often quite good. A large party working on a dam at Lavamund was comfortably housed and enjoyed good camp conditions including hot showers daily. Eighty men working in a brick factory lived in well-lit and heated rooms of specially built barracks...two hundred men working for an engineering firm had single-tier beds with three or four blankets, ample space for sport, flower and vegetable gardens – in the words of the ICRC delegate, 'a model camp'.[6]

In Britain too, life for prisoners of war could be easy enough. In the Second World War Hans-Joachim Thilo recalls how he was given two days arrest for refusing to accept an order that prisoners were not to attend services at the village church: a very light sentence for a very odd offence:

> But I do not recollect getting so much to eat in all my time as a P.O.W. as during those two days. Every ten minutes my English guards turned up and brought me food and drink and cigarettes *ad lib*.[7]

Nevertheless, whatever the circumstances, the first reaction of the captive is shock, difficulty in believing what has happened and, more importantly, what is happening now. The essence of this feeling is well summed up by Krishna Nehru Hutheesing. She and other Indians found the experience shattering in an especially vile system. I have mentioned her first shock when she was first imprisoned and she was locked in a cell with three women grievously disfigured by leprosy. Later, she reflected on her experience:

> Though personally I did not suffer as many others did during imprisonment, I found the lack of human touch, the insolent way we were talked to, and the oppressive atmosphere of the place, at times became unbearable. The very air seemed different from that of the outer world. It was full of menace, violence, meanness and graft and there was always cursing on one side and cringing on the other. A person who was at all sensitive was in a state of continuous tension with their nerves on edge. Trivial matters would be upsetting and a piece of bad news in a letter or in a newspaper which had been smuggled in made one ill with anxiety. Those outside found relief in action and in various activities and so gained some sort of equilibrium of mind and body. In prison there was no outlet. Bottled up and repressed a one-sided and perhaps rather distorted view of happenings, was inevitable.[8]

Yet captives adjust and often the speed with which they do is phenomenal.

Arthur Koestler, even though he was under a supposed sentence of death, found that he was immediately beginning to take stock, and to come to terms with where he was, and then describes, typically, what the new captive does next:

> First of all he gives a fleeting look round the walls and takes a mental inventory of the objects in what is now to be his domain:
>   The iron bedstead,

The wash-basin,

The W.C.,

The barred window.

His next action is invariably to try to pull himself up by the iron bars of the window and look out. He fails, and his suit is covered with white from the plaster on the wall against which he has pressed himself...he makes some more laudable resolutions: he will do exercises every morning; and learn a foreign language; and he simply won't let his spirit be broken.[9]

Ian Watt, a prisoner of the Japanese on the Burma Railway, reflects on how prisoners adjust. He says that no other word is adequate:

I cannot find any other term to describe the perspective of my experience time has brought. Unconsciously we adjusted and adjusted so completely that we were, in a queer sort of way, rather happy; and the ultimate reason for this seems to cast a light on life in general.[10]

Rose Giallombardo recounts how an American woman prisoner expressed the same reaction: to accept the inevitable, and try to forget the life of freedom which has been lost:

The first thing that an inmate has got to do is to divorce her mind from outside. It's got to be a void as far as the Free World is concerned. You can't think about outside – not if you're going to do this time. It takes a while to go from one extreme to the other – to go from the normal to the abnormal. It's a shock to the system. It's hard to do – to blank out everything – the ties you have out there. It's not easy to do this. But you push them far back in your mind so you can do this time. To do successful time you must. You close out anything real – anything to do with the Free World. You face reality in the prison.[11]

In the same prison, Alderson in West Virginia, prisoner Helen Bryan is given similar advice: 'Whatever you do, don't think. It's bad to think by yourself, but it's hell to think when you're in Lockup. So, remember, don't think.'[12]

Bryan found, though, that she had to work out a way of coping with sleeplessness, a constant worry of the imprisoned:

> The agenda always carried three main points, but the subtopics varied. The first heading was persons. I chose some one person, a relative or a friend or someone I admired from a distance, and ponder upon his personality and character in an effort to determine why and how he had influenced my life. The second heading was places. I would think of the many places I had been in my life and the resulting satisfaction or joy gained therefrom, whether it was a simple picnic in the woods or a visit to a South African chieftainess in her kraal. The third heading was labelled The Future, the question which obsessed me most. Such 'thought control', I was convinced would give content to the long hours before the bliss that was sleep would envelop me.[13]

Dietrich Bonhoeffer constantly reviews his situation, and maintains a quite remarkable sense of optimism. He was a Lutheran pastor, and an opponent of the Nazi regime. He was arrested in April 1943 and confined in the military Tegel Prison in Berlin. His letters from prison are full of optimism about his potential fate, although what he wrote may well have been coloured by his wish to assure his parents that he would be safe. So, he writes to them that:

> I have now had four weeks in prison, and whereas I had no difficulty from the outset in accepting my lot consciously, I am getting used to it in a natural, unconscious sort of way. That is a relief, but it raises problems of its own, for I have no desire to get used to this sort of life, and it would not be right to either.[14]

He is here expressing the same kind of thought as occurred to Oscar Wilde when he was told in prison that he should be patient. He retorted that he could be patient because patience was a virtue, but what was needed in prison was apathy and apathy was a vice.

Prison, though, produced for Bonhoeffer the eternal experiences, including the acceptance of what previously would have been unthinkable:

> However much I get used to the external conditions of prison life, it doesn't seem quite natural. It is quite interesting to watch this gradual process of self-adaptation. I was given a knife and fork to eat with a week ago – a new concession – and they seemed almost unnecessary, it had become so natural to spread bread, etc. with a spoon. But there are other things which are so irrational, e.g. the actual state of being in prison, that it is impossible to get used to them, or at least very hard.[15]

He experiences the creeping force of institutionalisation, although he does not name it as such. He wonders what is happening to his emotions:

> This is my second spring in prison, but a very different one from last year. Then all my impressions were still fresh and vivid, and both joys and hardships were felt more keenly. Since then something has happened which I should never have thought possible – I have got used to it. The only thing that puzzles me is, which has been greater, the growth of insensitivity or the clarification of experience?[16]

After almost two years, another feature of institutionalisation appeared. He wrote to his parents of his apathy – just as Wilde noted – and he begins to wonder if he is thinking properly:

> However hard I try to be patient and understanding, I sometimes feel it is better not to write any letters, but to keep silent. For in

the first place my disordered thoughts and feelings would only give birth to wrong words, and secondly what I write would be very much out of date by the time it reached its destination. It costs no little effort to keep to the facts, to banish illusions and fancies from my head and to content myself with things as they are.[17]

Bonhoeffer expresses the constant belief that he would soon be charged and acquitted, but this did not happen. There was to be no peace for him. After a perfunctory hearing, he was hanged at Flossenburg on 8 April 1945. Only a month later, Germany surrendered.

Part of the 'adjustment', and one which takes effect quickly, is the acceptance of what would previously have been regarded as an intolerable situation. Very soon after his incarceration, Arthur Koestler, typically, found his standards going downhill:

> I remained so until the afternoon, and then became even more cheerful when the door opened and the kindly old warder and an assistant dragged in a straw mattress. It was a dirty old mattress, and the straw sagged and stank, but when it had been laid over the iron springs and I had stretched myself out on it, I felt in all my aching joints how marvellously comforting it was compared to the iron springs which cut into the flesh.[18]

Primo Levi was conscious of how quickly he deteriorated, but to him it made sense and was all part of the process of thinking differently:

> I must confess it: after only one week of prison, the instinct for cleanliness disappeared in me. I wander aimlessly around the washroom when I suddenly see Steinlauf, my friend aged almost fifty, with nude torso, scrub his neck and shoulders with little success (he has no soap) but great energy. Steinlauf sees me and greets me, and without preamble asks me severely why I do not wash. Why should I wash? Would I be better off than

I am? Would I please someone more? Would I live a day, an hour longer? I would probably live a shorter time, because to wash is an effort, a waste of energy and warmth. Does not Steinlauf know that after half an hour with the coal sacks every difference between him and me will have disappeared? The more I think about it, the more washing one's face in our condition seems a stupid feat, even frivolous: a mechanical habit, or worse, a dismal repetition of an extinct rite.[19]

In prisons in modern China, some prisoners have the same feeling of degeneration and the inescapable feeling that they cannot escape it, even though they are conscious of what is happening. They:

Recall a nagging fear of losing their identity, of general regression and devolution, and of becoming less than human, or even no longer human. They would sometimes realize that they were losing the virtue and decency so crucial to their former sense of identity within society. Zhang Xianliang admits to having resorted to scheming and deception in order to obtain a bit more food; he was aware of his degenerating and decaying sense of self, yet could not do anything about it.[20]

In 1914, when the First World War began, some 4000 mainly British men and boys were interned in Germany. They wound up in a camp on a disused airfield called Ruhleben, outside Berlin. It is a paradox that the German Ruhleben translates into English as 'Peaceful Life'. J. Davidson Ketchum wrote an exhaustive account of the camp, using the pseudonym Denton in the book to describe his own activities there. He describes the feelings of the prisoners upon capture:

As Ruhleben asserted its undeniable reality, it was the past that tended to become remote and unreal. Not for several weeks was it possible to knit the two together intelligibly, and meanwhile the prisoner found his concept of himself strangely shaken. Which was he – the respectable solicitor and suburban householder, or the unshaven, straw-splattered outcast, picking up the last scrap of potato out of a rusty bowl?[21]

In Ruhleben, which seemingly was full of people who had high standards, those standards soon deteriorated:

> Existence was on a primitive level, and clothes, conduct, and speech were rough and uncompromising. Garments were as warm and durable as possible; these were the only standards, and no one tried any longer to dress fashionably or eccentrically. Comradeship was not felt to require politeness, and in the congested barracks contacts were forthright and brusque. A man entering a crowded doorway uttered no 'Excuse me!' but simply shouldered his way in; if a messmate left his property on your bunk you threw it on the floor.[22]

D'Harcourt is another who reports how a person's expectations and standards sink without realising it. At one point, he is sent to the 'little camp'. The bunks designed to hold ten, held twelve or thirteen sick men, and: 'There they lay, stained and spattered with excrement, dying and waiting to die'… 'the filth and stench were indescribable'. Yet such is the power of the institutional process that this French aristocrat could conclude: 'Once I had become accustomed to the stench and the filth and the wretched food of the little camp, I realized there were many advantages in being there.'[23]

To this physical reality is added another which is crucial to the smooth running of an institution. Captives must do as they are told, and without question. The institutional system is expert at inducing such obedience, as T.E. Lawrence goes on to observe:

> This learning to be sterile, to bring forth nothing of our own, has been the greater half of our training and the more painful half. Obedience, the active quality is easy. We came in wanting to be very obedient and we are pathetically grateful to Taffy

for ordering us about from dawn till dark. The common tone and habit of the camp helped us and taught us obedience, atmospherically.[24]

Zeno found the same:

I have not made a decision, except a few negative ones, for many months now, and as prison slowly unfolds in front of me I am beginning to think that I shall never be called upon to make one during the whole of my sentence. That is part of imprisonment, in many ways the hardest part.[25]

If there is any sign of hesitation in being compliant, the system has a means of ensuring it. Every captive is faced with the appearance of people in uniform, both staff and other captives, with no notion of where they have come from or how they will behave. And to every captive comes the fear of physical beating, perhaps to death. As with everything else, the degree of certainty of this fear will depend upon the reasons for incarceration and the traditions of the captors. Even if the captives do not have experience of imprisonment, they will know that many thousands of captives have died at the hands of the captors. For Pierre d'Harcourt there was real danger, as always for those locked up by totalitarian regimes. In his case, there was a good chance of meeting violence since he was first consigned to a Gestapo prison. As well as the usual apprehension experienced by prisoners, there was the distinct likelihood that he might even be killed.

Brendan Behan, later a famous writer, was only 16 when he was sentenced to Borstal for the possession of explosives. He was a convinced Irish Republican – he was later sentenced to fourteen years by an Irish court for the attempted murder of two policemen – and here he was in a British gaol. This was at the beginning of the Second World War, and so naturally he was surrounded by staff and prisoners who hated him. Even though he was not in the same kind of danger as, say, a prisoner of the Japanese, he still faced the possibility of attack. He knew because of his offence at a time of war that he was an object of hate. Hard as he was: 'I was not defiant of them but frightened.'[26]

Even a powerful figure like Nelson Mandela soon lost confidence in the face of likely staff violence:

> The captain pointed to Aaron Molete, the youngest of the four of us and a very mild and gentle person, and said, 'Why is your hair so long?' Aaron said nothing. The captain shouted, 'I'm talking to you! Why is your hair so long? It is against regulations. Your hair should have been cut.'[27]

At this, Mandela tried to interfere, and immediately experienced the absolute fear of the defenceless prisoner. The captain: 'began to advance. I was frightened; it is not a pleasant sensation to know that someone is about to hit you and you are unable to defend yourself.'[28] Mandela knew that even though he was a boxer and could have defended himself, the penalty would have been considerable, and at this stage in his imprisonment, unknown.

Some captives face extreme, life-threatening conditions. Perhaps the most poignant example is that of the prisoners of war of the Japanese. Here they had to face the very issue of survival, and Russell Braddon, himself a prisoner, expresses this very succinctly:

> Many thousands of men survived periods of captivity which all existing medical knowledge clearly stated to be impossible to survive. It was not, however, their exotic diet alone which kept them alive (they were eating cats, dogs, and snakes): complimenting this diet there had to be a pigheaded and totally unreasonable will not to die... This – it must be noticed – is quite different from the will to live, which too often ignores the presence of death. The will not to die recognizes that death is at hand, acknowledges frankly that death is right to expect another victim, and then refuses to become such a victim. Survivors of Buchenwald and Dachau acquired this will exactly as survivors of the Thailand Railway acquired it. Nazis were no less perplexed

by it than were the Japanese: and no one can properly understand it who has not experienced it.[29]

Another prisoner of the Japanese – and they are plentiful – agrees. Ian Watt writes how they learned to be vigilant so that you were not punished because of some caprice on the part of the guards. There was, though, a strange consolation, and one that many captives of the Japanese felt, faced with weird, unpredictable behaviour. Ian Watt expresses this belief forcefully: 'They were so different from us that our belief in ourselves was never challenged; we regarded them, not as real human beings, but as malign and unpredictable lunatics.'[30]

This quality of unpredictability seems to have been a characteristic of Japanese guards, and is often commented upon as being especially difficult to handle:

> The Japanese methods, when overt, varied between brutal and direct (as at Selarang), and subtle – but dangerous in their ambiguity. The strict adherence to POW rules and regulations was an insurance against what Galleghan termed the 'illogical temper and brutality of the Japanese'.[31]

Despite all of these terrors, captives want to survive. There is often thought of suicide, sometimes fulfilled, but this is usually rejected. Zeno considers it, but in the end decides not to:

> It is true that I would sooner be dead than where I am. It is true that I toy with the idea of self-destruction as a sleepless man might toy with his sleeping pills. Death has become the father-figure of my middle age.[32]

Captives often consider suicide as a way out of the hell in which they find themselves. It is remarkable that more do not carry it through. The 16-year-old Stuart Wood was one of many who considered self-destruction:

I foresaw further punishment in that silent cell down below with nothing to eat or drink but bread and water, and my mind began to explore means of avoiding it. What could I do? – strangle myself? Lay my head on the floor and, by pulling the heavy bed-board down upon it, dash out my brains? But if instead of killing me it injured my head so that I became an imbecile or went mad? My mind shrank from that possibility just as it shrank from the utter finality of death.[33]

Suicide is part of the process of self-analysis which is common in people who are locked up. They often wonder just why they are where they are, and if there is any point in going on.

When the shock is over, prisoners soon begin to think, and reflect on their relationship with the outside world. Russell Braddon tells us that the prisoner of war has an immediate and particular problem. It is facing guilt about having surrendered. There are degrees of this. The man who is unconscious when he is caught will feel less guilty than someone who has ammunition left, even if he is in a hopeless position and that carrying on fighting would mean certain death:

Every prisoner-of-war, sooner or later – and there is always plenty of time – has to pass judgement on himself on many charges: but none will acquit himself of one of those charges at least – that he no longer fights the enemy while his country does.[34]

This 'sombre and humbling knowledge comes early in captivity… Thereafter the prisoner adjusts and compensates.'[35] A principal consolation is that, unlike criminal or political prisoners, he has not committed offences against his own people: 'They are and will be ostracised: I will always be a respected member of my own community.'[36]

Some emphasise the intensely personal nature of the decisions to be made in a new and hostile environment. Ian Stewart was an army medical officer (MO) and a prisoner of the Germans in the Second World War:

In prison all distinctions become clear. I came to despise the cliché that there is good in all men. Most I found to be capable of nobility. Others were worthless, some evil beyond forgiveness.[37]

Zeno was an intelligent and well-educated man, and furthermore he was at the beginning of a life sentence. He spends a good deal of time considering his position, and is able to articulate his conclusions: 'certain lines to be adopted if I am to get through the indeterminate years which stretch out ahead of me. I must protect myself or I shall go under.'[38]

Dostoevsky is another who found that he entered another stratum of society when he went to prison, and once again he reminds the reader of the peculiar difficulties facing captives from a higher class. Of his fellow prisoners, he writes:

I sometimes felt myself hating these fellow-sufferers of mine. I would envy them and curse their destiny. I envied them because they were among their own kind, were companions to one another and understood one another.[39]

His fellow Russian prisoner, Alexander Solzhenitsyn, some hundred years later, felt the same suspicion and hostility, and believed that he had dealt with one aspect of the problem: Who could be trusted?

On the other hand, the sensor relay helped me distinguish those to whom I could from the very beginning of our acquaintance completely disclose my most precious depths and secrets – secrets for which heads roll…during all those seventeen years I recklessly revealed myself to dozens of people – and didn't make a misstep even once.[40]

Some become extremely introspective. Amongst these is L.H. Morrison, who worked in the Malay Civil Service, and was imprisoned by the Japanese in 1941, spending time in Changi Prison (which is still in use as a prison) in Singapore, and on the Burma Railway. He considers how he can survive:

> The most important conviction which I gained – and of which I already had ample evidence – was that the real enemy is within oneself... The real enemy is self-preoccupation... You find yourself on shifting sands, frantically trying to feel firm ground. And you panic, you go to pieces – unless you have got something to hold you together.[41]

In his case, he believes God came 'to the rescue'.[42]

One way in which captives adjust to this humiliation is to reify it into something which is good for them, in part as a way of coping, and in part as an expiation for their crimes. Zeno is an example: 'For the fiftieth time I resolve to accept the daily humiliations as part of my punishment, but I know I shall not keep this resolution...I tell myself that I must learn humility.'[43]

It is this odd resolution to develop humility which Zeno considers a solution to the sense of regret he feels for ending up where he is:

> In my cell I find that humility I longed for when I came here first. Outside of it my stupid pride predominates. Years ago, I denied that there was any person in the prison on whom I could model myself. That was true then, but I feel that it is no longer. I have found the model, and when I am in his company I am conscious that he has the humility I seek. His virtues create similar virtues in me. It is strange that he should be the man whom the law, by the very severity of the sentence it imposed on him, should have considered to be the greatest criminal of all.[44]

The man in question was George Blake. He was sentenced to 42 years by a British court for spying in the 1960s, but escaped, provoking an outcry, several reports – notably one by Lord Mountbatten – and a seismic change in British penal policy. The most important of these changes was the subordination of 'reformation' as a goal of the system to the supreme reassertion of 'security'. Blake escaped to Moscow and was never recaptured.

But people cope, will not surrender their souls and build belief systems to help them. The fact that people are able to do so was a source of wonder to the well-educated Peter Wildeblood suffering the captive life:

> I never found one who could accept the fact in the sense of settling down to a permanent monotonous routine which would not vary during the next thousand or two thousand days. They simply refused to believe that in, say, 1960 they would still be sitting in this dark, smelly place still watching the dart-players and wondering if their cell-floor were clean enough to pass muster.[45]

Oscar Wilde was sentenced to two years hard labour for homosexual offences in 1895. His trial and conviction was a focus of national and international interest, and, indeed, still is. As might be expected, his reflections upon the experience are heartfelt and articulate:

> Suffering is one very long moment. I have lain in prison for nearly two years. Out of my nature has come wild despair; an abandonment to grief that was piteous even to look at; terrible and impotent rage; bitterness and scorn; anguish that wept aloud; misery that could find no voice; sorrow that was dumb. I have passed through every possible mood of suffering.[46]

> For a year after that was done to me I wept every day at the same hour and for the same space of time. This is not such a tragic thing as possibly it sounds to you. To those who are in prison tears are a part of everyday's experience. A day in prison on which one does not weep is a day on which one's heart is hard, not a day on which one's heart is happy.[47]

But he goes on in a spirit of self-realisation very reminiscent of d'Harcourt and Zeno. Central to this is this strange need to embrace humility:

> But while there were times when I rejoiced in the idea that my sufferings were to be endless, I could not bear them to be without meaning…and suffering least of all. That something hidden away in my nature, like a treasure in a field, is Humility.[48]

> I have got to make everything that has happened to me good for me. The plank bed, the loathsome food, the hard ropes shredded into oakum until one's fingers grow dull with pain, the menial offices with which each day begins and finishes, the harsh orders the routine seems to necessitate, the dreadful dress that makes sorrow grotesque to look at, the silence, the solitude, the shame – each and all of these things I have to transform into a spiritual experience. There is not a single degradation of the body which I must not try to make into a spiritualising of the soul.[49]

Mrs. Jeanty-Raven was arrested by the Gestapo in 1943 in Belgium for helping a British airman. Her way of dealing with a hideous situation is remarkable. Her main concern is to avoid that self-pity which she believes is so destructive:

> Coming from my wonderful home and life, a prison cell was a knock-down. All I did was to cry almost non-stop, or to curse. Came the day, however, when I thought that this was self-destruction and, if I was to face a trial and somehow survive, this, certainly, was not the way to do it. I was sorry for myself, I did not deserve all this, I had been a good mother, a good wife, I was only trying to win the war etc… 'I', the hateful 'I' was all over me and the first thing to be done was to kill it.[50]

This Jeanty-Raven did to the extent that she accepted her lawyer's advice to be 'irresponsible', which meant to feign insanity. By doing this, because of the complexity of the law, her husband's certain death sentence might be commuted. She agreed, convinced the authorities that she was insane, and spent over a year in horrendous circumstances in several psychiatric establishments before release. It is a story of huge bravery. Tragically, her husband was executed anyway.

A somewhat unusual collective response to the new situation can be seen in Ruhleben. Here, the prisoners coped collectively by encouraging a sense of 'Britishness': 'The whole code was summed up in the significant phrase, "Be British!", and no other injunction had comparable force as long as the camp lasted.'[51] This appeal should be seen in the context of the times. In 1914, the British Empire was at its peak, and the British were sure of their superiority. There were 80 prisoners from Africa, the West Indies, India and the Middle East. They lived in what were called the 'Niggers' Barracks'. The camp regarded them as 'amusing and irresponsible children'.[52] White people played cricket against them, but one prisoner, a South African, refused to do so. Thus this report of resort to jingoism is totally convincing. It is also an example of how the bringing in of social baggage helps survival.

Another universal experience, against which defence has to be found, is boredom. Ian Watt, prisoner of war of the Japanese, gives it a high priority on the list of problems: 'The worst phase of being a prisoner of war is boredom.'[53] Twenty years before, in the United States, Leopold found:

> The long period of being locked in one's cell from Saturday afternoon until Monday morning is one of the most disagreeable experiences in prison… What to do with oneself, how to put in the long, dragging hours becomes a problem. One can only sleep so many hours.[54]

There are many ways of coping with this overwhelming nightmare of boredom. Some captives engaged in very personal methods. Peter Elstob, prisoner in the Spanish Civil War, describes how he tried:

I devised a schedule for passing the long days. In the morning I would do strenuous exercise until I was utterly exhausted and then throw myself on the plank and try to sleep. But this didn't work too well for after a few minutes of rest I was wide awake again. I'd look at my watch and see that the whole thing had taken only twenty minutes.

I discovered a device whereby some time passed quickly. I made lists. All the books I had ever read, all the people I had ever known, all the houses I had ever lived in. The plays I'd seen and who was in them and where. I would pick a date out of the past and try to establish exactly where I had been and what I had done on that day.

And so four days passed.[55]

Russell Braddon, in his discussion about his time in prisoner of war camps, recounts a similar phenomenon:

The prisoner invariably sets about committing infallibly to memory the *modus vivendi* he knew outside captivity. He will torture his mind, and interrogate all his friends, until he has remembered the position and name of every main building in the city that to him was home. He will narrate to his friends, and repeat endlessly, every detail of his past life, and then listen to their similar reconstructions. He will reconstruct for them the plot of every book he has read, every play or film he has seen, and then listen to their similar reconstructions.[56]

It is remarkable but not surprising that 'brainy' captives (as they were called) seek the same resource. K.P. MacKenzie, a prisoner of the Japanese in Rangoon Prison in Burma, is one of many who decide that intellectual exercise is crucial. He:

formed the habit of trying to while away the time by recalling to my mind passages of poetry memorised in my school days. The lines:

> *Stone walls do not a prison make,*
> *Nor Iron bars a cage.*
> *Minds innocent and quiet take*
> *That for a hermitage.*

Would haunt me. They would keep running through my mind and I could not stop thinking about them for hours at a time.[57]

Dostoevsky, like other highly educated captives, found the deprivation of intellectual stimulation intolerable. He tried, as did like-minded people, to keep mentally alive by using his inner resources: 'Living without books, I had perforce become immersed in myself; I had set myself questions and tried to solve them, had at times been tortured by them.'[58]

Edith Bone, in solitary confinement for just over seven years, provides an amazing example of adaptation to a vile situation. Consigned to a dungeon in Hungary she wrote that:

> Having been brought up under the influence of a father whom I greatly admired and who was a disciple of Marcus Aurelius, I didn't mind the cold and darkness very much, and there were compensations.
>
> For instance, I liked to sing, and I know a tremendous lot of songs, but from infancy I had been laughed at and teased for my abominably out-of-tune singing by other youngsters with a truer ear and a better voice. Here I could sing to my heart's content; it had both the charm of being strictly banned by prison rules and the attraction of putting the screws into a cleft stick if they heard me; for, if they wanted to stop me, they had to crawl down an iron spiral staircase on which their iron-shod boots made a racket fit to wake the dead. By the time they got to the bottom there would be no singing they could stop, only a prisoner surprised out of deep sleep.[59]

This is an example of another phenomenon I shall examine later: the captive working out ways to beat the captor.

She goes on to say:

> I suffered from the icy cold, but not from the dark, and the freedom from external impressions it and solitude afforded was in fact welcome. After the fourteen months I had spent in the battle of wits against the various kinds of secret police officials, I at first merely rested; that is I did not as yet feel inclined to think out the implications of the position in which I found myself. I compiled an anthology of poetry in five languages, for which I drew stringent rules: only complete poems could be included, with a maximum of three missing words acceptable. A lot of long-forgotten material was thus drawn to the surface, to my own great surprise. My next enterprise was to translate selected poems from one language into the other; in this connection I discovered that rhymes came easily to me, thus stimulating an ample production of doggerel which gave me much amusement in the time to come.[60]

Eugene Heimler, sent to Auschwitz because he was a Jew, tried something rather unusual. He decided to chronicle life in the camp. Not only did this give him an interest, but it was also a weapon, if a secret one, for which prisoners are constantly searching, to use against the guards: 'It was a private victory, too, over the SS guards, who never knew I had them under observation.'[61]

John Hoskison, an English prisoner, also kept a diary, albeit for a different reason:

> With the frustration of not knowing how long I would have to remain in Wandsworth, I decided it would be a helpful mental exercise to start keeping a diary of anything interesting that took place – although being locked up on my own for such long periods meant that not a great deal happened. Occasionally I would leap up when I heard a whistle blown by a guard, signifying a fight,

but apart from mealtimes and exercise (when it wasn't raining), it was a lonely existence. When I look back and read some of the entries I realize what a bad state I was in.[62]

As time goes on routines are established, an especially important one being work. It might be supposed that work could help to alleviate boredom. After all, there must be different kinds of work. Some can indeed be pleasant, such as that performed by prisoners of war in Britain in the Second World War, or the gentle pace of replacing glass panes which was Brendan Behan's job at one time. Unfortunately, the more usual problem that captives experience is that the work they are given, if it is not positively dangerous as it could be in the Gulag, is boring. This, added to the intrinsic tediousness of 'doing time', increases immeasurably the suffering of prisoners. The problem with institutional work is that it is variously pointless (often deliberately so), time wasting and is not motivating.

Even in the relative comfort of an English open prison, the feeling of boredom is paramount: 'At first I thought it was another Butlin's,' said one man. 'But now it seems so pointless to me.'[63]

> Strangely, within two months of arriving at Ford (an open prison), many of the men confess the frustrations and the boredom are such that it appears to be more of a punishment than the Scrubs... They say they are in prison but not in prison. As they play with wires in the light industry section, or plant trees in the horticultural area, they feel they are wasting their time.[64]

Zeno goes to work in the canvas shop and asks a prisoner what he should do. The advice he is given is standard, not only in prison, but notoriously in the armed services, as we shall go on to see. Zeno is told:

> Do! I can tell you what to do in ten seconds flat. Look you fold it here, press down with this block of wood to crease it, and then again, here, here, and here. That's it. You're a trained man. Of

course you could work up your speed a bit, but there's no point in it. You'd just work yourself out of a cushy job. I could do enough in a morning myself to keep the shop going for a month. Bloody silly, isn't it man?[65]

In the military, avoiding work is a highly developed skill. Servicemen are expert at *seeming* to be working. T.E. Lawrence writes of the experience of all servicemen:

'You're silly cunts, you rookies, to sweat yourselves' they'd say. Is it our new keenness, or a relic of civility in us? ... Impossible, therefore, to dignify a job by doing it well. It must take as much time as it can for afterwards there is not a fireside waiting, but another job.[66]

The monotony of prison work is not new. Of Joliet Prison, Illinois, in the 1890s, Sydney W. Wetmore (a prison clerk) wrote an account of the work carried out by women:

The women sit facing these windows all day long, their chairs are in an even row and they have great piles of stockings in their laps. With darning needles and raveled wool they mend and repair heel and toe, it is terribly monotonous work, a dreary routine, a truly penitential task.[67]

There is no doubt that nowhere was work harder than in Russian prisons. Yet there are many contradictions even in the life of Russian prisoners. Dostoevsky tells how his work party was detailed off to break up a barge. They sat about until 'the foreman, an NCO with a stick came over'. He ordered them to get on with their work, but they wanted an 'assignment', which seems to have been a plan. He refused and 'somehow everyone finally got up and trudged off down to the river with reluctant, trailing steps'. Still they prevaricated, and after a few desultory movements the foreman shouted again, 'looking in bewilderment at the twenty-strong crowd of men who did not know how to start work'.

Eventually, the men 'set to work, listlessly, reluctantly and clumsily'. At the end of this remarkable story, the foreman retires defeated and the works supervisor arrives, and he organises the work to the satisfaction of the convicts and they set to.[68]

There is the same problem of boredom throughout institutions where people have lost control over their activity. In one psychiatric hospital, a patient recalls:

> For every day, even though you are passionately unenthusiastic, you will be required either to weave or to carpenter or to paint or to work metal. At the very beginning of your illness you may actively dislike most of these splendid occupations: but you will have to practise at least one of them daily, and by the end of your treatment you will actively detest all of them.[69]

He goes on to say that: 'Of the lot, weaving is perhaps the most distasteful.' And he describes why in cynical terms: 'But you will continue to weave throughout the entire period, or receive an adverse report from those in charge, which is an even worse fate than weaving.'[70]

Jane Buxton, serving a sentence in Holloway Prison for demonstrating against nuclear arms, contrasts her work there with work outside:

> The working day seems terribly long. At the publishers, where my work was very interesting, the days fairly flashed by; but here where most of the work is monotonous, repetitive, or even quite meaningless, time goes by like a tortoise.[71]

Sometimes, working hard is supposed to affect promotion of some sort, and can be dignified by some impressive term, an example being in Joliet Prison, Illinois, where there was put in place something called the 'progressive merit system'. This was a signal to the commitment to rehabilitation which was fashionable at the time. But the all-conquering apathy of prison confounded the system and Nathan Leopold explains how this happens:

> In 1925 and 1926 I was clerk in the shoe shop… Each month it was the duty of the keeper in charge of the shop to fill out slips, but he delegated the duty to his clerk. My instructions were to grade every man 49 for workmanship and effort and 49 for conduct every month unless he had been punished by being sent to 'the Hole'. In this case he was to receive 45 for each of the two grades. Obviously, since every man received the same grade, regardless of whether he held a relatively important job and applied himself diligently or whether he slipped by with the minimum effort; there was, in the very nature of the system, no possibility of earning advancement.[72]

The system was a sham because, as Leopold says, 'the guards paid only the most perfunctory attention to it'.[73]

There are many problems surrounding the question of work for captives. Historically, it was important that they should not enjoy it. Thus, in the English prison system of the nineteenth century, the use of the treadwheel and crank and oakum picking was deliberately purposeless and strictly punitive. There is also the function of keeping prisoners busy, and then consonant with the notion of reform came the attempt to train prisoners in a useful trade which would increase the possibility of employment on release. There is not always such lofty ambition. In the Gulag, or in China, for example, prisoners function as slaves producing goods for the state.

Some captives, in the attempt to cope, engage in more open and communal activities. Even in the most dire of Japanese prisoner of war camps, classes would be organised: 'Some kind of learning seemed to be the aim of almost everyone in the camp.'[74] The organisation of classes, or participating in those which the authority provided, was a very common resort, and in some places had important long-term effects. Part of the struggle against the prison authorities (and the government) on Robben Island was over the right to educational facilities. In a 'normal' civilised prison system, it is axiomatic that education should be provided in the hope that this will increase the will and ability of prisoners to lead law-abiding lives. The captor of the political prisoner has no such ambition. Nowhere is that clearer than in Apartheid South Africa, where black people wanted a society which was inconceivable to the white people. Education was therefore pointless, or worse, even dangerous.

Yet after protests, including hunger strikes, and legal process, captive political prisoners on Robben Island did manage to set up educational as well as sporting and recreational facilities. The ban on tertiary studies which had been imposed in 1977 was lifted in 1981.[75]

Despite the unpredictable changes of rule from time to time, academic study became a deeply integral part of life on the Island. One prisoner, Moseneke, who obtained a university degree while there, observed: 'Many people have emerged to survive Robben Island largely because of their studying. It is one single thing that really keeps you together.'[76] A group of prisoners summed up the success of the home-grown education effort:

> In a matter of three to four years we had actually wiped out illiteracy on Robben Island. Completely. Everyone could read and write, at least in his mother tongue. As we moved on, we issued little wonderful certificates for every step he would have passed, the heading always being 'The University of Robben Island'.[77]

Jane Buxton reflects a common determination to take the opportunity to improve her education: 'I want to continue with my Norwegian studies in here, and will write to my kind landlady to see if she can find the books in my flat and send them.'[78]

Reading, in itself, is a vital consolation to captives. Erwin James expresses a commonly held view by prisoners:

Reading books, not surprisingly, is one of the most popular pastimes in prison. Modern prison libraries cater for almost every taste in literature… Certainly books have always been important to me in prison – especially at the beginning. Radio was fine: music, drama, documentaries, news. All brought comfort through the longest, darkest, hours of isolation. But nothing can focus a restless mind like a good book.[79]

James, after his 20 years in prison, demonstrates the importance of books and education. After his release in 1994, he made a career, begun when he was still a prisoner, *inter alia*, in journalism.

James praises 'modern prison libraries', but they were not always so good. Wilfred Macartney places considerable emphasis on the importance of reading. Facing the prospect of a long period of captivity, a man:

must work out some programme of distraction…the first decision he would almost certainly make would be to do a lot of reading… He would not suppose that any obstacle would be put in his way by his jailors to stop carrying out such an edifying programme.[80]

The reasons 'jailors' sometimes discourage reading are varied. Mostly they derive from the feeling that to allow prisoners such freedom is evidence of 'mollycoddling', against which some staff wage a relentless battle. Macartney was at the receiving end of this effort. He would be in for a shock because: 'his jailors would be so persistent in their efforts to stop his doing any serious reading'.[81] He began to understand why. Writing of his imprisonment in the 1930s, he eventually realised that the system was apprehensive about prisoners reading:

Only after repeated complaints did I grasp that the jailor in charge of the library was in fact doing just what most of his superiors wanted done in regard to the convicts' reading, which was to give them as little to read as possible.[82]

In more recent times, after the establishment of the Open University in Britain, prisoners took the opportunity to study for distance degrees. In doing so they were supervised by staff, some of whom resented the fact that the prisoners were provided with opportunities which they did not have.

The wish to punish prisoners beyond their mere incarceration is never far away in English culture. In 2015, a British government Tory minister, Chris Grayling, possessed of the notion that prison was too comfortable, decided to restrict or ban books for prisoners. The outcry was such from the public, especially from the world of authors, that this brutal plan was never carried out. The depressing aspect of this is that such a policy could be resurrected in a twenty-first-century country, often praised historically for the liberal base of its penal policies.

Reading brings huge benefits to prisoners as it also does to society, which presumably is what philistines such as Grayling do not want.

This enthusiasm for reading is true even for prisoners facing death. Madame Jeanne-Marie Roland de la Platiére was imprisoned for conspiring against the French Republic in 1793, and was eventually guillotined. She wrote books in prison, and here she tells us how important her reading was to her:

In the morning I studied the English language in Shaftesbury's Essay on Virtue, and in the poetry of Thomson. The sound metaphysics of the one, and the enchanting descriptions of the other, transported me by turns [*sic*] to the most touching scenes of nature. Shaftesbury's reason gave new strength to mine; while Thomson's sensibility, and his delightful and sublime pictures, went to my heart, and charmed my imagination.[83]

Many years later, another educated woman prisoner, Jane Buxton, felt the same and repeated the appreciation of the relief that books afforded:

> Here locked in a cell all evening, there is nothing else to do but read, so I really relax and enjoy it. Of course it is a tremendous escape and relief from the surroundings. To me, books really have a different effect in prison. I find that I get an extra fifty per cent of pleasure and personal involvement out of them.[84]

She was not the first woman to find consolation in reading in Holloway Prison. There was much argument between suffragettes and the prison authorities about which books they were allowed. Some of the decisions are inexplicable. Thus, Katie Gliddon was not allowed to have the *Golden Treasury of English Songs and Lyrics*.[85] On the other hand, another found that: 'Books that were perceived to oppose the double standard, to offer a critique of patriarchal values or to contain a feminist vision of the future…were taken into the women's prisons and read there by suffragettes.'[86] Again, Gliddon was able to read Mazzini, a famous Italian revolutionary, who was something of an inspiration to the suffragettes, but was probably unheard of by the censoring authority, and so allowed.[87] Sometimes books were authorised, sometimes obtained with the help of staff and sometimes smuggled. Gliddon explained that she was able to read Shelley because she had managed to take the book through reception 'sewn in the collar of her coat'.[88] Shelley seems to have been a favourite amongst suffragettes: 'since it offered a valve for "violent emotions" that continued to maintain "a subversive appeal" for adult women'.[89] Naturally, suffragettes wanted to write, but appeals for them to be allowed writing paper and pencils were denied since they were not 'political prisoners', a discussion to which I shall return. Despite this, they managed to smuggle out letters, but this was a risky business.

Lord Nevill was in Parkhurst Prison 30 years earlier. In 1898, after a trial which naturally attracted nationwide attention, Lord

William Beauchamp Nevill, a son of the Marquess of Abergavenny, was sentenced to five years penal servitude for financial offences. He was lucky, in that his imprisonment coincided with the reforming policies following the Gladstone Report of 1895, which challenged Victorian assumptions about the effectiveness of punishment. He wrote that:

> To many prisoners this provision for reading and writing was invaluable, and life would be scarcely bearable without it. Others who cannot read yet enjoy picture-books, and there are raised-letter books for the blind.[90]

Nathan Leopold, like most educated prisoners, found consolation in reading. In his autobiography, he goes into some detail about his reading.[91]

Dostoevsky was deprived of reading material for most of his time in prison. Despite this, he was to become a famous literary figure. Towards the end of his sentence, he was able to contact some old friends who lived in the town. They gave him money, arranged for letters home and, above all, got him books. As well as being a moving account of his contact with the written word again, it is also a reflection of how cut off a prisoner has been, and how apprehensive he must feel about the future:

> I had not read a single book for several years, and it is hard to describe the strange excitement I felt as I read my first book in prison. I remember that I began to read it one evening, after lock-up, and I went on reading all night, until daybreak.[92]

Another resort of the captive, if it is possible and available, is sport. In Ruhleben in Germany, where the prospect of release was uncertain because it was a POW camp:

> The picture must not be painted too darkly. During the afternoon improvised football matches were going on in the square,

surrounded by excited spectators; after lights out at nine there were 'singing and funny stories', in at least one loft. Shouting and cheering were frequent, and a certain boisterous elation was in evidence. This did not mean that the prisoners accepted what had been done to them, for resentment was strong and vigorously expressed.[93]

MacKenzie, as a prisoner of the Japanese in the Second World War, tells how even though the men were exhausted, they welcomed the physical training (PT) they were forced to do. This 'did at least make a break in the soul-destroying routine'.[94]

There is a remarkable amount of reminiscence about concerts. In camps, and even in closed prisons, there was much resort to concerts of various kinds. It might seem unlikely that Tsarist Russian prisoners were allowed to prepare and perform, with staff present as audience, but they were. This may have been allowed at Christmas to put off the possibility of idle prisoners getting up to mischief. Whatever the motive, Dostoevsky reports that such events were a great success. The prisoners behaved since: 'All that was needed was for these poor men to be allowed to live in their own way for a bit, to enjoy themselves like human beings.'[95]

In Changi in the Second World War, concerts were a critical means of survival. Indeed, R.P.W. Havers described theatrical productions as: 'For so long the staple of Changi's extra-curricular activities.'[96] As Japanese behaviour deteriorated towards the end of the war, concerts were a target of their increasingly erratic orders:

Have just heard that Takahashi the camp commandant has cancelled all entertainment owing to the 'ribald singing' of 'God save the King' in the hospital area. We are (hopeful) that the ban will be lifted again although there is nothing on which to base this hope unless it is the fact that Takahashi has always showed himself sympathetic and helpful.[97]

In the Vietnamese prison of war camps, as we will go on to see, there was, in theory, a ban on communication, attended by threats of dire punishment if the ban was broken. Despite this, prisoners managed to devise all manner of entertainments:

> We continued to create methods and systems for utilizing the time. At first we developed study courses, book reviews, entertainment, and language courses which we held covertly by talking from our separate cells. (By mid-1972 we were allowed to hold these together.) Every Saturday evening we would have a 'movie'. We had two guys who were especially gifted at describing the movies they had seen. Sometimes they would even give us movies that they had never seen but someone else has told them about.[98]

In the same Vietnam prison environment, American prisoners brought their memories of 'movies' to a fine art, by turning them into stories with which they entertained their fellow prisoners:

> Our most popular entertainments, however, were our productions of Sunday, Wednesday, and Saturday Nights at the Movies. I told over a hundred movies in prison, some of them many times over. I tried to recall every movie I had ever seen from *Stalag17* to *One-Eyed Jacks* (a camp favorite). Often running short of popular fare I would make up movies I had never seen. Pilots shot down during air raids in 1972 were a valuable resource for me. They had seen movies that I had not. Desperate for new material, I would pester them almost as soon as they arrived and before they had adjusted to their new circumstances. 'What movies have you seen lately? Tell me about them.' On first acquaintance, they probably thought prison life had seriously affected my mind. But they would give me a few details, and from that I would concoct another movie for Saturday night.[99]

Tobacco is an important factor, dividing even further an already fractured body of people. It is so important that it is justifiably included in this list of means of survival. It is often forbidden, which is a very harsh rule for smokers. It was not allowed (for women) in the Joliet Prison in the 1920s. In a Grand Jury Investigation in 1926, criticism levelled against the Superintendent was that she allowed women to smoke – 'a common practice' – which was 'strictly against the rules'. This, interestingly, did not apply to male prisoners, who were 'even given a weekly tobacco ration'.[100] In more recent times in most American prisons, tobacco is freely available.

Prince Kropotkin, in his French prison, explains that although smoking is severely punished, and the offender fined, prisoners managed to get hold of tobacco. He also notes a common problem for the management of prisons – corruption or 'trafficking' by staff:

> Yet everybody smokes or chews in the prisons. Tobacco is the current money, but a money so highly prized that a cigarette – a nothing for an accomplished smoker – is paid 2d and the 5d *paquet* of tobacco has a currency worth 4s or even more in times of scarcity. This precious merchandise is so highly esteemed that each pinch of tobacco is first chewed, then dried and smoked, and finally taken as snuff, although reduced to mere ash. Useless to say there are undertakers (contractors) who know how to exploit this human weakness and who pay half of the work done with tobacco, valued at the above prices, and that there are also warders who carry on this lucrative trade. Altogether, the prohibition of smoking is a source of so many evils that the French Administration probably will be compelled soon to follow the example of Germany and to sell tobacco at the canteens of the prisons.[101]

Varlam Shalamov, in his Russian prison, writes of the pain of not having a smoke:

It was really tough to lay your hands on tobacco and I should have quit smoking long ago. But even though conditions were what might be called 'appropriate', I never did quit. It was terrible even to imagine that I could lose this simple great convict joy.[102]

Rupert Croft-Cooke describes the dangers attendant upon restrictions on tobacco. This can lead to unnecessary punishment, and, of course, to violence:

'Snout', or tobacco, is so scarce and therefore of such paramount importance in prison life that murders have been committed for an ounce of it, remission is lost every day for breaches of the regulations concerning it, screws risk their jobs to smuggle it, wives and other visitors take the chance of prosecution in order to pass it to prisoners and a whole commerce with important chiefs and many underlings thrives on it.[103]

There is no single cause of evil in prisons so active as this.[104]

Red Collar Man also draws attention to the disproportionate amount of punishment which is drawn down on offenders. At the time of his imprisonment, smoking was banned in English prisons:

The one almost universal form of misconduct in prison which is the cause of eighty per cent of reports made by the warders against the lags, can be told in a single word – 'snout'. Snout is the convicts' word for tobacco, and chewing is most popular amongst them although smoking has some followers. Of course it is easier to have a chew than a smoke as there is much more danger of discovery attached to smoking. It must be done in your own cell and the smoke must be blown into the ventilator, an unsatisfying and uncomfortable procedure.[105]

An almost universal feature of prison life is that tobacco replaces money as currency. In Egypt, 'In prison, cigarettes become a currency of exchange, a replacement for money. Every service is compensated with a certain number of cigarettes.'[106]

In Auschwitz, a rough tobacco called Mahorca was one of the currencies. Not only was this used within the prison, but it was also used to trade with free civilian workers:

> Among the ordinary prisoners there are not many who search for Mahorca to smoke it personally; for the most part it leaves the camp and ends up in the hands of the civilian workers of the Buna. The traffic is an instance of a kind of '*kombinacja*' frequently practiced; the prisoner, somehow saving a ration of bread, invests it in Mahorca; he cautiously gets in touch with a civilian addict who acquires the Mahorca, paying in cash with a portion of bread greater than that initially invested. The prisoner eats the surplus, and puts back on the market the remaining ration. Speculations of this kind establish a tie between the internal economy of the Lager and the economic life of the outside world.[107]

Middle-class prisoners are often surprised at what are, in fact, the perfectly normal features of prison life. In Britain, for example, where in modern times smoking is allowed, prisoners cannot afford to smoke as many cigarettes as they want. So there are 'barons' who lend tobacco at interest. Some staff believe this is related to the outside, in that money is transferred by people outside the prison, and the tobacco is then handed over inside.

Like so many prisoners in their reminiscences, Peter Wildeblood, as well as noting how important tobacco is, mentions the role of the 'baron':

> Since tobacco was the common currency, the attitude of prisoners towards it provided a faithful reflection of the attitude to money which he had had 'outside'. The miser hoarded his 'snout' as carefully as though it were a bag of gold; the cadger devoted all his ingenuity to borrowing other people's fag-ends; the spendthrift smoked like a chimney all through the week-

end, and then went without until Friday; the financial wizard created a capital of two ounces and an interest-rate of 50% per week, Men fought over a cigarette as they would have done over buried treasure.[108]

Red Collar Man was a baron, and he describes how he operated. As he was a 'trustie', he could move freely about the prison, and notably had access to the kitchens, since he collected food for prisoners undergoing punishment. If such a prisoner or his friends had tobacco, 'they could send me some and I would endeavour to smooth their punishment... I would give food for a chew of tobacco.'[109] He would do this by hiding food in the man's cell while the officer escorted him elsewhere.

So valuable is tobacco as the currency in prisons that sometimes staff are corrupted by it. Kropotkin notes this, as I have mentioned, but it is common everywhere. They 'traffick', which means that they bring tobacco in at some risk to their jobs and arrange payment by friends or relatives outside the prison. Such trading can be lucrative.

Rather rarer, but often present in writing, is discussion about alcohol. This again depends on the country. In the accounts of Russian prisoners, for example, discussion about vodka is never far away. Indeed, it seems to have corroded the entire system. It is imported from the outside, or made in the prison, and is widely used as currency. Chekhov notes how a cohabitant woman will leave her man for another if the latter, *inter alia*, has more vodka.[110] In other systems, such as the British, it is used more as a placebo against the prison situation.

There has been in more recent times another form of substitute currency. As the use of drugs has become more widespread in society, prisoners frequently refer to the use of drugs in prison. In England one authority writes that, 'Drugs illegitimately obtained and retained are the prized currency of illicit prison barter systems.'[111] Prisoners will go to considerable lengths to obtain drugs, even if the chances of not being caught are minimal. Thus in 2016 in Ranby Prison in

England, 'Prisoners muscled their way into a wing office at HMP Ranby in Nottinghamshire to take back legal highs.'[112]

> Inmates seized drugs from staff at a prison that is at risk of being 'overwhelmed' by a flood of so-called legal highs, an inspection report has revealed.
>
> Prisoners muscled their way into a wing office at HMP Ranby in Nottinghamshire to 'forcibly' take back a package containing new psychoactive substances (known collectively as NPS) that has just been intercepted by officers after being thrown over the walls. Watchdogs also disclose that some prisoners under the influence of NPS were left with fellow inmates who were asked to check that their condition did not worsen as health services struggled to treat the most seriously affected... It follows warnings that NPS is now the most serious threat to safety and security in Britain's prisons. There have been reports of officers falling ill after inhaling fumes from substances used by inmates.[113]

At the beginning of the twenty-first century in England, the use of drugs began to dominate the concerns of staff and those members of the public who were interested in prison affairs. There were frequent press reports of the widespread use of drugs and the often dire consequences. There were also reliable reports of the lengths to which prisoners would go to obtain them, including the use of 'drones' to fly in supplies. John Hoskison's account of his time in prison in the mid-1990s is dominated by the obsession with drug use. This episode seems to have been usual:

> That night was the most frightening of my life. When the lights went out Jimmy began an orgy of drug-taking. He rolled a taper about five foot long, and stuck it to the ceiling with some old porridge he'd scraped out of the rubbish box. It hung down above his head like a stalactite. After preparing the foil and the heroin, he lit the taper which burned at a ferocious rate even

though tightly rolled. The whole cell glowed red in the light of the flames. The grotesque shadow of his bent-over body, as he maniacally sucked in the fumes was etched on the wall and looked like the devil at play. It was a scene from hell.[114]

Despite every device to make life tolerable, adjustment has to be made to low standards, indignity, absence of choice and a host of other singular matters. And this has to be done in the context of a very alien community. Even with every effort, and the many physical and mental diversions the prisoner may pursue, in the end the process of what is called 'institutionalisation', begun with reception procedures, is effective. Some captives who have enough experience of this find it impossible to ever regain their independence. Norman describes how this happens:

One of the reasons the nicks are so full, is the wonderful security one feels there, you do not have to do anything for yourself. You are fed, clothed and housed, the price of cause is your freedom, but to quite a lot of geezers doing bird this doesn't worry them at all.[115]

Koestler recognised this feeling at once: 'This morning there was nothing to get up for; no work awaited me, no mail, no duties. For the first time I experienced that curious feeling of freedom and irresponsibility which is one of the illusions of prison psychosis.'[116]

Dostoevsky describes how a fellow convict seems irredeemably in the grip of this 'psychosis':

He had set himself up in the prison as though he intended to live his entire life there: everything that surrounded him, from his mattress and pillows to his eating utensils, was solidly arranged as though it was meant to last for a prolonged stay. I doubt if he ever thought about his release.[117]

El Sa'adawi found to her surprise and horror that she was beginning to forget about release. Everyday life soon began to eclipse thoughts about release. There were:

> Other matters. No sooner would the *shawisha* open the door to the cell than I would run out to the enclosure to dry the clothes I'd washed, and to dry out my mattress and blanket. I would start to believe that I was not waiting, that I had been born here and would die in the same place.[118]

So the captive adjusts to living with other people. How can this group of people be described? Is this a society? Or a community? Among the standard criteria for a society is that there should be a large element of friendship and tolerance, and there should be general consensus about common interest. In the case of the captive group these are hardly central features. So, depending on definitions, community may be more accurate if this means the mere fact of living together for the same reason, but with little else in common, provided that such a definition takes account of the fact that there are social relationships in the captive group, even if these are characterised by hostility. The next chapter looks in detail at this group which has been thrown together.

Notes
1. Giallombardo *op. cit.* p.99.
2. Shalamov, Varlam. *Kolyma Tales.* p.16.
3. Breed *op. cit.* pp.53–54.
4. Wood *op. cit.* p.243.
5. *Ibid.* pp.243–244.
6. Barker *op. cit.* p.99.
7. Thilo, Hans-Joachim. 'The Christian Church Comes to Life' in Moir. p.120.
8. Hutheesing *op. cit.* p.123.
9. Koestler *op. cit.* p.77.
10. Watt *op. cit.* p.140.
11. Giallombardo *op. cit.* p.135.
12. Bryan, Helen. *Inside.* p.13.
13. *Ibid.* p.125.
14. Bonhoeffer, Dietrich. *Letters and Papers from Prison.* p.15.

15. *Ibid.* pp.26–27.
16. *Ibid.* p.39.
17. *Ibid.* p.57.
18. Koestler *op. cit.* p.86.
19. Levi *op. cit.* p.46.
20. Williams *et al. op. cit.* p.168.
21. Ketchum, J. Davidson. *Ruhleben: A Prison Camp Society.* pp.32–33.
22. *Ibid.* p.97.
23. d'Harcourt *op. cit.* p.126.
24. Lawrence *op. cit.* p.181.
25. Zeno *op. cit.* pp.32–33.
26. Behan, Brendan. *Borstal Boy.* pp.124–125.
27. Mandela, Nelson. *Long Walk to Freedom.* p.406.
28. *Ibid.*
29. Braddon, Russell. 'Surrender, Like Marriage' in Mikes. p.57.
30. Watt *op. cit.* pp.146–147.
31. Havers, R.P.W. *Reassessing the Japanese Prisoner of War Experience: The Changi POW Camp Singapore, 1942–5.* p.117.
32. Zeno *op. cit.* p.70.
33. Wood *op. cit.* p.35.
34. Braddon *op. cit.* p.49.
35. *Ibid.*
36. *Ibid.*
37. Stewart, Ian McD. G. 'What Sort of Charity?' in Moir. p.159.
38. Zeno *op. cit.* pp.35–36.
39. Dostoevsky *op. cit.* pp.305–306.
40. Solzhenitsyn *op. cit.* p.186.
41. Morrison, Leonard Haslett. 'Reality Regained' in Moir. p.79.
42. *Ibid.*
43. Zeno *op. cit.* p.57.
44. *Ibid.* p.156.
45. Wildeblood *op. cit.* p.142.
46. Maine, G.F. *The Works of Oscar Wilde.* pp.857–858.
47. *Ibid.* p.881.
48. *Ibid.* p.858.
49. *Ibid.* p.860.
50. Jeanty-Raven, M.H. 'Without frontiers' in Moir. pp.57–58.
51. Ketchum *op. cit.* p.75.
52. *Ibid.* p.118.
53. Watt *op. cit.* p.146.
54. Leopold *op. cit.* p.88.
55. Elstob *op. cit.* p.69.
56. Braddon *op. cit.* p.59.
57. MacKenzie, K.P. *Operation Rangoon Jail.* pp.80–81.

58. Dostoevsky *op. cit.* p.354.
59. Bone, Edith. 'Solitary Confinement' in Moir. p.36.
60. *Ibid.* p.37.
61. Heimler, Eugene. 'Children of Auschwitz' in Mikes. p.8.
62. Hoskison *op. cit.* p.88.
63. Breed *op. cit.* p.59.
64. *Ibid.*
65. Zeno *op. cit.* p.28.
66. Lawrence *op. cit.* p.63.
67. Dodge, Mara L. *'Whores and Thieves of the Worst Kind': A Study of Women, Crime, and Prisons, 1835–2000.* p.46.
68. Dostoevsky *op. cit.* pp.121–123.
69. Bryan *op. cit.* p.203.
70. *Ibid.* pp.203–204.
71. Buxton and Turner *op. cit.* p.42.
72. Leopold *op. cit.* p.83.
73. *Ibid.*
74. Watt *op. cit.* p.149.
75. Deacon, Harriet. *The Island: A History of Robben Island 1488–1990.* p.139.
76. *Ibid.* p.112, quoting an interview with Dikgang Moseneke.
77. *Ibid.* p.112.
78. Buxton and Turner *op. cit.* p.26.
79. James *A Life Inside op. cit.* p.103.
80. Macartney *op. cit.* pp.194–5.
81. *Ibid.* p.195.
82. *Ibid.*
83. Scheffler *op. cit.* p.12.
84. Buxton and Turner *op. cit.* p.118.
85. Schwan, Anne. *Convict Voices: Women, Class, and Writing about Prison in Nineteenth-Century England.* p.158.
86. *Ibid.*
87. *Ibid.* p.160.
88. *Ibid.* p.161.
89. *Ibid.* p.162.
90. WBN (Lord William Nevill). *Penal Servitude.* p.126.
91. Leopold *op. cit.* pp.150–151.
92. Dostoevsky *op. cit.* p.353.
93. Ketchum *op. cit.* p.24.
94. MacKenzie *op. cit.* p.80.
95. Dostoevsky *op. cit.* p.203.
96. Havers *op. cit.* p.146.
97. *Ibid.* pp.146–147.
98. Risner, Robinson. *The Passing of the Night: My Seven Years as a Prisoner of the North Vietnamese.* pp.229–230.

99. McCain, John, with Salter, Mark. *Faith of My Fathers*. p.330.

100. Dodge *op. cit.* p.145.

101. Kropotkin *op. cit.* p.291.

102. Shalamov *op. cit.* p.112.

103. Croft-Cooke *op. cit.* p.157.

104. *Ibid.* p.160.

105. Red Collar Man. *Chokey.* p.168.

106. El Sa'adawi *op. cit.* p.81.

107. Levi *op. cit.* p.86.

108. Wildeblood *op. cit.* p.142.

109. Red Collar Man *op. cit.* p.163.

110. Chekhov, Anton. *The Island of Sakhalin.* p.158.

111. Carlen *Criminal Women. op. cit.* p.165.

112. Sandhu, S. 'HMP Ranby Prisoners "Muscle into" Office to Take Back Legal Highs, Report Finds.' *The Independent*, 25 February 2016.

113. *The Daily Telegraph*, 25 February 2016.

114. Hoskison *op. cit.* pp.82–83.

115. Norman *op. cit.* p.81.

116. Koestler *op. cit.* p.82.

117. Dostoevsky *op. cit.* p.322.

118. El Sa'adawi *op. cit.* p.98.

— *3* —

A Community?

Fyodor Dostoevsky is one of many when he points out that the world of a captive society is, by its nature, a world of its own:

> Here was our own world, unlike anything else; here were our own laws, our own dress, our own manners and customs, here was the house of the living dead, a life like none other upon earth, and people who were special, set apart.[1]

One hundred and twenty years later Brian Stratton, serving nine years for robbery in Parkhurst Prison in England, echoed exactly that observation:

> A prison is a world within a world, it has its own rules and regulations quite apart from those laid down by the Prison Department; it has its own currency, tobacco, and on some occasions its own justice.[2]

Another English prisoner had a very different background from Stratton. Taki Theodoracopulos is the son of a Greek millionaire, a self-described playboy and a gossip writer. He was convicted in 1984 of possession of heroin and sentenced to four months. But he, too, echoes the view that people in captivity do not form a coherent group:

Prisoners, and in particular black prisoners, I found, have a victim-fixation complex, despite the absolutely objective treatment cons receive inside. No one, not even the worst recidivists I came into contact with, ever admitted to feeling guilty or to having been at fault. In prison there is no feeling of community whatsoever. Everyone is out for himself... Only two moods compete in prison – apathy and hostility. At bottom, everybody feels lonely yet craves solitude.[3]

In 1943 in the United States, Jim Quillen was sentenced to 45 years for kidnapping two people in an attempt to escape from a robbery. He was released on parole in 1958. The idea of a 'community' is firmly demolished by Quillen. He served most of his captivity on Alcatraz, but he was also imprisoned in San Quentin. He was returned to the latter prior to his final release, and noticed that:

Today the prison was controlled in many aspects by the young, vicious, and terroristic gangs who inhabited the prison. Individual problems were settled not by the individual, but by the gang. Disputes were not settled face to face, but often by a silent knife in the back wielded by someone unknown to the victim. Inmates not involved in gangs found it wise and prudent to be ever-watchful, careful with what they said, where they went, and with whom they associated. Gang members were easy to offend and responded with violence.[4]

Nathan Leopold in Illinois, with his considerable experience, puts it more mildly, but makes the same point:

Actually the people incarcerated in a penitentiary do not form a homogeneous group; the only thing they have in common is that they have been convicted of felonies. Any theory that tries to embrace all the individuals is doomed to failure just because they have so little in common.[5]

In the Berlin prison, Ruhleben, during the First World War, prisoners felt the same: 'The camp was no longer a mere cage full of prisoners; it was a spatial pattern intersected by many barriers, barriers invisible to an outsider but real and effective to the men.'[6]

In short, it is a mistake to assume that the body of captives is a 'society', as that term is commonly understood.

This is despite every attempt by the system to enforce conformity and uniformity; captives bring with them all their social baggage. The divisions and groupings in the wider free community are maintained inside the prison. Thus are found affiliations of race, of religion, of political orientation, of regional loyalties, and the discrete divisions within the criminal groups which depend on the status of the crimes which are committed. There is one very notable exception to the importation of structures and values intact, and that is a curious reversal of social hierarchy.

Two of the outstanding examples are those of Russia and England. In the former, whether in Tsarist or Soviet times, the rigid social divisions of the free society are turned on their head in prison. There, the aristocrats were treated with contempt and often cruelty by lower-class captives. In the case of England, the situation is best exemplified, but not exclusively, by prisoner of war camps, especially in the Far East in the Second World War. Here the officers tried to maintain the formal relationship with the 'other ranks' which were the linchpin in the 'free' army. But the situation was now very different. In captivity, initiative, physical strength and character are the determinants of hierarchy, especially in obtaining food and other commodities. Formal rank and circumstances of birth become irrelevant. This was exacerbated when military officers behaved badly and selfishly, as we shall go on to see.

Although there are few of the positive characteristics of a society or community, a possible common denominator is a shared dislike or hatred of the staff – a constant refrain in Frank Norman's account. But we shall go on to see that this hatred is moderated by experience and the need to survive. In any case, as Norman readily reports:

There is one thing in the nick that cannot be blamed on the commissioners and that is your fellow prisoners. It is well known that you have to watch the men in grey far closer than those in blue and trust them less.[7]

He then describes how he left tobacco lying about and it was stolen: 'I do not blame who ever did take it I blame myself leaving it where someone could nick it, after all that's what prison's are for. Theives!'[8] This would seem a rather trivial example of the lack of 'fellowship', until we remember the critical importance of tobacco throughout many prison systems.

Even though stealing is despised and the 'sanctions' for those caught are severe, it is a commonplace of captive life. A Norwegian prisoner deplores such behaviour:

He is a bad fellow-inmate... He steals from the others. X had ten crowns in real money in his wallet...and Y went in alone, stayed there for a little while and came out again... Later X was going to play cards for money, and then the money was gone... it's difficult to complain about it, since human money is really not allowed in the institution.[9]

In the American Civil War, prisons there quickly emerged an underclass of thieves:

We now formed the acquaintance of a species of human vermin that united with the Rebels, cold, hunger, lice and the oppression of distraint, to leave nothing undone that could add to the miseries of our prison life.
These were the fledglings of the slums and dives of New York.[10]

Stuart Hood was an officer in the Highland Light Infantry when he was captured by the Italians during the retreat from El Alamein in 1942. As a prisoner, he recalls much more serious selfishness because it became the habit of formerly decent men:

> It was a cold hungry place where at times the veneer of education and acquired codes of conduct wore thin. Men stole bread from each other and bickered over cigarette stubs or over the size of a helping of maggoty rice.[11]

Race is the dominating divider in any prison system set in a plural or multi-racial society. In any prison system, that race which is in a minority, and therefore at the bottom of the hierarchy in a free society, is over-represented amongst captives. The one exception was that of South Africa and, more generally, of colonial regimes during the days of white supremacy, where black people were in the majority in the free community. This disproportionate number of minority groups who are locked up is true at the present time in, for example, Britain, Australia, New Zealand and the United States. A representation of this fact can be seen from the not so well-known figures of the captive numbers of Native Americans:

> Native Americans are only 0.6 per cent of the total population, yet they comprise 2.9 per cent of federal and state prison populations. The disproportion of imprisoned Natives is more clearly seen at the state level, where they account for 33.2 per cent of the total state (prison) population in Alaska, 23.6 per cent in South Dakota, 16.9 per cent in North Dakota, and 17.3 per cent in Montana compared to approximately 15 per cent, 7 per cent, 4 per cent, and 6 per cent of the overall state populations respectively.[12]

In England there is a similar pattern. Quoting official Home Office figures, Pat Carlen notes that, in respect of women: '16 per cent of all British nationals in prison in June 1995 were from ethnic minority groups':[13]

84 per cent were white; 13 per cent were black; 1 per cent were of Chinese or other ethnic appearance. This compares with the general female population of England and Wales (British nationals aged 15–65) of whom 95 per cent were white 2 per cent were black, 2 per cent were South Asian and 1 per cent were Chinese.[14]

There was a prison on Rottnest Island off the coast of Western Australia. From the 1830s until the beginning of the twentieth century, it was used exclusively for Aboriginal prisoners. These were often convicted of offences such as cattle stealing, which to the Aborigines made little sense, since any animal roaming seemingly had no owner and could be hunted. Aborigines continue to be disproportionately represented in Australian prisons for a variety of more modern, by European standards, offences. Thus there are Aboriginal prisoners convicted of physical assault, outlawed by European legislation, but in tune with traditional custom. In marked contrast to this numerical dominance of black and minority prisoners in criminal prisons, most prison staff in all the countries mentioned are white.

The divisions of race are very pronounced in some state prisons in America. In the Dwight Women's Reformatory in Illinois, the 'cottages' in which the women were kept were desegregated in 1960, but one woman who was locked up there after that draws attention to the fact that segregation was still in operation, and this was just one manifestation of discrimination: 'Blacks did the serious manual labour. We worked outside. We were the garbage collectors, worked on the laundry truck. The white girls had the light jobs, while they treated us like men. So it was basically segregated cottages.'[15]

Although there was not, in the 1960s, such segregation in the federal prison at Alderson, white women brought with them the same attitudes about race which were commonly held in society at large:

The physical proximity with Negroes is also quite distressing for many white inmates; especially acute is the fear of contamination from the communal use of bathing and toilet facilities. As one white southern inmate put it: 'It was hard to use the rest room, the shower and to eat with them. In the beginning I wiped off the toilet seat, and in the shower I would let the water run a long time before I used it.'[16]

These remarks were made in the early 1960s.

In the same prison as the one Giallombardo is describing here – Alderson in America, the only Federal prison for women – another prisoner, Helen Bryan, notes the same distaste. She reports white prisoners as saying: 'Isn't it awful for white and coloured girls to be eating in the same dining room? Before long they'll be putting the coloured girls in the same cottages with us and that's when I'll make bush (abscond).'[17]

In the late 1960s a member of staff of the University of Northern Illinois, Dae H. Chang, taught a number of extension classes in an unnamed state penitentiary in that state. As a result, the students wrote a number of essays which were published under the title *The Prison: Voices from the Inside*. There are a number of constant themes, one of which is homosexual behaviour, which I will deal with later, and another is racial hatred. Since in the United States race is the most sensitive social issue, it is one that is imported into prison. One account will illustrate this dominant and divisive strand in this prison, and one supposes by extension in all the prisons of the United States. The prisoner begins with a common disclaimer:

Before I came to the penitentiary 16 months ago I had no real racial prejudices. Upon being exposed to strong racism from both blacks and whites, I realized it was part of the adaptation process. Racial factors entered into everything from seating at meals to sporting events.[18]

This prisoner, and others, claims further that white officers will do everything to excuse black behaviour. This is for a variety of reasons, including the fact that the dominance of the blacks, through violence, leads to some kind of peace in the prison. The staff are also afraid that the blossoming cause of civil rights will undermine any attempt they make to assert authority. In the same prison, another prisoner describes overt racism: 'The best job assignments are held by white inmates, except for a few "token positions" that were awarded to Negro inmates.'[19]

George Jackson was well known in America in the twentieth century for his militancy in the black power movement. In 1960, aged 18, he was charged with stealing $70 from a petrol station. Advised to plead guilty, he was given a sentence of one year to life. He had two previous convictions. He spent ten years in Soledad Prison in California, over seven of those in solitary confinement. Then he was accused of murdering a white guard. He underwent a long trial, which was never finished because two days before his final hearing, Jackson was shot by a guard while allegedly attempting to escape. Naturally, he has plenty to say about race in prison:

> When I hit the yard in December '62 the brothers were lining up in the rain, outside the protection of the shed that covers half the upper yard. The Mexicans and whites had occupied all the lines under the shed. They would save long stretches of space for friends who never showed. So I had a picture on my first day there of the old slave, wet and trembling while these other people relaxed with plenty of room under the shed. The brothers were mainly concerned with avoiding any trouble, since the pig invariably will shoot at the black face in a black and white altercation... The blacks had to sit in the rear of the TV room on hard, armless, backless benches while the Mexicans and whites sat up front on cushioned chairs and benches with backrests!!! Now check this, if one of those punks was in his cell or in the shower, no one could sit in his seat and certainly no black dared sit there, I'm serious!!! All of this taking place in front of a uniform and a large, bold-print sign in English and Spanish that read 'No Saving of Seats Allowed'!!![20]

Jack Abbott, a white prisoner, seems to have had a different experience, and consequently his perception is different:

> In some cases, the prison regime will give privileges to blacks and Chicanos and Indians which they deny to whites... They implement this in many ways. They can use inmate organizations called 'culture groups'. These groups are given resources not available to others of races not of a certain 'cultural group'... Another way is by harassing *only* one race – more times than not, *today* it is the *white* prisoners who are being tortured and discriminated against.[21]

The observation has been made, by Luana Ross, that there is racial animosity between Native American and white prisoners in the Women's Correctional Centre of Montana:

> Prisoner relationships are definitely tense at the WCC, and ignorance of Native American culture spills over into the interactions between Native and white prisoners. For instance, one Native woman's religion is ridiculed by her three white cellmates who call it 'voodoo'. The term *voodoo* is also used by a guard in a write-up issued to a Native prisoner who threatened to 'hex' the guard. While voodoo is a recognized and credible religion, in this instance the designation is used as a racial slur.[22]

In England at the end of the twentieth century, as more and more black people were imprisoned, there was increasing tension. In the twenty-first century, such tensions are being exacerbated by the rising percentage of non-white prisoners. Taki recalls how:

> Two West Indians have been screaming abuse at everything and everybody throughout the night. I can tell they're Rastafarians by the racist tone of the abuse they're heaping out. Two whites, meanwhile, are giving it back to them in spades, no pun intended. The shouting lasted almost until dawn and by the time

they become too exhausted to go on, I've picked up a large new vocabulary of racial insults.[23]

John Hoskison, from a white, English middle-class background, was astonished when he first went on 'exercise' in his prison to see that: 'the other hundred or so sat on the ground at one end, forming two distinct groups: black and white'.[24] Later, at Coldingley Prison:

> Over seventy per cent of the inmates were black and for the first time in my life, I was part of a minority group. It didn't matter to me (we were all in the same situation), but it surprised me.[25]

In the event, it mattered a good deal since the black prisoners seriously affected his sleep, and his mental health because of the soaring noise of their ghetto blasters. Further, as he explained to a visitor: 'The black guys – they run the place. In fact they run the whole prison. All the officers are scared stiff of them; they daren't lift a finger because they're too quick off the draw at crying discrimination.'[26]

The purest forms of race division and race hatred were to be found in the prisons of South Africa during the Apartheid regime. Many black people were imprisoned for political offences. I have already recounted some of Nelson Mandela's reminiscences but there are others. One was Caesarina Kona Makhoere, who was imprisoned for five years following the Soweto uprising of 1976: she had spent a year before that in solitary confinement awaiting trial. The difference in the ways racial groups were treated of course reflected the situation in the wider society:

> When it came to white prisoners, things were different. We could see some white prisoners; they were feeling at home. All white prisoners had the chance to choose what type of shoes they wanted. They had stylish shoes and sandals, and the dresses were all smart. You would not be able to identify anyone of them as a prisoner.[27]

After describing the appalling prison food, she writes that at her table was a prisoner whose: 'Diet was completely different. When we questioned her different diet the answer was: "She is Coloured. So she's getting a Coloured diet." So it goes without saying that what Aminah Desai ate was considered too good for us blacks.'[28]

It is difficult to place in any exclusive category the following situation after the fall of Singapore in 1942, although race seems to be the main factor in the divisiveness which followed. Amongst the thousands of allied prisoners rounded up by the Japanese were many Sikh soldiers who were serving in the British Indian Army. At the same time, there came into being an anti-British force called the Indian National Army (the INA, but by the British the Indian Renegade Army), which sided with the Japanese. Many of these Sikh soldiers joined the INA, and there was a certain amount of sympathy for them amongst the Allied troops because it was believed they realistically had no choice. This sympathy quickly evaporated when the Japanese ordered that the prisoners should salute the Sikhs who were placed on sentry duty. Major Shean expressed the general view with his usual vigour:

> We are absolutely livid – the Japs have ordered us to salute renegade Sikh sentries. We all want the G.O.C. (General Officer Commanding) to say NO to the Japs., but he hasn't done so. I think it's the only time. We salute Japs. as our legitimate capturers but the last straw is to have to salute traitors. I'm buggarized if I'm going to and hope I won't be shot. There have already been several nasty incidents and beatings up and the G.O.C. has sent in a 'protest'. But the Japs. merely use our 'protests' for toilet paper.[29]

The last straw was the presence of Sikhs in the execution party which shot four prisoners who had attempted to escape.[30]

The divisions in Ruhleben were considerable, but were inevitable because of the random nature of the population, and persisted throughout the history of the prison. The most notable divide was between those who were pro-British and those who were 'German minded'. This latter group eventually had to be segregated because of the animosity between them and the others. As well as this central split, there were separate quarters for German citizens, Jews, 'Negros' and boys. Apart from these major classifications, the backgrounds of the occupants of most of the 'boxes' varied a good deal.[31]

In Ruhleben, we see an overlap between race and nationality, and this is echoed in other accounts. Ravensbrück was the only German Concentration Camp for women. Located some fifty miles north of Berlin, it held many thousands of prisoners from the usual wide variety of backgrounds. There were German and Austrian communists, gypsies, Poles, Russians, 'asocials' (prostitutes) and ordinary criminals; Resistance fighters from the occupied territories; and Jews from all over Europe. A very large group was the Jehovah's Witnesses. In the history of the Camps, the resistance of the Witnesses, and their suffering, is much undersung. In the autumn of 1939, over half the camp consisted of them,[32] and they consistently refused to work because the work was directed towards the war effort. All they had to do to get their release was to sign a form renouncing their faith. Only a small number did so.

The camp put people together indiscriminately, which is to be expected when the Nazi regime regarded all the inmates as scum, whose differences were of no significance, except that some were even more despicable than others:

> There had always been 'slums' of a sort in the camp-blocks more cramped and dirtier than others, usually towards the back, and occupied by asocials, Gypsies and others at the bottom of the heap… Most Russians and Ukrainians were brought to the slum blocks, as were the Jews who were arriving again at the camp. All the French were brought here automatically. There were no exceptions: the French countesses, teachers, generals' daughters, 'volunteers' and prostitutes were all *Franzosensäue.* [33]

There were the same national divisions in Tsarist Russia. Dostoevsky writes about the Poles in his camp, who kept themselves away from other prisoners.[34]

Added to the questions of race and nationality is the matter of religion, and sometimes all three are intertwined. In Stuart Hood's camp in Italy in the Second World War, there were the same religious divisions as there were in free society, notably 'the Catholics, who were favoured by the Italians…the…Anglicans…and the Dutch Reformed South Africans'. The latter provide a good example of how captive societies do not leave their culture at the prison gate. They were 'deeply entrenched in fundamentalist attitudes, citing the Old Testament as the doctrinal basis for their racialism'.[35]

A remarkable example of the effect of importing religion is recounted by Frank Gallagher. He was one of a number of prisoners, detained without charge by the British in 1920, and sent to Mountjoy Prison in Dublin. There they organised a hunger strike which was, incidentally, a success and they were released. One tactic used to try to break the strike was to refuse Catholic Absolution to anyone on the verge of death. When the priest told Gallagher this:

> I had to think it all out when he had gone away. The issues he had raised, although subconsciously I felt them to be false, were tremendous issues, reaching out into eternity, reaching in into the very center of the soul. There were momentous political issues as well. If the men were refused Absolution, the strike might collapse. It was the only thing that could break us… But with the shutting up of the prison on Saturday the spiritual unrest became almost unbearable… Even now the thing stands as a shadow within me, darker far than the shadow of death.[36]

As well as race, religion and nationality, captives are divided by political affiliations. Palestinian prisoners in Israeli prisons are just one example of captives who are divided by deeply held political beliefs. These depend upon religious orientation, political affiliations, educational background and other factors. It is not surprising that their beliefs were firm: after all, many have risked their lives in their cause. With the connivance of the authorities the captives are ruled by faction leaders, factions which mirrored those of the free Palestinian community: 'The actions, practices, and rituals of the prison community are constantly compared with the parallel ones of the larger Palestinian community in the occupied territories, based on each organization's view of Palestinian society.'[37]

Nashif gives an instance of how this worked in practice. Writing of the allocation of jobs, he explains: 'At first these roles were designated by the prison authorities, and later by the community itself. Each faction allocates captives to work in the prison facilities proportionally to the number of its members in the specific prison.'[38] Like other commentators, Nashif puts the best possible construction on these arrangements: '[By the early and mid-1980s] the dynamic of redefining the social and material networks shaped by the prison to serve the needs and purposes of the community of captives was highly developed.'[39]

However, in a group which is so highly charged politically, it is extremely unlikely that there are not stresses and tensions, and prisoners bear witness to that. There was anger, for instance, over the behaviour of censors:

> For example, I saw the censor (appointed by the Palestinian organisations) in the prison...as you know several Hebrew papers were sent to us, one of them was *Ha'olam Hazeh*, and in this magazine there were lots of scenes and photos of almost full nudity. Now the censor comes and surveys it. He has ink, so he covers the photos with the ink, so that when the magazine is read by the different prisoners nobody will see it... Of course, who sees it? The censor...ohhh...the censor sees what the others do not see.[40]

> ...then in 1986 came TV...and the censorship worked even more than with the books...where there was a scene he would turn off the TV, and the moment it had ended he would turn it on... This

whole issue created a bad atmosphere, it didn't take seriously the people who were watching the TV, and expressed mistrust in the prisoner's ability to take responsibility for himself. [41]

There has always been in the recorded history of captivity the separation both *de jure* and *de facto* of Jews. There are sometimes expressions of a wish for separateness by Jews. In Ruhleben there was also official segregation. The two or three hundred Orthodox Jews were separated 'within a week of internment, ostensibly for dietary reasons'. They were put in 'the oldest and dirtiest of the stables', and separation seems to have 'marked Barrack 6 off as a distinct social unit'.[42] Once again traditions prevailed, and a Jewish prisoner wrote:

> Barrack six was a sort of byword in the camp, invariably uttered in a tone of contempt. On the only occasion I visited the camp Cinema Palace there appeared upon the screen the figure of a grey-bearded old Jew gloating over a heap of coins, and at once somebody called out 'Barrack Six!' and a guffaw of laughter swept the room.[43]

There were, though, feelings which could have turned into nastiness. A notable instance was food. Kosher meals were sent in by members of a Berlin synagogue, and when food became scarce in the city, Jews were allowed to cook their own food. The result was that: 'The camp, however, pictured Barrack Six as living in luxury while Christians lined up at the soup kitchens.'[44] This anti-Jewish feeling was fostered by the camp newspapers, which commonly displayed 'many anti-Semitic witticisms'. In addition, Jews 'set themselves up as dealers in everything from cups of tea to jewelry'. The outcome was that: 'the Jews remained an outgroup as long as they lived in their barrack'.[45]

In Dostoevsky's prison, there was much excitement when it was learned that a Jew, the only one, was coming in. He quickly set up as a money-lender, but despite that: 'Everyone really seemed fond of him and none of the men ever harmed him.'[46] One of the strange paradoxes of the nineteenth-century Russian prison empire was that

Jews were allowed out to go to the synagogue, and Fomich, the Jew in Dostoevsky's prison, did so: 'All in all he lived in the lap of luxury.'[47] Nor is the modern English prison exempt from the historic attitudes towards Jews. In his English prison, a captive, Wilfred Macartney recalls: 'There is a good deal of anti-Jewish feeling in prison.'[48]

Even among the Jews there can be found historic and persisting divisions, as there is amongst Jewry in the free community. These are imported and perhaps exacerbated because of this most desperate of circumstances. In Auschwitz, Primo Levi tells us:

> Everyone knows that the 174000s (their prison identity numbers) are the Italian Jews who arrived two months ago, all lawyers, all with degrees, who were more than a hundred and are now only forty; the ones who do not know how to work, and let their bread be stolen, and are slapped from morning to evening. The Germans call them *zwei linke Hände* (two left hands), and even the Polish Jews despise them as they do not speak Yiddish.[49]

One of the most persisting of the 'invisible' divisions in the captive community, especially where British captives are concerned, is that of class. It is fair to say that this is the dominant theme of most of their literature, which is not surprising since it is mostly written by members of the British middle and upper classes, who reveal themselves riven by factions.

In Ruhleben, even though conditions were cramped, there were not as many disputes as might be expected. This we are told is because of the virtues of the middle class:

> The habitual reserve of the Englishman, while discouraging intimacy, is entirely compatible with politeness, good feeling, and regard for others. And it involves, further, a high degree of self-control-invaluable in avoiding such quarrels as often convulsed more intimate boxes.[50]

It should be added that this expression of belief in the superior behaviour of the English is rarely to be found in other accounts of prisoner of war groups.

Perhaps the strongest sense of camaraderie would be expected in prisoner of war camps. MacKenzie applauds this frequently in his reminiscences, claiming only that there were exceptions: 'All the men stood firm; only a handful let down the side and they were actuated by neurasthenia rather than by malice.'[51] In other camps, Changi for instance, there were times when morale was high. Havers analyses an event called 'The Selarang barrack square incident', which centred upon the insistence by the Japanese that captives sign an agreement not to escape. They refused at first, and this led to a potentially lethal situation which eventually was resolved.[52]

Even an ordinary Signalman (Private soldier) testifies to the decency of some prisoners, but mentions that the actions of some others were not so praiseworthy:

> It used to be said in the Camps along the route of the Burma-Siam Railway, 'It is every man for himself here', but in actual fact nothing was further from the truth. We depended so much on each other for encouragement, morale-boosting, and, in numerous instances, for very survival. Sick men would be tended by their mates encouraging, often bullying, them to cling on to life when the vital spark burned low. An egg purchased from a man's meagre 'pay' or something stolen from the Japanese stores to supplement the starvation rations that were the norm even for the sick.
>
> Of course, there was another side to the coin. Adversity brings out the best in some people, and the worst in others. Most camps had their quota of racketeers who would turn any situation to their own advantage. By and large, however, our miserable circumstances gave rise to fellow-feeling the like of which I have never met elsewhere.[53]

Much has been written about prisoners of war of the Japanese. The narrative is dominated by the fact that the attempt by officers to import class and rank differences was challenged, and that the experience of MacKenzie, and others, of camaraderie was rarer than one might expect. It is hardly a matter for surprise that faced with a demand for the maintenance of military hierarchy, lower ranks would resist this. There are several possible explanations. The lower ranks resented the fact that the senior people, as they saw it, were responsible for the situation in which they found themselves, but now insisted on the maintenance of privilege. Nor could they respect officers who, in a situation of great deprivation, arrogated to themselves the best of everything. Russell Braddon, a prisoner himself, is direct. He reminds us that even in this vile captivity there were serious hatreds:

> How to explain that one can't hate enough a brigadier who wore the red tabs of rank and did nothing but sell worthless dollars for what he hoped foolishly would be valuable I.O.U.s? That one can't hate enough the private who sold malarial patients water? The sergeant who did not stand between his men and the enemy's guards – though he was quick enough to insist that his men stood to attention for him? How to explain that one can't hate enough the brother officer who wouldn't wash and therefore crawled with lice that spread disease?[54]

The traditions of the British class system broke down because they were irrelevant in this novel situation and those with initiative and skills, even criminal ones, were the survivors. In Changi a Colonel Shortland lamented:

> For every two that played (the game) one did not, and the blackleg houses ate enormous meals while the honest ones went short. And in every house the greedy and undisciplined retired to their corners...the result was an atmosphere of suspicion that ruined all effort to organise a decent communal life.[55]

Such behaviour seems to have been commonplace amongst officers, judging by the amount of commentary on it.

The picture which emerges of officers' behaviour is not complimentary, not widely known, and when revealed is likely to be bitterly resented by those believing in the utter integrity of the British middle class. Major Shean is very critical of their behaviour:

> Owing to the loss of so many men up country and overseas the o/c i/c [Officer Commanding In Charge] British and Dutch Cemetery cannot get enough labour to keep the place up. They called for volunteers from the area which holds about seventy officers: we got seven volunteers! … A few hours a week pottering in the cemetery and yet the buggers won't give up hogging it on their beds.[56]

Another Major, Gillies, comments that when there was a disagreement about the distribution of food, in this case eggs, which were in short supply: 'I was always under the impression that we were fighting this particular war to put a stop to totalitarianism but that evidently doesn't apply to this particular POW camp.'[57]

When the prisoners were moved to Changi Main Prison, officers were issued with new clothing. This was a cause of ill feeling because some felt 'the "haves" are going to lose kit to the "have nots"':[58] that is those who had a lot did not want to share it.

A medical officer (MO) draws attention to the fact that officers try to fiddle their medical classification:

> The trouble is that there are so many slackers among the officers that they try and get their medical categories lowered by the M.O. and the M.O.s have, regrettably connived at this to a large extent. It isn't easy of course for a young Captain, say, to tell some old burbler of a Col. that there is damn all wrong with him except lack of guts and of course if the M.O. is a Regular, he has to think of his future…there are some 1200 officers here and at least

1000 of them are complete washouts in one respect or another by now, whatever they may have been before being POWs.[59]

Changi Camp, was, by all accounts, a slightly more comfortable place than the Railway, although it became much worse as the war went on, and especially after the prisoners were moved to Changi Main Prison. Officers above the rank of Colonel were moved to bases further north, initially Formosa. Major Shean wrote about the reaction of lower ranks:

> It is probably a day unparalleled in Br. Military history that so many senior officers have left their troops and staff and left so few regrets behind…it's very sad and never before have I seen so many senior officers thoroughly despised.

At one time, Changi prisoners who had money were asked to lend it to the government. A Sergeant Romney tells us that the response was likely to be poor because there was a 'feeling among many, rightly or wrongly', that the money would be used to 'finance officers' food purchases'. [60]

It is almost beyond belief that one of the concerns of the officers at Changi was that they might lose their batmen. Not just any batman, but a particular individual. In this account, Major Shean himself is the object of criticism:

> The loss of batmen was considered to be a serious issue for some. Major Shean, a regular soldier, and the other officers in his mess stood to suffer when 'Freeman (Shean's batman) was picked…to go up country along with Dolman, our head gardener…
>
> But we had a protest mass meeting and eventually our two head cooks were detached as they were asking for a transfer anyway. This is the time I have been on the verge of losing Freeman and I hope this luck will hold.

Havers' comment on this episode is apposite, even if restrained, and contains the paradox that Shean, who so often complains about the behaviour of officers, is the subject of criticism himself:

> In a situation, such as Changi, where the efficient utilisation of scarce rations was absolutely crucial, the willingness of Shean and his fellow officers to lose two experienced cooks seems particularly short-sighted when set against the value of the duties a batman could provide.[61]

Ian Watt was another of the 80,000 allied prisoners captured by the Japanese, and he, too, discusses animosity which arose from the continuing division between officers and others: 'At first, I think, most men tended to resent the fact that the usual sort of military procedures went on under quite different conditions.'[62]

Leonard Haslett Morrison, a prisoner in Changi and on the Railway, observed the damage done by the attempt to maintain what seemed to be irrelevant relationships: 'Regimental rivalries persisted. Class distinctions – Officers and Other Ranks – dominated. And a suspicion of one's own kind, much more lethal than a hatred of the enemy, ate away like a cancer at the heart of our P.O.W. societies.'[63]

A very good example of the persistence of the culture of the outside world can be seen in the attitude towards the class system in the English prison system. Middle-class prisoners, apart from the fact that they are likely to find conditions a good deal more intolerable than lower-class prisoners, also commonly do not regard themselves as criminal at all. Prisoners of war, most inmates of Concentration Camps and some of those locked up because of their political beliefs where they have not engaged in violence, clearly are not. This is a complicated question to which I shall return. Some who have broken what they consider to be unjust laws, such as Oscar Wilde or Peter Wildeblood, have nevertheless broken the law as it stood at the time.

Some proclaim that they should never have been convicted at all. Derek Williams is one such. In a cell with two thieves, he is reported as having:

wanted to tell the owner of this chattering face, which mouthed some obscenity every other word, that he wasn't like him at all. He had not made a penny unlawfully, that he had even been honest in filling in his weekly expenses sheet. He wanted to make the point that he was not a criminal, and that normally he would not want to be seen talking to somebody like him.[64]

Williams had been sentenced to two years for conspiracy to defraud.

As well as this curious belief that they are not 'real' criminals, middle-class prisoners usually find themselves horrified by prison life. They are appalled at the enforced proximity of such 'rough' people, a circumstance about which they can do nothing:

> 'I couldn't even adjust to the language,' said one polite middle aged, middle-class man. 'Everybody swore. It was vile and filthy. I was horrified by the whole experience. It seemed like another age. It's so Dickensian. It really is unreasonable, the whole thing. Most of all I hated being locked up…it is ghastly, filthy. There is rubbish lying about. Cells are inches thick in cigarette ash. And to top it all you are thrown in with all sorts of people.'[65]

Brian Breed, writing about white-collar criminals, records how they resented the fact that the English system, which made some allowance for their feelings by setting certain prisons aside for them, was allowing this privilege to be undermined. Ford is such an open prison, to which were consigned white-collar criminals:

> Among those who had offended before and been sent to prison, there were a number who had been to Ford before… Almost to a man they thought that 'it had gone down' considerably over the last few years. A typical comment was: 'They'll let anybody in here now. Once upon a time it was only top offenders, almost entirely white collar men who had committed decent crimes. Today anybody, even people who have committed quite ordinary offences are allowed in.'[66]

After all, they had not knocked anybody over the head and stolen their wallet, they had not raped somebody, they had not caused anybody real harm. They would be safe members of society when they got out, they would not be a menace, and certainly they did not need to be locked away to safeguard society.[67]

On her journey to Holloway, Jane Buxton, convicted of demonstrating against nuclear policy, furnishes another example of insistence that certain offenders are not offenders at all, when she regrets that: 'We couldn't call out "Ban the Bomb" or display our C.N.D. badges to show that we were not really criminals.'[68]

Another female prisoner, Sheila Bowler, sentenced to life for murder, was eventually acquitted and released when her case was retried. She expresses distaste for the behaviour of some of her fellow prisoners:

Wednesday 15 September 1993
Very rude people at the back when a representative of the Mothers' Union stood up to speak. I helped the chapel-cleaner, a lady from Mauritius, prepare tea for twenty-nine people. Some of them behaved like animals and were taking eight biscuits at a time. They know nothing about manners![69]

Prisoners who were probably merely aspirants to the English middle class affected disdain for fellow captives. 'Red Collar Man' was convicted in 1930 for an unnamed offence and given seven years. He served his sentence in Parkhurst Prison on the Isle of Wight where, incidentally, he found himself in contact with W.F.R. Macartney, whose account features in this book. His *nom de plume* arises from the fact that he was a 'trusted' prisoner, and the title of his book was chosen because he worked in the punishment area of the prison nicknamed 'chokey'.

Red Collar Man describes how a pretentious prisoner, and one who he comes to hate, explains his feelings for his fellow prisoners:

They are mentally feeble and physically unsound and it is beyond me why they should not be rendered sterile by law… It needs no violent exercise of the wits to realize that these men are of no value and are nearer to animals than to gods… The lack of mental concentration of these men makes it impossible to hold any sort of argument with them, and as for their moral side – they have none… I don't believe anyone from the outside world can imagine what an awful calamity it is for men of decent feeling, even if they have only a little of that left, to be plunged into this living hell of male whores, murderers, blackmailers and thieves; to suffer years of persecution from having to listen from day to day to their foul speech.[70]

The speaker was convicted of abortion.

British captives, especially when overseas, took their class feelings with them wherever they went. J. Davidson Ketchum relates how, when the 4000 British prisoners were settling in at Ruhleben, all consciousness of social rank and class disappeared, There was 'solidarity' based upon a recognition that the majority were British, and that fact was paramount. But, as it became clear that they were going to be imprisoned for a long time, social awareness returned. Whereas in the very early days people moved about socially quite freely, talking to anybody, very soon: 'The innate reserve of the Englishman soon manifested itself even in captivity, and we felt in time we must not address a fellow-prisoner without an introduction lest we be snubbed.'[71]

In Ruhleben, what Ketchum calls 'economic differences', which he might have added were based on class, led to a quite remarkable development. In April 1915, just five months after internment, a 'Summer House Club' was established by some 'well-to-do businessmen':

the club's amenities were modest; a few small rooms for reading and for card playing, a fenced garden for deck chairs, and a white-coated steward who served tea, Oxo, and synthetic lemonade. But the quota of a hundred members was quickly reached.[72]

But, 'So incongruous an innovation as the "Snobs' Club" aroused much biting comment.'[73] And the 'Barrack Captains', prisoners set in authority over others and of whom we will learn more 'were rarely seen except in business suits'.[74] Bad language, too, something of a major irritant for some, although used by everybody at the beginning, soon became eschewed by those of a higher class. One prisoner was worried: 'I wonder how much bad language I shall use when I leave this place. Ruhleben talk is shocking and is bound to leave a stain.'[75] It was a 'stain' brought into the camp by what one prisoner called 'the lower stratum of our community'.[76]

Even young Borstal boys are conscious of class difference, and how this is more important than the commonalty of being locked up. Brendan Behan reflects on class difference. He describes the situation, by no means unusual, of a boy not from the lower class:

> He was dead lonely, more lonely than I and with more reason. The other fellows might give me a rub about Ireland or about the bombing campaign, and that was seldom enough, and I was never short of an answer, historically informed and obscene, for them... I had the same rearing as most of them; Dublin, Liverpool, Manchester, Glasgow, London. All our mothers had done the pawn-pledging on Monday, releasing on Saturday... But Ken they would never accept.[77]

The depth of feeling about social difference will depend on the status or the notoriety of the prisoner. Oscar Wilde is one of many who reflect on these differences:

> Of course I know from one point of view things will be made different for me than for others; must indeed, by the very nature of the case, be made so. The poor thieves and outcasts who are imprisoned here with me are in many respects more fortunate

than I am. The little way in grey city or green field that saw their sin is small; to find those who know nothing of what they have done they need go no further than a bird might fly between the twilight and the dawn; but for me the world is shrivelled to a handsbreadth, and everywhere I turn my name is written on the rocks in lead.[78]

There is another view, based on experience, but it is unusual, to put it mildly. Jane Buxton served a sentence in Holloway for anti-nuclear weapons protests. She saw no evidence of snobbery:

> I think that there is a very good feeling amongst the prisoners, and an almost complete absence of class barriers, which is wonderfully refreshing…on the whole the sense of community and comradeship is very good… I suppose the two categories of prisoners whom one excludes from the all-embracing fellow-feeling are the very pro-officer and priggish informers and those who have committed particularly beastly crimes.[79]

It is not only in English prisons that class divisions and snobbery are imported. In Alderson, the American federal prison for women, not only is race imported, but so is class antagonism. Helen Bryan recounts a conversation she had with a fellow prisoner:

> Don't tell me you don't mind them. Their backgrounds are so different from yours and mine. I don't mind their coarse language and swearing, but I do resent their bad English – always those double negatives. I only hope during my time here I won't start talking the way they do. And the way some of them eat! I know they're hungry. I am, too, but there's always enough for everyone and they do try to have the tables set and served nicely, and a girl ruins everything by grabbing.[80]

Even in the misery of a Concentration Camp, people were aware of their status. A Ravensbrück prisoner, a doctor, 'loathed the constant company of riff-raff', but she phrased her misery carefully in her censored letter home:

> I wish I could be built so that stupidity and dullness wouldn't bother me as much, but I just can't help it. It may sound paradoxical but with time one wishes to be a hermit instead of always being around people.[81]

In Tsarist Russia, as may be expected, social divisions were especially pronounced. Dostoevsky, himself a nobleman, accepts the reality of this: 'I was naturally drawn towards men of my own class, to the "noblemen"... particularly in the early days.'[82]

Perhaps a supreme example of the importation of 'normal' social relationships is described by Dostoevsky. It is a good example of how these relationships survive: in this case, even superseding the devastation of the Tsarist prison. He writes of the convict Sushilov:

> He used to wait on me. I also had another attendant. Right at the very beginning of my term, during the earliest days, Akim Akimych recommended one of the convicts, a man called Osip, to me, saying that for thirty kopecks a month he would make my own meals for me every day if I disliked the prison food so much and had money to buy my own.[83]

After the Revolution, and the establishment of the Gulag, there was still a division between the political and criminal prisoners but now it was to become even more rigid, and dangerous.

Even slight regional differences create division, as Behan, an Irishman in an English Borstal found out: 'You're a good boy, Paddy, and the boys like you. The London boys do, and they're the only ones that matter.'[84]

Yet there can be solid friendships amongst captives. In her study of American women prisoners, Giallombardo observes that:

There can be found in prison communities very close relationships between two people who trust each other and importantly, share possessions. In Alderson there were two such close relationships. One was that between 'rap buddies', and the other between 'homeys'. The relationship between the latter is based upon the fact that they are from the same geographical area, and is more complex. Thus they will share possessions, but there is no sexual involvement.[85]

Such a close relationship could be found in the English Borstal and here the term for the pair was 'chinas'.

It is a truism to say that relationships between people who in the past have found friendships and trust difficult, in captivity discover the basic human need for companionship. Brian Stratton, having completed a nine-year sentence, reflects on the friends he was leaving, even though in restrained terms:

> I said my goodbyes on the Thursday evening. It's a bit choking to experience these goodbyes, particularly with Timmy Noolan, who is a close friend of mine. He shook my hand and told me to look after myself and be lucky.[86]

These main divisions which I have described were exacerbated in situations where captives had legitimate access to money. This meant that they could of course buy better food and other luxuries. In Ruhleben, for example, prisoners were allowed to receive money from outside, and this led to division:

> Until regular relief payments started, half the population was almost destitute while the rest had money, and this gave rise to a flood of pecuniary transactions. For the wholesale sharing of the first few days almost vanished with the appearance of community groups; not that Ruhleben's generosity had dried up – it was always there to be called on – but because new social

barriers had made men reluctant to accept help save from their own circle of friends. It smacked of 'charity'.[87]

There are other structures in the captive society which create friction. These include the distinction between political and criminal prisoners (to which we will return) hatred of certain kinds of offenders, such as those who abuse children, and the evolution of a market in banned goods such as drugs (a fairly recent development), tobacco and alcohol which leads to the accumulation of power in the hands of some captives. I have discussed the place of drugs, alcohol and tobacco in an earlier chapter, but the hatred shown to some offenders by other offenders can be illustrated by the following episode.

Brian Stratton was accused of attacking a child molester. Prisoners regard offences against children with especial disgust. Prisoners, like everyone else, have a protective instinct about children and they feel especially unable to help because they are locked up. They feel intensely that the victim could have been their child. Stratton explains what happened in this case:

> I heard a bit of a commotion downstairs and went down to see what was going on. Lying on the floor of the washroom was a particularly horrible sex con…who was doing fourteen years for raping an eight year old blind girl.

Stratton, naturally, has no sympathy and indeed is flippant about the attack:

> I suspected foul play had occurred. What made me suspicious was the hole in the top of (his) head, plus the fact that the washroom was splattered with blood all over the walls and floor. Whoever had obliged (him) must have supported a football team that wore red and green colours, for they had also emptied a tin of green paint all over him. It was quite a colourful effect – the blood running out of his head and mingling with the green paint making a nice shade of mauve. I should have been a

forensic expert because my thoughts were 'Ah, ah, this is a water paint, otherwise it wouldn't have mixed with the blood.' Having satisfied myself that [he] had been well and truly obliged in the fashion prescribed for child rapists, I went back upstairs and carried on reading the newspaper which, by pure chance, carried an article about a new kind of treatment for sex offenders. I knew that Blundeston was progressive, but I was a bit surprised that the new treatment had arrived so quickly for [him] to get it before lunch.[88]

When Stratton was interviewed about the attack, and was told that the man could die of his injuries: 'I replied "Good, he is no loss to anyone."'[89]

John Hoskison, as part of his learning about prison culture, is told what happens to 'nonces':

'...When they're found out they're done.'

'How do the guys find out though?'

'Screws tell 'em, they hate "bacons" as much as us.'

'And then they're plunged?'
    Guido lay down on his bed and kicked off his shoes. 'Plungin's a stabbin', but depends on what they've done. Sometimes it's a bucket of boilin' water with sugar in it thrown over their bollocks – rips all the skin off, fuckin' terrible that is. Saw it done to a geezer in Albany once, bloke died of a heart attack, good riddance though if you ask me.'[90]

Stanley Cohen and Lawrie Taylor discuss the attitude of long-term English prisoners to sex offenders. Many of those sent to Durham were not just ordinary sex offenders, but those whose activities had drawn national outrage. They were kept on a separate, secure part of the long-term wing in Durham Prison, and had little contact with

the rest of the prisoners. Cohen and Taylor were conducting classes
on the wing:

> We were completely unsuccessful in our attempts to invite
> men from the top floor down to our classes on the lower. The
> 'lower' class objected declaring that the others were 'monsters' or
> 'animals', although they recognised the hypocrisy or at least the
> irony involved in the application of such crude labels. As David
> said: 'We know it's a prejudice, but we just have to differentiate
> ourselves from them.' Gradually, however, we became aware
> that this was not an absolute differentiation. Some softening
> of the rejection takes place over time. Some sex offenders are
> eventually admitted to limited interaction, although not chosen
> as intimates, whilst others are still rigidly excluded. A sexual
> offender, whose 'madness' is regarded as passive, for example, and
> who displays a certain pathetic quality is more easily tolerated
> than an offender who has committed a similar crime but who
> exhibits a certain self-consciousness about what he has done or
> displays an ideological arrogance about his pre-prison deviant
> life style.[91]

There is a very special segment of the captive group, much despised,
but without whom the system would falter. These are the people who
spy and inform for the staff. They go by a variety of terms: 'grasses',
'coppers', 'squealers', 'snitches', 'rats'. They collaborate, of course, for
favours, which can range from getting easy jobs to time off a sentence.

Erwin James was amazed to learn that the English system
endorses the practice of informing. He went to the library and read
a book on prison law:

> It made spectacular reading. Staff were instructed that prisoner
> informants should be offered rewards such as incentive bonuses in
> their pay; the promise of positive recommendations to the parole
> board; transfers to preferred prisons; or even recategorisation,
> perhaps to open conditions, where town visits and home leaves

were possible. The part that really caught my eye was the paragraph explaining that the best informants were 'prisoners who have the respect of other prisoners and who are regarded as above suspicion'. 'It's like a rats' charter,' said the magazine editor. Jack sprang to mind...[92]

Men like Jack rarely give any serious thoughts to 'rehabilitation'. Did he gamble that, by betraying the secrets of the wing, prison officials would overlook the image and reward him in some way? It seemed a perilous strategy. Life on the landings could be dangerous indeed for an informer exposed.[93]

Informers are very cunning, since prisoners are always suspicious and are always watching for evidence that someone cannot be trusted. A Norwegian guard gives an example of how they can operate:

They might, for example, come over and grasp for your keys, and when you tell him you mustn't do that, the inmate says that many people have keys here, and mentions a name. They probably come to guards they like. If they don't like the guards, they don't say anything. But they often go to the doctor, perhaps. Take Y, who was released a while ago: inmates think he got out by informing on others... They might think they get advantages. They don't get much, but sometimes we give them a little.[94]

They are so contemptible that Brian Stratton equates them with 'sex cases':

Of the twenty odd cons working in the kitchen only about half-a-dozen were trustworthy as far as I was concerned. The rest were grasses and grovellers. Blundeston, in fact, was a haven for both police and prison informers and child molesters. They get sent to Blundeston from every nick in the country because it is figured that at Blundeston they are less likely to get hurt for their sins, owing to the fact that as the nick is so free and easy nobody would risk getting chucked out of there back to Parkhurst for 'doing' a grass or sex case… Admittedly, the grasses are encouraged to pursue their particular vocation, informing.[95]

When Helen Bryan had only just arrived in Alderson Prison, a prisoner gave her some advice: 'Never snitch on a girl no matter how much they bug you. That's the worst thing you can do here – squeal.'[96]

This was very sound advice because the risks are great and the punishments severe. In a maximum security Norwegian prison, a prisoner reports that:

> There is a lot of informing in this place. I don't know who does it; I would like to know, because if I knew, the, – . If X and Y and I here knew it, we would really give them hell.[97]

The hatred of informers is another of the universal features of captivity. John Hoskison, having been part of a cell search for drugs, decides not to tell what he knows: 'Eventually, the officers let me go, realizing I'd learned about prison justice – the fear of being labelled a "grass" is worse than anything they could throw at me. I was almost sick with relief.'[98]

Rupert Croft-Cooke tells us of a conversation he had with a very 'hard' prisoner about informers:

> 'They tell me,' I once said to Mike as we squatted side by side on a tepid radiator in the Old Rec, 'they tell me you'd think nothing of killing a man, Mike.'
>
> 'Not a grass, I wouldn't,' said Mike at once, the cool evil in his voice very convincing. 'But that's not a man. I never go armed on a job or anything silly like that. But anyone who grassed on his firm, I'd do. Well, you've got to, haven't you? Else where would you be?'
>
> As usual Mike's logic was deadly.[99]

In the Tsarist prison, the kind of punitive action envisaged and approved of by Mike was realised:

> Two hardened vagabonds in the Omsk fort had been planning an escape when, only days before their intended departure, their fetters were tightened and the guard strengthened. The two men spent months investigating who had tipped off the prison authorities. They came to suspect their cellmate and, over a couple of nights, they removed the planks that covered one of the walls in their cell and dug a shallow grave inside the wall. On the third night, they seized the man while he slept, stopped up his mouth, shoved him into the grave and buried him alive. The following morning, when the cell was opened at roll call, the guards could find no trace of the convict and assumed that he must have made his escape in the night. The entire prison knew what had happened to the informer but no one reported the crime.[100]

This is an illustration of the fact that the staff cannot possibly know what is happening in the captive community, even if there are informers. Such 'justice' was perpetuated in the Gulag. In that crucible of every dismal feature of captivity, especially in the chaos following the death of Stalin in 1953, those who reported on their fellows paid the ultimate price. After the arrival of an especially violent and organised prisoners' group at a special camp called Gorlag, 'they murdered four camp informers with pickaxes within a few days of their arrival'.[101]

It must have been a matter of despair for the radical black American George Jackson to acknowledge that there were 'rats':

> You see every time a rat does get put away, the prison authorities always release a different reason for the attack, never that he was an informer. Their purpose for holding the truth is that they don't want to discourage other potential rats and the truth would aid the convicts in the psychological war-con against cop.[102]

Primo Levi in Auschwitz is one of many who is disappointed that there are people who will, in his word, betray, friends, but sees why:

> If one offers a position of privilege to a few individuals in a state of slavery, exacting in exchange the betrayal of a natural solidarity with their comrades, there will certainly be someone who will accept. He will be withdrawn from the common law and will become untouchable.[103]

Despite the dangers, informers are found everywhere in prisons, indeed it has been suggested that the system is dependent upon them. A famous warden of Joliet is supposed to have claimed: 'Whenever you see three inmates standing together, two of them are mine.'[104] In those prisons housing political prisoners who ostensibly are suffering for commonly held beliefs, there are informers. Even Robben Island is not excepted:

> Apart from being monitored by the warders, the political prisoners were also spied upon by some of the common-law prisoners, as well as by informers from within the political community. 'There are informers on Robben Island too,' notes Alexander, 'men who for diverse reasons have left their organizations (or been expelled) and are collaborating with the authorities.'[105]

In Andersonville, where American Civil War prisoners constantly tried to tunnel their way out, there was an especial problem with informers:

> Another problem connected with tunneling was the number of spies and traitors among us. There were many – principally among the N'Yaarker crowd who were always ready to betray a tunnel, in order to curry favor with the Rebel officers.[106]

Nor is informing confined to the captives. Lord Nevill, writing about his experience as a prisoner at the end of the nineteenth century, mentions an unusual aspect of this when he claims that junior staff also gossip to senior staff about their juniors.[107] Since the staff as well as captives live in a fairly confined world, often in adjacent 'quarters', and in a system of quasi-military rank where there is promotion to be gained, this allegation is perfectly credible.

Before leaving the shape of prison society, mention must be made of a very pathetic section of that society. As well as men and women, children have been imprisoned, often with monstrous results. Children are imprisoned sometimes on an extensive scale. In the Gulag there were several categories of child captives. There were those who were the products of the civil war, or disastrous policies such as collectivisation, and there were street children. And there were children who were born in the camps since: 'If love, sex, rape and prostitution were part of camp, so too, it followed, were pregnancy and childbirth.'[108] Anne Applebaum writes further that: 'The treatment of children in juvenile camps hardly differed from the treatment of their parents.'[109]

Those who were babies or very young naturally suffered great neglect and were especially vulnerable to disease and abuse. The results of their experience were predictable, and are recorded by observers. One wrote that the children:

> All displayed a frightening and incorrigibly vengeful cruelty, without restraint or responsibility... They feared nothing and no one. The guards and camp bosses were scared to enter the separate barracks where the juveniles lived... If one of the prisoners' criminal leaders were gambling, lost everything and had staked his life as well, the boys would kill him for a day's bread or simply 'for the fun of it'. The girls boasted that they could satisfy an entire team of tree-fellers. There was nothing human left in these children.[110]

Gustav Herling agrees and is horrified at the juveniles he meets in prison:

Juvenile delinquents, like the boys in the cell, are the plague of the Soviet prisons, although they are mostly never found in labour camps. Unnaturally excited, always ferreting about in other men's bunks and inside their own trousers, they give themselves up passionately to the only two occupations of their lives, theft and self-abuse…only later I discovered that the *bezprizornye* ('the homeless') constitute a most dangerous semi-legal mafia, organized on the pattern of Masonic lodges, and surpassed only by the more powerful organization of 'urkas', or criminal prisoners.[111]

D'Harcourt observed a similar phenomenon in Buchenwald. The children in the camp were 'all very young, aged perhaps between the ages of three and ten'.[112] 'There was something terrible about them.'[113]

There were children who were truly pathetic. Although these examples are drawn from Tsarist prisons, and within those the especially horrific Sakhalin Island, their situation is nonetheless vile because of that. Examples are recorded by Chekhov:

I found adolescent girls in the guards' quarters, and when I asked them who they were, they said 'I am a cohabitant.' You enter the quarters occupied by a guard, and you find a man who is thick-set, well-fed and fleshy, his waistcoat unbuttoned and wearing squeaky new boots; he is sitting at a table and drinking tea. A pale fourteen-year-old girl with a weary face sits at the window. He usually call himself a non-commissioned officer, a senior guard, and says that the girl is the daughter of one of the convicts, that she is sixteen years old, and is his cohabitant.[114]

Writing of prostitution, which on Sakhalin was indistinguishable from simple slavery, Chekhov reports:

Because of the tremendous demand, neither old age, nor ugliness, nor even tertiary syphilis is an impediment. I met a sixteen-year-old girl on a street in Alexandrovsk, and they say she has been engaged in prostitution since she was nine years old. The girl has a mother, but a family background on Sakhalin does not always save a young girl from disaster.[115]

It can be seen that the 'community' of captives is divided into largely irreconcilable groups who will abuse, hurt and kill each other because of any difference, whether colour, religion, sex, class or age. Such divisions are not surprising, considering what a mixture is to be found in any captive group. 'Politicals' are especially drawn from every kind of background, as Paul Ignotus found. He was in a prison in a highly repressive state, Hungary, and writes that there was the most mixed group of people:

> There we were, counts and bishops, ci-devants of all classes and denominations, former generals of the Nazi machine which set out to conquer the world, former generals of the resistance against the Nazi machine. Former officers of the political police holding us under its thumb; a whole universe of smartness and counter-smartness, now ragged, stinking and miserable.[116]

There were men from 'the *gendarmerie* or the *Gestapo* or the Red or White political police... A far gentler group than these were the old noblemen of the former privileged upper-middle classes.'[117]

Amongst the latter there was even 'Prince Esterhazy, the top magnate of ancient Hungary.'[118] All brought their perceptions of their place in the civil hierarchy into prison with them. But as well as making out in this torrid world, and working out ways to find a place amongst people not of their choosing, captives also have to deal with the people charged with keeping them locked up. This requires very special skill, and the ways in which these skills have been developed over time and place deserves special consideration.

Notes

1. Dostoevsky *op. cit.* p.27.
2. Stratton *op. cit.* p.9.
3. Taki. *Nothing to Declare: Prison Memoirs.* p.202.
4. Quillen, Jim. *Inside Alcatraz: My Time on the Rock.* p.318.
5. Leopold *op. cit.* p.178.
6. Ketchum *op. cit.* p.111.
7. Norman *op. cit.* p.56.
8. *Ibid.*
9. Mathiesen, Thomas. *The Defences of the Weak: A Sociological Study of a Norwegian Correctional Institution.* p.127.
10. McElroy, John. *Andersonville: A Story of Rebel Military Prisons.* p.44.
11. Hood, Stuart. 'The Narrow Grave' in Moir. pp.106–7.
12. Ross, Luana. *Inventing the Savage: The Social Constructions of Native American Criminality.* p.89.
13. Carlen *Sledgehammer op. cit.* p.54
14. *Ibid.*
15. Dodge *op. cit.* p.252.
16. Giallombardo *op. cit.* pp.26–27.
17. Bryan *op. cit.* p.256.
18. Chang *et al. op. cit.* p.193.
19. *Ibid.* pp.63–64.
20. Jackson, George. *Soledad Brother: The Prison Letters of George Jackson.* pp.219–220.
21. Abbott *op. cit.* p.152.
22. Ross *op. cit.* p.155.
23. Taki *op. cit.* p.100.
24. Hoskison *op. cit.* p.31.
25. *Ibid.* p.96.
26. *Ibid.* p.106.
27. Sheffler *op. cit.* p.101.
28. *Ibid.* p.102.
29. Havers *op. cit.* pp.58–59.
30. *Ibid.* p.70.
31. Ketchum *op. cit.* p.135.
32. Helm *op. cit.* p.50.
33. *Ibid.* p.262.
34. Dostoevsky *op. cit.* p.92.
35. Hood *op. cit.* p.106.
36. Coogan, Tim Pat. *On the Blanket: The Inside Story of the IRA Prisoners' 'Dirty Protest'.* p.80.
37. Nashif, Esmail. *Palestinian Political Prisoners: Identity and Community.* p.85.
38. *Ibid.* p.55.
39. *Ibid.* p.57.

40. *Ibid.* p.87.
41. *Ibid.* p.88.
42. Ketchum *op. cit.* p.115.
43. *Ibid.*
44. *Ibid.* p.116.
45. *Ibid.* pp.116–117.
46. Dostoevsky *op. cit.* pp.149–150.
47. *Ibid.* p.148.
48. Macartney *op. cit.* p.136.
49. Levi *op. cit.* p.55.
50. Ketchum *op. cit.* p.135.
51. MacKenzie *op. cit.* p.168.
52. Havers *op. cit.* p.77.
53. Rossiter, Ray S. 'An Unforgettable Experience' in John Nunnely. p.161.
54. Braddon *op. cit.* p.68.
55. Havers *op. cit.* p.33.
56. *Ibid.* p.87.
57. *Ibid.* p.155.
58. *Ibid.* p.140
59. *Ibid.* p.141.
60. *Ibid.* p.41.
61. *Ibid.* p.85.
62. Watt *op. cit.* p.143.
63. Morrison *op. cit.* p.80.
64. Breed *op. cit.* pp.14–15.
65. *Ibid.* p.52.
66. *Ibid.* pp.60–61.
67. *Ibid.* p.74.
68. Buxton and Turner *op. cit.* p.2.
69. Devlin, Angela and Devlin, Tim. *Anybody's Nightmare*. p.206.
70. Red Collar Man *op. cit.* pp.161-2.
71. Ketchum *op. cit.* p.49.
72. *Ibid.* p.178.
73. *Ibid.*
74. *Ibid.* p.51.
75. *Ibid.* p.53.
76. *Ibid.*
77. Behan *op. cit.* p.232.
78. Maine *ibid.* p.861.
79. Buxton and Turner *op. cit.* pp.111–112.
80. Bryan *op. cit.* p.139.
81. Helm *op. cit.* p.34.
82. Dostoevsky *op. cit.* p.321.
83. *Ibid.* p.96.

84. Behan *op. cit.* p.153.
85. Giallombardo *op. cit.* pp.117ff.
86. Stratton *op. cit.* p.129.
87. Ketchum *op. cit.* p.101.
88. Stratton *op. cit.* pp.68–69.
89. *Ibid.* p.71.
90. Hoskison *op. cit.* p.34.
91. Cohen, Stanley and Taylor, Laurie. *Psychological Survival: The Experience of Long-Term Imprisonment.* p.74.
92. James *A Life Inside op.cit.* p.82.
93. *Ibid.* p.81.
94. Mathiesen *op. cit.* p.125.
95. Stratton *op. cit.* pp.60–61.
96. Bryan *op. cit.* p.13.
97. Mathiesen *op. cit.* p.124.
98. Hoskison *op. cit.* p.81.
99. Croft-Cooke *op. cit.* p.194.
100. Beer, Daniel. *The House of the Dead: Siberian Exile under the Tsars.* p.180.
101. Applebaum *op. cit.* p.438.
102. Jackson *op. cit.* p.214.
103. Levi *op. cit.* p.97.
104. Dodge *op. cit.* p.230.
105. Deacon *op. cit.* p.122.
106. McElroy *op. cit.* p.77.
107. WBN *op. cit.* p.158.
108. Applebaum *op. cit.* p.292.
109. *Ibid.* p.302.
110. *Ibid.* p.305.
111. Herling *op. cit.* p.14.
112. d'Harcourt *op. cit.* p.139.
113. *Ibid.*
114. Chekhov *op. cit.* p.194.
115. *Ibid.* p.202.
116. Ignotus, Paul. 'Assisted by Thugs' in Mikes. p.33.
117. *Ibid.* p.34.
118. *Ibid.* p.36.

— 4 —

Dealing with the Staff

Although there are enormous complications in relationships in the captive community, *the* most important relationship is that between the captive and the captor: between the prisoner – the 'con', 'crim', inmate, fish, and the gaoler – the 'screw', the 'bull', the 'vache', the dubsman, the officer, the guard. These groups of people face each other day in, day out, and both sides (and they are sides) know that to exist, there has to be a way of making compromises. They have to find accommodation for their conflicting interests. J. Davidson Ketchum interned at Ruhleben, soon realised that:'The soldiers are getting to know us better now, and we all get along together. England and Germany were at war – that was never forgotten – but within the camp a pattern of co-existence had to be worked out.'[1]

In this discussion of the relationship between captor and captive, the basic assumption from the beginning is that there is hostility on both sides. This is expressed forcibly by a black woman prisoner in America in 1961. She is writing to the Superintendent:

This is the third time I have written to you... Is it because I am a Negro and a prisoner here that justice here means nothing? Is it that a prisoner is wrong because they are prisoners? Is it that you have warders here that think they can do no wrong? If we have to follow rules why don't warders follow yours?[2]

As well as hostility there is an aura of fear. Not only do captives feel fearful but so do captors. It is axiomatic that those in charge of captives were often in danger, often great danger. In the early sixteenth century, it is recorded how the Warden of the Fleet Prison in London was attacked:

> Sir John Whitbrooke strook him on the head with the sharpe end of a hammer, whereof one cleft was before broken off and the other cleft newly whet, giving fower wounds to the skull and some bruses before the Warden could close with him…the Warden could have beaten out Whitbrooke's braynes with the hammer but that he was neither wrothfull nor daunted… (the prisoner took a stiletto out of his pocket and stabed the Warden's deputie cleane through the middle of his hand which notwithstanding it was dressed by a good chirurgion) did rankle upp to his shoulder, and was likely to have killed him; he also stabbed the porter of the howse directly against the heart and drew blood, but it pierced not; he stabbed the gaoler into the hand and twice through the sleeve of his dublett.[3]

To understand the complexities of this relationship it is necessary to know how the purpose of locking people up has changed in many countries in the last 150 years. In the universal traditional situation, the dynamics of the relationship between captor and captive were simple. There was a head of the institution supported by custodial staff, with occasional intervention from doctors. The simple task was to confine the prisoner. In many civilised countries from the eighteenth century, and especially in the twentieth, that dynamic became more complicated. As a consequence of a growing belief that the misbehaviour of captives could be 'corrected', dramatic changes were made in policy in penal institutions. England led the field, but even Tsarist Russia began to consider the idea of 'reform' as an alternative to sheer punishment.

When the institution aspires to more complicated goals than containment or punishment, there is a change in the expectation of staff behaviour. Now, even basic grade uniformed staff were expected to see reformation as part of their job. There is a shift on the part of senior staff (and sometimes the community) from identifying with the staff on the ground, to an expectation that inmates must be changed, and must therefore be 'understood'. If this 'change' is not being achieved, the view becomes that it must be the fault of the staff, not of the inmates, or for that matter of the institution. The enormity of this change can be gauged from this exemplary case from a psychiatric hospital. If a member of staff asks 'difficult' questions, then:

> The frequent mode of temporizing was for the senior to listen to the problem carefully, discover some evidence of a 'personal problem', 'transference problem' or some other possible psychiatric difficulty manifested by the questioner, and avoid any action in the matter of responsibility by suggesting or implying that more work was needed on the staff member's personal analysis.[4]

Such beliefs became reified into policy. The most important Prison Commissioner in English penal history, Alexander Paterson went further, incidentally, as the staff saw it, seriously eroding their authority. He wrote that if prisoners continually complained about a member of staff he: 'Would presently be watched without his knowledge and quietly tested, and dealt with accordingly.'[5]

The final complication in the life of the institution was the establishment of specialist departments – psychological, educational, vocational and so on – designed to further these new aims. This has meant that both captor and captive have another set of relationships with which to cope in what was, in the first place, a complicated, not to say tense, environment. There are many illustrations of the effects of these changes in the extracts quoted in this book. So the relationship between captor and captive became even more complicated, where countries aspiring to develop civilised penal systems placed an extra conflict in the role of basic grade uniformed staff. Now they were supposed to be involved in reformation and rehabilitation as well as ensuring security.

This conflict, of course, is evident to the captives. To a cynical George Jackson:

> It is the function of the uniform to hold a man here. This means they do the key work, the searching, beating, killing. The individual with the tie and white shirt (really just another type of uniform) determines what we'll eat, what bullshit academic and make-work programs we'll have. He presides over the silly group therapy games that always end in fights or snitch contests. Oh, and he also makes out board reports.[6]

Jackson, predictably, and consistently, expresses unadulterated hatred for all staff, custodial or 'therapeutic':

> San Quentin was in the riot season. It was early January 1967. The pigs had for the last three months been on a search-and-destroy foray into our cells. All times of the day or night our cells were being invaded by the goon squad: you wake up, take your kicks, get skin searched, and wait on the tier naked while they mangle your few personal effects. This treatment, fear therapy, was not accorded to all however. Some Chicanos behind dope, some whites behind extortionate activities were exempted. Mostly it came down on us.[7]

Naturally, every kind of relationship it is possible to imagine exists between captive and captor. The former can suffer brutality at one extreme – to be dealt with in detail later – and can find extraordinary kindness at the other.

There are also national factors which seem to affect the relationships between captor and captive. Thomas Mathiesen, in his study of Norwegian prisons, compares the attitudes of Norwegian long-term prisoners with their counterpart in the United States:

Answers to the question 'How often do you have a fairly long talk with guards in this institution?' indicate that in the preventive-detention institution 64 per cent of the inmates have such contact with guards once a day or more often. Only 6 per cent claim that they never have such contact with guards.[8]

In America, on the other hand, things are very different:

Several descriptions of American institutions indicate the presence of a central norm amongst inmates, that has been formulated as follows:

Never talk to a screw! The high frequency of contacts in the two Norwegian institutions suggests that this norm hardly exists in these institutions. This interpretation is strongly substantiated by observational and interview material. With the exception of the specific norm banning informing, I can give no excerpts from interviews indicating a ban on contact with guards.[9]

Mathiesen concludes by reporting that over half the Norwegian prisoners interviewed 'thought guards ought to have more contact'.[10]

One of the most famous of English prisoners was Oscar Wilde. Not only did his imprisonment prompt some excellent literature on his part, but he publicly espoused the cause of penal reform. When he was released from Reading Prison, Oscar Wilde wrote a letter to the *Daily Chronicle* (28 May 1897) which has become something of a legend in the English Prison Service, and in the tortuous history of penal reform. It shows that even in the harsh world of the Victorian prison system there were staff who could be kind, in this case, for the individual who tried to be generous, disastrously so. The letter begins:

I learn with great regret, through the columns of your paper, that the warder Martin, of Reading Prison, has been dismissed by the Prison Commissioners for having given some sweet biscuits to a little hungry child. I saw the three children myself on the

Monday preceding my release. They had just been convicted, and were standing in a row in the central hall in their prison dress, carrying their sheets underneath their arms previous to their being sent to the cells allotted to them... They were quite small children, the youngest – the one to whom the warder gave the biscuit – being a tiny little chap.[11]

Wilde goes on to say what a kind man Martin is, and as an example of this describes how a prisoner with violent diarrhoea was refused permission to empty his chamber pot because prisoners were not allowed to leave their cells after half-past five. Martin, absolutely against the rules, emptied the man's pot himself: 'Martin did this act of kindness to the man out of the simple humanity of his nature, and the man was naturally most grateful.'[12]

Wilde goes on to commend the new governor of Reading, thus again demonstrating the amount of power wielded by the head of a penal institution. Wilde here also hints at another phenomenon, which is that some heads can be popular *both* with staff and inmates:

He has altered the spirit in which (the rules) were carried out under his predecessor. He is very popular with the prisoners and with the warders. Indeed he has quite altered the whole tone of prison life... Under his predecessor the system was carried out with the greatest harshness and stupidity.[13]

This was the first of two letters Wilde wrote to the paper. In them he describes the misery of prison life, especially for children, of whom there were many.

His criticisms were typical of a groundswell of disapproval of English prison policy, accompanied by agitation from reform groups, and from within the Prison Service at the end of the nineteenth century.[14] Eventually in the twentieth century the system changed.

Wilde, writing about the influence of governors, raises a critical question about the captive regime: Can a head of the institution make any difference to the lives of captives? The heads of penal establishments themselves often wonder if what they do, and say, makes any difference. To find out the answer we have only to listen to what prisoners say. Wilde, as we have seen, is one of many to reflect on that influence.

Jane Buxton in Holloway felt compelled to protest about the fact that women were knitting material which was then unpicked. Being from a class that knew where power lay, and being in a system which allowed her to act, she went to the top:

> A few days ago I booked to see the Governor about that knitting on the First Offenders' Wing. She hadn't known about it, and agreed that that it must be demoralising to knit something that is merely going to be unpicked... The Governor was very nice about the complaint, and even thanked me for telling her (an extraordinary thing to happen to a prisoner).[15]

Zeno spends a good deal of his narrative discussing the governors of Wormwood Scrubs in London. Most of his account is charged with ambivalence and inconsistencies, which is only to be expected because the environment of captivity is never stable: 'If I am honest, I must admit that on reflection the majority of the governor grades I have come into contact with have been decent men.'[16]

He seems especially to approve of those governors he identifies as reformers, and who are quite happy to flout instructions from Prison Headquarters, and who will brook no opposition to the regime from reactionary uniformed officers. He names the governors. He meets Governor Tom Hayes for the first time:

> I look at his eyes, and for the first time since my arrest I feel a sense of security. They are steady and honest. I feel at once I am meeting a man, and not another of *them*. I sense that this man will not lie or prevaricate.[17]

For a man facing a life sentence with little to hope for, this is an unusual statement.

Rupert Croft-Cooke, on the other hand, is very much more critical than Zeno:

> Whereas the uniformed screws are, usually, a decent, reasonably conscientious, indeed rather likeable crowd, the higher ranks are for the most part an inadequate collection of misfits who seem to drift into the prison service for lack of a brighter alternative.[18]

But again, at least in the historical English tradition, and we will go on to see, in other traditions too, there seems to have been exceptions, as Croft-Cooke concedes, but even in this case there were weaknesses:

> Ben Grew, the Governor at Wormwood Scrubs was an exception. He had a conscience and was a man of breeding. But even he had not sufficient knowledge of what went on in his prison; for example, to eradicate the abuse he rightly detested most, the securing by certain prisoners of illicit privileges. A system flourished under his governorship, and, I feel sure, out of his ken, by which one man who had been at the Scrubs for a long time and had learnt all the foibles of the screws, could attain a position of comparative comfort and authority by carrying out secretarial and menial duties for officers who were glad to be relieved of their work.[19]

What Zeno constantly emphasises is the view that the English reformer is continually restrained by London, but he also stresses, as captives commonly do, that the head of a penal institution is immensely powerful, and can influence a regime for good or ill: 'His name is on every man's lips, his actions and orders are being discussed at every hour of the day. Gilbert Hair has said this, Gilbert Hair has done that.'[20]

But on one occasion this governor for whom Zeno has so much respect behaved badly. A concert had been arranged with performers from outside. Attendance at such events was normally voluntary, and a group of prisoners decided they did not want to go. But the governor decided to make it compulsory, and those who refused to go were subject to punishment. This consisted of removal to another part of the prison, where they were kept in their cells for 17 out of 24 hours. It was especially unjust because they were not formally charged and not given a hearing. Thus Zeno experienced the *disadvantage* attending the power of the head: that there is no appeal against the arbitrary use of that power.[21]

Wilfred Macartney agrees with this perception of the power of the head: 'He now came into chokey, and there was no doubt who ruled in Parkhurst.'[22] He relates how Governor Clayton on several occasions made a difference to a prisoner's life through his generous actions. And his influence permeated the whole prison: 'While Clayton was governor, assaults and floggings almost ceased in Parkhurst.'[23]

This illustrates the driving force behind the collective behaviour of basic grade staff. They watch for signs of how the Head wants the institution to be run, and will remarkably often tailor their behaviour to follow his lead. Stratton recalls that his first governor who was: 'a Quaker, hated violence of any kind, and not once during his term as governor did any prisoner get beaten up in the punishment wing'.[24]

The total experience of English prisoners appears that they agree on the power of the governor. But Ministers responsible for penal establishments can exercise more power if they wish, and if they intrude into the day-to-day management of prisons, which is unusual, they must be obeyed. In the mid-1990s, a Conservative Home Secretary was appointed called Michael Howard. He became painfully famous for his simple-minded mantra: 'Prison Works'. After escapes and disturbances, and the inevitable 'Review', there was the opportunity for Howard to placate his critics in the right-wing press, and apparently to do what they wanted, which was to 'tighten up' the prison system. The then Director General of the Prison Service records what followed:

> Severe curtailment of home leave with entirely new criteria being applied, a major crackdown on drugs with the introduction

of drug testing, and a wholesale restructuring of privileges for prisoners based on the principle of earning through good behaviour.[25]

Nor was this all. There was to be more handcuffing of prisoners, for example, a matter to which I will return in discussing cruelty. Of especial relevance to this discussion of the power of the governor, is the unseen effect that, as a result of Howard's interference, they became very nervous of using their judgement: a judgement in constant demand in a prison. A senior female governor describes the fear which became endemic:

> Previously officers used their discretion more than they do now. Because of the blame culture that's around at the moment, discretion is a word that's not used. If you deviate from the straight and narrow now – and I'm only talking about circumventing some of the pettier little rules – you're more likely to get sacked. This blame culture is making all staff consider their own positions. There are Governors who still take risks, but at tremendous personal risk, tremendous personal risk.[26]

American prisoners commonly write about the difference the change of the warden can make. Nathan Leopold describes the arrival of Major Henry C. Hill in 1929:

> His avowed purpose was to see first to security; there were to be no escapes. But once this had been provided for, it was his wish to grant the men every privilege and every liberty consistent with safety. He was no worshipper of the status quo; he was not afraid to innovate. But don't get the idea he was a softie or that he could be taken advantage of.[27]

His personal instruction to the guards was: 'Their punishment is the loss of their liberty. They are not to be punished further unless their conduct makes it necessary.'[28] This sentiment was enshrined by the great English reforming Prison Commissioner, Alexander Paterson, who wrote that: 'Men come to prison *as* punishment not *for* punishment.'[29] Amongst the simple improvements that Hill introduced were a shop, where prisoners could buy luxuries, 'talking pictures' and a much extended library and education service.

In San Quentin, California, Warden Clinton Duffy, upon his appointment as Warden in 1940, immediately began to make fundamental changes. In one of his first acts he demonstrated the power which could be exercised by the person in charge in many penal institutions, perhaps especially at that time in the United States. He knocked at the door of the senior uniformed officer in the prison:

> The house was occupied by Captain Ralph New under whom guards had used the dungeons, the straps, and the rubber hose so much that they had cost a warden his job. Captain New came to the door when I knocked, and I told him I had just been appointed warden.
>
> 'I've heard that,' he said shortly.
>
> 'All right,' I said. 'I'm making some changes, and as of this minute, you're through.'[30]

Duffy is widely regarded as a reformer, and the catalogue of changes he made must have been difficult to implement in the political mood of the times, or in any times, since those locked up are deemed to deserve it. Duffy's radical activity included the abolition of the dungeons – 'My first official act'[31] – the abandonment of bread-and-water punishment and generally a constructive program of recreation and education. He was also an early and persistent advocate of the abolition of the death penalty.

Also in the United States, in 1929, after about eight years as superintendent of Joliet Women's Prison, the reformist Elinor Rulien was dismissed. This followed a change of political government accompanied by agitation by junior staff who disapproved of her methods. Generally, despite Wilde's claim about the power of the

Head, junior staff – if they fear any move to lessen their authority, or to make the exercise of it more complicated – can thwart reform, provided they can coordinate their resistance. But captives too can make their views felt. On the day she left the job the prisoners rioted and 116 prisoners signed a letter to the *Joliet Evening News* addressed to the departing superintendent:

> Like a mother you forgave us time after We, the inmates of this division, offer you this momento [*sic*] as a token of our earnest regret at the hand fate has dealt us in removing you from our midst… We wish to say that in losing you, we feel that we will have lost an interested friend, as well as a good, considerate official. Briefly, you have been a 'good fellow' and a 'square shooter'. And we feel that…no one can do more for us than you have done. To us you have been kindness personified… We realize that many of us haven't always been what we should have been, and a few of us have been just impossible, and yet you, with your keen knowledge of human nature and fair judgement, have always shown us consideration, dealing with us mercifully when many times we deserved drastic time.[32]

L. Mara Dodge points out that it is remarkable that the chief organiser behind the writing of this letter was a very troublesome African American woman, constantly in trouble for: 'fighting, refusing to obey orders and in other ways resisting disciplinary officers'.[33] She had just finished a term in solitary for her part in a riot.[34] The letter is a remarkable tribute.

It seems that even in the nineteenth-century Russian prison camps it was possible for a decent man to be in a position of power. Dostoevsky gives an example:

> Lieutenant-Colonel GG-v was a real godsend to us… The convicts did not simply like him, they adored him, if such a word may be used in the present context. How he managed to do it, I have no idea, but he won them over right from the start.

'He's our father, we don't need our own!' the convicts used to say time and time again.

The fact that he 'was a thoroughly debauched individual' seems to have been irrelevant, since 'he was kind to the convicts, kind almost to the point of tenderness, and he really did love them as a father…'. Such popular men seemingly do exist.[35] Probably more typical was the Major who was the overall head of the prison. This was a man: 'Distinguished by a mode of thought that ran quite counter to that of the rest of mankind… A man such as the Major must forever be bearing down on someone.'[36]

A consolation for the convicts must have been that this individual was removed from office.

Even a prisoner like Caesarina Makhoere, usually a relentless critic of the system, commends the Head of her South African prison, Brigadier Venter:

He agreed with most of the complaints we raised against his staff and usually promised to solve any one of our problems. And, honestly, he did… When the staff behaved badly towards prisoners, he would stop them and even remove them from the section.[37]

She still wonders about his motives: 'Being head of the whole prison he worried about his good record, I suppose.'[38] Nevertheless:

He regarded other people as human beings, with the result that whatever he said was not lightly taken. At no stage did he use an iron hand towards a prisoner; instead he preferred to talk to and understand a person.[39]

Even in the vile conditions of the camps of the Confederacy in the American Civil War, there could be found Commandants who treated the captives with some consideration. McElroy, in his summary, concludes that: 'The commandant of the prison – one Captain Bowes – was the best of his class it was my fortune to meet.'[40]

And, as we have seen, an almost perfect statement of the power of the head is made by Dodge, of Superintendent Rulien in Illinois who introduced a wide range of improvements in the living conditions of her prisoners, as well as establishing constructive activities.[41]

Of course, if the presence of a humane head of the institution makes a difference, so does the presence of a cruel one. A notably cruel one was in that most cruel of systems, Tsarist Russia. His name was Major Nikolayev and he was the Warden of Dué Prison on Sakhalin for seven years. Amongst his studied cruelty:

> He also placed convict offenders in barrels and ordered them to be rolled along the shore. 'You know, when they roll that sweetheart around for an hour, the fellow becomes as gentle as silk'…When the major was about to give a thrashing to a convict, he announced that the man would not come out of it alive, and, in fact, the offender died immediately after the beating.[42]

It must have been of consolation to some that he was eventually sentenced to penal servitude himself.[43]

Even on the brutal Robben Island, a change of head transformed lives dramatically, in this case for the worse:

> There was a regression in conditions, however, in the early 1970s with the arrival of a new Commanding Officer, Colonel Badenhorst, when a reign of terror was reestablished. After Badenhorst left the Island in 1972, conditions once again began to improve slowly.[44]

The same characteristics are seen in the behaviour of the Warden of the Illinois penitentiary:

> He is a man that appears to be an enemy of us inmates rather than a friend. All his comments are criticism of what he thinks

we inmates should be doing while here at the institution… His staff eagerly reacts to the examples he sets.[45]

Apparently of the same Warden it is remarked that: 'In my opinion he is selfish, unreliable and unqualified to have a job of being Warden.'[46]

Oscar Wilde was another who found one of his governors, Colonel Isaacson, very harsh. He said to a friend in a classic Wildean aside:

> Not that Isaacson was cruel, but that he had no imagination, as once he would have said that Isaacson was absurd. To someone else he said that Isaacson could not eat his breakfast until he had punished somebody.[47]

None of these can be compared with some of the brutal Heads recorded by United States captives confined in the prisons of the Confederacy in the American Civil War. One infamous example was a Captain Henry Wirz. He was the Commandant of 'the interior part of the prison' and so was in charge of crucial areas of the Andersonville prisoner of war camp in Georgia from 1864 until the end of the American Civil War in 1865. The man in overall charge of prisoners was Brigadier John H. Winder: 'To whose account should be charged the deaths of more gallant men than all the inquisitors of the world ever slew by the less dreadful rack and wheel.'[48]

Winder died before the end of the war and so was never brought to account. Instead, it was Wirz who was arrested in April 1865 and charged with injuring the bodies and destroying the lives of soldiers in the military service of the United States. John McElroy, a prisoner of war, describes his first sight of Wirz:

> There has been a good deal of misapprehension of the character of Wirz. He is usually regarded as a villain of large mental caliber, and with a genius for cruelty. He was nothing of the kind. He was simply contemptible, from whatever view he was

studied. Gnat-brained, cowardly, and feeble natured, he had not a quality that commanded respect from anyone who knew him. His cruelty did not seem designed so much as the ebullitions of a peevish, snarling little temper, united to a mind incapable of conceiving the results of his acts, or understanding the pain he was inflicting.[49]

Winder and Wirz were not the only people regarded as responsible for the conditions of Andersonville, but when McElroy was moved, it was the memory of these two which was uppermost: 'We escaped for a while from the upas-like shadow of Winder and Wirz, in whose presence strong men sickened and died, as when near some malign genii of an Eastern story.'[50]

The list of Wirz's cruel acts was long and included hunting men with dogs, starving the men and exposing them to atrocious weather. Of particular – and some thought, of gratuitous brutality – was his shooting of prisoners who crossed the 'Dead Line'. This was a mark short of the perimeter fence which prisoners were not to cross. It was alleged that some who were shot were mentally disturbed or that they had strayed by accident. In any case the guards were only too willing to open fire.

He was sentenced to death and hanged, an action which was, and remains, a matter of dispute. His defenders say, variously, that others were as guilty, that Confederate prisoners had been treated equally badly, that the situation with regard to food, for example, was not within his control. For his part, Wirz advanced the classic defence that he had only been obeying orders. With regard to the Dead Line, this was, he said, a perfectly ordinary security measure. The controversy about Wirz was so pronounced that despite his execution as a 'war criminal', a statue was erected of him in Andersonville.

When it comes to more junior staff, the 'screws', those with whom captives deal with day by day, there is of course a wide variety of view. Perhaps the remarkable thing is that there are any compliments at all. A lot will depend on the culture of any institution at a given time, and this is especially true of the United States, where regimes can swing violently following political change in the local government. Jack Henry Abbott writes that staff, in his experience, had absolutely no redeeming feature:

> The pigs in the state and federal prisons – especially in the judicial system – treat me so violently, I cannot possibly imagine a time I could ever have anything but the deepest, aching, searing hatred for them. I can't begin to tell you what they do to me. If I were weaker by a hair, they would destroy me.[51]

In an Illinois penitentiary, another prisoner says that: 'I find that the officer's here care little less than nothing about the inmates.'[52]

Such views are found throughout the world in captive memory. Caesarina Kona Makhoere was sentenced to five years for political protest which she served in several South African prisons. She had no good to say of the lower ranks of staff:

> Warrant Officer Smith was a real bitch. She was a bully, clumsy, and most of the time when she came to work she was drunk... We prisoners were worst off with her. She would look at us as if we were things coughed up and splashed against a dirty wall. A black person was not expected to talk back to her... Then there was Captain Callitz, who must be the most stupid person I have ever come across. A tall Afrikaner woman, she kept repeating again and again that there were rules and regulations to be observed.[53]

Paul Ignotus was imprisoned by the Communist regime in Hungary in 1949. His perception of the staff was definite, and no doubt immoveable: 'Soon the gaoler, a piece of sub-human omnipotence in uniform, would be coming round.'[54] And when reflecting on the lesson captivity has taught him, 'that one should be humble', a frequent theme in this book, he concludes that: 'The lesson would have been slower if I had not been assisted by the thugs of the

Political Police.'[55] And for him it was utter contempt for the staff that was an important tool for survival:

> Were we impressed by our masters, the new top dogs? They struck us all as being far coarser, clumsier and more ludicrous in their omnipotence than anything we had seen or imagined. We had only contempt for them, laughing at their pompous solecisms and shuddering with disgust at their crudeness and cruelty…(they) proved themselves attractive to prisoners who, irrespective of their political leanings and background, fell prey to social fascination.[56]

Pierre d'Harcourt's study of one of his captors was more serious and a good deal more sombre. Of one of these, he writes that he was: 'the most interesting man at Neue Bremm', and one of the two worst SS men there. In civilian life, he was a butcher and had a good business. Outside the camp he was regarded as:

> sensible, hard-working and kind; a good fellow, a worthy citizen, and a pillar of the local community… At his trial, after the war nothing could be discovered in his past to explain the sophisticated and elaborate cruelty which he displayed at Neue Bremm.[57]

The savagery of this man, strange to say, intrigued d'Harcourt. He specialised in creeping up on men in the latrine, wearing rubber soles or slippers. He would bring a cudgel down on head and shoulders and kick the man on the buttocks and in the groin 'to the sound of ecstatic cursing and shouting. Many who entered that W.C. never came out alive.'[58] Such brutality will be discussed at greater length in another chapter.

Lady Constance Lytton had experience of several prisons in early twentieth-century Britain because of her activities in the suffragette movement. Like other captives, her opinions of the uniformed staff varied from time to time and place to place. However, in Walton

Prison, Liverpool, she had little good to say about them: 'Most of them treated me like dirt.'[59] This animosity may have been because they disapproved of her cause, but it may have been because of class antagonism. Although she had 'disguised' herself as 'Jane Warton', supposedly a working-class woman, her accent and manner would have been impossible to hide.

Many years later, another female English prisoner, Chris Tchaikovsky, is even more severe in her criticism of the London Holloway staff:

> Some were ex-army women, dragon closet-lesbians who would put you on report for hugging another woman if the mood took them... I hated them. They were cruel, mocking, loathsome, abnormal, deferential, conformist half-wits...it was in there, on my first sentence, that I learned that women as vile as screws existed.[60]

Another English female prisoner attributes the violence amongst inmates, including her own, to the behaviour of staff. This is part of a theme which appears throughout captives' accounts. It is, variously, that staff do not prevent prisoners being harmed by other prisoners, or that they actively encourage such violence. When Josie O'Dwyer was sent to Borstal:

> I was terrified. This time there was real reason to be afraid. An air of viciousness pervaded the whole place. The tougher you were the better. If you weren't tough people insulted you and took your cigarettes off you. You had a dog's life.[61]

She means, of course, that the other inmates are stealing from her, but she nevertheless blames the staff: 'It's the way the prison officers ran it which made it like that.'[62]

Later, when serving a sentence in Holloway, she attacked a prisoner called Myra Hindley, a notorious child murderer and one of the most hated women in British criminal history both amongst prisoners and in the wider community. She had been convicted, with Ian Brady, of the brutal murders of children in the 1960s. When O'Dwyer had finished with her:

> She was quite a mess. I'd knocked her teeth lose at the front, she had to eat through a straw for about six weeks. Her nose was crossed to the left side of her face, I'd split her lip, her knee and her ear, and she had two black eyes.[63]

In excusing this violence, she blames the staff for encouraging her to do it: 'It was: like "Here's half an ounce of tobacco, Josie" – It wasn't until the Assistant Governor came down that I realised I had done something wrong.'[64]

Taki probably represents a typical English prisoner's view in that he reflects the truism that some staff are decent, some are not. Thus, after he is moved to a different cell in Pentonville in London, he comes across an officer who leads him to say something negative:

> The screws, too, leave something to be desired. One of them, Officer Williams, doesn't unlock me when the bell rings for work as he notices that my cell is messy, and my bed undone. When I explain to him that I've just moved in, he grunts and tells me that I won't be unlocked until lunchtime. I try to explain further, but Williams, a big brute of a man, slams the door shut and walks away. I sit on the edge of the bed, feeling very sorry for myself, until anger at the injustice of it sets in.[65]

Officer Williams, by Taki's account, was exceptional. Other staff Taki found were different:

> Christmas is two days away, and I would have liked to give a present to the three men who were kind to me while I was in D-wing – Mr. Wrigley, Mr. Holliday (two officers) and Sid – but I have nothing. The deadening effects of materialism will not interfere in my relationship with those men... I think about this

as I jump up and dress quickly, to avoid another confrontation with Williams...[66]

Now, despite some objectionable characters and a cruel guard or two, I feel at home here. Especially when I'm alone in my cell or in the gym. Mr. Heavy and Mr. Leggett, Mr. Wrigley and Mr. Holliday are like my uncles.[67]

It is difficult to know whether Taki has simply become inordinately dependent on staff, as the effects of institutionalisation take effect, or whether these simply are decent men.

Zeno is another interesting example of classic ambivalence about staff. This ambivalence is not surprising since across the endless range of custodial staff it is possible to find every variety of behaviour imaginable, and Zeno sums this up very well, giving us a picture of a varied group, some of whom are cruel bullies while others are reasonable, kind even: 'On the faces of some of the screws an animal brutality, a shallow-eyed insensitivity that is hard to imagine as being wholly human... On the faces of a few of them, a very few, traces of occasional compassion.'[68]

Not all English prisoners would agree with the generous remarks quoted by the English prisoners above. On his transfer to an open prison, Walter Musgrave, a 'white-collar' offender, wrote: 'The place had no need for walls or wire or even for the galaxy of grim-faced warders in blue who seemed so busy but did so little.'[69]

It is impossible to make any general statements about the relationships between captor and captive. What is remarkable though is that considering the power that captors can wield, there is so much comment which is favourable. All the competing emotions inherent in the relationship were summed up by Rupert Croft-Cooke:

Most of all a man's pride may be hurt by his relationship with the screws. The majority of these, as I have said, are decent men who interpret their duties with humour, sympathy and fellow-feeling. They do not seek to take advantage of an unnatural situation, and they get through their years of service, much as the prisoner gets through his sentence, with as little fuss as possible. What is shameful is not in fact that they *do* ill-treat, domineer over or humiliate prisoners, because (with one or two exceptions I shall describe) they do nothing of the sort, but that they *can* do so. The prisoner has no remedy against a malicious screw... The screw is a despot, whether he wants to be or not, by the very nature of his calling. The prisoner's awareness of this is in itself a degradation.[70]

Despite this generic humiliation, Croft-Cooke goes on to write of what can only be called empathy:

From most of those I knew I remember small acts of kindness and consideration. If these are trivial so are most details of the unnatural life of prisons and trivial things have tremendous effects on men in that highly strung condition... I remember an ex-Palestine policeman who took me half across the prison and up to my cell on the 'fours' one night because I wanted to write instead of sitting through a concert by amateurs. And I remember other kindly acts.[71]

Wilfred Macartney was 28 when he was convicted in 1928 on charges of obtaining information calculated to be useful to an enemy. He was sentenced to ten years penal servitude. His initial experience of staff was that they were reasonable:

The general control of the convicts, was in charge of a jailor nicknamed by the prisoners 'Gentleman Smith' and he was certainly a splendid fellow. Coming to Wandsworth with a heavy sentence is a sombre business, and the administrative details consequent upon conviction are tedious and exasperating to the nerves. Gentleman Smith certainly helped to lessen and ease the strain.[72]

Macartney, though, with his considerable experience, goes on to say that this officer was exceptional, and that jailors varied:

> The Wandsworth jailor seems to be hand-picked from the prison service for his reactionary attitude to the treatment of prisoners. These jailors were certainly the worst lot I met in my 'lagging', and between them and the convict Gentleman Smith frequently stepped to stop a liberty being taken with a man who has got enough on his plate.[73]

After Wandsworth, Macartney was transferred to Parkhurst on the Isle of Wight. Considering his heavy sentence, his summary of the staff is rather remarkable. 'Many of the jailors took considerable risks and went out of their way to be decent to the men in their charge,'[74] and he gives examples:

> The changing governors: the stern and bleak Y---; Clayton, humane, sardonic, and cunning, with a real place in his heart for the underdog. The deputies: Saunders, Marriot, J. Ennion, nicknamed 'Jumbo', the best-natured and kindest jailor who ever walked.[75]

Wilfred Macartney, who can criticise as well as commend staff, recounts a remarkable case of decent behaviour by staff. At the time he was working in the prison hospital, and since Parkhurst is on an island in the southernmost part of Britain, visiting can be prohibitively expensive:

> It is not unusual for some jailor to put up in his own house the wife or mother of a convict dying in the gaol hospital, and not just for one night only, but sometimes for several days; and when this occurs the visitor is always treated with an exquisite courtesy.

> I have known this happen on several occasions; and in one case when a woman from the distressed areas, almost destitute, whose

son was dying in gaol, arrived in Parkhurst with only a single fare, she was put up by a warder, and a general subscription amongst the jailors paid her fare back to Durham and gave her a few shillings over.[76]

Despite his criticism mentioned above, when he was ill and in hospital Stuart Wood writes: 'Now that I lay stretched helpless on my back everyone was gruffly kind to me, so kind, indeed, that in my weakness I often cried softly into my pillow with gratitude.'[77]

He then goes on to make remarks about warders, which are akin to those noted later by Peter Wildeblood:

I have formed some very sincere attachments among prison warders, and they for me, I am sure. I was always quiet, courteous, respectful and well behaved, not because I feared them or from any spirit of servility, because I have never been servile, but because I understood the condition of their lives, and because, with few exceptions, they have always treated me as a man. I owe many little kindnesses to warders…it has been my misfortune to hold some warders in complete contempt for their inherent brutality, lack of principle and meanness, and my pleasure to entertain for many of them a genuine liking and respect.[78]

There are other accounts of their experience given by English prisoners which often record quite flattering remarks about staff. Brendan Behan was only 16 when he went to Borstal. He was lucky, since he was sentenced to a term in what was at the time (the early 1940s) the world model of penal reform. The Borstal system, which took its name from the village in Kent where the first such institution was established in 1902, had developed into an unparalleled attempt to reform young offenders. Staffed by officers in civilian clothes, and modelled in part on the English public school system, it was the expression of a singularly British belief, and firmly located in the British and European tradition, that young criminals were not entirely to blame for their behaviour, and, above all, that that behaviour could be changed. In the cynical late twentieth century, that belief held little sway, and the Borstal system was abolished in 1982.

Behan had only good to say about the Borstal staff. He had been refused permission to go to Mass, because he was a member of the IRA and normally would have had to wait until all the Catholics came back before he had his breakfast. His officer decided otherwise: "'Well, 'ere's your breakfast then!" He was a nice old bloke, for that morning anyway and added: "anyway Paddy, you get your scoff now and don't 'ave to wait an hour and 'alf for it".'[79]

At one point, Behan was invited to join in an escape attempt by another inmate. He declined: 'Not just now, I wouldn't. The screws were all right, and I liked the other blokes. It wasn't like Walton and lastly, though I didn't like saying it to Ken, I didn't like double-crossing the Governor.'[80]

Earlier, when they were being transferred to Borstal from the maelstrom of Walton Prison, Liverpool, he received his first taste of the possibility that both the English and the prison staff might be human:

> The screw got newspapers and gave us all the cigarettes we wanted and in great excitement the train pulled out for London... Harty talked to one of them. A Liverpool man like himself, and they talked together like two old working men about their wives and the screws' kids, and Harty's wife and the kid to come, and complained about their in-laws, and talked about how hard it was to get a house and all to that effect.[81]

Peter Wildeblood – who had every reason to be bitter, since he served a sentence for homosexual offences under a highly controversial law – singles out individual members of staff of whom he approved. When he is released after what was a very humiliating experience: 'At ten minutes to eight the gate was opened. The early shift of warders were coming on duty. Many of them had been my friends, and I shook hands with half a dozen of them.'[82]

His summary is positively complimentary:

It is astonishing that the Prison Service should contain so many decent good-hearted men. In every prison there are, of course a few cranks and bullies who are quite obvious to everyone and should have been weeded out long ago. There are also a great many who merely do what they are paid to do, in a kind of bovine trance-state which is strikingly like that of some of the long-term prisoners…fortunately, in addition to the bullies and the robots, there exists a small body of warders – almost, one might say, an underground movement – which is perhaps the most potent force for the reform of criminals which exists today.[83]

As with Rupert Croft-Crooke, the senior staff though do not get off so lightly: 'I wish I could say the same of the Principal Governors, Deputy and Assistant Governors, for it is in their hand that the real power lies.'[84]

Constance Lytton, like most captives, came across all sorts of staff. Having complained about staff at Walton Prison in Liverpool, this is a remarkable encounter she had in the prison hospital in Holloway, a prison about which there are so many adverse comments made by prisoners. She was upset after a visit from her sister, and she was crying:

The wardress heard me and before long she came and stood by my side. I expected a scolding. She seldom took any notice of the patients till morning, and I knew it was her business to reprove me, but on looking up at her face I saw that the customary mask-like expression had vanished. She was kind, she enquired tenderly why I was crying, sat down on my bed and held my hands, told me that my sister would not remember my reproaches but would be unhappy if she knew of my present distress. She did not laugh at me, she showed as much sympathy as a friend. It was a great surprise. She stayed talking to me in whispers for a considerable time, though looking continually towards the door as if in fear of being detected in a kindness, for through the night as well as through the day, she was liable to unseen inspection through the locked gate and open door, or through the spy-hole of the door when it was closed. I was most deeply grateful to her, it was a delightful discovery that underneath her rigid exterior she was an unspoiled human being.[85]

Then follows one of the strangest events recorded between captive and captor in prison reminiscences. Cynics may read every kind of innuendo into this, but as always the feelings of the captive are paramount, and it is her feelings which must be respected:

I longed to return her kindness and ventured to propose that I should rub her chest to ease her hacking cough. At first she would not hear of it, but at last, after I had fetched some ointment from the bed-head of one of the patients who had a cough, she consented and allowed me to open her dress. She seemed much afraid and told me she would probably be dismissed if we were seen... I would gladly have talked to her all night about prisoners, the working conditions of wardresses, her own life, but this, of course, was forbidden. She soon went back to her table, her face resumed its former expression and I never again held any intercourse with her... This kind act of the night-wardress remains as one of the sunlit flower patches of my time in Holloway.[86]

Another suffragette, Gliddon, on hunger strike, recalls that the matron was 'a nice intelligent woman', and that the wardresses on her ward were 'charming' and 'make things as easy for [the prisoners] as possible'. A year later, Harriet Kerr expressed something akin to gratitude towards and solidarity with the female prison workers, as she wrote in a secret letter in 1913:

Baths also I am cut off from during hunger strikes, but the wardresses are really great dears and bring me the best equivalent they have… They would also bring me books if they dared, but someone would discover it and tell on them and I should hate to get any of them into trouble.[87]

Other women prisoners in England seem to be notably tolerant towards the staff. Margaret Turner, who served a sentence in Holloway Prison in England in the late 1950s for demonstrating against nuclear weapons, reports some almost felicitous experiences with staff. On one occasion, she tried to teach an Austrian prisoner who could not speak English. There were all sorts of obstacles to her doing this but:

> Luckily one of the officers in K wing is a sympathetic person and this week she has bought out of her own money a few text books for Helga to teach herself English. We are all enormously grateful to her for this personal kindness, but it's a pity officialdom has to be so heartless.[88]

On one occasion, Margaret Turner has to select some shoes – for a prisoner with little choice, this was a big issue: 'I mentioned the kind officer who let me take some time to choose some shoes. It's surprising how one gets to feel disproportionately grateful for the smallest kindness here.'[89]

This is Turner's summary of the staff:

> We are finding that many of the officers are kind and friendly, especially the younger ones… I think I had expected them all to be rough, wispy-haired harridans.[90]
>
> I must say I immensely admire the way some of the officers here, especially the younger ones, just hit exactly the right note with the prisoners. They are friendly and human, sometimes even humorous, without losing any authority.[91]

Another prisoner, Jane Buxton, convicted of the same offence, writes: 'I haven't told you about the second officer in charge at the factory, who is a really a very kind and sweet person.'[92]

Not all the officers were so humane. Of one she writes a depressing account of how one mature woman could behave to another:

> We work hard and try to do everything we're told, yet somehow it seems we can never do anything right. I am the particular *bête noire*. Today I have been told to take the silly grin off my face, and that it gives her the willies to look at me. Civil answers seem to annoy her almost more than anything. Sometimes I try to stick up for myself and say something in an upright way, but before I've got half a dozen words out, she chips in and starts talking back at me.[93]

Erwin James, writing about his life sentence, has a chapter entitled 'Memories of Officer Bill': 'Bill had been an officer for twenty-five years. He was laid back and always courteous to prisoners. Everybody liked him… I heard that Bill passed away the other week… It was sad news.'[94] James is allocated a prison officer, whom he calls 'Fairman', to help him prepare a 'release plan'. Once again their relationship seems to have been positively cordial. As they talked:

> He reminded me of how good it could be just to be an ordinary, decent human being. His was the kind of life I had hankered after before coming to prison, but I had never discovered the means by which it could be achieved… In fact by the end of our talk I felt that perhaps he did, after all, possess more than a little understanding of what it might be like to walk in the shoes of somebody serving my kind of sentence… Fair play to him, I remember thinking as he walked me back to my cell.[95]

In a totally different world, that of a Communist regime, was captive Edith Bone. Her summary, after over seven years in solitary confinement, is almost unbelievably balanced:

What I myself consider more interesting were the discoveries I made about the people surrounding me. They were all supposedly my mortal enemies, out for my blood. In fact, they were doing a routine and rather distasteful job because it offered material advantages which outweighed the unpleasantness.[96]

Even in that model of inhumanity, the Gulag, there was behaviour which captives want to praise:

> It is impossible to write of Soviet labour camps without paying tribute to the kindness and helpfulness of the hospital nurses. Perhaps because, at least in the daytime, they lived in more human conditions, although they returned to the barracks at night, or perhaps because the hospital was the only place in the camp where it was still possible to help human suffering – whatever the reason, the nurses treated us with such tenderness and devotion that we looked upon them as beings from another world, whom only some trick of fate had forced to live with us and share all the hardships of our slavery. The human atmosphere of the hospital also affected free men. The camp chief, Samsonov, always exchanged a few words with each patient during his inspections, and the severe voice of Yegorov, the free head doctor (it was said that he too had once been a prisoner), became warm and gentle whenever he stopped by a sick man's bed.[97]

Kind the doctors may have been, but they were as corrupt as everyone else. Gustav Herling goes on to describe how the doctors would be bribed to allow relief from work, especially women, who would 'in return visit the doctor at night in the small duty room', and how the *Urki* would pay for a drop of alcohol or other drugs:

> In such camps the doctors were a social *élite* unequalled in its style of life, its opportunities and even its orgies, and the efficiency of a camp medical mafia was improved by the participation of the

free head doctor, who usually had himself been a prisoner, and who appropriated a major share of the spoils.[98]

Such occasional decency as Herling described was not confined to the rather special environment of the hospital. Herling goes on to tell of experience in the more everyday situation of work:

> In some brigades, too, the degree of friendship between prisoners and their guard was so close that, as soon as they were out of sight of the guardhouse, the 'strelock' put his rifle on his shoulder and began to chat pleasantly with the last few pairs. This insignificant expression of human feeling gave us not so much the pleasure of raising ourselves from humiliation and contempt, but rather the excitement at an infringement of prison rules. Occasionally the guard treated his brigade with politeness, and even showed signs of a rudimentary guilty conscience towards them. Therefore the days when the guard of a particular brigade was changed were amongst the most memorable for the prisoners and were eagerly discussed in the barracks. Some time had always to pass before a fresh understanding could develop between the slaves and their new overseer. It was quite a different case if the escorting guard looked upon the prisoners as his natural enemies and treated them accordingly; that brigade did not miss the slightest opportunity of annoying him and making his work difficult.[99]

When Mohamedou Slahi was in his Jordanian prison, hardly noted for a liberal regime, and before his 'rendition' to Cuba, and when he had every reason to be bitter and afraid, he writes:

> It was categorically forbidden for the guards to interact with the detainees, but they always broke these rules. They recounted the latest jokes to me and offered me cigarettes, which I turned down because I don't smoke. They told me about the other detainees and their cases and also about their own private lives, marriage,

children and the social life in Jordan. I learned almost everything about life in Amman speaking with them.[100]

When he was sent to Guantánamo, his relationship with his American guards was even more surprising. Despite the beatings, the 'cold cell' and other tortures, a curious, if ambivalent, bond was formed: 'They started to make me repair their DVD players and PCs, and in return I was allowed to watch a movie…we slowly but surely became a society and started to gossip about the interrogators and call them names.'[101]

One taught him chess and several played with him. But he was never allowed to forget who he was. Playing chess, he made a mistake and was admonished: 'You should build a strategy, and organize your attack! That's why the fucking Arabs never succeed.' And when he said, 'If I were you,…,' the guard got angry and said, 'Don't you ever dare to compare me with you, or compare any American with you!'[102]

Even in the vileness of the Egyptian prison there were kindly staff. For an Egyptian intellectual like Nawal el Sa'adawi, having to submit to what must have been a peasant's experience, the adjustment was swift, and no doubt surprising. But an even greater surprise was to come:

When I told the *shawisha* (wardress) that I could sleep only on a straight wooden board, she left the cell and was gone for a while. When she returned, she was breathing heavily, and Dhuba was in tow carrying a wooden board. The *shawisha* had come across it in a storehouse in the prison, and she presented it to me as a gift.[103]

Shawisha Nabawiyya astonished me sometimes by taking courageous stands in which she stood firmly on the side of right and showed no fear of the prison administration's power. Unlike the other *shawishas*, she did not accept any bribes. Nor did she allow a prisoner to be beaten, even if the senior official in charge ordered her to do so.

'Once I obeyed the order and beat a prisoner in the correction cell,' she said. 'Then I went home, and I felt a pain around my heart. I stayed home for a week, sick, and since then I have not beaten any prisoner. Even if they threatened to dismiss me, I would never beat a prisoner. I quarrel with my son when he beats a cat or dog – so what about a human being?'[104]

There can be no situation so conducive to stress as a hunger strike, both for captives and captors. One such was in Mountjoy Prison, Dublin. Yet even here a prisoner manages to find something good to say about staff. A warder, McCrane, discusses the situation of the hunger strikers with a prisoner:

'Well, McCrane?' (the prisoner asks)
'Brennan and Darcy are very bad. Brennan is going, I think. Some of the others are weaker. O'Connell has those fainting fits again. Rogers vomited half the night and is like a ghost.'
'Thanks, McCrane. By the way, what do you think's going to happen?'
'I don't know; some of you are going to be let die, sure enough.'
'We are ready for that, McCrane…'[105]

Two doctors this morning…Dr. Hurley's smile has completely worn off. He looks quite changed…aged… Sat on my table after Dr. McConnell had gone out…
'Now, Gallagher,' he said, 'I want you to get your brain working. No man has died yet. Some of them cannot live any longer. Brennan is nearly gone. Two of the men in the hospital are dying. Some of the later arrivals in A. Wing are likely to go under any minute. I have got this thing through up to now without a death.' (I smiled with my eyes only: he is too kindly a man to hurt.)[106]

This conversation took place in, ostensibly, a most hostile and dangerous situation.

The situation in the English prisons, even at the beginning of the twentieth century, was a good less threatening, and the complaints are often much less serious. In Lord William Nevill's account, he explains that the governor is limited in his power by visiting magistrates and the prison directors. But he then goes on to disprove his point by saying that a new governor would not allow prisoners to receive a reference book called *Whitaker*. A prisoner appealed to a director who told him 'there was something in the book which was deemed undesirable for prisoners to read'. Nevill writes that:

> I have since searched Whitaker from cover to cover, and I think it would be very difficult for the prison officials to point out where the undesirable information is given…shortly after this all leave for having books from outside was withdrawn.[107]

Despite this annoyance, which of course in the claustrophobia of the prison was important to Nevill, his verdict on the officers is complimentary:

> In the course of nearly four years' experience I came in contact with a large number of officers of one kind or another, and, with a few exceptions, I formed a high opinion of them personally, and also of the methods on which they worked…[108]
>
> With regard to the warders and assistant-warders, taking them as a body, I do not think they could possibly be improved upon. It was a wonder to me that they got such a good class of men to join the prison service.[109]

The American federal prisoner Helen Bryan's approach to her imprisonment is remarkable. She tries to understand and to accept the prisoners who are from a very different background, and her attitude to the staff is generous. It could be of course that the staff at this prison were exceptionally mature and reasonable towards the captives:

> My contact with officers was limited to approximately twenty-five women who might be considered a representative cross-section of the staff. I expected to find the officers hard, unfeeling, and, where I was concerned, scornful and possible prejudiced. None of these expectations was realized. Two outstanding qualities characterized them. First, their unflagging concern for the welfare and future of the girls, and second, their fairness and justice in dealing with us... I experienced their ceaseless care of us in the cottage and I saw that their attitudes towards us were based primarily on their concern for the individual and for the smoothest and happiest functioning of the group... I think that generally the girls themselves would have said the officers were more fair than unfair... Although the officers I knew displayed a solid and continuing interest in us, their attitude was detached and impersonal and never for a moment could we forget they were officers... A considerable number of officers were from the South. I was, therefore, more than surprised to see them manifest no racial prejudice of any kind... I was convinced that the officers exercised the same fairness and consideration towards the Negro girls that they showed us.[110]

In those countries where there was no tradition of reasonable care for captives, the recorded experience is almost without any consolation. But, even in the hell of the Japanese prisoner of war camps, there were occasional acts of kindness. And, obviously, to the captive in the Japanese camps, but not only there, in dealing with absolute deprivation, kindness is an experience which in freedom cannot be properly understood:

> A Japanese mess orderly, a man whom I saw once only. He [by which the writer means God] chose a man who was prepared to forget self and his life to bring me life – the food which I so

badly needed in an awful week of deliberate starvation imposed by the Kempeitai. That a man should put his head in a noose as a calculated risk for another, and an enemy at that, jolted me out of the vicious circle of my self-preoccupation.[111]

Nor was this the only Japanese whose kindness and bravery was recounted by the same prisoner, L.H. Morrison, in his experience in Changi and on the Burma Railway. Again, the context is almost beyond belief. This was the Japanese army, drilled to obey orders, and taught that what they did was important and based on principle. And yet even here staff would take risks, even though their actions could only bring trouble. It need hardly be said, though, that such compliments are rare in the reminiscences of captives of the Japanese.

Also rare are reported cases of decent behaviour by guards in prisons in Vietnam. But there are some. John McCain, a pilot, and later after his release, a very distinguished Senator in the United States, was a prisoner left for the night tightly bound with ropes:

> A short time after the guard had left me to ponder my bad attitude evening, this guard entered the room and silently, without looking at or smiling at me, loosened the ropes, and then he left me alone. A few minutes before his shift ended, he returned and tightened up the ropes.[112]

There were other rare, but very welcome instances of kindness by a member of staff in Vietnam:

> One night Larry was awakened by the sound of his cell door opening. A guard approached his cot… Larry lay still, pretending to be asleep, wondering what the guard was up to, not knowing whether to be frightened or not. He opened his eyes as much as he dared, not enough so that the guard could see they were open. To Larry's amazement, the guard was gazing down at him with one of the saddest, most sympathetic expressions he had ever seen on anyone; the man's face was a map of kindness. He

was holding a blanket. Larry had not been issued a blanket. The guard came close, slowly lifted Larry's head, put the blanket beneath it, smoothed it, then laid his head back down on the blanket, so gently he was hardly aware that it happened. Then the guard turned away and tiptoed out of the cell, closing and locking the door as quietly as he could.[113]

There are several ways in which captives keep the staff at bay. Sometimes the way is intensely personal, and the staff will never know of the protest, but the captive does. Even though he had not eaten or drunk for 36 hours, Koestler made a decision to resist:

> So I poured the coffee down the W.C., and the bread too, after having broken it into little pieces. In doing so, I had the impression that I was again taking an active part in the course of events, that I was putting up some sort of a fight; and this thought had a calming effect. I crouched on my wire-mattress and tried to go to sleep.[114]

There are instances where, especially if the prison or camp is chaotic, prisoners could do what they wanted, apparently without the knowledge, or perhaps with the connivance, of staff. An early example of captives doing what they please occurs in an account of the lives of confined Catholics in Wisbech Castle in England at the end of the sixteenth century:

> Sometimes also I had an opportunity of celebrating the Holy Mysteries, for from the lower room (which was inhabited by Catholics) in the dead of night we were enabled to obtain vestments by a rope which was let down from our window, and in the early morning, before the wardens and other prisoners were awake, we returned them in the same manner.[115]

Another commonly recorded experience is the curiosity that the prisoners may find staff a source of unending interest, bemusement, fascination and disgust. Prisoners even find staff laughable. Frank Norman describes an officer the prisoners called 'fighting Fred'. He was a source of endless amusement because of his idiotic boasting about his achievements. He:

> Was a black belt at judo (every blow a death blow) as he used to say, he had trained boxers, and had been a boxer his-self, he had also trained wrestlers and been a wrestler. On top of this he was once a lumberjack, a bally dancer, a female impersonator, a bricklayer, carpenter, gas man, probation officer, artist, writer, sculptor, not only had he done all these things and was a master of them, he had also done anything you said you had done…if Fred said he killed an Elephant with his bare hands, well that's just what he did and who were we to dispute it. After all if we did he might find something to nick us for but we didn't want that…we told him that he should realy be in the C.I.D. but we could get any farther than sudjesting it as it seems he had already been in the C.I.D. and had solved more cases than enough, so we just gave up.[116]

Captives will not be completely obedient. There is always enough spirit left to try to resist the oppressive nature of regimes personified by the staff. There is a whole galaxy of ways to ridicule, annoy or even manifestly protest in ways that the captors are never aware of. One way is only hinted at by Brendan Behan: 'I have him bitched, balloxed and bewildered, for there is a system and a science in taking the piss out of a screw and I am a trained young man at it.'[117]

In Ruhleben, one of the prisoners describes how they would drop a mug on the stone floor, which would send up a cheer, which in turn would bring the guard shouting for silence. They would then wait until he was back in his cubicle and drop the broken pieces again: 'It simply infuriated him.'[118]

Sometimes captives would court danger and they would bait staff even if such actions could provoke a lethal response. This happened in a prisoner of war camp in the Second World War:

Even in a society where captives and captors share a similar culture, the young and wildly frustrated among the prisoners will be inclined to do everything in their power to annoy their guards... The Poles before us had been far worse; unfortunately for us they had used the windows to shout rude remarks at the sentries and if possible drop things on their heads. The result was the sentries were apt to fire at anyone they saw near a window whatever they were doing there.[119]

Even in the Confederate prisons of the Civil War captives would try to laugh at the guards' expense, though this could be extremely dangerous. John McElroy tells of one way of doing this:

Late at night, when everybody would be lying down, and out of the way of shots, a window in the third story would open, a broomstick, with a piece nailed across it to represent arms, and clothed with a cap and blouse would be protruded, and a voice coming from a man carefully protected by the wall, would enquire:
'S-a-y, g-uarr-d, what time is it?'
If the guard was of the long suffering kind he would answer:
'Take yo' head back in, up dah; you kno hits agin all odahs to do dat.' Then the voice would say, aggravatingly, 'Oh, well, go to –you—Rebel--, if you can't answer a civil question.'
Before the speech was ended the guard's rifle would be at his shoulder and he would fire. Back would come the blouse and hat in haste, only to go out again the next instant, with a derisive laugh, and,
'Thought you were going to hurt somebody, didn't you. You ---------But Lord, you can't shoot for sour apples; if I couldn't shoot no better than you, Mr. Johnny Reb, I would-----'
The guard's shots caused a turn-out of the guard but all they would find 'everybody up there snoring away as if they were the Seven Sleepers'.[120]

It is quite remarkable that in such situations captives could try to make fun.

K.P. MacKenzie relates how, even in the squalor of the Japanese prisoner of war camps, they managed to put on variety shows. The star comic turn: 'would never lose an opportunity of getting in a sly dig at the guards if he could do so without their understanding what he was about'.[121]

Despite the horror of a Concentration Camp, captives can still find solace in mocking the guards. Sarah Helm reports on the behaviour of a group of women prisoners in Ravensbrück:

> Prisoners like nothing more than to fool the guards, break the rules. Some groups were so good at it that they almost didn't care about the SS at all. It once happened that a prisoner smuggled a wonderful azalea branch out of the nursery into the political prisoners' block. The theft was discovered because the commandant's fresh flowers were not delivered that day. But the theft was so well organized that the smugglers were not discovered, which gave them great happiness.[122]

Some captives seem almost obliged to defy the system. K.P. MacKenzie recounts how a fellow prisoner of the Japanese:

> Took some terrible bashings from the jailers who did not like his independent fearless spirit. Several times he was made to stand to attention, bare-headed in continuous rain or in the broiling sun, for several hours because he failed to bow to the Japanese. Birse was an inspiration to us all…he almost invited the Jap guards to beat him by his habit of visiting solitary and other blocks to bring any small extras, that he could steal from the kitchen where he worked, to those prisoners who were in need of them.[123]

Brendan Behan describes the expertise of an Irish prisoner who delighted in infuriating the staff by singing martial songs, and at the same time imitating the sound of a pipe band:

He was able to roar in a whisper... For a time the screw stood on the steps in amazement looking round and straining his ears to catch the faint but rhythmic and persistent drone of Callan's piping. The he screwed up his eyes and spoke through his teeth.

"Oo's making that bleeding noise, eh?'

Of course the officer got the wrong man.[124]

Zeno describes a fairly harmless but joyful way in which they made fools of the officers. They are allowed to play bridge but no other card games. They, of course, play poker, and an officer might approach and ask why there is no movement of the cards. He will be told that they are waiting for someone to bid: 'I have seen a screw stand for ten minutes watching four silent, unmoving players, and in the end move off down the hall with a shrug. Time means less to us than to them: we can always outwait them.'[125]

And that is what many captives do: as Zeno says, they 'outwait' the staff. They are in no hurry, but at the same time survival means developing relationships of some kind with the captors in order to live. There are too other cruder ways of defiance. This can consist of withdrawal of labour, abuse, physical attack (remarkably rare) or riot. All of these of course attract severe punishments.

One of the most moving accounts from a captive about a member of staff, and furthermore a captive who was under sentence of death, comes from a victim of the Nazis. Krystyna Wituska (1920–43) was a member of the Polish underground when she was arrested in 1942. She was guillotined in 1943. Her letters to her parents are full of courage without a sign of doubt, anxiety or self-pity. Her last letter reads:

You will receive this letter after my death... Don't despair beloved parents, be brave dearest Mummy. Remember that I watch over you and grieve over every one of your tears. But when you smile, I smile with you.

May God reward you for the love and care with which you
have enveloped me. Farewell, dearest parents, farewell Halinka.
Your Tina.[126]

In this same letter she writes:

[This letter] will be sent to you by a person to whom we are
immeasurably indebted. She has been our friend and our
guardian. At great personal risk, she tried as much as possible
to ease our difficult fate; she shared with us whatever she could,
never asking for anything in return. We called her our 'Ray of
Sunshine,' because whenever she came into our cell, she brought
her joy and laughter. We became friends with her daughter. You
saw her once, Daddy; do you remember?

I only regret that I will never be able to repay her for
everything that she did for us, for her dear heart of gold. She was
especially fond of me and I loved her as one can only love one
who offers a hand when you are truly in need and never thinks
of this as charity, but only as something normal. Please don't
forget her.[127]

The woman to whom she refers was a German prison guard, Hedwig
Grimpe, who worked in the Alt Moabit Prison in Berlin. As she
promised, after the war she delivered Tina's letter to her parents.[128]

There is a critical but strange midway world between captor
and captive, and it is occupied by those captives who achieve or
are accorded authority and upon whom the staff rely to help them
control the population. It is this lamentable phenomenon which I
now consider.

Notes

1. Ketchum *op. cit.* p.177.
2. Dodge *op. cit.* p.276.
3. Jessop, A. (ed.) *The Economy of the Fleete.* pp.29–30.
4. Stanton, Alfred H. and Schwarz, Morris S. *The Mental Hospital: A Study of Institutional Participation in Psychiatric Illness and Treatment.* p.39.

5. Paterson, Alexander. His articles in *The Times* were collected and printed in his book *Our Prisons*.
6. Jackson *op. cit.* p.217.
7. *Ibid.* p.241.
8. Mathiesen *op. cit.* p.136.
9. *Ibid.* p.137.
10. *Ibid.*
11. Maine *op cit.* p.897.
12. *Ibid.* p.900.
13. *Ibid.* p.903.
14. *Ibid.* pp.897ff.
15. Buxton and Turner *op. cit.* p.160.
16. Zeno *op. cit.* p.194.
17. *Ibid.* p.120.
18. Croft-Cooke *op. cit.* p.62.
19. *Ibid.*
20. Zeno *op. cit.* pp.48–9.
21. *Ibid.* pp.90ff.
22. Macartney *op. cit.* p.64.
23. *Ibid.* p.155.
24. Stratton *op. cit.* p.9.
25. Carlen *Sledgehammer op. cit.* p.107.
26. *Ibid.* p.113.
27. Leopold *op. cit.* p.164.
28. *Ibid.*
29. 'Alec Paterson 1884–1947: An Appreciation' by Gordon Hawkins, privately published, no date.
30. Duffy, Clinton. *San Quentin: The Dramatic Story of an American Penitentiary.* p.49.
31. *Ibid.*
32. Dodge *op. cit.* p.141.
33. *Ibid.*
34. *Ibid.*
35. Dostoevsky *op. cit.* p.331.
36. *Ibid.* p.183.
37. Scheffler *op cit.* pp.98–99.
38. *Ibid.* p.99.
39. *Ibid.*
40. McElroy *op. cit.* p.12.
41. Dodge *op. cit.* p.143.
42. Chekhov *op cit.* p.196.
43. *Ibid.*
44. Deacon *op. cit.* p.98.
45. Chang *et al. op. cit.* p.96.

46. *Ibid.* p.135.
47. Ellman, Richard. *Oscar Wilde.* p.466.
48. McElroy *op. cit.* pp.54–55.
49. *Ibid.* p.59.
50. *Ibid.* p.194.
51. Abbott *op. cit.* p.54.
52. Chang *et al. op. cit.* p.134.
53. Scheffler *op. cit.* p.98.
54. Ignotus *op. cit.* p.28.
55. *Ibid.* p.43.
56. *Ibid.* pp.33–34.
57. d'Harcourt *op cit.* p.89.
58. *Ibid.* pp.89–90.
59. Scheffler *op. cit.* p.231.
60. Carlen *Criminal Women op. cit.* p.32.
61. *Ibid.* p.142.
62. *Ibid.*
63. *Ibid.* p.158.
64. *Ibid.*
65. Taki *op. cit.* p.54.
66. *Ibid.* p.56.
67. *Ibid.* p.138.
68. Zeno *op. cit.* pp.20–21.
69. Musgrave, Walter. 'Warrant to Nowhere' in Mikes. p.128.
70. Croft-Cooke *op. cit.* pp.95–96.
71. *Ibid.* p.221.
72. Macartney *op. cit.* p.34.
73. *Ibid.* p.34.
74. *Ibid.* p.107.
75. *Ibid.* pp.37–38.
76. *Ibid.* p.184.
77. Wood *op. cit.* p.130.
78. *Ibid.*
79. Behan *op. cit.* p.107.
80. *Ibid.* p.231.
81. *Ibid.* pp.144–145.
82. Wildeblood *op. cit.* p.172.
83. *Ibid.* p.155.
84. *Ibid.*
85. Lytton *op. cit.* p.111.
86. *Ibid.* pp.111–112.
87. Schwan *op. cit.* pp.168–169.
88. Buxton and Turner *op. cit.* pp.108–109.
89. *Ibid.* p.67.

90. *Ibid.* p.41.
91. *Ibid.* p.120.
92. *Ibid.* pp.83–84.
93. *Ibid.* p.137.
94. James, Erwin. *The Home Stretch: From Prison to Parole.* pp.105–106.
95. *Ibid.* pp.114–115.
96. Bone *op. cit.* p.38.
97. Herling *op. cit.* pp.103–104.
98. *Ibid.* p.109.
99. *Ibid.* p.46.
100. Slahi *op. cit.* pp.175–176.
101. *Ibid.* pp.326–327.
102. *Ibid.* pp.327–328.
103. El Sa'adawi *op. cit.* p.86.
104. *Ibid.* p.132.
105. Coogan *op. cit.* p.74.
106. *Ibid.* p.75.
107. WBN *op. cit.* pp.64–65.
108. *Ibid.* pp.69–70.
109. *Ibid.* pp.80–81.
110. Bryan *op. cit.* pp.257–259.
111. Morrison *op. cit.* p.79.
112. McCain *op. cit.* p.228
113. Hubbell *op. cit.* p.57.
114. Koestler *op. cit.* p.84.
115. Thomas, J.E. *House of Care: Prisons and Prisoners in England 1500–1800.* p.15.
116. Norman *op. cit.* pp.118–119.
117. Behan *op. cit.* p.366.
118. Ketchum *op. cit.* p.97.
119. Barker *op. cit.* p.121.
120. McElroy *op. cit.* pp.33–34.
121. MacKenzie *op. cit.* p.161.
122. Helm *op. cit.* pp.83–84.
123. MacKenzie *op. cit.* p.76.
124. Behan *op. cit.* p.125.
125. Zeno *op. cit.* p.77.
126. Scheffler *op. cit.* p.59.
127. *Ibid.* p.449.
128. *Ibid.* p.59.

— *5* —

Prisoners in Authority

One of the most important dynamics of the captive life is the transfer of authority from staff to inmates. This can be 'informal', which is to say some captives will simply assume it. We will see examples of this in the Russian Gulag and in the English Borstal system. This informal authority can be achieved by the prisoners through their reputation, which may be brought in from the outside or may be accorded by the staff, who recognise that without such informal delegation, control and indeed administration would be difficult or impossible.

Earlier generations of captives and captors saw this as normal and acceptable. The Marshalsea was a debtors' prison in London, and exemplifies the long-standing practice of giving prisoners authority. Jerry White sets out some of the rules and regulations in that prison:

Enforced by a committee of nine with a chairman, all elected by the 'court', a meeting of all male prisoners held on Mondays at noon, non-attenders facing a fine of 3d… The court also elected the secretary month by month and the master of the ale room… The committee had a judicial function too, deciding 'all matters in dispute which may happen to arise in the college between the members thereof'. Opposing parties and any witnesses were heard and the committee's decisions 'considered final'. Prisoners not abiding by the committee's decision were fined 2s 6d. Those refusing to pay had their names and offences posted 'in the ale-room and other most conspicuous places in the college', chalked on the walls, broadcast loudly in the yard 'by the crier', were sent to Coventry and refused entry to the ale-room and its privileges.[1]

John Dickens, a prisoner and the father of Charles Dickens, is probably the best known of those elected to be chairman.[2]

Writing of the Marshalsea and such delegation, White sums up the universal danger of the practice: 'Democracy could, however, turn swiftly to tyranny.'[3] One prisoner at the beginning of the nineteenth century, Giles Hemens, refused to accept that 'tyranny':

> Hemens would have a terrible time there. He refused to suffer in silence. His case exposes the dark side of debtor democracy and the undercurrent of violence flowing beneath that neat copperplate script of the 'College Regulations'. And his exposé had serious consequences for those nominally in charge of the gaol.[4]

Such delegation is not consigned to history. It continues everywhere, officially arranged, and the result is invariably cruelty and misery. If this is so, then why are prisoners set in authority over others?

The most positive motive is a belief that by allowing captives to exercise responsibility, they will learn about how decisions are made. This will, in some way, teach them about community responsibility, and the complications of living in harmony with other people. Supposedly, it is also an exercise in democracy, from which the captive community can learn. Such faith derives from the belief in 'reform'.

But the main reasons for the abrogation of power are those of exigency. It is impractical to employ enough staff, certainly of the right calibre, to control unruly inmates. There are never enough staff to exercise complete control over the inmates, and so prisoners are recruited to help. Staff need help, and that help comes in the form of the considerable resource of the body of prisoners. The strongest are picked for their strength, regardless of their moral integrity (or more likely their lack of it), and they will be those who have their own best interests at heart, and advance them above all else. Such promotion has the added advantage of dividing the strength of the prisoner body; indeed it serves to weaken it. Unfortunately, however tyrannical the staff may be, in any prison there is no tyranny like that which is exercised by fellow inmates. This entire exercise of course accords with the primary need to keep order. This is clear from the Russian practice:

> Prisoners governed themselves through an intricate web of traditions and practices overseen by the commune... A stable and extended version of the *artel*, that self-governing organisation of convicts in the marching convoys en route to Siberia, the prisoners' commune operated in all penal settlements along similar lines...each one would elect an elder, or *starosta*, responsible for administering funds paid into a central kitty and for negotiating with the central authorities. The prison warders... would then deal with him directly.[5]

The fortuitous need for both economy and punishment, always a signal aim of captive establishments, was made clear in the case of how Palestinian prisoners were controlled:

> As for the Ramleh prison, my clients there informed me that the condition of Arab prisoners and detainees had deteriorated when Jewish criminal prisoners were appointed to guard over them, instead of people from the Prison Authority. These 'guards' do their utmost to embitter the Arabs' lives, so that as to get a reduction of up to a third of their own terms, as they had been promised. The Arab prisoners – who did not want to resign themselves to more working hours, to humiliating treatment, to being prevented from studying, to being prevented from buying things at the canteen – are victims of the punishments which are then imposed by the authorities.[6]

In China, in modern times, inmates were put in authority as part of the drive to meet production targets, which is a fairly unusual reason for delegation. This is how the system was devised so that these targets were met:

> Each inmate group chief (*zuzhang*) implements on an individual basis among the prisoners in his specific group. The grade of an individual prisoner's food ration depends upon the degree to which the production quota is fulfilled or undershot…such prisoners have served in a mediating role between the camp administration and rank-and-file prisoners, thereby developing a relatively keen sense of how the camps are run on a daily basis… the prison administration's dependence upon such inmate chiefs to help control other prisoners has often enabled cell tyrants (*yuba*) to lord it over the rank-and-file like criminal kingpins.[7]

In considering the simple taking-over of power by captives, the Russian Gulag is a very good example of a situation where strong prisoners are allowed to exercise almost unlimited power. Menachem Begin describes his experience where the *Urki*, the criminal, as opposed to the political, prisoners ruled:

> They called him Redbeard. He was in jail for murder. He was head of the *Urki* and was held in genuine high esteem by the criminal prisoners… Even the sentries were afraid of him.[8]

In Cook County Jail, Illinois, in the United States in the 1960s, there was the same informal take-over of power by the strong. Cook County was not exceptional. The practice described there was, and is, common in the United States:

> Each Cell Block was run by three inmates, the strongest, and no officer ever came inside the cell block. During the time I was on H-4 (two months) no officer ever came inside. The officers allowed the count to be taken by the three strongest inmates, the

food was distributed by these inmates, the cells assigned when they became available, etc.[9]

Even in a camp for British prisoners of war, individuals, regardless of rank, could somehow manipulate themselves into a position of considerable influence. This was possible because of the breakdown of the rigid military hierarchy:

> At the Dulag (writes J.V. Webb) the British liaison officer was an Airborne sergeant who was captured on D-Day and who had by the beginning of September 1944 achieved a very powerful position. He was in charge of the distribution of Red Cross parcels, and always had unlimited cigarettes to exchange with newly arrived prisoners for their gold rings, wrist watches or other valuables.[10]

A more restrained, but equally threatening example of informal power can be found in the English Borstal system. Here there was a phenomenon called the 'daddy', a young man who because of his strength and connections could bully and terrorise weaker inmates. Brendan Behan tells us how he benefitted from their protection: 'Dale had not so much mouth out of him since he'd come down to Feltham. They went round very quiet men for fear of Murray and Lovely Ball and the terrors.'[11] Murray, Behan goes on to point out, 'was the daddy of them all', and the others would do things for him to keep on the right side.[12]

The history of *officially* according power to prisoners in Britain has a long history. The motive for this seems to have been, in historical times, mainly financial, but the ill effects of the practice had been noticed and deplored as part of the movement to reform in the eighteenth century. In 1835, an Act named after the Duke of Richmond forbade the use of prisoners as staff. A measure of how the system relied on them can be gauged from the fact that as a consequence of the Act, in the Coldbath Fields House of Correction, there had to be recruited: 'eighty-two new officers under the designation of sub-warders'.[13] Such prohibition did not end the formal handing over of power to captives.

The giving of authority to captives took off during the early part of the twentieth century when the English prison system became the world model for notions of penal reform. From being a repressive regime, in its day itself a model, if a harsh one, of penal policy, it set an example of faith in the potential for change in even the most seemingly hopeless cases. But the 'trustee' prisoner predated the 'reformist' ideology. In 1852 at Dartmoor, a notorious establishment, a carefully supervised 'red collar' man appeared. He was the prototype of that legendary figure in the English prison: the 'red band', part of a system of which it was claimed: 'The main purpose was not to save staff, or to facilitate administration of the prison but to introduce a reforming agency in convict prisons.'[14] Eventually authority seeped into the system and in 1921 at Camp Hill Prison on the Isle of Wight, the 'honour party' was set up. These were groups of prisoners working without supervision inside the walls. Then, in Wakefield Prison there was a peak in the reformative urge. This owed a good deal to the public school/Oxford tradition, when a super red band called a 'stroke' was set up, who was the head of a 'crew' of prisoners who wore blazers with crossed oars:

> Their job is not to command the crew but to set the pace: each mess of some ten men has its stroke, and in this prison each mess has its own small room where it eats and lives, and the stroke sees to it that the standards of the prison and the mess are maintained – but he has no disciplinary authority and no special privileges or remuneration.[15]

Brendan Behan had early experience of being at the receiving end of power given to prisoners under such systems. He worked in the mail bag shop in Walton prison in Liverpool and two prisoners were in charge of assessing the work the prisoners did. They disliked Behan, and constantly rejected his work, with the collusion of the officer who called him 'a stupid Irish bastard'. One of these prisoners was called James and Behan defined him, in colourful language, as 'a proper white-livered whore's melt'. Behan decided to attack him, and he gave him a severe beating. Behan 'was delighted, thinking of James, and him going round a walking advertisement to the other bastards to leave me alone'.[16]

There was also in the Borstal system a 'leader system'. These were appointed by the staff and had power, limited in theory but considerable in practice. While the existence of 'leaders' in Borstal, for example, could be, and was, of help to staff, a considered view would be that at the source of bullying and other abuses there was the leader system and the protection it gave to the perpetrators. Mark Benney was a 16-year-old who wrote about his experience of Borstal in the 1920s. Of the leader system, he writes:

> The discipline was kept by a body of 'leaders,' under the direction of a 'house-captain,' who were chosen from among the lads for their general capability. These 'leaders' had a little court of their own where they were allowed to try cases of minor defection and impose small punishments. While this gave an opportunity for individual persecutions, on the whole leaders managed their adjudications with a rough-and-ready justice that served its purpose.[17]

But he goes on to describe how leaders could abuse their position. This abuse was of little interest to the staff, as long as control was maintained, and usually there was little the inmate could do to stop it:

> The leader of the landing on which I lived came to me one day and asked if I would like to be his 'orderly'. (Leaders were allowed to have orderlies to clean their room. The job was coveted by new arrivals since, although it involved unpleasantly menial duties, comparable to a 'fag' in a Public School, it carried with it such privileges as surreptitious cigarettes, freedom from more unpleasant duties, and being unlocked when the rest of

the landing was shut up in their rooms.) I assented eagerly, and ascribed the favour to my winning personality.

But one afternoon, while most of the lads were in their rooms and I was seated on the leader's bed cleaning his shoes, he came in with a curiously embarrassed look on his face and sat himself beside me. He sat for a moment without speaking, then placed a tentative hand on my knee. Awkwardly, I moved away. He was a very big-built chap.

'Come on, be a sport,' he said.[18]

Benney resisted, and threatened to tell the Housemaster. In return, the Leader threatened him with a report to the Housemaster. Eventually Benney threw the shoes down and left, with an oath. But he paid a price: 'For the next couple of months I was continually appearing before the Leaders' Court on fictitious charges.'[19]

Yet in spite of the opportunity of abuse the system offered, uniformed staff have always liked it. Even unrelenting critics of the prison system in England, such as the founding General Secretary of the Prison Officers Association, Harley Cronin, approved of the idea. He said, in one of his many absurd statements that: 'The trust reposed in leaders and red bands was very rarely abused.'[20] This is not a view to which prisoners or staff would subscribe, but as may be seen from the tone of his book, Cronin was not likely to believe anything a prisoner said about anything, including any experience of abuse of power.

It is very common for captives in every system to be appointed formally to assist the staff in the administration of the system. In the French penal colony of Guinea the result was mayhem. This did not matter, any more than it did in the Gulag or the Concentration Camp, because there was no policy of care for vulnerable prisoners. But sometimes the victims fought back. In the French colony:

It should be explained that in certain prisons the warders were assisted by 'provosts', i.e. convicts who served the administration and were chosen by them from among those who had turned informer. Though enjoying certain privileges themselves, such men did not hesitate to discipline their fellow prisoners, and this was a terrible day of reckoning. Armed with small knives which they had contrived to hide, the victims of the 'provosts' set about them with the warders looking on helplessly. When night fell, fifteen wounded men were picked up and carried off to hospital.[21]

Kropotkin describes how, in the same way as in the French colony, in the metropolitan French prison of Clairvaux, staff completely handed over authority to the prisoners:

> At nine the light are diminished. During the night each dormitory remains under the supervision of *prévôs* who are nominated from among the prisoners and who have the more red lace on their sleeves, as they are the more assiduous in spying and denouncing their comrades.[22]

The danger of giving authority to captives is universally agreed. A group of the Moncada rebels imprisoned in Cuba, before the 1950s revolution, were removed to a part of the prison set aside for mental patients. This was as a punishment for singing a revolutionary song when President Batista was visiting. In charge of them was a prisoner, the: 'grim figure of *Cebolla* (Onion), a cretin serving a term of over a hundred years for murders committed outside and inside the penitentiary'.[23] This, despite the fact that the Law specified that: 'Prisoners could be chosen for these auxiliary functions "only when their record shows they are not dangerous".'[24] Mencía goes on to say: 'The prisoners thoroughly despised him. He was short, chubby, and big-bellied, completely bald, and had small round eyes that were almost lost in his pudgy face.'[25]

Naturally, such prisoner guards were hated. In Alderson women's prison in West Virginia certain inmates were delegated to carry out semi-staff jobs. These were called 'cops' or 'lieutenants'. They had more authority than, say, the English red band, because they reported other prisoners for breaking rules. This of course made them very unpopular with other prisoners: 'Here is an open-and-shut case of identification with staff values, and the inmate cop's actions deny the solidarity of the inmate body and weaken the bonds of interdependence which bind them together.'[26]

Solzhenitsyn also describes a formal arrangement where prisoners were chosen to be guards: 'Among those who could survive were the Ordners – the internal camp police or Polizei – chosen from among the prisoners.'[27] The result was that: 'Here you are in the hands of *the trusties*'.[28]

In the prisoner of war camps of the Far East, considerable authority was given to the captive military hierarchy. Even here there was resentment and disgust at the behaviour of captives who were given authority over others. At one point in the Changi Camp in July 1944, a Lt. Col. Newey was appointed by the Japanese to command the camp. As part of his determination to enforce discipline on his fellow prisoners, he opened up punishment cells:

> What were described as 'incorrigibles, thieves, and offenders against Camp Orders' were restrained in the gaol area for an indefinite period. Treatment in the correction cells included the Japanese punishment of standing for long periods.[29]

An example of a punishment was that awarded to a Gurkha officer Lt. J.I. Smith. For playing a musical instrument on an unauthorised day he was sentenced to three days solitary confinement. He was to be locked in a cell without any bedding and was to receive one meal a day. When the Japanese commander was removed, Newey was relieved of his command, which led fellow prisoner Major Shean to write: 'The only good thing arising from his (Takahashi's) departure is that arch-bastard Newey has also resigned.'[30]

As prisoners often suspect, fellow captives who are given authority often also perform the role of informers. In America in the past prisoners commonly worked in chain gangs, a system to which I shall return. We shall also see that the practice of working prisoners in chain gangs has been resurrected in recent years. In North Carolina in the early twentieth century:

> There are certain tasks in connection with every gang that must be done either by hired men or by prisoners not under the gun. For the purpose of performing these tasks each camp has a number of prisoners who are given a considerable amount of freedom… Trusties serve quite often as 'stool pigeons'.[31]

Very soon in Ruhleben an informal network of prisoners in authority was set up. These began as interpreters and became formally, and 'mysteriously', 'Captains'. Of course, the German Commandant wanted interpreters, and it was in this way that some were 'either volunteered or were pushed forward by others'. This was the modest beginning of the Captain's Committee, which became in a year the all-powerful government of the camp.[32]

So great was this power that the Germans issued all orders through the Captain of the Camp, and in turn all communication between the prisoners and the Germans went through the Captain's Office. The Captain of the Camp also became the official representative of the prisoners in dealing with the British and American governments. But there were objections: 'None of the captains had been elected to any such function, and the affront to democratic principles caused three years of bitter agitation.'[33]

The Civil War in America, and the consequent imprisonment of soldiers, is a case study of both of the dynamics of the captive society and the effects of handing over control. Gradually, the prisoners were accorded authority in the camp. Warren Lee Goss, one of the prisoners, reports that:

> From the time we arrived in prison we were continually troubled and annoyed by having our scanty clothes, blankets, and cooking utensils stolen from us. There were so many temptations, and so few restrictions thrown in the way of the perpetrators of theft that it became an evil, at last that must be checked.[34]

Apparently this developed into systematic gang theft and on one occasion, one of the thieves was caught. The question then was: What should be done with him? A prisoner called 'Big Peter' appeared and shaved off half his hair and beard: 'The incident narrated was the beginning of a power in camp to punish offenders, which finally provided us with an effective police organisation.'[35] The choice of the enforcer was, from the point of view of the staff, quite perfect:

> Pete was an uneducated Canadian – a man of gigantic stature and great physical strength, of an indomitable will, great good nature, and with innate ideas of justice, in the carrying out of which, he was as inflexible as iron. A blow from his fist was like that from a sledge hammer, and from first to last he maintained so great a supremacy.[36]

At one point it was clear that criminal gangs amongst the prisoners were murdering people, and the 'police' arrested them. They were tried, with all the ceremony of a civilian court, and sentenced to death. They were duly hanged, with the approval of Captain Wirz.[37]

The 'Raiders', who were the camp bullies, were eventually opposed and overcome by the 'Regulators'. McElroy writes of this seminal struggle. At the head of the Regulators was a Sergeant Leroy L. Key, 'one of the bravest men I ever knew'.[38] After a series of violent battles the Regulators held power, with the support of Wirz, who established a 'prison' for those 'arrested'. The most important of the Raiders were tried. Sergeant Key set up a court martial which seemingly was conducted justly, and as a result a number were sentenced to run the gauntlet, a number to wear ball and chains, and six were sentenced to death.[39] Running the gauntlet was a very dangerous matter, and: 'Three of the number were beaten to death. I saw one of these killed.'[40] Wirz summarised the procedure:

> 'I return to you dose men so Boot as I got dem. You haf tried dem yourselves, and found dem guilty – I haf had notting to do wit it. I vash my hands of eferyting connecte wit dem. Do wit

dem as you like, and may Gott haf mercy on you and dem'...
One of them gasped out:

'My God, men, you don't really mean to hang us up there!'
Key answered grimly and laconically:
'That seems to be about the size of it.'[41]

As always the situation deteriorated. Goss goes on to describe how the police were: 'Mostly of the class denominated "roughs", selected for their physical rather than mental qualifications, and in some cases became a greater evil than that which they were instituted to correct.'[42]

In the end the inevitable happened just as Goss expected:

I am sorry to record that in the Florence (S.C.) military prison when S. was acting chief of police, this kind of police force became for a while degraded tools in the hands of the rebels, and whipped men at their command upon the bare back for digging tunnels &c, for which dirty service they were rewarded with extra rations. I have entered thus particularly into details which were needful that the general reader should have, that he may realise in some degree the position of a prisoner at Andersonville, and to show that anything originally devised for our welfare might be perverted to our misery.[43]

Captive society during the Second World War is distinguished everywhere by rivalry between Communist and non-Communist prisoners. The former were always quick to try to get into positions of power. In the detention camps set up by the Allies to hold native-born Germans at the beginning of hostilities in 1939, the detainees were required to manage themselves to a large degree, and here the organising skills of the Communist group were demonstrated. Quite a lot of those fleeing Nazi Germany did so *because* they were Communists, and these formed quite a large proportion of the population of the camps. One prisoner in a camp in Canada, Werner Burmeister, explains what happened:

The detailed control, the allocation of food, and the preparation of meals, were all left to us. Kitchen and food stores therefore represented the commanding heights of economic power in the camp, and these had been quickly occupied by our communists, who had volunteered their services before anyone knew who they were.[44]

Perhaps the pinnacle of delegation to captives, if that word is not construed as associated with merit, was the system in the German Concentration Camps. Concentration Camps served a number of purposes. Some, like Auschwitz, were extermination camps. Others, such as Buchenwald, were sources of slave labour, although of course people were murdered there. In the former, authority was given to criminals, 'because the SS wanted chaos to reign'. In the latter the SS realised that the 'politicals', notably the Communists were more stable, and so were able to 'organise camp life much better than the criminals'.[45]

Primo Levi explains the delegation of authority, and, being Jewish he was naturally interested in the place of Jews in the system. He was depressed by what he saw, since a reasonable expectation might be that Jews, of all people, could expect a feeling of solidarity:

> *'Prominenten'* is the name for the camp officials... We are more particularly interested in the Jewish prominents, because while the others are automatically invested with offices as they enter the camp in virtue of their natural supremacy, the Jews have to plot and struggle hard to gain them.
>
> The Jewish prominents form a sad and notable human phenomenon. In them converge present, past and atavistic sufferings, and the tradition of hostility towards the stranger makes of them monsters of asociality and insensitivity.[46]

We have seen that in the Concentration Camps each category wore a coloured badge. Criminals wore a green triangle, and Levi explains how brutal they were in Auschwitz: 'Our effective masters in practice are the green triangles, who have a free hand over us, as do those of the other two categories who are ready to help them – and they are not few.'[47]

Eugene Heimler writes an interesting account of his change in status at a point when he became privileged. Because he became friendly with another prisoner who had access to Red Cross food, his diet improved and he began to look well. When he was transferred to Berga-Elster Camp, his appearance led to his appointment as *Vorarbeiter* (foreman) in the camp kitchen, 'one of the most coveted posts in the camp'. Thus he changed from being one of the unprivileged to being 'one of the leaders'. The change was traumatic:

> Now that I had managed to break free from such mass existence, I found myself feeling differently, acting differently, and of course eating differently.
>
> The opposite to regression is freedom: freedom of thought, and speech, freedom of action, freedom of movement. In the work camps of Buchenwald and Berga-Elster I regained some of these freedoms, except of course the freedom of movement – though even this was greater than before because I could move freely within the camp.[48]

Heimler then discusses how he exercised these freedoms. He could talk and discuss with a wide variety of people, and he could engage in another freedom: 'forbidden action'. This not only presented an opportunity to help others, but it was also a chance to fight the guards, a chance almost every prisoner has always taken. 'Forbidden action' consisted of the satisfying, if dangerous practice, of smuggling boiled potatoes to American and Russian prisoners of war: 'It was a risky undertaking, but each success was a personal victory over the enemy.'[49]

In Buchenwald the organisation of the camp was entirely in the hands of what Pierre d'Harcourt calls 'the prisoner bosses' – kapos – and much of his account of his time there is dominated by the enormous power they wielded. The relationship between the kapo and the individual prisoner was complicated indeed. When d'Harcourt was sent to Buchenwald, he found that the communists had established themselves as masters, and he quickly learned that he was under suspicion because not only was he not a communist, but he was a Roman Catholic. Two of the kapo's 'lieutenants' sought him out and told him he was lucky because he had been put into a block which had a Roman Catholic kapo. They explained to him that the kapos organised the labour details, including the dreaded draft for some distant labour project. If the kapo approved of someone, he could make sure he was not on the list: if you were on the list, it meant certain death. D'Harcourt's kapo was nervous that the top kapos who were communists might 'put a black mark against my name'.[50] So in turn he did not wish to seem close to d'Harcourt. He advised him to 'keep as quiet and inconspicuous as possible'.[51] Surely a massive understatement, is d'Harcourt's note that 'they left me feeling rather worried'.[52]

Just how identified the inmates who wielded authority in Buchenwald were with the SS is exemplified by d'Harcourt. The SS were very strict about religion, which was officially forbidden. This was another opportunity for the Communists to exert their control. If new Roman Catholic prisoners prayed publicly, experienced prisoners would: 'Warn them that even if the SS did not get to know of these public activities, the communists would, and that serious trouble would result.'[53]

A few days after his arrival, d'Harcourt received orders to report to a kapo in the labour office. This was the man who had total control over the organisation of prisoner labour. He was one of the most powerful prisoners at Buchenwald. D'Harcourt was shown into a living room, where the kapo, 'T', was sitting in an armchair, smoking and reading a newspaper. He was well turned out, in riding breeches, shirt and tie, and looked 'clean, fresh, and well groomed'. The visitor was invited to sit down, and to take a cigarette. 'It was extraordinary, like a dream.'[54]

For some ten days he went to the kapo every day. The interviews were affable, and consisted mainly of questions about his family life, his schooling – and about the underground. Pierre d'Harcourt answered truthfully, he says, because, as he told 'T', by now the information was out of date. At the same time 'T' made clear that the rules of the camp had to be obeyed.

The only variation in the routine was as surreal as the experience itself. Some prisoners had been found malingering and they were brought to 'T'. He appeared in breeches and singlet, and systematically used them 'as a boxer in training uses a punch bag'. Each got a beating and three men were knocked unconscious. 'T' was not angry, nor did he seem to take any pleasure in it. This happened regularly. D'Harcourt writes, almost humorously: 'He seemed to regard it in a matter-of-fact way as a convenient combination of disciplinary action and vigorous exercise.'[55]

What d'Harcourt did not know at the time was that these interviews had a deadly purpose, since, although he was not aware of it, he had been sentenced to death. But he was a member of a distinguished family, and his father, being well connected with Roman Catholic scholars throughout Europe, and well known as a friend of the German people, had approached a French cardinal. When this failed, the Pope and General Franco had been asked to intervene. Then the wife of the Hungarian premier approached Hitler personally, and d'Harcourt was reprieved. The kapo 'T' knew all this, and suspected that this marked the prisoner down as a reactionary. But another powerful prisoner, Eugene Kogon, a Roman Catholic German, was also very influential in the camp. He knew a good deal about the background, and while d'Harcourt was being 'interviewed', persuaded 'T' not to execute him.

Pierre d'Harcourt wrote of 'T' that he was 'one of the most remarkable men I have ever met'. After the war, d'Harcourt wrote to 'T', by then in a government post in East Germany. He replied and his letter: 'Ended with the cryptic sentence: "I hope, Comrade, you will remember the lessons of the camp."'[56] D'Harcourt's experience is a complete summary of the total authority held by prisoner kapos in Buchenwald.

Even after the war, the Communist ideology superseded all other considerations. It was a heartlessness perhaps derived from the very core belief of the Nazis: that some people were possessed of worth and others were worthless. D'Harcourt found that the Communists were convinced of this; not for racial, but for political reasons.

The power given to the kapos is documented in many scholarly accounts of the camps. The Commandant of Auschwitz, Rudolf Höss himself, commented on the 'powerful influence' exerted by the kapos.[57] And as the war went on, and more and more people were sent to the camps, the sheer weight of numbers and the shortage of able-bodied guards meant that in the workplace:

> They soon came to depend completely on the more cunning Capos [*sic*] who were, moreover, usually their intellectual superiors. This state of affairs resulted in a reciprocal covering up of all derelictions and transgressions at the expense of the prisoners in their charge and to the detriment of the camp, the enterprise or the firm.[58]

This despite the curiosity that guards and kapos were constantly told that they should not abuse prisoners.

The rivalry between Communists and non-Communists could be murderous in other places too. In the Korean War of the 1950s: 'In the Koje island camps in Korea, fanatical Communist prisoners murdered non-Communist prisoners in order to establish Communist control of the camps.'[59]

Ravensbrück was a Concentration Camp for women. The prisoner guards at Ravensbrück were as vicious as those in the male Concentration Camps. In Buchenwald the kapo hierarchy was eventually captured and run by Communists, but in Ravensbrück the criminal prisoners – the 'green triangles' – were selected. As is usual where criminals and 'politicals' are mixed, the former terrorise the latter. As well as imposing the strict discipline required by the SS, these women formed a network of spies. It is no wonder that Himmler said of the kapos generally: 'As soon as he doesn't do his job we make him return to his block with fellow prisoners and there they will beat him to death.'[60]

The most difficult decision of the 'blockovas' (those in authority in the women's camp) came when Koegel, the male Commandant of Ravensbrück, paraded them and told them that they had to select all 'The women who were sick or couldn't work, because they were going to be sent to a sanatorium.' 'Almost all of them [the blockovas] were beneficiaries of the political takeover of Kapo jobs earlier in the year.' As to whether they complied, 'it is difficult to know, because of the shame of admitting etc.'[61]

When Auschwitz opened its gates to female prisoners, Himmler ordered that 1000 kapos should be supplied by Ravensbrück, by now very experienced in using captives as staff. In Ravensbrück there was, after the autumn of 1939, a hierarchy of prisoner guards. The blockova was the block chief, the 'stubova' the room chief. Then there was the 'lagerläuferin' or camp runner. 'And a "head prisoner" was appointed. Margot Kaiser was the first to get the job. Her official title was lagerälteste camp senior, although the prisoners called her "*lagerschrek* – camp terror".'[62] At her trial she admitted beating to death at least ten women.

The politicals decided to collude with the authorities in Ravensbrück. It was a decision which was not made easily. After all, it meant working with the Nazis. But it was decided to capture the kapo jobs from the criminals who had earlier cornered them. This was a studied decision based on a realistic appraisal of the situation. It was decided that punishment in the 'bunker' (punishment block), punishment which the 'criminals' could engineer, would surely kill them, and one who had been there barely survived. Beatings and murders led to a meeting of communists, many of whom had long experience of imprisonment, and ways of coping with it. They agreed that there was no point in trying to win against the SS:

> But they could surely defend themselves against the likes of Margot Kaiser, the *Lagerschreck* and her green and black-triangle criminal kapos. Each one of those here had at some point

been sold out to the SS by one of Kaiser's 'bandits'... If the communists could somehow procure these kapo jobs their lives might improve.[63]

The way they did this was to steal cigarettes and alcohol from the stores and plant these on a green triangle block leader. The head guard was taken in, and removed all the leaders from their positions and replaced them with communists. Nobody worried about what might have happened to those who were displaced. The communists had got what they wanted.[64]

Even when Concentration Camp inmates were sent to work in factories, all the politics were transported with them: 'In some of the prison industrial plants, such as the "Gamma" lighter factory, Nazi convicts were allowed to enforce their own racial laws for the sake of efficient teamwork.'[65]

Nor was the power of life and death confined to what may be regarded as this extreme situation. Even in the relatively civilised and monitored British prisoner of war camps, German inmates managed to mete out justice. In a camp in Perthshire a German prisoner was tried and lynched by fellow prisoners because he informed the staff about an escape.[66]

In the Gulag there was a similar situation to that of the Nazi Concentration Camps. Here, the authorities placed the 'thieves-in-law' in authority over the politicals: 'whom the thieves naturally loathed'. This system operated from 'about 1937 until the end of the war', when the authorities decided to crack down on criminal prisoners. Until then, as a prisoner described:

> They did not work but they were allocated a full ration; they levied a money tribute from all the 'peasants', those who did work; they took half of the food parcels and purchases from the camp commissary; and they brazenly cleaned out the new transports... All the ordinary criminal inmates of the camp – and they made up the majority – hated them intensely.[67]

It was to be expected that a figure such as Nelson Mandela in South Africa would exercise informal control over his fellow captives, and so he did. He explains how it happened. Regardless of the nature of the regime, staff and prisoners have to achieve some accommodation. This was well understood by Mandela:

> I always tried to be decent to the warders in my section; hostility was usually self-defeating. There was no point in having a permanent enemy amongst the warders… We had one warder at the quarry who seemed particularly hostile to us. This was troublesome, for at the quarry we would hold discussion among ourselves, and a warder who did not permit us to talk was a great hindrance.[68]

Mandela's solution was to ask a prisoner 'to befriend this fellow'. One day the warder asked the prisoner to let him have his jacket so he could sit on it. 'Even though I knew it went against the comrade's grain I nodded to him to do it.'[69]

And here we have, in a sentence, the most important, and the least known, of the dynamics of life in prison: the authority exercised by prisoners. Mandela furnishes other examples. He tells the story of a 'Coloured' warder, who would slip the prisoners sandwiches and tobacco. Mandela organised the distribution of these, but one heavy smoker was unhappy about his share and his protests jeopardised the supply because the warder became nervous.

The result was that:

> I thought it necessary to punish Tefu. I said, 'Now, look you have jeopardized our supplies. You are not going to have any tobacco or sandwiches tonight. You have almost lost us these privileges. So we are cutting you off until you improve.'[70]

That sanction brought him into line: 'Tefu was always difficult, but from that point he behaved much better.'[71]

It has been explained that the policy of giving prisoners authority is not always driven by exigency, because of the shortage of staff. Nor is the motive invariably one designed to break up any united front which prisoners might develop. In more civilised systems, this is a policy based variously on the idea that the experience of exercising responsibility is a contribution to reform, and is an effective way of communicating what prisoners are feeling: not always seen as giving in, or 'mollycoddling'. The United States, with its huge population and wide variety of ways of locking up people, has produced some pioneering examples of handing over authority to prisoners in the belief that such a policy will lead them to experience the use of power and exercise it wisely. We need to be reminded, however, that it is widely assumed that prisoners have no rights, and in the view of the wider community must suffer whatever comes their way as a by-product of their deviancy. It is not only prisoners who are watched suspiciously by the community for evidence of 'mollycoddling'. Even psychiatric patients must be so regarded:

> It is nevertheless important to emphasise the generally Spartan character of hospital life in order to combat the fear we have referred to as being expressed with remarkable frequency by those associated with a mental hospital – the fear of 'making patients too comfortable'.[72]

A famous Warden who tried a scheme of prisoner democracy was Thomas Mott Osborne.[73] He was a wealthy man, and well known and active in Democratic political life. In 1913 he became Chairman of a new State Commission for Prison Reform in New York State, and to try to understand the nature of prison life he 'served' a prison sentence as 'Tom Brown'. This action not only bewildered the public, but led to the derision which was to greet all his attempts at reform. While Chairman he experimented at Auburn Prison with the idea of self-government for prisoners in the form of a Mutual Welfare League. In 1914, he became Warden of New York State's Sing Sing Prison, in modern times reborn as the Ossining Correctional Facility.

It was here that he set up another Mutual Welfare League, through which he gradually devolved considerable authority to the prisoners. An elected committee of prisoners met, suggested improvements and administered punishments, including for striking, attempts to escape and even assaults on staff: extremely serious offences with which the Warden had previously dealt. There were, too, other less dangerous innovations: an end to the rule of silence, lights were left on longer at night and cinema was moved from Saturday to Sunday, which had been an excruciatingly boring day.

There had been involvement of prisoners in Sing Sing before Osborne's arrival, in the form of something called the Golden Rule Brotherhood. The Brotherhood is a very good example of what can happen if power is delegated to captives without a very secure framework. It was corrupt and mainly a vehicle for spying for the administration and for organising the trafficking of drugs and alcohol. The power behind the Brotherhood was a fraudster, an influential banker and ex-Congressman, who lived a life of luxury in the prison, and who, because Osborne curbed his activity, was to wreak his revenge. Osborne was charged with several offences, including dereliction of duty and sexual malpractices with prisoners. He was acquitted, but the whole squalid business, which was a mixture of disapproval of his methods and a tangle of political intrigue, led him to resign from the Wardenship in 1916, and over the next few years the reformative ideas he had introduced petered out. Osborne though was not finished with prisons. In 1917 he was made Commander of Portsmouth Naval Prison, and he was there for two and a half years. Here too he objected to brutality and unnecessary intrusion into the lives of the inmates. And he introduced a raft of reforms.

Osborne's idea was tried in Stateville Prison, Illinois, in the early 1930s by Warden Hill. It is difficult to believe that experienced Wardens did not know of the potential for disaster in such ventures. But the prisoners knew and were apprehensive. Nathan Leopold was a prisoner at the time, and writes a predictable account of what happened:

In some ways it sounded good. But a good many of us were afraid that it would not work out too successfully. First, there was the matter of electing the 'senators' as we called them. There were still a good many cliques and mobs in the prison; they would, in all likelihood, be able to dominate the election. Then, it would be very hard to get much concerted action on the part of the men selected. Cons are great individualists, and it was questionable whether they would be willing and able to subordinate their private ambitions to the general good...we had guessed right. The committee met with the warden twice or three times. After these few sessions Warden Hill decided that it was a waste of time and disbanded the committee.[74]

Nevertheless, inmates did exercise authority for a time, for example as orderlies, as teachers and as librarians.

A classic example of the risk taken by giving prisoners authority occurred in Singapore in the 1960s. Following a determined effort by the government to tackle the problem of gangsterism in the Chinese Secret Societies, an experiment was tried on Pulau Selang, an island off the coast. To this island were dispatched hundreds of 'detainees', given indeterminate sentences, but with the condition that they could be freed if they showed that they were prepared to be law-abiding. To this end, the island was developed as a constructive environment, with productive work and a good deal of freedom. There was a small staff and the prison relied on freed ex-detainees, called 'settlement attendants', to keep order.

In July 1963, there was a riot on the island, and the Superintendent, Daniel Dutton, was murdered in a most brutal manner, together with three other staff. At the subsequent trial, Major Peter L. James, the Director of Singapore Prisons, said that he doubted if any secret society gangsters could be rehabilitated. But Dutton had been convinced otherwise, and was equally sure that the idea of employing ex-prisoners as guards was sound. James, though, was much more realistic:

He had also opposed the appointment of ex-Pulau Senang detainees as settlement attendants. In his opinion, to employ ex-prisoners in a position of authority in a prison system was wrong. It was quite possible that a detainee could find that he was being supervised by a settlement attendant who was, or had been, a member of a rival secret society.[75]

In the subtitle to his book on the subject, Alex Josey describes the events as: 'The Experiment that Failed'.[76]

There have been many other occasions when the handing over of authority to captives has been a deliberate policy as part of a rehabilitative programme. Writing in 1912, the first Superintendent of the Detroit House of Correction, Z.R. Brockway, explained his idea. He was one of the most enthusiastic believers in the devolution of authority in the history of prison reform:

> The experiment of engaging prisoners in monitorial and mechanical supervision and in educating their fellow prisoners, as it was conducted at the Detroit House of Correction during my Superintendency, was ennobling to the prisoners who were so assigned, and at one stage of the experiment it seemed feasible to establish in such a municipal prison (at least in the details of its administration) a system of almost complete self-government.[77]

Brockway was also the first Superintendent of the famous Elmira Reformatory in New York. Here again he writes with enthusiasm of his methods:

> The reformatory became like a garrison of a thousand prisoner soldiers; more of the prisoners were utilised in the details of management, and prisoners to the number of nearly a hundred were given some military rank. They were assigned to participate in governing by service as monitors, instructors, inspectors, patrolmen, record clerks, etc. The military control was, at one time, so completely by the prisoners that on one occasion at the

evening dress parade of the regiment, with a thousand men in line (no citizen but myself was present to observe it), the whole command from colonel to corporal was composed of prisoners.[78]

Such experiments did not last. The reasons by now are obvious.

In truth, the motives for giving authority to inmates were more traditional than might appear from the resounding theories about 'democracy', or the benefits of teaching prisoners how to exercise responsibility. There was often the central reason, already discussed, of expediency. In the Clinton Farms, later known as the New Jersey Reformatory for Women, a system of prisoner involvement in the administration of the institution was introduced in 1914. It was admitted that the motivation was: 'The insufficient physical accomodations of the institution and the small staff compliment permitted no more than minimum security so that some form of student government honor system was necessitated.'[79]

The system seems to have persisted though, unlike that tried in many other American institutions. A common experience was that of the New Jersey State Reformatory. In 1913 the Superintendent introduced 'a tentative form of inmate self-government'. He reported that:

> There was organised a Council composed of thirty of the inmates elected by the inmates themselves. The duty of this Council is to assist in the discipline of the institution. They give particular attention to the keeping of order on the tiers, and to suppressing conversation with regard to crime and to preventing profanity... The power has been given to the Council not to administer punishment in any way, but to deprive inmates whose influence is harmful from the privileges of the yard and from entertainments.[80]

The Superintendent consulted the inmates after a year 'as to whether or not they desire to have the plan continued another year'.[81] The response was unequivocal and unsurprising:

A feeling had grown that there had been more or less unfairness by 'The Council'. Politics to some extent had entered from time to time in the selection of the councilmen, so that the two plans of being governed by council or officers of the institution were now put squarely before the young men for a decision as to which system of government they preferred. The result of their vote was overwhelmingly in favour of being governed by the officers rather than inmates… [They felt] that it was better for them that the institution should return to the original plan of being governed by the appointed authority of the institution and hence the council disbanded.[82]

This is only one example of the failures in this ideal recorded by J.E. Baker. Osborne's Mutual Welfare League at Auburn, to which reference has been made, established in 1913: 'continued to function…until 1929, but its original purpose and procedures were deflected throughout the years'.[83] In one report it was stated:

that the Mutual Welfare League was deeply involved in the riots of 1929 at the Auburn Prison and ceased operations thereafter. Leadership apparently had fallen into the hands of inmates who should not have been elected to represent others as they had actually strong-armed their way into leadership.[84]

The Warden of Sing Sing in New York State, Lewis E. Lawes, who took over in 1920, was critical of the League he found there. Within a short time he abolished the League's Court since he found that: 'The better element remained aloof from the League, as a consequence of which it became the plaything of the less desirable men. On election day, apprehensively anticipated by the staff, the first-aid clinic was kept busy.'[85]

In the Westchester County Penitentiary the 'Effort League' had disciplinary powers over other inmates. By the early 1930s it died out because: 'It reportedly deteriorated into "kangaroo courts".'[86]

Such then are the variety of ways that some captives accrue power over others. As we have seen, these range from stealing to murder. The total penal experience is that this seemingly inevitable process is malignant, and adds immeasurably to the misery and pain of imprisonment.

Notes

1.   White, Jerry. *Mansions of Misery: A Biography of the Marshalsea Debtors' Prison*. p.196.
2.   *Ibid*. p.199.
3.   *Ibid*. p.147.
4.   *Ibid*. p.233. White draws upon the research work of Angus Easson.
5.   Beer *op. cit*. p.179.
6.   Langer, Felicia. *With My Own Eyes: Israel and the Occupied Territories 1967–1973*. p.132.
7.   Williams *et al. op. cit*. pp.83–84.
8.   Begin *op. cit*. p.187.
9.   Chang *et al. op. cit*. p.49.
10. Barker *op. cit*. p.124.
11. Behan *op. cit*. p.98.
12. *Ibid*.
13. Webb, Sidney and Webb, Beatrice. *English Prisons under Local Government*. pp.103–104.
14. The National Archive, Kew, London, HO45/15189/570791/1984.
15. Fox, Lionel. *The English Prison and Borstal Systems*. p.152.
16. Behan *op. cit*. pp.76ff.
17. Benney, Mark. *Low Company: Describing the Evolution of a Burglar*. p.219.
18. *Ibid*. p.223.
19. *Ibid*. pp.223–224.
20. Cronin, Harley. *The Screw Turns*. pp.51–52.
21. Péan, Charles. *The Conquest of Devil's Island*. p.164.
22. Kropotkin *op. cit*. pp.281–282.
23. Mencía, Mario. *The Fertile Prison: Fidel Castro in Batista's Jails*. p.67.
24. *Ibid*.
25. *Ibid*. pp.67–68.
26. Giallombardo *op. cit*. p.115.
27. Solzhenitsyn *op. cit*. p.218.
28. *Ibid*. p.543. Original emphasis.
29. Havers *op. cit*. p.159.
30. *Ibid*. p.160.
31. Steiner, Jesse F. and Brown, Roy M. *The North Carolina Chain Gang: A Study of County Convict Road Work*. p.52.

32. Ketchum *op. cit.* p.25.
33. *Ibid.* p.100.
34. Goss, Warren Lee. *The Soldier's Story of His Captivity at Andersonville, Belle Isle, and Other Rebel Prisons.* p.1850.
35. *Ibid.* p.1860.
36. *Ibid.*
37. *Ibid.* p.1920.
38. McElroy *op. cit.* p.100.
39. See *ibid.* pp.106ff. for an account.
40. *Ibid.* p.108.
41. *Ibid.*
42. Goss *op. cit.* p.1920.
43. *Ibid.* p.1934.
44. Burmeister *op. cit.* p.95.
45. Heimler *op. cit.* p.17.
46. Levi *op. cit.* pp.96–97.
47. *Ibid.* p.39.
48. Heimler *op. cit.* p.19.
49. *Ibid.* p.20.
50. d'Harcourt *op. cit.* p.117.
51. *Ibid.*
52. *Ibid.*
53. *Ibid.* p.135.
54. *Ibid.* pp.118–119.
55. *Ibid.* p.119.
56. *Ibid.* pp.118–122.
57. Krausnick, Helmut and Broszat, Martin. *Anatomy of the SS State.* p.233.
58. *Ibid.* p.235.
59. Barker *op. cit.* p.124.
60. Helm *op. cit.* p.51.
61. *Ibid.* p.132.
62. *Ibid.* p.51.
63. *Ibid.* p.79.
64. *Ibid.* p.80.
65. Ignotus *op. cit.* p.36.
66. Barker *op. cit.* p.124.
67. Applebaum *op. cit.* p.263.
68. Mandela *op. cit.* p.497.
69. *Ibid.* pp.497–498.
70. *Ibid.* p.411.
71. *Ibid.* p.412.
72. Stanton and Schwarz *op. cit.* p.54.
73. For an account of his work, see Chamberlain, Rudolph. *There is No Truce: A Life of Thomas Osborne* passim.

74. Leopold *op. cit.* p.196.
75. Josey, Alex. *Pulau Senang: The Experiment that Failed.* p.39.
76. *Ibid.*
77. Baker, J.E. *The Right to Participate: Inmate Involvement in Prison Administration.*
     p.34.
78. *Ibid.* p.38.
79. *Ibid.* p.56.
80. *Ibid.* p.48.
81. *Ibid.*
82. *Ibid.* pp.47–48.
83. *Ibid.* p.51.
84. *Ibid.*
85. *Ibid.* p.54.
86. *Ibid.* p.63.

— 6 —

The Wonderful World of Communication

Captives want to know what is happening to each other, what is happening to their families and generally what is going on in the world. In captivity everywhere prisoners develop means of communication. The staff will often wage an endless, but fruitless battle to try to stop this. Included under the term 'communication' is verbal contact between prisoners, and their constant attempt to stay alive to events in the outside world, mostly, but not solely, through letters. For example, Second World War prisoners made radios, and in the twenty-first century, illegally held mobile telephones have provided a new challenge for staff. There is another way of communicating: if captives are very lucky, they may receive visits.

One of the most dreaded features of prison is the ban on free communication between prisoners. This is very common and has been institutionalised historically as the 'silent system' or 'the separate system'. The justification for this policy takes many forms. Sometimes the rationale is that it forces reflection upon one's previous behaviour, and causes what the American 'penitentiary' set out to do: 'bring that calm contemplation which brings repentance'.[1] Sometimes it is explained as a device to prevent 'contamination' of one prisoner by another. It is sometimes starkly punitive, as it was in the Victorian English system. Here a long sentence began with several months of isolation.

The purpose of silence and its companion, separation, is very complicated. In some monastic orders, such as the Trappists, it can be strictly observed to induce contemplation. In that Order, there is the basic ingredient of seclusion. One of the central tenets of the rule of St. Benedict is that they: 'may not leave the cloister without permission...they may not receive letters or gifts from outside except by special permission of the abbot'.[2]

Denys Rutledge, a monk, explaining St. Benedict's Rule, writes that:

> The monastery is to have a gate, be physically cut off from the rest of the world with a 'wise old man' always in attendance...the intermediary between the community and the rest of the world is of considerable importance; first impressions are lasting.[3]

When an English prison officer is appointed to be gatekeeper, he is advised that his is one of the most important positions in the prison. He is the public face of the prison.

In the terrifying Russian fortress of St. Peter and St. Paul, Prince Kropotkin describes how the authorities there tried to stop communication:

> The floor of the cells is covered with a painted felt, and the walls are double, so to say; that is, they are also covered with felt, and, at a distance of five inches from the wall, there is an iron-wire net, covered with rough linen and with yellow painted paper. This arrangement is made to prevent the prisoners from speaking to one another by means of taps on the wall. The silence in these felt-covered cells is that of a grave.[4]

In Dwight Reformatory in Illinois during the 1930s, an ex-inmate recalled: 'We had to walk in silence two-by-two. Take a certain route even if another way was closer.' They were escorted by male guards. She continued: 'The only way we could talk to each other was mumbling. You'd learn to keep your head looking straight and talk out of the side of your mouth.'[5]

This interference with ordinary contact is one that prisoners find insufferable, and which universally they are determined to break. Pierre d'Harcourt writes with feeling about just how intolerable solitude is, but as always, because of his optimistic personality, he finds consolation:

> In its way solitude is an enriching experience, and it was as well that I was able to find it so, for I was to be in solitary confinement for two and a half years. The first effect it is likely to produce on one is an examination of the conscience. Every now and again it is necessary to take stock of oneself, but in normal circumstances few of us give ourselves the time to do so... The solitude of prison is an excellent climate for establishing one's interior balance sheet and for that internal dialogue which is a necessary function of spiritual life.[6]

He goes on to observe how there can even be a physiological consequence of silence, even if a person, as he does, can find some redeeming features in the absence of verbal or visual contact with other people:

> We had to wait in the yard for some time and were able to talk quite freely because the guards were not on the alert. This was a tremendous, almost overpowering experience for me, for I had not talked face to face with anyone for more than two years. The mental excitement soon began to tell on me. My head ached and I felt sick and dizzy, as a child might feel after too many rides on the roundabout at the fair.[7]

Prisoners very soon devote time to developing ways of breaking down the barriers. Some are very simple. In his Afghan prison, Mohamedou Slahi, in the early stages of his detention by the

American government, notes: 'When we spoke, we covered our heads so guards thought we were asleep, and talked until we got tired.'[8]

Constance Lytton, in the English system at the beginning of the twentieth century when a silence rule was still in place, describes how it was possible even to engage in soundless communication:

> Intercourse by means of speech being forbidden, the language of the eyes becomes perfected. Inquiry, interest, fellow-feeling, loyalty, encouragement, sympathy of the best, all these emotions are expressed in prisoners' eyes in a way that outbids the meaning of words and the intonations of the voice.[9]

When Stuart Wood was in prison, talking was forbidden, so he tells us of the universal skill of talking without moving a muscle:

> Old hands have learnt to communicate with each other by talking without moving the lips or head, and the best method is to keep one's eyes fastened on the screw and talk to the man in front or behind out of the side of the mouth, keeping the lips under control much in the same way that a ventriloquist does. I learnt to talk like that, although it is very risky.[10]

Among the many surprises which Peter Wildeblood experienced was the prisoners' skill at talking without appearing to talk. This was one of the few amusing contacts with fellow prisoners which he relates:

> As usual the air was buzzing with ventriloquial conversations. 'How you doing Pete?' asked my neighbour, a dwarfish bald Cockney whom I had not met before. It took me a moment to find out who was speaking, since the words seemed to be issuing from his ears.[11]

Other ways of making contact seem very improbable, but faced with the ban on ordinary means of communication, and given the ingenuity and time prisoners have, even the most bizarre are credible.

One of the classic methods is tapping on walls or pipes. Pierre d'Harcourt describes in detail how he and a neighbour developed a system.[12] Soon they were able to carry on a conversation and exchange information. But even more ingeniously they were able to play chess. In a sad postscript, he adds: 'But my neighbour was taken away one morning… I do not know what became of him, but I should like to tell him he won the last game.'[13]

The use of tapping is universal in those prisons which seek, without success, to demand silence. Because it is common, there will be much discussion of it here. Another captive of the German Gestapo, Dietrich Bonhoeffer, also describes tapping: 'It was past midnight when Canaris returned to his cell after a prolonged absence. Knocking on the wall, he signalled to his neighbour, Colonel Lundig, a Dane, who had survived, that the end was near.'[14]

Wilhelm Canaris was a German admiral who was summarily convicted of treason and who was executed on 9 April 1945, the day after Bonhoeffer was also executed, both at Flossenburg.

Jane Buxton, serving a sentence for anti-nuclear weapon protests, quickly worked out how to contact a fellow protestor:

> When first we moved to D wing, Margaret and I tried to communicate with each other by tapping on the wall, as our cells are next door. Unfortunately we have both forgotten our Morse Code from Girl Guide days. But I thought of dividing the alphabet into four groups of six or seven letters with different numbers of taps, because there are four distinct sounds we can get – a knife, a tin tray, a hairbrush and a shoe.[15]

Constance Lytton, another prisoner of conscience, relates how:

> We passed the time recommending to each other various dodges of how to keep in touch while in prison. Knocks on the cell wall with a brush or boot, and at the hour when the wardresses went to meals it was said to be possible to communicate by speaking on the hot water pipe, which runs through all the cells, at the

point where it touches the wall. We were to maintain the right to talk to each other at associated labour. Mrs. Pankhurst had obtained the right to speak to her daughter when they were in prison together. Otherwise the silent rule, at all other times we were told, was very rigidly enforced.[16]

Using structural defects is common. Mark Benney describes what happened when he first settled in his cell in Chelmsford Prison, where he was serving 18 months hard labour for burglary:

> I was startled by a sibilance coming, apparently, from the corner of the cell. I looked round at the hot-water pipes running along the wall under the window, but could see nothing untoward. The sibilance occurred again, taking the form of a distinctly human 'Hey!' Suddenly I realised: it was the prisoner in the next cell calling through the cracks in the wall made by the passage of the water pipes… 'I'm doing three days bread and water. We're all on it in this wing… This is a nick, this is! It's a proper bloody hell, I can tell you. An' I've got to do three years here.'
>
> A warder passed along the landing, and so we scurried away from the pipes.[17]

Sometimes notes are passed. An Irish Fenian prisoner of the late nineteenth century, Thomas Clarke, wrote how:

> Throughout the whole time we stood loyally by each other and as I have said, were in close and constant communication with each other. Never a week passed but I received a note from John Daly – and some weeks two or three notes – and he received the same from me. This went on for eleven years. As with Daly, so with Egan for the eight years he was with us. Tell that to the prison authorities and they would say it was utterly impossible. But, we too had reduced our business to a scientific system – it was diamond cut diamond. At all events they never had the satisfaction of catching notes with either of us.[18]

Tim Pat Coogan, the historian of the IRA who wrote about this episode, goes on: 'It would have meant thirteen days punishment for the writers had the notes been found. But Clarke for sixteen years never even kept a pencil on his person. The black lead was buried in the floor of his cell.'[19]

On Robben Island, some of the more 'extreme' prisoners were kept in single cells so that they could not communicate with those in communal cells. But as usual prisoners found ways around the enforced restrictions:

> The prisoners soon found ways to overcome the divisions, and there was always communication, although it was often slow and interrupted because of the illicit methods that had to be used. One common method was to wrap messages in plastic and put them in the drums of food which all had to go through to the kitchen serving the entire prison.[20]

In fact, on Robben Island the prisoners went so far as to form a communications committee. They devised various ways in which to pass information. They collected empty matchboxes that the warders threw away. They invented a code and sent messages in a secret compartment hidden in the box. This would then be picked up by the 'general' prisoners. Another method was to hide messages in food drums. In isolation, a prisoner would strap a message to the inside of the toilet bowl: another political prisoner would then deliberately get into isolation and pick up the message.

Books were another way to send information. When he was in prison in Jordan, Mohamedou Slahi, who was to end up in Guantánamo, had access to a library of books 'though some of it is meant as propaganda for the king':

> The best part about the books was that detainees used them to pass messages back and forth, solacing each other by writing good things inside the book. I didn't know any detainees, but the

first thing I always did was to sift through a book looking for messages. I memorized all of them.[21]

Solzhenitsyn describes how their repellent librarian would always check their books when they returned them:

> They were examined in case we had left pinpricks or dots underneath certain letters – for there was such a method of clandestine intramural communication. They might come to us and say that they had discovered pinpricks. They were always right, of course; and, as always no proof was required. And on that basis we could be deprived of books for three months.[22]

Prisoner communication can, however, be disastrous, since false information can be carried as effectively as true. Brian Stratton gives an excellent example. Two prisoners had been sent to the punishment cells. The story quickly circulated that they had been beaten and 187 prisoners arranged a sit-down strike. They refused to move and were forcibly removed, in the process being hurt, often badly. Brian Stratton was sitting in his cell when:

> I heard the guy next door banging on the wall. It was one of the two geezers we had arranged the sit-down over. I went up to the window to hear what he was saying. 'Brian, Brian, are you all right mate?' came his voice. 'I'm not feeling all right' I replied. 'What are you doing up here? You are supposed to be down the chokey in a terrible state along with Johnny Schofield. That's why the trouble started because we heard you both got a kicking'. 'No, mate. They never touched us when we went down. We are both O.K.', he said. The grim irony of the situation hit me then. I started to laugh though it hurt. We had given the screws a chance they had been longing for to kick seven kinds of shit out of us and the two geezers over which it had all started had never had a finger laid on them in the first place.[23]

Even when captives can communicate, there can be some very curious effects. Kropotkin relates a completely unexpected side-effect which, in his experience, somewhat diminishes the joy of human contact. Once again, the method used is tapping:

> If conversation with neighbour prisoners (by means of light knocks on the wall) is possible, it is a relief, the immensity of which can be duly appreciated only by those who have been condemned for one or two years to absolute separation from all humanity. But it is also a new source of suffering, as very often your own moral sufferings are increased by those you experience from witnessing day by day the growing madness of your neighbour, when you perceive in each of his messages the dreadful images that beset and overrun his tormented brain.[24]

There are many accounts of how captives of different sexes managed to communicate against formidable barriers. Although in the Gulag for most of its history there were plenty of outlets for sex, consensual and violent, when the sexes *were* segregated they nevertheless managed to communicate. This was done by sending notes through the agency of prisoners in the camp hospital where the sexes were mixed. They also set up:

> A 'mailbox' in the railway work zone where the women's brigades laboured. Every few days, a woman working on the railroad would pretend to have forgotten a coat, or other object, to go to the mailbox, pick up what letters had been sent, and leave letters in return. One of the men would pick them up later.[25]

Also from the Gulag comes an account by Eugenia Ginzburg after 18 years of confinement. She writes how a prisoner in the next cell was tapping on the wall, but she and her colleague could not understand the code. When they went to the washroom, they noticed that the shelf was covered with powder and had the word 'Greetings' written on it. They then tapped 'Greetings' and they were able to decipher the code: 'In it the alphabet is divided into five rows of five letters each. Each letter is represented by two sets of knocks, one slow, the other quick. The former indicates the row, the latter the position of the letter.'[26] From that point, they were able to communicate extensively, exchanging news and views.

At the turn of the nineteenth century in America, in the main, the female prisoners were separated from the male: 'entirely separate and apart'.[27] But despite physical barriers, women found ways of communicating with men, sometimes with the help of male trusties.

Kate Richards O'Hara, a socialist anti-war activist incarcerated at the women's unit of the Missouri State Penitentiary in 1919, described the severe punishments that female prisoners risked in order to relay messages to their incarcerated husbands and boyfriends. She explains that 'communication between the inmates of the men's and women's departments is more frightfully and fiendishly punished here than any other thing'.[28] Likewise, illicit communication between male and female prisoners was never entirely cut off at Joliet. In 1926, one visitor observed a woman confined to her cell as punishment for: 'Flirting with the men in the hospital "on the other side" despite the fact that 'two stone walls and a thoroughfare intervene.'[29]

In the same prison, one of the incessant battles between staff and prisoners was waged, yet again over communication: 'The prison files are full of confiscated messages ["kites" in prison slang].' Edna Wyeth goes on to admonish a new inmate in 1961:

'Do you know if it wasn't for Phyllis Adams we'd both be on the floor (in segregation) right now? Mrs. W went through the garbage and picked up a piece of my kite to you. Phyl reached out & took it out of her hand, said it was a letter from home she had torn up! Then Phyl went through the trash & picked out all the pieces to me and I flushed them... Do you know these screws and guards go through the garbage regularly?'

What is more, the punishment that Biedermann imposed – sending copies of confiscated notes (including love letters) to the inmates' families – was so deeply humiliating that inmates sought to avoid it at all costs.'[30]

This was of course what the deeply unpopular Mrs Biedermann (the Superintendent) wanted.

In many systems captives are allowed to receive and send letters. The importance of these letters to captives can be imagined. There are two major functions of this: keeping in touch with families and keeping aware of what is going on in the world outside. There is a third, and that is using the mail as a means of illicit communication.

As Cohen and Taylor point out, it is especially difficult for very long-term prisoners to keep in touch with family and friends outside. In English prisons the number of letters is restricted, so too are the people to whom prisoners may write. If an outgoing letter contains any information or opinion to which staff object it can be withheld, as can any incoming letter which is considered not suitable. As well as this set of structural obstacles, there is the likelihood that relationships will cool, a feature of all penal experience:

> Old gang loyalties quickly disappear once the leader or the lieutenant has been inside a few years and there is a growing problem in retaining contact with wives and children. You suddenly realize as Roy said that 'you want *their* letters more than they want *yours*'. There are occasional passages in outsiders' letters which suggest that they have not read the prisoners' letters too carefully, or that events have forced the contents out of their minds. Either way, a sense of the unilateralism of the relationship grows upon the lifer. A concern about how long it will last begins to undermine the reassurances which accompanied the initial separation.[31]

Prisoners of the Japanese were desperate for news from outside, but their guards were erratic and unpredictable in this respect as in others. Nevertheless, contact was made. Prisoners received mail in 1944, even though it was postmarked 'with dates varying from four to twelve months previously'.[32] The Japanese also allowed wireless messages to be sent, and BBC messages were received. There was another way of getting news:

> The POWs were well provided for with accurate and up-to-date news about the world and the war via a number of secret radios. These had been present in the camp since the beginning of captivity and, despite many searches, had never been discovered.[33]

Naturally, a principal concern of prisoners of war is whether their relatives and friends know what has happened to them. In the Japanese camps, in part because of the well-publicised reputation of the captors for unpredictable behaviour, the captives were especially anxious that news should be sent home about their position. Some assurances were given that people at home had received information, but this proved to be of doubtful reliability. Only after ten long months after the surrender of Singapore: 'did the first news from home arrive at Changi'.[34] The situation remained a source of anxiety since: 'Ultimately, the reception of mail at Changi was infrequent, and the Japanese only allowed mail to be sent from Changi on five separate occasions.'[35]

In Germany in the Second World War the prisoners received *The Camp*, which purported to give 'news' to prisoners. The first issue in July 1940 announced that: '*The Camp* will, however, true to its name, serve you with the news, good or bad, in a simple and straightforward manner.'[36] Of course, it did nothing of the sort, but prisoners were able to find out news by listening to the BBC on secreted radios 'to which most camps in Germany had access'.[37] Barker tells of one prisoner's account of how this was possible. In this case, three men would go to the library, taking advantage of the fact that the lighting there was on the same circuit as the German administrative block. They would then listen to the news, make shorthand notes, take them back to the barracks and distribute information around the camp.

In Vietnam, American prisoners were allowed to receive and write letters. But their reception was erratic, and they would sometimes be interfered with by censors:

> Letters and packages from home had been great morale boosters in prison – which was the reason the Vietnamese seldom let us receive them. Most men received little mail until 1969. If we were in punishment at the time they were being distributed, they kept them. They usually rifled the packages so that we averaged getting less than half of what had actually been sent. And for some perverse reason, they refused to let some of the men receive any.[38]

Outgoing mail was censored, and this caused difficulties because the censors' English was poor, and there were especial problems if the letter contained American idioms:

> I wrote among other things, 'Kathleen, you're my candle in the window'…when the letter came back the sentence was deleted and they had me in for a quiz because of it. They were sure it was some code or phrase with a double meaning.[39]

There was a considerable anti-war movement in the United States, since some parts of American society disapproved of the war for a variety of reasons and there were many violent protests. Part of the anti-war movement was the Committee of Liaison with Families of Men Detained in Vietnam: COLIAFAM. This organisation arranged with the Vietnamese government 'to be exclusively authorized to process letters and packages to the POWs'.[40] Because many families refused to deal with an anti-war group, correspondence suffered, and prisoners received fewer letters than if COLIAFAM had not intervened.

When it comes to odd but effective clandestine practice, a prisoner in Batista's Cuba recalled:

that Miret picked up the ball in surprise and, not attaching any importance to it, kept on talking while he nonchalantly took it apart. When the stuffing came out, they saw it consisted of pages of paper covered with tiny handwriting... Curiosity led to surprise: the pages contained a message from Fidel.

This was how the first rudimentary yet effective means of communication was set up between Fidel and the rest of the Moncada prisoners on the Isle of Pines. Paper or rubber balls containing messages were thrown back and forth between the enclosed prison yards. It is said that sometimes an obliging prison guard helped out in this original form of correspondence, returning the balls when they fell short and landed on the roof.[41]

This was not the only way in which the Cuban revolutionaries kept in touch. Indeed, the Batista prisoners were amongst the most determined of captives to defy the ban:

Other means of communication were also found to link those inside the prison walls with each other and with the outside world. On visiting days, messages were slipped in between the layers of the bottoms of matchboxes. Despite the restrictions, freedom could not be muzzled. Messages were inserted in clothes, cigars, and food. Common prisoners cooperated. Guards took messages and even someone in the director's office helped out. Both brief notes and longer messages circulated in these ways.

Even the ordinary mail was used, outwitting the prison censor. Between the lines of ordinary letters to relatives and friends, Fidel wrote with invisible ink-lemon juice, from lemons sent along with other food, not arousing the slightest suspicion. Heat applied to the white paper brought forth the brown tracing of Fidel's instructions to compañeros along with damning denunciations.[42]

In April 1954, Fidel told his sister about the system and hinted at the ultimate purpose of much of this secret communication. It was to revise his speech in his defence at his trial which was to become, in the judgement of pro-Castro historians, a cornerstone of revolutionary theory. It was distributed as *History Will Absolve Me*, only after considerable risk. Whatever its value, it is a remarkable example of how prisoners can communicate: 'The document containing the revolutionary program that would lead a people to freedom was drawn up in a Cuban prison cell.'[43]

Many penal systems allow visits. Of course, they vary in nature from those where communication is by telephone through a glass partition to those where conjugal relations are allowed. But they are all valued by captives. This is the view of 'Jimmy Dunn', a pseudonym of an American captive:

> Visits are important to a lot of guys for a lot of different reasons. I know I dig mine, even if they are only from my old man nowadays. I'd like to get down south where you can really have some good visits; lay out on the lawn, eat that good chicken or whatever else your people bring. And if you can get a broad up there to see you, you can even get a little rubbin's.
>
> Any of the old-time cons in the joint will tell you that visits are the worst thing you can have in the penitentiary, because they say all they do is put you on a bum kick. But I'm suspicious that the only reason they say that is because they aren't getting any visits. Generally, there isn't anybody, left to visit them. But I haven't gotten that far yet, to the point where I think visits are bad. I may someday, but in the meantime, I'll just keep my visits.[44]

John Hoskison, in his English prison, is another prisoner who wonders about visits and whether they may lead to regrets about having them at all. Having been visited by his partner and his father:

> Back in my cell I lay on my bed and considered the age-old question: is it better to experience elation and excitement, that will invariably be followed by depression, or go through life taking no risks? Their visit had been brilliant, but the knowledge that

it would be two weeks before the next was intensely depressing. Some prisoners preferred never to have visits: they were simply too painful. But for me the pleasure far outweighed the pain. If a phone call was the equivalent of being watered and fed, Bronya's and my father's visit amounted to an emotional banquet.[45]

Gustav Herling writes about 'The House of Meeting' in the Gulag. This was the place where captives could receive visitors and *inter alia*, enjoy conjugal relations. These visits could take place: 'Only after the most complicated and trying procedure had been undergone by the prisoner as well as his family.'[46] There are many reasons why prisoners refuse to have visits. In this case, just one hurdle for the political prisoner is:

> The cruel, discouraging paradox of this situation is that during the hearings at the N.K.V.D. the petitioner must do everything to convince the interrogator that he has broken all relations with the prisoner and eradicated all emotional ties with him.[47]

For those who manage to be visited, there is the familiar depression when the visit is over:

> I only know that I often heard sobbing as I passed by the house of meetings, and I believe that this helpless, spasmodic weeping relieves their tension and expresses for the wretched human tatters, now dressed in clean prison clothing, all that they may not say in words.[48]

As soon as they begin to relate to each other, the visit is over, and predictably the pain is considerable: 'That is why prisoners, after their return from the house of meetings, were lost in thought, disillusioned, and even more depressed than before the longed-for visit.'[49]

Some very detailed accounts of the scale and variety of means of communication come from American prisoners in Vietnam:

Fortunately, the Vietnamese – although they went to extraordinary lengths to prevent it – couldn't stop all communication among prisoners. Through flashed hand signals when we were moved about, tap codes on the wall, notes hidden in washroom drains, and holding our enamel drinking cups up to the wall with our shirts wrapped around them and speaking through them, we were able to communicate with each other. The whole prison system became a complex information network, POWs busily trafficking in details about each other's circumstances and news from home that would arrive with every new addition to our ranks.[50]

In early January, we were relocated to another end of the camp, a place called 'The Corn Crib.' We had neighbors in the cells on either side of ours, and for the first time we managed to communicate with fellow POWs. Our methods were crude, yelling to each other whenever the turnkeys were absent, and leaving notes written in cigarette ash in a washroom drain. It would be some time before we devised more sophisticated and secure communication methods.[51]

An unusual communication is reported on one occasion. A prisoner called Jerry Denton agreed to be interviewed by a Japanese reporter in what was to be a propaganda broadcast on behalf of the Vietnamese:

The Japanese reporter lost no time in getting the interview broadcast, and Jerry appeared on U.S. network television in June. In addition to his remarks, he had blinked out in Morse Code with his eyes a message that was picked up by American Intelligence and by many others who had been radio operators during the century's wars. The message: *torture*.[52]

Prisoners very soon devote time to developing ways of breaking down the barriers. Some of these seem very improbable, but faced with the ban on ordinary means of communication, and given the ingenuity and time prisoners had, even the most bizarre are feasible. There seems to be no limit to the imagination of the prisoners:

> One day, after Lockhart had washed his extra pair of pajamas in the bath area, Bob watched him hang them on a line in the courtyard. Later, he washed his own extra pajamas, hung them on the line next to Lockhart's, and slipped a note into a pocket of Lockhart's pajamas.
>
> For four days he watched through the crack in his door, but Lockhart never went near the laundry... Finally Lockhart approached the clothesline. A guard with him reached up to see if the pajamas were dry, felt the pocket, found Shumaker's note.[53]

The guards in Vietnam were especially obsessive about preventing communication between prisoners, and any discovery would lead to very unpleasant punishment, even the threat of death: 'If you talk, you will be shot on the spot. No communication.'[54]

Robinson Risner, an American Lieutenant Colonel who was shot down in September 1965 and imprisoned for seven-and-a-half years, writes about the sort of punishment that could be expected:

> Rod Doremus called to me through his window, and while I was talking to him the guard came in and caught us. He took me back to my cell, opened up the leg stocks and started to put me in them. I really made a big fuss saying, 'Don't put me in those stocks!' He could not understand English but made a sign that I had been talking. I said, 'No! No!' I was singing, and began to sing for him. He stood there perplexed. He was a civilian medic and evidently not too hard-nosed. But I had been talking and he was supposed to do something to make me uncomfortable, so he was going to put me in stocks. Luckily, I argued him out of it.[55]

Later Risner was to learn the high price of communicating with his fellow prisoners. He had tried to send a message on the bottom of his plate so that the prisoner who washed up could know he was surviving. The guard happened to read it. The guard they called Mickey Mouse said:

> 'You have broken the rules by trying to communicate. Now you will be severely punished.'

> He produced a couple of pads about an inch thick and as big as silver dollars. They were made of something like horsehair. The guards put them over my eyes, and by wrapping bandages around my head, forced the pads back into my eye sockets. It seemed as if they were driving my eyeballs right back into my head. I was sure they were ruining me and making me permanently blind. They took my legs out of the stocks. I was barefooted with my wrists bound behind me. They were already tingling from the circulation being cut off… The worse they treated me, the greater my determination not to talk.
>
> I did feel pretty weak, though. Thirty-two days in the stocks without any walking to speak of had made me pretty unsteady. The lack of any food but bread and water, combined with diarrhea, had really sapped my strength.[56]

This was only a beginning. They pushed him outside and he fell into ditches, then they took him back inside and tightened the ropes on his arms and legs and beat him:

> At a certain point, my right shoulder began to slip out of its socket. With a slight pop it felt as if it came out. I saw bright lights and my ears rang. The guards were oblivious to my pain.[57]

This went on until he agreed to cooperate. He did so in the usual way, which was to tell them what they already knew, or to lie. This period of torture was one of many which Risner endured.

 Despite such punishment, the captives did not give up their attempts to communicate. They did this by boring small holes into walls, by learning: 'to talk to each other by putting our heads in the vents and throwing our voices'.[58] They whispered, often using walls as echo chambers. They also wrote notes which they managed to pass in various ways, such as on trays which the prisoners washing up could remove. On one occasion, this led to yet another round of punishment for Risner. A particularly cruel guard they called Big Ugh discovered a note with the inevitable results.[59] The American prisoners devised the most unlikely ways of communicating: 'What they had not learned was that having a handcuff between us was just like a telephone. All either of us had to do was move the handcuff or put pressure on it, and we could communicate.'[60]

The most sophisticated method of communication was a series of 'taps', described in detail by Hubbell. This is the most elaborate set of 'taps' I have found recorded, and those with a special interest in the subject will find his account intriguing.[61]

There were other developments, some of which were very odd. One of these was a series of coughs and spits, which caused no comment since the staff were constantly doing both. In addition, Risner reports that two other prisoners 'retaught me Morse code' and it seems that this was used.[62]

Such risks and the violent punishments which followed discovery of communication systems are commonly reported by prisoners of war. In one Japanese camp, there are many examples of fearlessness, and an utter refusal to obey the rules about communication: 'Finnerty succeeded in maintaining contact with us, getting extra quantities of food smuggled into the solitary cells and transmitting news by signal (he was an expert signaller), at considerable personal risk.'[63]

Perhaps one of the most intricate, determined and successful systems of communication in captivity is that recorded from Palestinian prisoners locked up by the Israeli government. An account of this is written by Esmail Nashif. He begins by reminding the reader why captors do not want to allow communication:

Prison is meant to disconnect its inmates by isolation; at least, this is the aim of its builders and owners. By contrast, the inmates of the prison seek incessantly to communicate and to reconnect themselves to each other and to their society. The channels of communication of the imprisoned are excellent locales for examining the contested sites of the material culture.[64]

The Palestinian 'political' prisoners use a number of familiar ways of communicating. These:

> can be classified into: (1) written materials; (2) verbal communication; (3) signs other than the written and the verbal, such as knocks, hand gestures, facial expressions, and so forth. For example, in one of the central prisons the captives used the water and sewage pipe systems to deliver messages through knocking.[65]

Once again, the presence of the universal 'tapping' system is in evidence. There is an important dimension to the Palestinian system of communication. It was essential that the captives kept in touch with the organisations to which they belonged outside the prison. One prisoner, whose job it was to write letters, explains how:

> I used to hide many letters in my clothes…for example, one of the nice places I used is the upper folded side of my shirt… I used it many times, and the folded parts of the pants, you know…but nothing is like the *cabsulih*, it is the total secrecy… I was old so I couldn't carry it, but I helped to prepare it.[66]

> The *cabsulih* gradually came to be the most important vehicle for the transfer of knowledge in and out of the prisons. It carries letters, books, articles, poems and military orders, among other kinds of information. The processes of its preparation, circulation, and consumption necessitate well-organized and coordinated groups of senders and receivers.[67]

This is such a complicated matter that it is worth repeating what Nashif describes:

The *cabsulih* is made in two stages. First, the message is written, preferably on greasy paper, like that used in wrapping food, as this causes less damage to the ink and the paper itself in its trip round the bodily fluids.

The size of the paper is important: 'it should not be more than half A4 in size'.

Then comes the work of writing the message. The professional *cabsulih* writers use the *msamsam* (the Arabic word for sesame) style of writing. This is very small hand writing that can rarely be read by the naked eye.

A prisoner, Murad:

Used to read *cabsulihs* and rewrite them in regular handwriting as part of his organisational duties… Each organization had specific cadres who were responsible for reading the *cabsulihs* received from the prison. The techniques of decoding, as Murad tells us, were known and institutionalized at the organizational level.

The paper must be folded 'very tightly', and then there is the method of concealing and transferring the message:

The *cabsulih* might be put in the mouth under the tongue, put in the rectum or swallowed. While the latter two are more frequent, the mouth is mainly used in family visits. Under the watchful eyes of the prison guards, the *cabsulih* is delivered from mouth to mouth while kissing across the netting that divides families from inmates.

If a prisoner is transferred or released, there is an opportunity to deliver the message:

Upon arrival at his destination, the political captive extracts the *cabsulih* from his defecated materials and delivers it to his addressee. Sometimes a *cabsulih* might occupy several bodies before it reaches its destination.

One prisoner exemplifies the success of the system:

My wife received around sixty *cabsulihs* from me…it was the whole book that I wrote in the prison…when I was released I unwrapped it and started to copy the book… After two months *Fursan al Intifadah* (*The Knight of the Intifadah*) was published and it reached most of Palestine.[68]

It can be seen from all of these accounts that the determination of captives to communicate will generally overcome the interminable and futile attempts of staff to prevent it. As I have shown, punishments could be, and still are, cruel and the next chapters detail the wide varieties of cruelties found in all penal systems.

Notes

1.   Grünhut, M. *Penal Reform.* p.46.
2.   Rutledge *op. cit.* p.141.
3.   *Ibid.*
4.   Kropotkin *op. cit.* pp.93–94.
5.   Dodge *op. cit.* pp.207–208.
6.   d'Harcourt *op. cit.* pp.56–57.
7.   *Ibid.* p.76.
8.   Slahi *op. cit.* p.23.
9.   Lytton *op. cit.* p.168.
10. Wood *op. cit.* p.56.
11. Wildeblood *op. cit.* p.118.
12. d'Harcourt *op. cit.* p.59.
13. *Ibid.*
14. Bonhoeffer *op. cit.* p.182.
15. Buxton and Turner *op. cit.* p.66.
16. Lytton *op. cit.* p.59.
17. Benney *op. cit.* pp.322–323.
18. Coogan *op. cit.* p.32, quoting from T.J. Clarke *Glimpses of an Irish Felon's Prison Life.*

19. *Ibid.*
20. Deacon *op. cit.* p.100.
21. Slahi *op. cit.* p.176.
22. Solzhenitsyn *op. cit.* p.215.
23. Stratton *op. cit.* pp.19–20.
24. Kropotkin *op. cit.* pp.74–75.
25. Applebaum *op. cit.* pp.291–292.
26. Scheffler *op. cit.* p.141.
27. *Ibid.* p.130.
28. *Ibid.* p.131.
29. *Ibid.* pp.130–131.
30. *Ibid.* pp.223–224.
31. Cohen and Taylor *op. cit.* pp.77–78.
32. Havers *op. cit.* p.149.
33. *Ibid.* p.151.
34. *Ibid.* p.108.
35. *Ibid.* p.49.
36. Barker *op. cit.* p.90.
37. *Ibid.* p.91.
38. Risner *op. cit.* p.253.
39. *Ibid.* p.255.
40. McCain *op. cit.* p.280.
41. Mencía *op. cit.* p.104.
42. *Ibid.* pp.104–105.
43. *Ibid.* p.104.
44. Manocchio, Anthony, and Dunn, Jimmy. *The Time Game: Two Views of a Prison.* p.190.
45. Hoskison *op. cit.* pp.55–56.
46. Herling *op. cit.* p.91.
47. *Ibid.*
48. *Ibid.* p.93.
49. *Ibid.*
50. McCain *op. cit.* p.211.
51. *Ibid.* p.202.
52. Hubbell *op. cit.* p.177.
53. *Ibid.* p.41.
54. Risner *op. cit.* p.126.
55. *Ibid.* p.29.
56. *Ibid.* p.92.
57. *Ibid.* pp.92–93.
58. *Ibid.* p.71.
59. *Ibid.* p.187.
60. *Ibid.* p.126.

61. Hubbell, John G. *P.O.W.: A Definitive History of the American Prisoner-of-War Experience in Vietnam, 1964–1973.* pp.44–45.

62. Risner *op. cit.* p.65.

63. MacKenzie *op. cit.* p.87.

64. Nashif *op. cit.* p.41.

65. *Ibid.* p.54.

66. *Ibid.* p.58.

67. *Ibid.*

68. *Ibid.* pp.59ff.

— 7 —

The Studied Organisation of Cruelty

One persistent feature of accounts of prison life is the relating of stories of cruelty and brutality by staff and prisoners. There are varieties and degrees of abuse and cruelty. They can be divided into those that are legal, however deplorable, and those that are not. These range from the use of pejorative names and other forms of emotional bullying, physical assault which can be minor, if it is possible to describe any physical assault as such, or more sustained attacks leading to serious physical damage or murder. Very common indeed are the imposition of hunger, rape and exposure to extremes of temperature. We have already dealt with some acts of brutality visited by prisoners on each other as a consequence of the delegation of power to prisoners, but there are some which are especially brutal and which are enabled because of the murderous nature, indifference or laxity of staff.

This and the next chapter are about the punishments and cruelties that have been visited on people in captivity. I will deal first with the several organised forms of captivity in the nineteenth and twentieth centuries which were, and in some cases still are, especially monstrous, and in the next chapter with cruelty administered legally to individuals, and cruelty which is illegal, capricious and carried out by individuals.

No one country has a monopoly of the cruel treatment of its captives. England has examples of such treatment, albeit in the centuries before the nineteenth century. Perhaps the inescapable fact is that cruelty is an intrinsic part of penal systems, and that it is only by considerable effort that the pressure to revert to abusive treatment can be resisted. One example, taken from English experience, will illustrate both abuse and how pressure, given the existence of a liberal tradition, can contain it.

In 1729, a Parliamentary Committee, set up to investigate conditions in British gaols, went to the Marshalsea Prison in London, as bad as any in the country. On the 'Common Side', which is where the poorest prisoners were, they found overcrowding, so that:

> Half the prisoners lay in hammocks suspended above those who had to lie on the bare floor. The 'Air is so wasted' that prisoners had been stifled, 'several having in the Heat of Summer perished through want of Air'… In the women's sick ward were seven 'miserable Objects lying on the Floor, perishing with extream Want'. In the men's sick ward they found eleven 'miserable Men', living skeletons as they must have been, in a terrible condition: three or four lay between the legs of trestles on the floor; three or four lay over them on boards resting on the trestles; and over them lay three or four more in hammocks… The committee understood that before this, 'a Day seldom passed without a Death, and upon the advancing of the Spring, not less than Eight or Ten usually died every 24 hours'.[1]

Conditions were somewhat better for those who could pay, on the 'Masters Side', but the total picture which emerged of English prison life was as bad as could be imagined.

Similar conditions can be found in more recent times, and, as we shall see, even in the present day. The case of North Korea is special because of the unredeemed level of brutality which is reliably reported as being endemic there. Even allowing for the hostility felt towards the regime by the West, there can be no doubt, and no surprise, that the treatment of both political and criminal prisoners there is amongst the worst in recorded history. The evidence, not only from ex-prisoners but from organisations such as Amnesty International, is overwhelming. Prisoners are beaten, raped, executed and murdered. Nor is this a matter of history as there is no sign of any change, since there seems little prospect of any alteration in the political situation. It may be assumed that every example of cruelty set out in these chapters can be found there.

We have seen many instances of brutality in several penal systems, but since the brutality was, and is, systemic, I will now look more closely at the organisation of five examples. These are the Chinese penal system, the Russian complex, Nazi Concentration Camps, the Japanese prisoner of war institutions and French Guiana. We have seen that there are examples of kindness and compassion even in these. But they remain in history as loathsome, cruel machines, which stand as examples of human degradation, especially in regard to the behaviour of the guards. The Russian and Chinese examples, it may be noted, are still thriving. The difference between these examples and most of the other prisons I have discussed is that in Russia and China deliberate and extreme cruelty was, and is, visited upon individuals. In the case of the five listed brutality was, and in some cases is, endemic, indiscriminate and murderous.

Associated with all of these in respect of the utter neglect of humane behaviour, is the treatment of captives by the Americans in Guantánamo Bay. Joseph Hickman was a Staff Sergeant in the US Army, and a guard in Guantánamo. He wrote a book about the murder of detainees there:

> As I flew to Gitmo in 2006, I knew because the enemy fought differently than in previous conflicts... Gitmo seemed like a legitimate solution for holding non uniformed enemy combatants in a new kind of war. When I heard people complain about the legality of the place, or the Bush administration's actions, I thought they didn't understand the new, harsh realities facing America. I also believed that while the United States's actions

might not conform to the letter of the Geneva Conventions, they upheld the spirit. I trusted my government and my military to uphold basic American principles of decency.[2]

The ill-treatment of captives in Guantánamo may reasonably be bracketed with the Nazi or Gulag camps because it was, and as far as can be discovered still is, explicitly directed by the government. So there were media reports in 2017 which claimed that prisoners there would no longer be force fed, the argument being that the refusal to eat was a choice they had made and therefore they should not be surprised at the consequences. So, they must die. Unlike the case of North Korea, much of what goes on in Guantánamo is in the public domain, as in this example:

> Under the plan, which was implemented in fits and starts throughout the fall and finally, with the signed authorisation of Defense Secretary Rumbeld, in a harrowing fifty-day barrage starting in November, military interrogators subjected Qahtani (a prisoner) to a round-the-clock regime of extreme sleep deprivation, loud music and white noise, frigid temperatures, stress positions, threats, and a variety of physical and sexual humiliations.[3]

The evidence which follows is drawn principally from the *Guantánamo Diary* of Mohamedou Ould Slahi. His case, and his experience, are typical, and such treatment has been widely and reliably reported. He is a Mauritanian who was living in his own country in September 2001. He was then thirty and he was arrested and questioned, and then released, by Mauritanian police. In November he was questioned again and at the end of the month he was, in the curious word which came into use, 'rendered' to a prison in Amman. 'Rendition' is an American euphemism for illegally moving captives without charge, and without lawful authority, from country to country. Here he was questioned for over seven months. In July 2002 he was again 'rendered', this time to Bagram, an American base in Afghanistan. This is yet another American location which attracted condemnation because of its treatment of captives, some of whom were murdered. In the way in which, as we see throughout this book, authorities are skilled at inventing terms which conceal what is actually going on, this location was described as the Bagram Theater Internment Facility. This begs the question as to what was being 'facilitated'.

In August 2002 Mohamedou Slahi was flown to Guantánamo. In 2015 he was still there – having suffered all the cruelty set out above – and has never been charged, and this, despite a Court ruling that, because of his Habeas Corpus Appeal, he should be released. His continued detention was hailed by the *New York Daily News* in March 2010 under the heading: 'Keep the Cell Door Shut: Appeal a Judge's Outrageous Ruling to Free 9/11 Thug'. The editorial opined that: 'It is shocking and true: a federal judge has ordered the release of Mohamedou Ould Slahi, one of the top recruiters for the 9/11 attacks – a man once deemed the highest-value detainee in Guantánamo.'[4]

Slahi was recommended for release by the Periodic Review Board in July 2016. He was eventually released in October 2016 and returned to Mauritania. The fact that the numbers involved are not vast in no way diminishes the horror or the illegality of their treatment. Nor does the lesser scale reduce the shame brought by such treatment on the Administration of the United States.

The Chinese penal system exemplifies all of the most loathsome features of other systems which have organised brutality. Cruelty came to a peak under Chairman Mao: 'Mao would not merely follow Stalin's lead in building a larger and more economically ambitious prison camp system than the Russian czars, or the Chinese emperors had ever contemplated attempting.'[5]

He declared that he would 'remould' Chinese reactionaries through 'forced labour' and 'propaganda' into 'new men'.[6] This 'remoulding' became a central plank of penal policy. Like in the Russian and German camps, the number of 'political' prisoners was a measure of the scale of the repression.

As in the Russian system, the Chinese wish to make an economic success out of convict labour was a failure. Nor was the idea, found in both systems, that convicts would settle sparsely populated areas realised. This was because the convicts, far from being rehabilitated, were in wretched health, were often personally quite unsuited to pioneering work, and their treatment did not usually cause rejection of their political beliefs but often reinforced them. The basic belief was, of course, flawed. There was nothing to 'remould' since: 'By the 1980s, approximately half of the PRC's [People's Republic of China] camp inmates were openly denying that they had committed any crime, the confession of which had long been viewed as a starting point for successful remoulding.'[7] In the event, with respect to economic targets, this has been a failure: 'A 1990 PRC study conceded that the production output of these prison enterprises in 1988 covered no more than 8% of the costs required to maintain the system.'[8]

In the Chinese prisons and camps were to be found all the unpleasantness which is inevitable in inhumane captivity. Prisoners were always hungry, for example:

> Liu notes that the ordinary prisoners' soup was typically made of partly rotten vegetables that no ordinary customers would buy at the market. It would usually lack edible oil, which is an extremely important but often missing nutritional component in the practically meatless camp diet.[9]

And when we examine such systems one universal horror is the presence of vermin in such vast numbers as to lead not just to considerable discomfort, but a serious danger to health:

> Especially at night, bedbugs would commonly crawl up from cracks in the floor and floorboards and drop onto prisoners from the ceiling. Already weak from malnourishment and hard labour, most inmates have also had their resting hours interrupted by the irritating bites of bedbugs or other blood-sucking vermin...

Zhang does recall seeing hungry inmates pick off lice and munch them down.[10]

As may be expected, torture is a feature of the Chinese regime and in many cultures it continues to be an acceptable way both to punish and to extract information:

> Though technically illegal, the torture of prisoners by PRC guards and cadres has been widely practised during the Deng-Jiang Era, even in 'advanced' and prosperous cities such as Beijing and Shenzhen. Judge Zhang Xin has estimated that 90% of the early 1990s inmates in the Shenzhen Detention Centre were tortured during their interrogations in order to squeeze a confession out of them. (The traditional bamboo or wooden bastinado) has lost much ground to the high-tech electric shock baton or taser since the 1970s.[11]

And there are other instruments of torture, usually reported as commonplace. Despite the efforts of international organisations torture may still be described as usual in many countries.

None of this concerned the authorities in China, since as in Russian and German Nazi camps, staff were trained to believe that the captives were sub-human: 'Metropolitan prison administrators' common failure to supply prisoners with such basics of hygiene as a wash basin and soap fits into a long-standing pattern of neglect directed at the less-than-human "elements" under their custody.'[12]

In China, solitary, the universal use of which I shall discuss at length later, was used frequently and for long periods. Just one example is that of a prisoner who spent two years of his twenty-six 'at the bottom of a dry, and totally dark well'.[13]

Although the term Concentration Camp is normally associated with Nazi Germany, as the British are often reminded, the system was used in the Boer Wars at the end of the nineteenth century by the British, in an attempt to control the Boer guerrillas. The man responsible was a British General, and a national hero, Herbert

Kitchener. As part of an increasingly desperate strategy, he herded women and children into camps, and ordered farms and livestock to be destroyed. Some three thousand miles of barbed wire surrounded the camps. What happened was reported by Emily Hobhouse, a famous campaigner, horrifying some of the British public:

> While the military ran the camps (until November 1901) the death rate was 344 per 1,000, falling to 20 per 1,000 in May 1902. The families were deprived of clothes, bedding, cooking utensils, clean water and adequate medicine. Children often had to lie on the bare earth exposed to unbearable heat. By October 1901, 80,000 Boers were living in these camps – a number which swelled to 117,871 in the eleventh month. 20,177 inmates died, most of them children.
>
> Kitchener appears to have been indifferent to the suffering he caused in South Africa.[14]

Nor were the camps of the Second World War the first use the Germans made of the practice of herding people and killing them. At the beginning of the twentieth century South-West Africa (present day Namibia) was a territory colonised by force, and illegally, by Germany. In 1904 the Herero and Nama peoples revolted because of the brutality of the invaders, and after many died of hunger and starvation, thousands were rounded up and put into Concentration Camps, where many died. The whole episode is generally agreed to be the first genocide of the century.

Very soon after the Nazis came to power in Germany in 1933 they established a network of Concentration Camps. Always supreme in the operation of the camps was Heinrich Himmler, who created the camps: 'As legally independent administrative units outside the penal code and the ordinary processes of the law.'[15] Theodor Eicke, the Commandant of one camp, Dachau, wielded huge influence in the creation of the camps, an influence which finds its parallel in the contribution of individuals to the establishment of the Gulag. Eicke became especially important after his appointment as Inspector of

Concentration Camps in 1934, where: 'his personal influence on the future organisation and "spirit" of the SS guard formations was second only to that of Himmler's'.[16]

Those sent to the camps were initially designated enemies of the state, for example the earliest inmates of Auschwitz were 'political' Poles. By the summer of 1944, it was a centre of extermination. Very quickly, the groups swept up increased in number and variety. From 1935 the pacifist Jehovah's Witnesses were confined, and beginning in 1937 those now held in 'Protective Custody' included 'work-shy elements'. Others defined as anti-social groups were beggars, gypsies (who suffered especially), pimps, habitual criminals and male Jews with criminal records. At the same time, it was decreed that inmates of the camps should be made to work, and eventually factories were built near the camps for this purpose. In 1942, the importance of economic activity was recognised, with the establishment of the SS Economic and Administrative Office. This 'controlled the economic enterprises of the SS and administered the concentration camps'.[17]

The next development was the consequence of German territorial expansion when anti-social elements from, for example, Austria, had to be accommodated. And then there developed the major 'question' of the Jews. An important point in the removal of Jews was what is called *Reichskristallnacht*, the famous pogrom of 9 November 1938. After this, about 35,000 Jews were sent to the camps.[18] Most of them were confined for a short period, being released upon promising to emigrate.

After the outbreak of war in 1939, extremely harsh measures were enacted to be used against those who were a danger to the state, especially members of left-wing parties. And it was the Concentration Camp which was to become the place in which increasing numbers of executions were carried out. The position of the Jews presented a paradox for the Nazis. This was because the 'solution' – the Final Solution – adopted at the notorious Wannsee Conference in Berlin, in 1942, to exterminate the Jews, was in conflict with the need for slave labour.

Before he even arrived at his camp, Buchenwald, Pierre d'Harcourt describes his treatment on the journey to a 'Reprisal' camp, Neue Bremm:

> We had hardly stepped out on to the platform when the SS fell upon us as if they had gone beserk. Yelling like lunatics, kicking and pummelling us, they chained us into couples, and then drove us like cattle into a long line. In the confusion one of the prisoners, an old general fell down. It was obvious that he had injured himself badly; in fact afterwards we discovered that he had broken his arm. The SS stood over him and kicked him until he managed to get to his feet.[19]

Ravensbrück was rather special since, as has been mentioned, it was a Concentration Camp for women. It was some fifty miles north of Berlin and it was full of the familiar bestialities. A survivor told of an especially heartless episode. One of the stubova (room chief) allowed a sick, three-year-old Gypsy girl to sleep because she was ill: 'The girl was discovered by the SS man Johann Kantschuster. "He grabbed the child by the hair, took her to the lake, and drowned her."'[20]

The women were subjected to savage beatings on naked flesh. But this proved to be hard work for those administering it, and prisoners were invited to help. The incentives offered were removal from the punishment block and extra food: 'There was no shortage of volunteers.'[21] It may be noted that in Tsarist prisons there was the same solution to the same problem. In those prisons there was so much flogging that convicts were induced to flog their fellows.[22]

There was a Doctor Sonntag at Ravensbrück. Doctors, perhaps unexpectedly, were the largest single group of professionals who agreed to help in the Nazi programs. His arrival in the camp heralded an even more vicious routine:

> On his first day they all watched as he passed down the line of waiting women, kicking the weakest with his boots, or lashing out with his stick at any cries of pain. He made one woman

undress and kicked her in the stomach. What horrified the women was not only his brutality, it was the smile on his face.[23]

Some idea of the scale of murder in the camps may be gauged from one figure from Ravensbrück. In 1941, of the 6544 captives at one time, 'nearly one third of Ravensbrück women were to be "mercifully killed"'.[24]

Even in the Concentration Camps system, at least at the beginning, there were objections to systematic brutality. In 1934, in the early days of the camps, at Hohnstein Camp, which at the time was run by the SA (Sturm-Abteilungen), charges of torture and other forms of brutality were brought against 23 members of staff, including the Commandant. The *Gauleiter* of Saxony, the Nazi overlord, intervened, recommending that the charges should be dropped as the case would damage the Nazi Party. But the Reich Minister of Justice declined:

> The form of ill-treatment reveals a brutality and cruelty in the perpetrators which are totally alien to German sentiment and feeling. Such cruelty, reminiscent of oriental sadism, cannot be explained or excused by militant bitterness however great.
>
> Light prison sentences were passed on all the defendants, but the Nazi Party both gained its revenge, and learned a lesson. Some of the jury were expelled from the party, Hitler pardoned all the guilty, and there was duly built into the regulations for the camps the severity for which they are notorious.[25]

The end of the Second World War brought the era of the Nazi Concentration Camps to a close, and many of those who had carried out atrocities were tried and punished, a process which is continuing in the twenty-first century.

The behaviour of the guards in Japanese prisoner of war camps in the Second World War became notorious. As well as Japanese, there were Korean and Taiwanese guards, and it is generally agreed amongst ex-prisoners that, although the Japanese were savage in their behaviour, the Koreans were worse. Since the numbers of Japanese guards were greater, it is they who are exposed for their cruelty:

> We were continually disturbed, both by day and by night, by Nip sentries. They would come along the corridors, very often in rubber boots, and would stop outside the gate of a cell. The occupant would then have to bow to the sentry in Japanese fashion. This was a particularly subtle form of torture, for it prevented us from getting any proper sleep. If one did not immediately rise and bow as soon as the Jap appeared, however silently he might have approached, one was beaten up. I remember, on one occasion, two officers in cells not far from mine were caught asleep by a sentry. He roused them, took them out of their cells and ordered them to slap each other until one collapsed. The winner was then knocked about by the sentry until he too collapsed.[26]

The relative mildness of this treatment can be judged by the fact that the narrator, a British officer K.P. MacKenzie, described this as 'subtle'.

The conditions under which the prisoners suffered have passed into legend. The events in this account can only be described as commonplace:

> We were living crowded together in in wretched conditions; we existed in mud and filth throughout the hot and humid monsoon season for six months of the year; we roasted on gravel and cement in the broiling sun; we wore the scantiest of clothing, mainly *fundoshis*; we had no headgear and most of the men, except for a few who had wooden sandals, had to go about bare-footed. We were ill-treated and had no food suitable for Europeans. There was very little water available for washing or cooking and a really cold drink was a luxury we never experienced. There was no electric light, no fans or punkahs. In spite of all this, the B.O.R.s [British Other Ranks] were expected to march on the hot tarmac roads and visit all parts of Rangoon as working parties.

The squalor, stink and misery of such conditions, depressing and humiliating, took a heavy toll and the plight of the sick and suffering cannot adequately be described by any words that are at my command.[27]

Colonel K.P. MacKenzie, the writer of these words, was one of the many thousands who suffered at the hands of the Japanese and he is, not surprisingly, very bitter about it. He has his beliefs about why they behaved so badly. He believes that, although the Japanese proclaim that they are superior to all other races, they cannot convince themselves that they truly are. And so they set out to humiliate others to convince themselves that they are. They also imitated what they saw as the manner and style of Europeans, with pathetic results: 'The average Jap guard in Rangoon regarded himself as a fair imitation of the European. What he succeeded in being was a tenth-rate caricature of a third-rate Continental comedian, giving the impression of an Englishman.'[28]

The most notorious camps were those along what is known as the Burma Railway. This ran from Bangkok to Moulmein, and on it worked some 80,000 mainly British, American, Dutch and Australasian prisoners who had been captured in Malaya and Indonesia. There were similar camps in other parts of the Japanese Empire, and the cruelty there is referred to in other parts of this book.

Russia has a long and shameful history of the indiscriminate way people were captured and the way in which they were brutalised. Even allowing for the fact that for most of its history Russia was a primitive society, the treatment of its delinquents was remarkable, even after the Enlightenment had swept throughout Europe, and even though there were half-hearted attempts to 'reform' the system.

The region which has always symbolised this brutality is Siberia. Since the fifteenth century millions of Russians and inhabitants of the Empire, notably Poles, have been exiled there. Especially during the nineteenth century, the presence of large numbers of turbulent Poles threatened the stability of the penal estate and even of Siberia itself. Other captives included thieves, murderers, religious dissenters, vagabonds and above all political opponents of the state, many rounded up after the frequent insurgencies of the eighteenth and nineteenth centuries. There were also those exiled because they had shown 'themselves to be intemperate', or 'guilty of immoral conduct'[29] or simply 'incapable'.[30] A justification for this wholesale expulsion of people, apart from the overwhelming purpose of punishment, was the idea that the exiles and released prisoners would develop the territory. Concomitant with this noble aim was a conviction that by settling the country: 'They would discover the virtues of self-reliance, abstinence and hard work. In practice, however, the exile system dispatched into the Siberian hinterland an army not of enterprising settlers but of destitute and desperate vagabonds.'[31]

Not only did this theory fail in the most spectacular fashion – the same curious and contradictory dual purpose took root in Imperial China, and with the same consequences – but, in Tsarist Russia, it turned Siberia into a lawless savage land where nobody was safe from the depredations of escaped convicts, and the latter were themselves the victims of summary justice by the peasantry. When their sentences were completed, if they were alive, they could be allowed to 'settle', or with difficulty, obtain permission to return to European Russia.

For many years, the captives had to walk to their prisons and camps. The distances they had to march from European Russia to Siberia were enormous. Daniel Beer writes an account of the march:

> The convicts walked all year round. During the intense heat of the summer, those at the rear of the marching column choked on the great dust clouds raised by hundreds of tramping feet. On the open steppe, the treeless horizon and cloudless skies offered no respite from the burning sun. Dehydration and sunstroke saw many convicts collapse as they marched. The autumn rains brought only temporary respite from the heat before they turned the roads into a churning quagmire through which the convicts squelched knee-deep. Late September would already bring the

first searing winter frosts. At 20C below, the breath froze onto the men's beards, forming chunks of ice; at 30C below, the cold burned the lungs.[32]

Those thought to be dangerous were handcuffed:

And they wore heavy leg fetters connected by a chain that ran through a ring attached to a belt. They were then shackled in pairs to a pole, later replaced by a chain, to prevent escapes. When one collapsed, all had to stop; when one had to defecate, all had to attend.[33]

The scale of their suffering may be gauged from the time the journey took:

The majority of prisoners travelled from distant Russian provinces, and to reach their assigned locations took two years. However, if they had fallen ill and had been hospitalized, it could take as many as three years. There were examples of some convicts taking four or five.[34]

The eminent writer Anton Chekhov visited and inspected camps in the nineteenth century, notably those on Sakhalin Island, and sums up the total experience of extreme captivity after his visit:

We go to another ward. Here again is that horrible misery which can no more be hidden under all these rags than a fly can be hidden under a magnifying glass. It is a beastly existence, it is nihilistic, a negation of proprietary rights, privacy, comfort and restful sleep.[35]

The brutality and inefficiency of the Tsarist prison system, which probably reached its zenith on Sakhalin, is set out by Chekhov, whose report, whilst it was of interest in Russia was probably of little consequence, which is not surprising when the enormity of the penal empire is remembered:

> Even now we find officials who think nothing of beating a convict over the face, even when he belongs to the privileged class, and when a convict has failed to remove his cap quickly enough, he is told 'to go to the guard and tell him to give you thirty lashes'... not every warden knows exactly how many prisoners live in the prison at any particular time, exactly how many are fed from the common kettle, how many have escaped and so on.[36]

Yet, despite the chaos of the convoys the convicts established 'artels', which were convict committees that dealt with the guards, kept discipline and helped with the smooth running of the operation. Their first march was the beginning (and for many the end) of their suffering. When they eventually arrived, there are countless accounts of the conditions under which these millions lived. In the Nerchinsk mines, the most feared in all of Siberia:

> The barracks housing them were, one inspector noted, 'falling down, poorly designed...terribly cramped, badly maintained and filthy'. In some of the mining settlements, between eighty and a hundred and twenty men were crammed into such buildings, measuring nine square metres, in which 'there was neither order nor fresh air. Destitution and squalor reigned everywhere.[37]

Although I deal with the sexual abuse of women later, in the context of the Russian system the matter deserves special mention. The authorities were well aware of the explosive situation where large numbers of men were deprived of the company of women. At various times they tried to compel wives to join their husbands in exile, and there are famous cases where noble women did so voluntarily. The abuse of women (and, for that matter, men) more properly qualifies as brutality both by officials and captives, and so must be mentioned here. Women began to suffer as soon as they joined the marching convoys:

Despite the fact that most female convicts had no history of vice, the assumption of officials was that all female convicts were prostitutes even before they entered the marching convoys. In 1839, one Polish exile, Justynian Ruciński, observed at first hand how every female exile was obliged to take a lover in the marching convoy. The choice of a partner was not her own, though, but that of the highest bidder among her 'suitors'. If a woman rejected the proposed union, she 'was subjected to terrible reprisals'... On several occasions Ruciński 'witnessed horrible rapes in broad daylight'.[38]

The plight of convicts on Sakhalin Island is another penal legend. Sakhalin is in the North Pacific, between Russia and Japan, and has historically been a matter of dispute between the two countries. Life was so wretched on Sakhalin that for most of the settlers, it was no better than that of the convicts. Indeed it was so bad that many returned to the mainland as soon as possible.

In the 1860s the first convicts were sent there. By 1897 the 'total exile population had swelled to 22,000'. The lives of the women, and of the children, on Sakhalin deserve a special place in the annals of the horror of captivity. Of the roughly 4000 women on the island, about two thirds were female convicts and the rest were free-status women (wives who had followed their husbands or were the peasant offspring of exiles).[39] Chekhov calculated that the ratio of men to women was 100:2.[40] As well as convict women there were free women who 'came to remedy their husbands' lives and lost their own'.[41] They were a truly unhappy group, appalled at the climate and the broken promises of a joyful life.

When a party of convict women arrived at the island:

They are accompanied ceremoniously from the pier to the prison. The women, bent under the weight of bundles and knapsacks hanging fore and aft, stagger along the road, pale from seasickness, while mobs of women, men, children and office workers follow behind, like the troops of people who follow comedians at a fair...

peasant settlers follow the crowd with obvious and honourable intentions: they need housewives…the clerks and guards need girls…(the settlers) are permitted to enter the women's barracks and they are left there with the women. The suitors wander around the plank beds, silently and seriously eyeing the women; the latter sit with downcast eyes. Each man makes his choice.[42]

Commonly, women were sent out as prostitutes by the 'cohabitants', but Chekhov regards a paradox in the relationship: 'She changes cohabitants frequently, selecting the one who is richer, or who has vodka, or she changes them out of sheer boredom, for the sake of variety.'[43]

Chekhov wrote a good deal about the misery of women on Sakhalin:

Even innocent women following their husbands were not spared this fate. In a continuing violation of the regulations that stipulated that women should travel separately from the men, they often found themselves locked up overnight together with hardened criminals. Exiles' wives were also sometimes forced into sex by criminals in the marching convoys or passed around by their spouses in exchange for money, vodka or physical protection.[44]

From these barbaric premises and their atmosphere where fifteen- and sixteen-year-old girls are forced to sleep beside convicts, the reader can judge in what disrespect and contempt women and children are held. They voluntarily followed their husbands and fathers into penal servitude, but how cheaply they are valued.[45]

Beer sums up their lamentable fate: 'Sakhalin's women became, in effect, the prisoners of prisoners.'[46]

The whole system was suffused with incompetence, and corruption, remarkable even for Russia at the time. St. Petersburg had little idea what was going on, and when told, the government either refused to believe it or did not know what to do. So from the moment of their march to Siberia the convicts were robbed by officials, identities were exchanged and no proper records were kept as to who was in the column. Sakhalin ceased to be a penal colony on 1 July 1906, not because the government eventually realised that it was both brutal and a failure, but because the Russians suffered a famous and humiliating defeat at the hands of the Japanese in the war of 1904–05.

After the fall of the Tsar in 1917, Siberia continued to remain the destination for millions of Russian prisoners and those of a variety of nationalities. The Gulag, a system of labour camps which dominated Soviet Russia, was the lineal descendant of the Tsarist prison network. The term 'Gulag' is derived from the Russian initials of the organisation which ran it: The Main Camp Administration. In the wake of the Russian Revolution, the Soviet government found it necessary to remove all those elements from society which it perceived as a threat to the New Order. In the beginning, as Anne Applebaum points out, the exact purposes of the camps were unclear. If there was a purpose it was to make the prisoners work, but initially it was not specified what this work was aimed to achieve. Although many were to die and be murdered in them, they were not, as some of the German camps were, camps for the specific purpose of extermination.

Equally vile was the treatment of people in the Soviet Gulag. The examples marshalled by Applebaum are prolific and it is difficult to select just one which illustrates the enormity of the inhumanity of the system. An extract from a report of 1933 is some indication of the horror of the Gulag. This was 'sent for the personal attention of Stalin' on the fate of 6114 peasants, who were transported to exile on an island in the Ob River:

The transport conditions were appalling: the little food that was available was inedible and the deportees were cramped into nearly airtight spaces…the result was a daily mortality rate of

35–40 people. These living conditions, however, proved to be luxurious compared to what awaited the deportees on the island of Nazino… There were no tools, no grain, and no food… The day after the arrival of the first convoy, on May 19, snow began to fall again, and the wind picked up. Starving, emaciated from months of insufficient food, without shelter and without tools… they were trapped. They weren't even able to light fires to ward off the cold. More and more of them began to die… On the first day, 295 people were buried. It was only on the fourth or fifth day after the convoy's arrival that the authorities sent a bit of flour by boat, really no more than a few pounds per person. Once they had received their meagre ration, people ran to the edge of the water and tried to mix some of the flour with water in their hats, their trousers or their jackets. Most of them just tried to eat it straight off, and some even choked to death. These tiny amounts of flour were the only food that the deportees received during the entire period of their stay on the island.

Three months later, 'nearly 4,000 of the original 6,114 "settlers" were dead'. Those who survived did so because they ate each other, and were subsequently charged with cannibalism.[47]

Existence followed the traditional pattern of captive communities; only conditions were much worse than in most other places. Life in the early camps was confused and charged with contradictions. Thus there were summary executions and even mass murder, but at the same time, and as late as 1924, the prisoners were performing plays and operas. A camp which was to become a model, Solovetsky, had a library of 30,000 books.[48]

In the early days, the Tsarist inheritance proved something of a nuisance. There were many reasons for this, but an important one was that in the Tsarist prison political prisoners had considerable privileges. These privileges included not being made to work and being able to correspond with sympathisers outside Russia. When the Soviet government started locking up their opponents, the captors carried on this tradition. The government wanted to stop this but, for a variety of complex reasons, it would prove very difficult.[49]

In 1930, because of the threat of boycotts by Western countries, the term *kontslager* (Concentration Camp) was changed to *ispravitelnotrudovye lagerya* (corrective-labour camps).[50] As in all states, as I mention from time to time, the words respecting the confining of people are carefully chosen, and meanings are manipulated.

Such a division of the captive population into political and criminal proved unworkable for many reasons. These included the natural resentment felt by the criminals, the authorities having to assuage constant complaints, and the fact that the politicals' refusal to work was utterly contrary to the Soviet ethic. So the position had to change:

> By the end of the 1920s the socialist politicals no longer had a unique status. They shared their cells with Bolsheviks, Trotskyites and common criminals. Within the decade politicals – or rather 'counter-revolutionaries' – would be considered not as privileged prisoners but as inferior ones, ranked lower in the camp hierarchy than criminals.[51]

Thereafter the politicals became 'enemies of the people' and after 1937, their wives and children were swept into the same category and were dispatched to the Gulag. As one of them said: 'We didn't have sentences, we were just "wives"' – technically: 'Member of the Family of an Enemy of the Revolution'.[52]

The end of the Second World War saw some changes made in the Gulag. The political prisoners were still around in huge numbers, and now many of these were: 'Red Army soldiers, Polish Home Army officers, Ukrainian and Baltic partisans, German and Japanese prisoners of war'.[53] These were not easily cowed, and those judged to be the most dangerous were sent to new 'special camps'. At the same time, the authorities lost patience with the anarchic behaviour of the 'criminal' prisoners, and the most troublesome of these were sent to new special prisons with strict security and a harsh regime.[54]

As the Soviet Empire expanded after the Second World War, one of the exports to Eastern Europe was the camp system. A curiosity was the establishment of two of these on the sites of former Concentration Camps: Sachenhausen and Buchenwald. To these were consigned people who were judged to be enemies of the new states.[55]

There seemed to be no end to the existence of the Gulag network. But then, in 1953, Stalin died. There was an immediate attempt to seize power by Lavrenty Beria, arguably the most powerful man after Stalin, which ultimately proved unsuccessful. But, in the short period while he tried, he began to reorganise the Gulag. As well as redistributing responsibilities for its administration, he also aborted more than twenty of the Gulag's flagship projects, on the grounds that they 'did not meet the needs of the national economy'. Of much more importance to the prisoners was his request:

> That an amnesty be extended to all prisoners with sentences of five years or less, to all pregnant women, to all women with young children, and to everyone under eighteen – a million people in all. The amnesty was announced on 27 March. Releases began immediately.[56]

A rapidly deteriorating situation in the Gulag, paradoxically, was made worse by this amnesty, since there was much anger on the part of people who did not qualify. So, the next few years saw widespread riots, strikes and takeovers by prisoners, which the authorities found difficult to control. Eventually, the patience of the administration was exhausted and control was regained, with much brutality and loss of life. An example is that of Steplag Special Camp, where in 1954, when the prisoners had taken over and presented a long list of demands: '1700 soldiers, ninety eight dogs, and five T-34 tanks surrounded the camp...the tank drivers had no qualms about running straight over those prisoners who advanced to meet them'.

[57] The rebellion was crushed at the cost of unknown numbers of dead and wounded. Khruschev made a famous speech in 1956, in which he attacked much of the system and after that releases and 'rehabilitation' took off: 'If 7,000-odd people had been rehabilitated in the three years preceding [Khruschev's] secret speech, 617,000 were rehabilitated in the ten months that followed it.'[58]

While the contribution of Gulag captives to the Russian economy was immense, there were many examples of projects devised by Stalin, which were of no use or were aborted after his death. Applebaum lists some of these, including a length of railway track 'constructed at great expense and at the cost of many lives [which] had not been used for three years'.[59]

The point has been made that the justification for these monstrous institutions (at least by the captors) was that they were economically successful. In fact, they were only modestly so and in some cases the suffering was pointless and the outcome of no use whatever.

The Burma Railway is another illustration of the large-scale futility of penal 'projects', and the shame of the human cost:

> Within weeks of the ending of the war the Line began welcoming its own end. It was abandoned by the Thais, it was dismantled by the British, it was pulled up and sold off by tribespeople...the Line welcomed rain and sun. Seeds germinated in mass graves, between skulls and femurs and broken pick handles, tendrils rose up alongside dog spikes and clavicles, thrust around teak sleepers, and tibias, scapulas, vertebrae, fibulas and femurs...of imperial dreams and dead men, all that remained was long grass.[60]

The history of the camps after Khruschev is about considerable agitation by dissidents which led to imprisonment, and when the reasons for this and the conditions under which prisoners were kept became known outside the Soviets, in the 1960s the authorities developed a new tactic. This was to claim that those locked up were mentally ill: 'the era of the *psikhushka* – the special mental hospital – had begun' [61] – another example of penal neology. MVD Order

No.020 of 1960 officially abolished the system but it lingered. In 1986 President Gorbachev granted a pardon to all political prisoners, and this effectively ended the vast network of political imprisonment, although the Perm political camps were not finally closed until February 1992.[62]

The many accounts written by those in the post-Stalinist era of prisoners show clearly that conditions would have been recognisable to prisoners of the Stalinist era.[63] Anne Applebaum visited the central prison in Archangelsk in 1998 and found that:

> The corridors were narrow and dark, with damp, slimy walls. When the warder opened the door to a men's cell, I caught a glimpse of naked bodies stretched out on bunks, covered in tattoos…about twenty men standing in a row, not at all pleased to have been interrupted… We spent more time in the women's cell… Women's underwear hung from a rope strung across the ceiling; the air was thick and close, very hot, and heavy with the smell of perspiration, bad food, damp and human waste. The women, also half-dressed, sat on bunks around the room and showered insults on the warder, shrieking their demands and complaints. It was as though I had walked into the cell that Olga Adamova-Sliozberg had entered in 1938.[64]

Judith Pallot, writing in 2002, underlines the fact that the Russian penal system has retained many of the features of its Soviet antecedents:

> While Russia continues to use the same network of penal institutions as it did during the Soviet period, the economic changes of the past ten years have meant that penal colonies have increasingly found it difficult to cover their costs, which has had a knock-on effect on the standard of provision for their inmates. There is a deficit of medicines, food products and clothes in Russian prisons which is exacerbated by overcrowded conditions, especially for those held in remand prisons. Mortality rates are

28 times and tuberculosis rates 58 times higher among Russia's prisoners than among the general population, and starvation and malnourishment are major problems. The current problems have been exacerbated by the sentencing policies of the Russian courts, which, as in Soviet times, tend to use custodial sentences for relatively minor offences in preference to alternatives such as fines and community service... Meanwhile, the collapse of the former order has been associated with an increase in the level of crime and the identification of new forms of criminality in Russia. All these factors have combined to swell the population of Russia's penal colonies. The peak in the prison population was in the period 1989-95 when Russia had twice as many people imprisoned as at the end of the Soviet period. Russia entered the twenty-first century with over one million people in penal institutions and, with 810 prisoners per 100,000 population the highest rate of incarceration of any country in the world.[65]

One striking parallel between the Nazi Camps and the Gulag is that individuals at the highest level took a detailed interest in their administration. We have seen that Himmler paid close attention to what went on, and so did no less a figure than Stalin. A similar parallel may be seen in the fact that two individuals in particular can be identified as the most important 'architects' of the camps. These were Eicke in Germany, and Naftaly Aronovitch Frenkel, paradoxically a Jew, in Russia. Yet another parallel lies in the fact that, in the same way as the SS in Germany took control of the Concentration Camps, so in the USSR the successive bodies of Secret Police created a private fiefdom. There must have been great monetary profit in these systems.

Several captives compare the Nazi Concentration Camp with the Soviet Gulag. The conclusion seems to be that, apart from those Concentration Camps devoted to extermination, life in the Gulag, as we noted earlier, was worse.

French Guiana (still part of Metropolitan France), in the north of South America, was originally a colony. It is a vast country, about one sixth the size of France, and the climate is atrocious. After the failure of attempts to settle it, combined with France's abolition of slavery in 1848, it was decided that it should be used to receive prisoners sentenced to transportation. This was not France's first use of transportation as a solution to anti-social behaviour, nor was France alone in using the removal of prisoners to distant lands. Britain had a very long record, beginning with the dispatch of people to the West Indies and America, and then, when America became independent, to Australia soon after Cook had 'discovered' the continent. In 1788, the famous 'First Fleet' sailed with 568 men and 191 women on board.[66] Many thousands of prisoners were to be sent from Great Britain. The last convict ship landed its cargo of 279 prisoners in Western Australia in 1868.

The public associates the French penal settlement in South America with Devil's Island, and the latter with the case of Captain Alfred Dreyfus. In fact, Devil's Island is a tiny island off the coast of the main penal colony, the smallest of a group of three. In French, the penal colony is called Bagne de Cayenne. Bagne means prison, and so the colony was regarded as one vast prison.

Alfred Dreyfus, an army officer, in a case which rocked France, was wrongly convicted of treason in 1894. Dreyfus was the only prisoner on Devil's Island, and when he first arrived:

> A stone cabin, four metres square, was built for the condemned man; the windows were barred; the door, also barred, opened into a lobby in which a warder was on duty night and day. Six warders, armed with revolvers, were told off to guard the prisoner, and relieved each other every two hours.[67]

Much worse was to follow. The British press announced that Dreyfus had escaped, and although a denial appeared in the French press, the relevant Minister, goaded on by the virulently anti-Jewish press, decided to act. The captive's freedom was to be further restricted:

He would no longer be permitted to walk in that part of the island which had hitherto been reserved for him, but only in the space immediately surrounding his hut. [He was then told] that he would be put in irons during the night. At the foot of his bed, which consisted of three planks, a bar of iron was riveted. It was shaped like a spit, with a pair of iron manacles in the middle, each fitted with a double lock. These were to encircle the prisoner's ankles.

At daybreak the warders released the prisoner, but when he first got up he could hardly stand. He was forbidden to quit his hut, in which he was now forced to remain day and night...in time his ankles became raw and bleeding and had to be surgically dressed. His warders, moved to compassion, secretly bandaged his feet before putting them in irons.[68]

Dreyfus asked why he was being so cruelly treated. He was told it was 'a precautionary measure'.[69] As presumably was the sloop permanently anchored off the island. This treatment was endured for almost five years before the persistent work, notably of his brother and friends in France, proved that he was not guilty. He was re-instated in the army and continued his career.

The Dreyfus Affair did not especially stir French interest in conditions in their penal colony. The focus of the case was the anti-Semitism which had caused the scandal in the first place, and the aftermath and writing since has focused almost entirely on the fact that a Jew had been so badly wronged. The lives of the other captives seemed to have excited little interest until the Salvation Army began a campaign in the 1920s.

As often happens with penal theory, the stated intention seems sound. Guiana needed settlers, France needed the income, criminals were able-bodied, and the ultimate argument was that this would give otherwise hopeless cases a chance of rehabilitation. As we have noted, the same theory failed in China and Tsarist Russia. On the other hand, something of this had happened in Australia, and the contribution of convicts to the development of Australia was considerable. In recent years, many Australians have come to terms with this odd heritage, and indeed rejoice in it.

To this end, of encouraging settlement in Guiana, one of the legal devices established was *doublage*. This meant that anyone sentenced to fewer than seven years had to stay for a further term, equivalent to the sentence. Anybody sentenced to longer sentences had to stay there for life. Even for those who completed their sentence there was little hope. If a free man wanted to return to France, or for that matter to North Africa since there were prisoners from there too, he had to pay his fare. This of course was usually out of the question. But in South America the circumstances were very different from those in, for example, Australia. There was, first and last, the remarkable climate, with its attendant diseases (including leprosy) and natural hazards of every kind. The effect on the captives was dire, and accounts are full of the misery they suffered.

Such an account was written by a Salvation Army officer who pioneered the work done by the Army in the 1920s. When Charles Péan arrived at St. Laurent-du-Maroni, the capital of the *Bagne* in 1928 he saw, at once, the typical life of the convicts. He was shown the camp depot:

> The huts where the convicts, shut away in groups of forty from six in the evening until six in the morning, lived their tragic communal life. What happened during the hours of darkness was beyond the imagination, but in the morning, when the guards (who were on duty only during the day) came to open the padlocked doors, sometimes a corpse was found, a knife between the shoulders or the stomach ripped open.[70]

Next he saw the punishment cells:

> Where convicts, their feet fast in irons, awaited their transportation to what were ironically known as the *Iles du Salut* (the Isles of Salvation). Several of these men were to be seen stretched out on bare boards in a state of indescribable filth.[71]

Then he witnessed the *doublage* system in practice. Their position was much worse than that of prisoners as the conditions of their 'freedom' were in many ways worse than those of close confinement:

> By far the greater number wandered about without shelter. More than ever before the *Bagne* was their prison. Some of them retained a vestige of civilization, and for clothing wore a pair of linen trousers of uniform cut as they worked unloading cargo in the blazing sun.[72]

There were convicts everywhere, some under guard, others ostensibly free:

> They wandered through the towns, hid themselves in the forest, worked in the gold mines, stole, killed, blasphemed, died. Their prison was as large as a sixth of France. Their gaolers were the impenetrable jungle, the deadly forest, the swamp, the sea, the sharks.[73]

In the town of St. Jean was a 'relegation area', where recalcitrant prisoners were sent:

> Here the seriously ill, the epileptics and the imbeciles lived without hope in a misery that beggars description…if the Penal Settlement was an *oubliette*, this camp was the *oubliette* of the Settlement.[74]

Yet, as is often the case in places of captivity, there are mesmerising contradictions. Péan came across a freed man, a *libéré*, well dressed, carrying a cane and self-confident, who announced that a group of them had founded a club – 'The Club of the expatriate *Libérés*'. The man went on to explain that:

> As you will have noticed, a man can regain his liberty and prove his worth by hard work and good conduct. He can even enjoy his

civic rights once again, but none the less he will continue to be ostracized by the civil population. It is almost unbelievable that we are not allowed to sit down in the cafes, and in the cinema we have to occupy special places. We are called 'Old Whites' or '*Popotes*' and are humiliated in a dozen different ways.[75]

Péan then visited the club house, which he found to be clean, with an array of newspapers and magazines set out, with a list of members and the rules of the club pinned to the wall. He was introduced to the 15 members of the club: 'all in the prime of life and correctly dressed.'[76] Unfortunately, when Péan returned to Guiana after an absence, he met the founder, the man he had met earlier, in desperate straits. He was ruined, diseased and had rejoined the thousands condemned to die.

Nothing changed until the intervention of the Salvation Army. After a report was published in 1924, a government commission was set up to examine what could be done, but this proved to be useless. Eventually, the Salvationists were given permission to work in the colony and there they established plantations and hostels, and at the same time worked on the problem of returning freed prisoners to France, and the total closure of the penal settlement. Predictably, the problems were enormous. There was opposition as well as support in France and in the colony: the settlers deplored the ending of cheap labour. The officers of the Salvation Army had to endure the same conditions as the prisoners. And the work with the convicts was extremely difficult. These were hardened and hopeless men, often violent and addicted to a venomous local rum called *tafia*. This was distilled and sold by the municipality, which made any attempt to restrict it impossible. In fact, Péan rates it as the main problem:

Unquestionably the real enemy of all the *libérés* was the *tafia* at 3.50 francs a litre. Some drank it to drown their misery. Many who were well-behaved became savage and vindictive under the effects of this neat rum. Pay day was crime day. The municipality sold five hundred thousand francs' worth per annum, solely for local consumption.[77]

Eventually, the Salvation Army put in place a system whereby men could earn money to put towards the cost of their repatriation, and in February 1936 the first shipload of men reached France. In September of that year, after considerable public discussion a committee was set up, and after six months a Bill was laid to abolish the penal settlement.[78] But progress was slow and was halted by the Second World War, when the colony, like Metropolitan France, was torn by political divisions and the conditions for the convicts worsened. After the war repatriation was resumed. In late 1952 the Salvation Army Captain was able to report that: 'There are no more libérés to send home from here. The two groups which have left are the last of the men.'[79]

The army continued to help those who were repatriated, since they faced problems which often overwhelmed them. Some, after all, had been in the *Bagne* for decades. The closing of the penal settlement must rate as one of the great humanitarian triumphs of the twentieth century.

The question which must always be asked is how any society could condone what came to be such slaughter in so many different situations, and how was it possible to find enough staff to carry out that slaughter? With regard to the recruitment of staff to carry out the work of destruction, like any system which confines 'undesirables' to prisons, the authorities must first identify personalities who would enjoy such work. We have seen that d'Harcourt, a Concentration Camp inmate, was, in a sense, fascinated by how a man who seemed to be perfectly normal was capable of carrying out such cruelty, much of it spontaneous and all of it pointless, apart, that is, from personal satisfaction. But even such men (and women) have to be assured that the work they are doing is for the public good.

At such persuasion the Nazi state was excellent. An economic crisis is fertile ground for propounding a belief that malign groups are responsible for that crisis. Such a crisis hit Germany after the

First World War, and very quickly the ancient European belief in the pernicious nature of the Jews, inflamed by the racial theories which had taken hold, especially in Germany, led to the inescapable conclusion that removal of the offenders was the only 'solution'. And 'Solution' it became.

To convince the guards to carry out their duties, terms of abuse are invented to persuade them that the victims are not human. In Ravensbrück, they were called 'communist whores', 'Slav vermin', 'Jewish bitches' and the Jehovah's Witnesses became 'religious hags': 'So "filthy" were these "Slavs" that when they first passed the Ravensbrück gates they were brutally scrubbed "clean" before being sent to the *Strafblock* and put on brick-throwing work "until hands were bloody and raw".'[80]

In Soviet prisons, even the terrifying juvenile captives were indoctrinated into abusing the political prisoners:

> When the 'children' came back from their instruction, our ears burned at the obscenities which they mixed freely with the stock phrases of Soviet propaganda. Accusations of 'Trotskyism', 'nationalism,' and 'counter-revolution' were constantly flung at us from their corner, the assurances that 'Comrade Stalin did well to lock you up,' or that 'the power of the Soviets will soon conquer the whole world' – all this repeated again and again with all the cruel, sadistic persistence typical of homeless youth.[81]

After the start of the Second World War, and through the 1950s, not only were the alien politicals such as the Ukrainians called 'collaborators', 'traitors' and 'spies', but they were also subjected to the multi-worded epithets at which the Russians seemed to be expert. These included 'snake-like, slavish dogs of the Nazi hangmen'.[82] Stalin referred to 'enemies of the people' as 'vermin', 'pollution' and 'filth', or sometimes simply as 'weeds' which needed to be 'uprooted'.[83]

Such was the fate of captives who were subjected to authorised, organised state brutality. Now we will examine staff behaviour sometimes allowed by systems, and that brutality which is unofficial.

Notes

1. White *op. cit.* pp.96–97 and passim for details of the Committee's findings and the consequences.
2. Hickman, Joseph. *Murder at Camp Delta: A Staff Sergeant's Pursuit of the Truth about Guantánamo Bay.* p.5.
3. Introduction to Slahi *op. cit.* by Larry Siems p.xxxv.
4. *Ibid.* p.xxx.
5. Williams and Wu *op. cit.* p.7.
6. *Ibid.* pp.7–8.
7. *Ibid.* pp.52–53.
8. *Ibid.* p.19.
9. *Ibid.* p.42.
10. *Ibid.* p.88.
11. *Ibid.* pp.94–95.
12. *Ibid.* pp.128ff.
13. *Ibid.* p.123.
14. Wilson, A.N. *The Victorians.* p.612.
15. See Krausnick and Broszat *op. cit.* passim for the astonishing way in which Himmler accrued power.
16. *Ibid.* p.175.
17. *Ibid.* p.292.
18. *Ibid.* p.202.
19. d'Harcourt *op. cit.* p.78.
20. Helm *op. cit.* p.63.
21. *Ibid.* p.98.
22. Beer *op. cit.* p.278.
23. Helm *op. cit.* p.7.
24. *Ibid.* p.12.
25. Krausnick and Brozsat *op. cit.* pp.166–167.
26. MacKenzie *op. cit.* p.61.
27. *Ibid.* p.88.
28. *Ibid.* p.148.
29. Beer *op. cit.* p.23.
30. *Ibid.* p.24.
31. *Ibid.* p.4.
32. *Ibid.* pp.32–33.
33. *Ibid.* p.736.
34. *Ibid.* p.35.
35. Chekhov *op. cit.* p.39.
36. *Ibid.* p.198.
37. Beer *op. cit.* p.86.
38. *Ibid.* p.42.
39. *Ibid.* p.251.
40. Chekhov *op. cit.* p.152.
41. *Ibid.* p.153.

42. *Ibid.* pp.153–155.
43. *Ibid.* p.158.
44. Quoted Beer *op. cit.* p.253.
45. Chekhov *op. cit.* p.73.
46. Beer *op. cit.* p.257.
47. Applebaum *op. cit.* p.88.
48. *Ibid.* pp.46ff.
49. *Ibid.* p.36ff.
50. *Ibid.* p.75.
51. *Ibid.* p.58.
52. *Ibid.* p.111.
53. *Ibid.* p.418.
54. *Ibid.* p.420ff.
55. *Ibid.* p.410.
56. *Ibid.* p.430.
57. *Ibid.* p.451.
58. *Ibid.* p.456.
59. *Ibid.* p.424.
60. Flanagan, Richard. *The Narrow Road to the Deep North.* pp.226–7.
61. Applebaum *op. cit.* p.487.
62. *Ibid.* p.500.
63. See *ibid.* pp.480ff for details.
64. *Ibid.* pp.511–512.
65. Pallot, Judith. 'Forced Labour for Forestry: The Twentieth-Century History of Colonisation and Settlement in the North of Perm Oblast'. pp.1057–1058.
66. Shaw, A.G.L. *Convicts and the Colonies: A Study of Penal Transportation from Great Britain and Ireland to Australia and Other Parts of the British Empire.* p.363.
67. Charpentier, Armand. *The Dreyfus Case.* pp.65–66.
68. *Ibid.* pp.81–82.
69. *Ibid.* p.82.
70. Péan, Charles. *The Conquest of Devil's Island.* pp.18–19.
71. *Ibid.* p.19.
72. *Ibid.*
73. *Ibid.* p.20.
74. *Ibid.* p.34.
75. *Ibid.* p.47.
76. *Ibid.*
77. *Ibid.* p.101.
78. *Ibid.* p.146.
79. *Ibid.* p.182.
80. Helm *op. cit.* p.49.
81. Herling *op. cit.* p.15.
82. Applebaum *op. cit.* p.256.
83. *Ibid.* p.112.

— *8* —

'Cruel and Unusual Punishment'

Cruelty towards captives has a long recorded history. In 1553, a distinguished man, Edward Underhill, was sent to Newgate Prison in London for writing an anti-Papist ballad. His wife petitioned for his release, but this could not happen until his health improved. Eventually he was released, but being unable to walk he was carried to a litter and taken home very slowly. It had taken just a month of the infamous brutality of Newgate to reduce him to such a state.[1]

Not all such cruelty is so devastating. Some acts are manifestly cruel, such as imposing physical hurt. But there are others which are more subtle, such as bullying which falls short of the infliction of physical pain. Perhaps a possible definition of 'cruelty' and 'brutality' would be any act which if inflicted outside captivity is either illegal or generally regarded as intolerable. Although such acts are regarded as both in prisons, and may strictly be illegal, prisoner experience is that redress is usually impossible. And in any case there may be a tradition and a culture that such behaviour is normal and probably deserved.

The mildest form of what might be called 'active cruelty' is verbal abuse, which is abuse nevertheless, and victims of it have testified how they have suffered from it. An example is drawn not from prison, but from another institution, which manifests many of the same social dynamics: the military. In this case, the verbal bullying borders on the physical. Anyone who has served in a branch of the armed forces will recognise how commonplace is this account by T.E. Lawrence:

> Our treatment is rank cruelty. While my mouth is yet hot with it I want to record that some of those who day by day exercise their authority upon us, do it in the lust of cruelty. There is a glitter in their faces when we sob for breath; and evident through their clothes is that tautening of the muscles (and once the actual rise of sexual excitement) which betrays that we are being hurt not for our own good, but to gratify a passion. I do not know if all see this: our hut is full of innocents, who have not been sharpened by my penalty of witnessing: – who have not laid their wreath of agony to induce: – the orgasm of men's vice.[2]

Lawrence's description of his Commanding Officer, and how the system allowed him to behave as he did, does not compete with some of the examples we will deal with later, but all the essential ingredients are there. What is remarkable is this seemingly immanent hatred lurking in some of those who control people:

> The day he first flew there, the aerodrome was ringed with his men almost on their knees praying he would crash. Such hate of a brave man is as rare as it is hurtful to the service. His character was compounded of the corruptions of courage, endurance, firmness and strength: he had no consideration for anyone not commissioned, no mercy (though all troops abundantly need mercy every day) and no fellowship…his officer friends urged that he was kind to dogs, and had the men's material interests at heart. It was that that hurt us most. We felt that we should be more considered than our food and our clothes. He treated us like stock cattle: so the sight of him became a degradation to us, and the over-hearing his harsh tone an injury. His very neighbourhood grew hateful, and we shunned passing his house.[3]

There is always a defence for such behaviour. In this case, it is defended as a way of teaching people obedience, the absence of which would lead to a complete breakdown in discipline.

There are accounts of humiliation which are even more personal. On Robben Island, there was a daily search called the *tauza*. This involved the prisoner dancing naked and jumping to dislodge any concealed object in his rectum. One prisoner, Dikgang Moseneke, recalls this: 'Few things can be as degrading as that.'[4] However another prisoner hinting at justification 'writes of knives that "suddenly flash-produced perhaps from some disciplined anus".'[5]

There are cruelties which are intrinsic, such as the cold. Predictably, Gulag prisoners were especial sufferers. Menachem Begin is somewhat amused at the reaction of newcomers:

> The sick were taken to the bath-house in their underwear, with nothing but a thin blanket over them. The new-comers wanted to know whether the patients went like that to the bath-house in the winter, too... The reply they received to their questions was the answer to all questions and problems in the correctional labour camp: 'You'll get used to it, and if you don't you'll die.'[6]

It is not only in extremely cold countries that prisoners suffer. Egyptian women in the Barrages Prison with Nawal El Sa'adawi complain that:

> I had started to get spinal pains due to sleeping poorly, the dampness of the ground, and the cold wind which came in at night through the bars with the end of autumn and the onset of winter.
>
> One night, a cellmate began to shiver from the cold. Her complexion grew pale and her limbs trembled uncontrollably. 'They've got to block up the doors and windows,' she said. 'I can't stay in this cell in the wintertime.'
>
> 'I'll die if I have to spend the winter here,' screamed another.[7]

The next common source of suffering is hunger. There are degrees of suffering caused by hunger. Common enough is the experience of Hanns Lilje, arrested by the Gestapo in August 1944:

> The second unpleasant discovery was the power of hunger. I already knew from the Lehrter Strasse that degrading feeling of hunger, as one watched the shadow of the prison wing opposite advance slowly, indescribably slowly, across the hot prison yard to the place, which, like a sun dial, announced the next 'mealtime', and, in between, the heroic and not always victorious struggle with the temptation to eat the next tiny cube of bread before time. But here it was different. Here hunger came with elemental power, like a heavily armed man who throws one to the ground. Until then I did not know what it was like to grow faint with hunger, and to raise oneself from one's miserable bed only with great effort and reeling steps.[8]

Another prisoner of the Gestapo also records her suffering. In Germany in 1944 a well-known writer, Luise Rinser, was arrested and charged with high treason and sent to Traunstein Prison. During the prolonged period of the investigation into the case against her, she suffered the usual indignities and privations, including hunger, which was overwhelming:

> Suddenly, though, a quite unheroic anguish overcomes me, a blind rage against this tyrannical regime, a wild anger at these walls, bars, and oaken doors, these hundreds of chains, bolts, locks, and security measures, this whole merciless system of dehumanization. I am dead tired. I cannot think anymore, nor write, hunger is devouring me.[9]

The effects of losing control over what you can eat is illustrated by the account by Sergeant Roxburgh, a prisoner of the Japanese at Changi, who does not complain about the quantity as much as the monotony of the diet: 'We get rice for breakfast, rice for dinner and more rice for tea and the ration is a full pint mug. There is no salt in it to give it a bit of flavour.'[10]

Such a diet would have been considered a luxury in the Gulag since, as always, we turn here to witness the suffering which attends extreme hunger. Here there was a category of captives nicknamed *dokhodyagi*, 'a term usually translated "goners"'.[11] Herling describes the state as 'someone who is dying by inches'.[12] Hunger makes people lose their dignity in other ways, too. Again, Herling writes that:

> It was the conduct of these hungry people that was most terrible. Although they might seem normal, they were half mad. Hungry men will always defend justice furiously (if they are not too hungry or too exhausted). They argue incessantly and fight desperately. Under normal circumstances only one quarrel in a thousand will end in a fight. Hungry people fight constantly. Quarrels flare up over the most trivial and unexpected matters: 'What are you doing with my pick? Why did you try to take my place?' The taller man attempts to knock his enemy down by using his own weight advantage – and then scratch, beat, bite… All this occurs in a helpless fashion; it is neither painful nor fatal.[13]

Varlam Shalamov's short stories about the Gulag, which are very autobiographical, are dominated by the pain of hunger. When a new group of captives arrive:

> How could they be told that they had never in their lives known true hunger, hunger that lasts for years and breaks the will? How could anyone explain the passionate, all-engulfing desire to prolong eating, the supreme bliss of washing down one's bread ration with a mug of tasteless, but hot melted snow in the barracks?[14]

One of the concomitants of starvation, which has caused untold distress, is disease. In Gustav Herling's experience in the Gulag:

'No attempt was made to cure complete physical exhaustion, various forms of hunger dementia, night-blindness, and advanced vitamin deficiency which resulted in ulceration of the body and loss of hair and teeth.'[15]

In the prisoner of war camps in the Far East, disease soon appeared as the diet became irregular.

The experience of hunger was similar in the prison camps of the Confederacy in the American Civil War. Not only was the food in short supply, but it was also often uneatable. John McElroy, a prisoner himself, writes: 'Scanty as this was, and hungry as all were, every man could not eat it. Their stomachs revolted against the trash.'[16]

Hunger was a constant feature of life for American prisoners in Vietnam. Robinson Risner writes about the time he was a dishwasher, where he had an opportunity to scrounge:

[The guard] watched constantly while I was washing the dishes to make sure I didn't get any extra food. If I caught him not looking, I would eat every scrap available, including that which had been partially eaten. If they caught me, I would have to pour everything out on the floor, which was filthy. It was virtually the habitat of rats. This was the room where for forty years guards had relieved themselves in a pit and where we emptied our waste buckets.

But despite the filth, as soon as the guards turned away or left, I'd pick up the scraps and devour them. There were times when I found banana peels that had turned black. They would be thrown in a corner where I knew the rats had nosed over them. If the guard wasn't looking, I would put them under my shirt, take them back to my room and eat them. I was so starved that anything with any substance or bulk was a blessing.[17]

Another source of distress common in prison systems is described by Edith Bone. She was a Hungarian arrested as a British spy when she returned to Hungary for a visit in 1949 and spent over seven years in solitary confinement:

There were, of course, plenty of unpleasant physical experiences; I was extremely dirty, could not change my clothes or underwear for months, with the result that my body was covered with painful running sores. I treated them with the medicated toilet paper I was given in woefully insufficient quantity.[18]

One result of filth was summed up by Menachem Begin with an especially vile example:

In the labour camp we had forgotten about clean shirts and had grown used to a shirt that swarmed with lice… And if you find lice on your body you will feel revulsion only at the first one, in it you will see the symbol of your downfall. Only the first louse will shake you out of your apathy, and move you to ask fearfully: 'To what have I been brought?'[19]

Another Gulag prisoner 'became obsessed' with lice: 'As a biologist he was interested in how many lice could subsist on a certain space. Counting them on his shirt he found sixty, and an hour later another sixty.'[20] The Gulag chiefs were aware of the dangers of disease coming from lice, and, as Anne Applebaum explains, fought a long and mainly unsuccessful battle to eradicate them.[21]

In Andersonville Prison in the American Civil War, there was a problem with fleas. One prisoner had a disagreement with a guard because he insisted on sleeping outside the tent because of them: 'I told him I would not and called him to witness and, hobbling back into the tent on my toes, I pulled back my sleaves and scooped up a handful off the tent floor.'[22]

It is to be expected that captives will have to share their cells with rats. A prisoner called Tápanes, one of Fidel Castro's compatriots, describes what happened when he decided he could not eat the disgusting food offered to him:

He offered me a tin dish of milk with some lumpy mush and, in a strident voice, said merely, 'Eat.' I told him I wasn't hungry –

in reality, I had completely lost what little appetite I'd had. He replied 'If you haven't eaten this in 15 minutes, I'll make you eat it. I'm *Cebolla*, the [inmate] head of this cellblock, and what I say goes.' With that he went out, slamming the door behind him.

Once again, I was alone with my thoughts – and with that dish of mush that I had absolutely no desire to eat. I thought about the situation and noted that there were several holes in each corner of the cell. I came up with what seemed like a brilliant idea: stuffing the food into the holes – all except the sweet potato which I would eat – so I could return the dish empty to that repulsive character. That night when I finally fell asleep, I was awakened by huge rats climbing all over me. My 'brilliant' idea of filling the holes with food had attracted a pack of them.[23]

American prisoners in Vietnam also write of the vermin with which they were surrounded:

The cell was grossly filthy. It seemed to be a gathering place for all the mosquitoes in the world. And the rats! Some were in the cell or running through it all the time. Others were different – a kind of whitish-gray, with webbed feet, and so big they could not squeeze through the wide gap at the bottom of the cell door. They would stick their heads down into the gap and look up at Larry. They had great white teeth. Sometimes, when they were staring at him, their tails, half as big around as a man's wrist, would curl under the door. When Larry was taken to empty his waste latrine bucket in this area, he would see the gigantic rats loping away from stools as large as those produced by big dogs.

There was an abundance of scorpions, too, large, greenish things that came up out of the toilet area and under the gap of the cell door looking for food. They looked like fiddler crabs, with huge claws swinging on their big tails.

And there were armies of big, fast ants. When Larry's food was brought in, he had to race to get it eaten before the ants overran it.

It was a place of horror.[24]

Another form of punishment, commonly legal in penal establishments, is the imposition of solitary confinement for short, long or indeterminate periods. In the past, solitary had been at the very centre of prison policy. In 1790, in the famous Walnut Street 'Penitentiary' in Philadelphia, prisoners served their time in solitary: 'to induce that calm contemplation which brings repentance'.[25] They never emerged from their cells. In England, this policy was much admired, since it not only caused the prisoner to reflect on his behaviour, but it also avoided the 'contamination' which was seen as one of the principal evils of the unrestrained association of prisoners. An alternative was the 'Silent System'. This is known in the history of penology as the 'Auburnian System' after the New York State prison in which it was the policy. Here, the prisoners worked in association but with a rigidly enforced rule of silence. The penal experience is that the silence rule is virtually unenforceable even with harsh penalties for breaking it, as we have seen in the discussion about communication. There was much finessing in the several regimes, with expert classic manipulation of the meaning of words. Thus the Separate System differed from the Solitary System because, although in the former:

> Each individual prisoner is confined in a cell, which becomes his workshop by day and his bedroom by night, so as to be effectually prevented from holding intercourse with or even being seen sufficiently to be recognized by a fellow prisoner... under solitary confinement...the prisoner is wholly deprived of intercourse with other human beings...[under the separate system] he is only kept rigidly apart from other criminals, but is allowed as much intercourse with instructors and officers as is compatible with judicious economy.[26]

Early attempts to introduce the separate system in Britain led to the criticism which persisted throughout the latter part of the nineteenth century and the beginning of the twentieth: that it was productive of 'a great number of cases of death and of insanity'.[27] Nor was this an isolated criticism. The reduction of the period of separation from 18 months to 9 in England, which became the standard length of separation, did not reduce the concern about the horrific effects of separation on the minds and bodies of captives. Edmund du Cane, the architect of the English Victorian system, confirmed separation for the first 9 months of their sentence as a policy inflicted on all prisoners. By the end of the nineteenth century (and the finish of Du Cane's iron rule), the system was slowly dismantled. The Gladstone Committee, reporting in 1895, was very critical of the English system and recommended *inter alia* that the policies of separation and silence should be ended. The Prison Commissioners opposed such recommendations, but the policy was by now utterly discredited.[28]

There is the usual plethora of slang terms used by prisoners to describe this practice of punishment by isolation: the hole, the block, the shelf, the cooler, Siberia (but not actually in Siberia). Officialdom, too, has a number of euphemistic phrases to describe the practice. America has a history of reaching out for words to improve the image of what is done to captives. Thus, over time, the prison has become a penitentiary, now it is a correctional facility. Nor is America alone in this. The Chinese government dropped the term *laogai* (meaning 'remoulding through labour discipline and production brigades'). In its place there is *jianyu*, which means 'prison'. But a government gazette noted after the announcement of the alteration in 1994 that: 'The function, character, and role of our penal institutions remains unchanged.'[29]

Again in America, solitary confinement is another example of word shift, where solitary is now dignified by the term Adjustment Centre. Here: 'The experiences in the Adjustment Centre are planned for treatment rather than punishment.'[30] One psychiatrist who tried to work in one – Soledad Prison in California – did not last long. The Centre was: 'Filled with the most concentrated human misery to which I have ever been exposed – torturing loneliness and yearning to meet another human being on equal terms, to talk as man to man.'[31]

He might have been describing the conditions experienced in solitary in many other American prisons. Jack Abbott tried to escape when he was about 21. He was caught and:

> The jailers reopened a cell that had not been used in twenty-five years and placed me in it under prison discipline – a starvation diet of a bowl of broth and a hard biscuit once a day. It was a *blackout* cell. I was given a canvas sleeping mat and the door was closed on me. There was an iron sink-and-toilet combined in the corner, and other than that there was nothing except about two inches of dust on the floor.
>
> It was in *total* darkness. Not a crack of light entered that cell *anywhere* – and I searched, in the days that followed, for such a crack along every inch of the floor and the walls. The darkness was so absolute it was like being in ink.[32]

Jack Abbott manages to communicate the very intense and complicated thoughts which absorb the solitary prisoner. He deals with the problem of how the mind can be occupied, since being in solitary is calculated to excite all sorts of fantasies and hallucinations:

> Then the mirages in the wasteland. You are from insanity; you are only living through an experience, an event. The mirages are real reflections of how far you have journeyed into that pure terrain of time. They *are* real. They bring the now out-of-place things back into the desert that was once the felicitous garden of your memory. *There a cherished woman passes into existence and you approach, draw close to her, and you touch her and she caresses you and then she vanishes in a shimmer to reveal the man masturbating that you have become and are caressing so tenderly. A beautiful flower is seen at a small distance and opens its radiant wings in a promise of spring among the dusty weeds. More suddenly than it appeared, it disappears to reveal a dark splotch on the wall in the fetid, musky cell.*

A brook bubbles over the dusty pebbles of the wasteland, promising to quench, to quench – and as you turn, it disappears in a flush of the toilet.[33]

Solitary, often in darkness, was a common experience of American prisoners in Vietnam. John McCain, as a perfectly average person, discusses the experience of being alone:

It's an awful thing, solitary. It crushes your spirit and weakens your resistance more than any other form of mistreatment. Having no one else to rely on, to share confidences with, to seek counsel from, you begin to doubt your judgment and your courage. But eventually you adjust to solitary, as you can to almost any hardship, by devising various methods to keep your mind off your troubles and greedily grasping for any opportunity for human contact.[34]

There is little doubt that solitary confinement causes some mental deterioration in even the most resilient personalities. When in 1970 my period of solitary confinement was finally ended, I was overwhelmed by the compulsion to talk nonstop, face-to-face with my obliging new cellmate. I ran my mouth ceaselessly for four days.[35]

Women were not saved from solitary because of their sex. In Dwight Reformatory for women, Illinois, as late as 1958, a prisoner with experience of prison in four different states wrote of the segregation unit: 'This place needs investigating. Women in punishment laying on the floor in below zero weather. On a naked floor. No food for 10 days. I'm trying so hard to stay out of trouble.'[36] L. Mara Dodge comments that: 'Although Emmerson exaggerated slightly, she was not far from the truth.'[37]

Some American judges have challenged many aspects of prison regimes, including the use of solitary. One ruled, after a hearing about San Quentin in California, that before being confined to solitary, a prisoner should be allowed a proper hearing with witnesses and so on. The response of the prison authorities was again to initiate a new description. The environment which had been called 'punitive segregation' was now 'administrative segregation'.[38] The fact is that solitary may have an administrative function, whatever that means, but it has an inescapably punitive purpose as Jessica Mitford found when she stayed in a Women's Detention Centre in Washington, DC, in the early 1970s to gain experience of being a 'prisoner'. She heard strange noises coming from solitary, here called the 'Adjustment Centre', and asked a member of staff what was happening: "'Oh, that's just Viola, she's in Adjustment for her nerves." "It doesn't seem to be doing her nerves much good." "Her trouble is she's mental, always bothering the other inmates. So we keep her in Adjustment."'[39]

Peter Kropotkin describes the reality of solitary from his 'two years and a half of personal experience' in a Russian prison:

> I do not hesitate to say that, as practiced in Russia, it is one of the cruelest tortures man can suffer. The prisoner's health, however robust, is irreparably ruined... The want of fresh air, the lack of exercise for body and mind, the habit of silence, the absence of those thousand and one impressions, which, when at liberty we daily and hourly receive, the fact that we are open to no impressions that are not imaginative – all these combine to make solitary confinement a sure and cruel form of murder.[40]

There is plenty of evidence of its cruel effects. Prisoners in isolation, even for a short statutory period, as in the English Victorian prison, recount how they began to lose a grip on their sanity. Sometimes 'solitary' can be a sentence in itself, often of very long duration. Anne Applebaum describes how in the 1930s prisoners could be sentenced to years of isolation. Nor is it only in America that euphemisms are marshalled to make solitary seem less cruel. In her description of how the uses of the Gulag were somewhat modified after the death of Stalin, Applebaum illustrates how those who lock people up in Russia engaged in the same deployment of neologisms:

'You are mistaken,' the novelist Yuli Daniel wrote a few years later (after 1960), in a letter to a friend. 'You are mistaken if you thought I was sitting in a prison. I was being "held in an investigative isolator", whence I was not thrown in the cooler, "but was installed in a punishment isolator".'[41]

Applebaum describes how solitary confinement was used after the apparent lessening of the harshness of the regime in the 1950s. Now captives could be sent for minor offences and the rule about a maximum of 15 days could be circumnavigated by removing a prisoner for a short period and then giving him a fresh sentence. A report in 1976 describes the punishment cells of Vladimir Prison, which illustrates that: 'These cells were comparable to anything invented by Stalin's NKVD.'[42]

Menachim Begin describes his experience in that Stalinist era with an account of his time in isolation:

> The seven days and the seven nights went by. The solitary confinement weakened me considerably, but taught me much. I learnt that there is a worse place than the prison cell, just as I learnt later that there is a worse place even than the solitary confinement cell... When I returned, when I went up to my cell, I was the happiest prisoner in the world.[43]

Everywhere the conditions of solitary are grim. The mere fact of solitary does not seem to penal administrators to be sufficient punishment. It has to be enhanced by making the environment intolerable. Warden Clinton Duffy of San Quentin describes the 'dungeons' before he abolished them in 1940:

> The dungeon was a black tunnel about fifty feet long, with seven small cells on each side. The ancient mass of rock and concrete had the musty odour of a tomb; no sunlight had touched its mouldy walls for almost ninety years, and the foul air had nowhere to go, for there were no windows and the cell doors

were hand-forged iron. Each cell was nothing more than a niche cut into the stone, and the walls and floor were bare. There was no light, no bed, no ventilation, no toilet facilities, not even a bench. There were sometimes three or four men in one cell, and there was no place to sit except a triangular block of concrete in one corner. Prisoners slept on the damp floor, with one blanket if they were lucky, and they got bread and water at the whim of the guards. I had to use a flashlight to take my notes, and for weeks afterwards I was haunted by the memory of the shrunken faces I saw in the dim light, the smell of the living dead, the drip-drip of moisture from the vaulted ceiling.[44]

It is common for captives to be treated harshly when in solitary, as this Illinois prisoner who worked in the solitary area relates: 'If an inmate gives the officer any kind of trouble his "pan" (food) will be cut or the officer will just forget to feed him.'[45] Like all accounts of confinement, it is difficult to believe that people could treat each other in such a manner, but the evidence is overwhelming.

The same horror could be found on Robben Island, the South African prison:

[The cell]…was no bigger than the toilet…and (it was) damp, dark, cold. No flush toilet, just a squat hole there for you and a little water. That is all. You get about fifteen minutes to go and have a wash in the morning and that's it. Otherwise you spend almost 24 hours in that cell alone.[46]

The imposition of solitary can affect captives without respect of persons. A former British Chief Constable, the highest rank in the police service, serving a prison sentence, was sent to solitary:

For four nights and three days… I found myself accommodated in an overheated and smelly cell with bare walls, a small, high window, red light in the ceiling and peephole in the door. There was a two inch thick straw mattress on the slightly raised platform, a wooden shelf to eat from and a lump of concrete like a tree stump as a seat. I had bedding but no pillow. I was allowed out of my cell to slop out and taken for exercise…behind the detention block. After a day I was aching all over from the hard mattress.

This man, William McConnachie, was punished 'near the end of his sentence for the offence of absenting himself for a few hours from his outside employment without the governor's permission'.[47]

It is rare indeed for a captive to express a wish for solitude, although they do, and upon reflection this need not be surprising. Nawal El Sa'adawi in her Egyptian prison is one who does:

I had imagined prison to be solitude and total silence, the island on which one lives alone, talking to oneself, rapping at the wall to hear the responding knock of one's neighbor. Here, though I enjoyed neither solitude nor silence, except in the space after midnight and before the dawn call to prayer. I could not pull a door shut between me and the others, even when I was in the toilet… As soon as the *shawisha* had opened the cell door in the morning, I called out to her. 'I want to be transferred to a solitary cell. I don't want to stay in this cell any longer.'

But the prison administration rejected my request. I came to understand that in prison, torture occurs not through solitude and silence but in a far more forceful way through uproar and noise. The solitary cell continued to float before me like a dream unlikely to be realized.[48]

Another who experienced pleasure from being alone was Gustav Herling. On one occasion, he was in the camp hospital, which was:

The only place, in camp and prison alike, where the light was extinguished at night. And it was there, in the darkness, that I realized for the first time in my life that in man's whole life only solitude can bring him absolute inward peace and restore his individuality. Only in all-embracing loneliness, in darkness which conceals the outlines of the external world, is it possible to know that one is oneself, to feel that individuality emerging, until one reaches the stage of doubt when one becomes conscious of one's insignificance in the extent of the universe which grows in one's conception to overwhelming dimensions. If this condition savours of mysticism, if it forces one into the arms of religion, then I certainly discovered religion, and I prayed blasphemously: 'O God, give me solitude, for I hate all men.'[49]

After one of her days in custody the suffragette Constance Lytton longed for solitude: 'I felt considerably exhausted still from the battering about the day before, and I had a craving to be alone. Unlimited hours of "solitary confinement" were the most desirable paradise I could vision to myself.'[50]

In the English system, 'solitary' was often accompanied by 'reduced diet'. There are occasions related by captives where this punishment added to solitary. Wilfred Macartney describes what happens when a prisoner was sentenced to bread and water, as he himself was. Breakfast was eight ounces of bread and a pint of water; mid-morning, another pint of water. At 4.30, another eight ounces of bread and more water is handed out. There is nothing more until the next day. All this time is spent in solitary confinement.[51]

In his Illinois prison, Nathan Leopold was caught with a pair of contraband pigeons. His punishment had an added element. The officer:

told me to step up and extend my wrists through the bars. When I had done so, he snapped the cuffs, one on each wrist, closed and locked the metal storm door, and went away. There I stood manacled to the bars of the door. Eight inches in front of my face was the black inner surface of the storm door. I could shift my leg from one leg to the other; I could push my right arm through the bars as far as the elbow and so turn to my left; I could push my left arm through the bars and turn to the right. That was absolutely all I could do.[52]

Each period of this chaining lasted three hours.

Chaining is a common feature of restraint and punishment. In Tsarist Russia, there was a very bizarre but much hated additional supplement, described by Chekhov:

> In the Voyedsk prison convicts are fettered to wheelbarrows... each is chained with manacles and fetters. From the middle of the manacles there hangs a long chain about three or four arshins long which is attached to the bottom of a small wheel barrow. The chains and the wheelbarrow constrain the prisoner and he moves as little as possible, which undoubtedly affects his musculature. Their hands become so accustomed to this that each slight movement is made with a feeling of heaviness and when the prisoner is finally released from his wheelbarrow his hands retain their clumsiness and he makes excessively strong sharp movements. When he takes a cup, for example, he spills his tea as though he were suffering from St Vitus' dance. At night while sleeping the prisoners keep the wheelbarrow under the plank bed. To facilitate this, the prisoner is usually placed at the end of the bed.[53]

In modern times, under United Nations Rules, widely ignored in many countries, chaining should be used under very limited circumstances and never for punishment. In spite of this, Amnesty International reported many cases of female inmates being chained, even while they were giving birth. Apart from the fact that in such circumstances attempts to escape are unlikely, this practice causes discomfort at best and serious damage at worst. In New York in 1998:

> They took the handcuffs off when the baby was about to be born. After the baby was born, she was shackled in the recovery room. She was shackled while she held the baby. Had to walk with

shackles when she went to the baby. She asked the officer to hold the baby while she went to pick something up. The officer said it was against the rules. She had to manoeuvre with the shackles and the baby to pick up the item. In the room she had a civilian roommate and she had to cover the shackles, she said she felt so ashamed… She said she was traumatized and humiliated by the shackles. She was shackled when she saw her baby in the hospital nursery (a long distance from the room). Passing visitors were staring and making remarks. She was shackled when she took a shower; only one time when she was not.[54]

There are legal punishments which are physically very brutal. In England, there persisted until recently two forms of legal beating. In the historical English system, men could be flogged with a cat-o'-nine-tales or a birch. For a flogging, a prisoner was spread-eagled on a 'triangle', his back bared, with a leather strap to protect his kidneys, and his head pinned so that he could not turn it. Wilfred Macartney tells of a prisoner, Tommy, he knew who was flogged several times:

> While the fearful scars wrought by the cat on his back and beneath his arms can never be eradicated, perhaps the memory of prison life will fade and Tommy, bravest of little men, will pass the rest of his life in freedom. Tommy is entitled to a happy life, and I think that if it comes to him Clayton [the governor] will have done his bit in the saving of one man from a death in gaol.[55]

Red Collar Man describes the procedure for flogging with the cat-o'-nine tails. A prisoner was sentenced to 24 strokes for assaulting an officer:

> [He] was stripped to the waist and mounted on the triangle. One warder strapped his left leg to the bottom cross-bar with a leather strap, while another did the same with his right leg. Meanwhile a third was binding his wrists together with a strap from which a long rope was carried to a pulley at the top of the

frame, thence down to another pulley at the bottom through which it was pulled tight and made fast so that his body was at full stretch. A canvas bag was placed across the top of his shoulders to protect his neck from the flying tails of the Cat.

Everything was now prepared, the flogger took his stand to one side of the triangle and, at a signal from the Governor, he commenced to flog. Between each stroke the Chief called out the number while the doctor watched to see how Pearson was taking it. He made no outcry, but took his punishment without flinching. Had he shown any sign of collapse the MO had power to stop the flogging and forbid any further strokes.[56]

Corporal punishment was gradually reduced in Britain in the early 1960s. In 1961, ten men were sentenced to a flogging, and seven of them received it. The last time prisoners were flogged was in 1962, when three out of those sentenced were flogged. In all these instances the birch was used. The year 1965 saw the last occasion when a prisoner was sentenced to the 'cat', but the sentence was not confirmed by the Secretary of State. Corporal punishment in prison was legally abolished in England under the Criminal Justice Act of 1967.

Some of the most extreme judicial physical punishments recorded by prisoners were administered in the Russian camps. From accounts, in the nineteenth century the amounts recorded are difficult to believe. There were at least two forms: the birch and running through a line of staff wielding wooden rods. Dostoevsky reports, without surprise, the sentencing of prisoners to as many as a thousand strokes, although not to be administered at the same time. When he was in hospital Dostoevsky saw several men brought in after beating:

The aid that was given usually involved the necessary process of frequently changing a sheet or shirt soaked in cold water and applying it to the man's lacerated back, especially if he himself was unable to look after himself. Another form of aid was the deft extraction of wooden splinters from the blisters.[57]

It may be noted that judicial flogging was approved, including, in several countries, the beating of women. All of these described above are legal punishments.

By far the majority of physical attacks on prisoners by staff are those carried out illegally. A very straightforward example is taken from Western Australia. In June 1968 there was a riot in the state's largest prison, Fremantle. As a result there was a Royal Commission, which reported in 1973, to investigate allegations, including charges of brutality by staff. One charge made was that during the riot an escaping prisoner was shot by an officer without reason. The latter claimed that the prisoner had refused to halt when ordered. The prisoner claimed that he had stood still. After studying the details, including the geography of the incident, the Commissioner believed the prisoner's version, and concluded that the officer was lying.[58]

Persisting staff brutality is recorded by Mohammedou Ould Slahi, a Guantánamo victim. He describes how, when he was being moved in the process of 'rendition':

> They stuffed the air between my clothes and me with ice-cubes from my neck to my ankles, and when the ice melted, they put in new, hard ice-cubes. Moreover, every once in a while, one of the guards smashed me, most of the time in the face…there is nothing more terrorizing than making somebody expect a smash every single heartbeat.[59]

Some very bad experiences are recorded by Palestinian women imprisoned in Israel, especially brutal because the victims are women. Such a woman, Wafa Albis, was captured by the Israelis and imprisoned for 'terrorist' offences:

> They interrogated me. Three female jailers struck me on the injured parts of my body with their iron sticks. This lasted for almost fifteen minutes and caused unbearable bleeding and

pain[60]...while I was interrogated for three months, I saw nobody but the criminal jailers who threatened to rape me. That was my worst nightmare. After that, the physical torture ended. They removed me to the next stage: psychological and medical treatment.[61]

There are plentiful examples of physical, unlawful cruelty in the chain gangs of the southern United States. These became a familiar and ultimately dominant feature of the penal system. They were useful in supplying very cheap labour for public works, especially roads and: 'There is evidence in some instances that the mill of criminal justice grinds more industriously when the convict road force needs new recruits.'[62]

In 1925, it was written that: 'the county chain gang still maintains its supremacy as a penal institution in the South'.[63] By 1995, the practice had petered out, but in the late 1990s chain gangs appeared again, however they only lasted for about a year. In one county in Arizona the chain gang was re-established for men in 1995 and for women in 1996. The year 2013 saw the practice still surviving in one Florida county, with prisoners chained round the ankles; this, despite a US Supreme Court ruling in 1996 that some forms of the chain gang constituted 'cruel and unusual punishment'.

Apart from the fact that chain gangs intrinsically are cruel, their history is charged with violence against prisoners. In the early 1920s, it was reported that a 'Negro' who had been sent to a gang:

Refused to work on the ground that he had wronged no one and it would be sinful for him to work. He was subjected to every form of torture that the superintendent of the camp could devise. He was beaten; he was chained in uncomfortable positions for long periods; he was chained behind a truck for a whole day – sometimes forced to walk, sometimes dragged. No treatment forced him to work.[64]

This individual was later sent to another gang, where the same thing happened. Eventually, he was found to be insane: 'but it was more or less of an accident that he was not killed before his condition was discovered'.[65]

Apart from everything else, there was a huge problem because of the nature of the staff employed on chain gangs. They seemed to have been universally of a very low standard in every respect, and it is not difficult to find cases such as this:

> In 1925 a chain gang official, locally called 'the walking boss', with a reputation of long standing for brutality, was dismissed by order of a Superior Court judge and indicted for murder. Almost immediately, and apparently without difficulty, he secured a position as a guard in a camp fifty miles from the one from which he had been dismissed.[66]

Such extraordinary outcomes are common because the authorities almost invariably supported the staff regardless of what they have done:

> In two well-known cases a prisoner died within a few hours of being flogged; and in a third case two prisoners died also within a few hours. In each case the county physician found that the prisoner had died from causes other than the beating he had received. The two last named, the physician said, had died from sunstroke.[67]

This excusing of the behaviour of staff was made a good deal easier because the bulk of prisoners on the chain were black.

Even in this dismal system there were individuals who tried to improve the lot of the captives. In 1926, it was reported that a C.W. Mayberry, Chairman of the Board of County Commissioners, decided to try to lessen the tyranny of life in the gang:

> There were no guards. The patrolman in charge had no gun of any kind, as he stated in the hearing of all his prisoners. The men sleep in a camp at night; but they are not guarded, chained, or

locked in. They wear no stripes or other uniform to distinguish them from other working men. They sometimes visit their families on Sunday. They report for work at seven o'clock on Monday morning.[68]

Under the Apartheid regime in South Africa, the beating of black prisoners by white staff is well documented. This story by Makhoere can be easily replicated. She had protested that she had not had her allotted time in the bath:

You know Mbomvana, this stupid wardress, had a boyfriend, one of the warders at Kroonstad. And her boyfriend, whose name was Roet, came with another man called Else. They swaggered into the bathroom, lugged me out of the bath, naked, water running off me. And they started smashing into me with batons. All over my body. They pulled me to my cell, one on each side, hammering me with their batons. They dumped me there like a sack of potatoes.[69]

American prisoners were routinely tortured by their Vietnamese guards and interrogators. This was sometimes in an effort to extract information, but also as a punishment, as in this episode in Hoa Lo Prison, called by the prisoners the 'Hanoi Hilton':

'For insulting the Vietnamese people,' the officer said, 'you must be punished.'
  Mentally Rod steeled himself. He was made to lie flat on his stomach. A guard slipped a loop of clotheslinelike rope around one arm just above the elbow, stood on the arm and pulled and cinched the rope until it could not have been made any tighter. In this manner several such loops were tightened around each arm. With the circulation thus cut off, Rod almost immediately lost all feeling below both elbows; he could not feel or move his hands and fingers.

Then one guard stood in the middle of his back while others began drawing his elbows together behind his back – the elbows do not easily come together behind the back, so this took some work.

When the elbows were tied tightly together, he was made to sit up in his bunk and his ankles were locked into the stocks at the foot of the bunk...

'Do you apologise to the Vietnamese people?' he asked.

Rod sat silent, stared straight ahead.[70]

Some broke under such strain; others gave false information or information that the Vietnamese already knew.

Ralph Gaither was a pilot, and on one occasion he whistled the Lord's Prayer, one of the many activities which were banned:

Ralph got away with a warning that time, but when he was caught tapping to Al Brudno, he was locked in torture cuffs and led from his cell through a trench, down into a one-man 'bomb shelter.' This hole in the ground was perhaps four feet square and seven feet deep. The Vietnamese had been using it for a cesspool and Gautier found himself ankle-deep in human excrement. He did not know whether the overpowering stench was worse than the pain from the cuffs.[71]

Writing by captives in English prisons abound with stories of physical attacks by staff. Red Collar Man was especially well placed to see any abuse of power by the staff because he worked in the punishment cells in Parkhurst Prison. He begins his assessment with a compliment:

In the majority of cases the warders at Parkhurst are good fellows, out to do a difficult and unpleasant job to the best of their ability [but] the behaviour of some warders to the convicts in their charge is a matter of constant wonder to me. They will often deliberately go out of their way to irritate a man into breaking out so that they can get him sent to chokey, or flogged if he loses his head and goes for them. It is chiefly the younger officers who are guilty of this deliberate teasing and bullying, and one can only suppose that it is due to their lack of experience. Captain Clayton, on taking over the Governorship of the prison in 1930, put a stop to a lot of this, and the warders became more careful, if not more humane in their handling of the convicts.[72]

But he reports some brutal incidents. On one occasion a young prisoner had 'smashed up', that is wrecked, his cell. The staff who removed him 'gave him a thrashing', and he was removed to a 'silent cell':

> As I entered the cell he was standing against the wall with only his shirt on. The jailer took the clothes from me and threw them at Ibbotson's head. As Ibbotson put up his hands to catch the clothes the jailer punched him as hard as he could in his stomach. Ibbotson curled up and the jailer slogged him on the chin as the poor fellow fell forward. 'And that's for luck'. He laughed, slammed the door, and left Ibbotson naked and in the dark, on the floor of the silent cell.[73]

Brian Stratton had later experience of 'chokey' in Parkhurst:

> The chokey screws at Parkhurst were as fine a bunch of pigs as it has been my pleasure to meet. Together, this little firm, provided they had got their kicking boots, weren't afraid to attack any poor prisoner who was unfortunate enough to be down the chokey.[74]

He goes on to describe how he, and others, were treated after a 'sit down':

> Every morning they were unlocked to slop out, one at a time; from the cell to the recess would be two lines of screws, each one with his stick in his hand, and the con had to walk or run the gauntlet with lead-loaded sticks hitting at him from all angles.[75]

Wilfred Macartney, over the course of a very long sentence, experienced many different kinds of behaviour from staff. We have seen that often relationships were good. But sometimes they were not: 'The great majority of the screws hate the brutality of the system, and yet become brutes themselves. Some, of course, enjoy being brutes, but most of them enjoy being brutes because their bread-and-butter depends on it.'[76]

Brendan Behan, although his experience of staff behaviour was mostly good, relates what happened on one occasion:

> After the Governor had gone we heard thumps and moans coming faintly from below stairs, from chokey.
>
> The Principal Officer, a thin water-shaven man, erect, slim and spotless and beribboned, turned his old eyes to Johnston, cocked his ear to the moaning with the air of a connoisseur, smiled and murmured appreciatively, 'Someone getting a clean shirt, Mr. Johnston'?
>
> A clean shirt was the beating they sometimes gave a prisoner beginning his punishment.[77]

On another occasion, Brendan Behan argued with the priest because the latter said that membership of the IRA, quite rightly in the view of the priest, meant excommunication:

> The officer said 'Get out you Irish swine'...and threw me out of the priest's office. Calling another officer Mr. Millburn said 'This -Irish swine–insulting-the priest-' Mr Mooney nodded, shocked, and hit me a blow in the face'. The punches they gave me in the ribs, in the kidneys, and once or twice they hit me across the face with a bunch of keys, but concentrated mostly in the guts and a few kicks in my arse, when they sent me sprawling across the room... [I] had a look in the mirror...my face was not too bad, and nothing noticeable, though my lip was cut on the inside where I got the blow from the bunch of keys and I could feel the blood going down my throat and sickening me. I was

also now being sickened and a cold clammy sweat was coming out on my hands, and on my forehead now in delayed reaction for the fright.[78]

Walter Musgrave, an adult and well-educated English prisoner, expresses his disgust at the complicity of the doctor in cruel behaviour by officers. Complaints about the collusion of doctors are fairly common in captives' accounts:

> The doctor knew quite well that it was the fight with two young warders, when I had refused to stand up and call them 'Sir' in the dormitory, that had caused the torn ligament in my arm. The same kind of 'accident' accounted for young Hobson's three cracked ribs, officially described as 'the result of a collision while playing football'. In fact it was caused by the numerous jabs of Fenner's truncheon in the damp silence of 'the chokey'.[79]

In the English prison women were not exempt from illegal beatings because of their sex. Josie O'Dwyer describes a visit from the 'heavy mob' – in the English system a special group of staff mobilised at times of unrest:

> When they give you a fucking good hiding they do get their jollies out of it and you can feel that they do. As they are carrying you to the block they are all reaching out for their pound of flesh-pinching you under the arm or on the inside of the thigh. One particular officer always steamed in and started poking you in the chest because she wanted you to hit her – that's what she got off on, the struggling and the fighting.[80]

Sometimes physical attacks are more routine than these seemingly casual examples. The treatment of Indian prisoners went beyond verbal bullying, although that was an important constituent. Krishna Hutheesing, who describes the wardresses as '"lifers" hardened by long terms in various prisons', writes how they were 'vicious, cruel and immune to any finer feelings for the young girls who had come there and whom they bullied and thrashed mercilessly'.[81]

Some of the most brutal treatment of prisoners has taken place in prisoner of war custody. One of the accounts to emerge from the Spanish Civil War of the 1930s was written by Peter Elstob. He lived a colourful life as a soldier in the Second World War, and as a writer and activist in the International PEN organisation. It was typical of his almost careless courage that as Secretary he went to Nigeria in 1967 during the Biafran War to seek the release of the writer Wole Soyinka. Elstob was the author of several well-regarded books on military history. His obituary in *The Guardian* (25 July 2002), summed him up as: 'one of those people born in the wrong century'.

Born in 1915, after an erratic education in part in America, he joined the RAF and trained as a pilot. He was dismissed, it is said, because he engaged in dangerous acrobatics, and shortly after that, in 1936, he went to Spain and offered his services to the Republican government. Somehow that government believed he was a spy, and so he came to be imprisoned mostly in a notorious establishment called Montjuich near Barcelona, and it is about his time there that he wrote a very racy account.

The situation in Spain was of course chaotic, and nowhere more so than in the prisons. His fellow prisoners were foreigners, priests (singled out for especially humiliating work, and one of whom who was in his 80s was executed) and fascists. These were young, usually in their teens, but this did not save them from being led out in groups over a period and murdered. Their leader was a young man nicknamed 'One-eye', and when his turn came he was treated brutally. He sneered at the guards, and then:

> The order had been given to fire and all fell except One-eye who was untouched…this was intentional cruelty on their part. The firing squad then reloaded and took aim again at the solitary figure singing at the top of his voice in the midst of nine dead ones. The second volley brought him down, but didn't kill him. All the shots went into his arms and legs. He lay on the ground

screaming with agony, and the captain went over to him and stood laughing above him.

'You don't sing so much now, do you?' he said and shot him through the head with a revolver.[82]

Even allowing that this was a brutal war, the behaviour of the guards was callous: 'They had the new automatic rifles and they were laughing and joking amongst themselves. Three of them were smoking.'[83]

In the Korean War waged between North Korea, with Chinese assistance, and South Korea, and America and its allies, there are records of ill-treatment. To former prisoners of the Japanese this would have come as no surprise, since, as we have seen, it was commonly said that the Korean guards in Japanese prisoner of war camps often outdid the Japanese in their brutality:

> The first step in this process was a specialized interrogation. 'Pak's Palace', near Pyongjang, was one of the worst camps endured by American POWs undergoing such interrogation. This North Korean establishment, which was outside the jurisdiction of the Chinese, had an exceptionally high mortality rate, and a reputation for the tortures inflicted on prisoners. The chief interrogator was a sadist, Colonel Pak... The Palace wanted military information and men were required to answer a questionnaire. Coercion began as soon as a prisoner refused to talk. Verbal abuse would be followed by threats, kicks, cigarette burns and promises of further torture.[84]

A common way of inflicting cruelty has always been by sexual attacks both by staff and other prisoners. Predictably these occurred when the sexes were mixed. A survivor of the Gulag describes what happened on the transport ships:

> They raped according to the command of the tram 'conductor'...
> then, on the command *konchai bazar* ('stop the bazaar') heaved off

reluctantly, giving their place to the next man, who was standing in full readiness…dead women were pulled by their legs to the door, and stacked over the threshold. Those who remained were brought back to consciousness – water was thrown at them – and the line began again. In May 1951 on board the *Minsk* (famous throughout Kolyma for its 'big tram') the corpses of women were thrown overboard. The guards didn't even write down the names of the dead.[85]

Such was the behaviour of some prisoners, in this case in Russia. It is debatable as to whether such behaviour is that of depraved prisoners, or whether this was another example of the transporting of a wider culture into the area of captivity. Such scenes were a commonplace of the behaviour of Red Army soldiers as they advanced through Eastern Europe in the Second World War.

There are reports of sexual attacks in every penal system. Apart from allegations of sexual abuse at the Federal Detention Centre in Pleasanton California, the women reported that: 'Among other things, that guards had taken money from male inmates in exchange for allowing the male inmates to enter the women's cells so that they could sexually abuse them.'[86]

In another 'civilised' society, there has been recorded an especially brutal piece of behaviour, this time by female prisoners in an English prison. A female officer reports that:

We have had such trouble here with women giving each other internals that with the shortage of staff we actually refused to unlock one evening, and it was subject to an inquiry. And there were literally chaplains, nurses and prisoners wanting to go on the investigation to tell them about the internal (vaginal) searching (by prisoners looking for hidden drugs) that was going on. I mean there were women going to the nurses with bruises between their legs where they had been forcibly held down, and too frightened to take it to the police.[87]

Commenting on this statement, Pat Carlen observes:

> When prisoners themselves complained to me about overcrowding, they did not mention fear of sexual assault by other prisoners as being foremost among their many worries, (though this may have been because those most in fear of 'decrutching' were those who other inmates may have had good reasons for suspecting of hiding contraband drugs on their persons, and who would therefore be very circumspect about drawing anyone's attention to their predicament).[88]

There is a variety of cruelty, which, while sexual in content, does not derive from the wish for sexual satisfaction, except incidentally, but is designed to hurt and humiliate the captive. One of the best documented examples of this practice comes from Guantánamo. There are several official US government reports which confirm the practice. The sexual humiliation and sexual assault of Guantánamo prisoners was often carried out by female military interrogators. Mohamedhou Slahi, the author of *Guantánamo Diary* describes his experience of this. Much of his account is 'redacted', another euphemism, this time meaning text being crossed out by censors:

> As soon as I stood up, the two [redacted] took off their blouses, and started to talk all kinds of filthy stuff you can imagine, which I minded less. What hurt me most was the forcing me to take part in a sexual threesome in the most degrading manner. What many [redacted] don't realize is that men can get hurt the same as women if they're forced to have sex…both [redacted] stuck on me, literally one on the front and the other older [redacted] stuck on my back rubbing [redacted] whole body on mine. At the same time they were talking dirty to me, and playing with my sexual parts… I am saving you here from quoting the disgusting and degrading talk I had to listen to from noon or before until 10pm… I kept praying all the time. 'Stop the fucking praying!

You're having sex with American [redacted] and you're praying? What a hypocrite you are!' said [redacted].[89]

This was not an isolated incident either in his experience or in that of other prisoners. On another occasion:

> That afternoon was dedicated to sexual molestation. [redacted] blouse and was whispering in my ear, 'You know how good I am in bed,' and 'American men like me to whisper in their ears,' [redacted] 'I have a great body'. Every once in a while [redacted] offered me the other side of the coin. 'If you start to cooperate, I'm gonna stop harassing you. Otherwise I'll be doing the same with you and worse every day. I am [redacted] and that's why my government designated me to do this job. I've always been successful.'[90]

The distorted mode of thinking which allowed the brutal treatment of Guantánamo captives is summed up by the final observation by the woman involved: 'Having sex with someone is not considered torture.'[91]

The most extreme form of physical attack, as we have seen, is systematic torture. This seems to be, broadly, of three kinds. The first is functional since it is designed to extract information. The second is carried out to humiliate often combined with pleasure. The third is excused for the reason that it is done in the best interests of the captive. Sometimes the motivation seems to be a combination of all three, as in the systematic approval of torture at Guantánamo, or in this next case.

Mashíd Nírúmand was in her late twenties when the Iranian government arrested her, with others, for being a member of the Bahá'í religion. Her experience was recorded by another prisoner, who was released:

> When they separated me from you I was blindfolded and taken to the basement, and they made me sit on a wooden table they

use when they whip people. I could hear people screaming and crying all around me… I simply told them, 'I will not recant or give you any names even if you tear me apart.'[92]

On 18 June 1983, she and nine other women were executed.[93]

Sometimes torture is justified as being for the good of the captive. An example is force feeding, common when there is a hunger strike, and this generally occurs amongst political prisoners. In the twenty-first century it is severely condemned, but nevertheless prisoners in Guantánamo were subjected to it, since there all generally agreed rules about the humane treatment of prisoners were ignored.

Perhaps the most notorious instances of force feeding occurred in England during the Suffragette protests of the early twentieth century. There were many occasions when imprisoned women resorted to the hunger strike, and their treatment aroused huge controversy. In 1910 Lady Constance Lytton was imprisoned, but she gave her name as Jane Warton to ensure that she would be treated like an ordinary prisoner. She went on hunger strike and was forcibly fed. Her harrowing account should be recounted in some detail:

I offered no resistance to being placed in position, but lay down voluntarily on the plank bed. Two of the wardresses took hold of my arms, one held my head and one my feet. One wardress helped to pour the food. The doctor leant on my knees as he stooped over my chest to get at my mouth. I shut my mouth and clenched my teeth… The sense of being overpowered by more force than I could possibly resist was complete, but I resisted nothing except with my mouth. The doctor offered me the choice of a wooden or steel gag; he explained elaborately, as he did on most subsequent occasions, that the steel gag would hurt and the wooden one not, and he urged me not to force him to use the steel gag… But I did not speak nor open my mouth… he finally had recourse to the steel… He found that on either side at the back I had false teeth mounted on a bridge which he did not take out… He said if I resisted so much with my teeth, he would have to feed me through the nose. The pain of it was intense and at last I must have given way for he got the gag between my teeth, when he proceeded to turn it much more than necessary until my jaws were fastened wide apart, far more than they could go naturally. Then he put down my throat a tube which seemed to me much too wide and was something like four feet in length. The irritation of the tube was excessive. I choked the moment it touched my throat until it had got down. Then the food was poured in quickly; it made me sick a few seconds after it was down.[94]

Women of course suffered from all the cruelties inflicted upon men. But in addition there were cruelties which only women could experience. The most signal of these, as well as the sexual violence which has been described, are pregnancy, concern about children, humiliation attending menstruation and distress arising from adherence to cultural norms.

It is not unusual for pregnant women to arrive in captivity. How they are dealt with varies enormously, according to factors which are customary in the society in which the captivity takes place. As is usually the case, it is in the Gulag that the most desperate conditions are found. In a report of 1949, it is stated that of the 503,000 women in the camps, 9300 were pregnant. Also in the camps at the same time were 23,790 women who had small children with them. In a rare moment of charity, leavened with expediency, it was recommended that mothers should be released early. 'From time to time such amnesties were carried out.'[95]

Conditions for these groups were as bad as for any in the Gulag system. Pregnant women were made to return to work as soon as they could. They were only allowed a short time to breastfeed; often this was inadequate, and when weaning there was no further contact between mother and child.[96] The problems of pregnancy and motherhood are not, of course, confined to the Gulag. Every penal system has to develop a policy around these issues. An example is furnished by Dwight Reformatory in Illinois:

Even though 225 Women gave birth at Dwight between 1931 and 1971, few kept their infants for long. In the 1960s mothers were permitted only a single hour-long visit each week with their babies, who were cared for by civilian nurses. Inmate mothers were encouraged to find an outside placement – with relatives or in foster care – within the first month.[97]

The classic lack of sympathy for captives, both because they should know what to expect and because they were inferior, was summed up by an administrator:

> Many inmates had so many kids they really didn't care about their new child. Many were bad mothers when they were out; their children were raised by their grand-parents... Most women only claimed they were interested in their children when they were incarcerated, not when they really had the chance.[98]

In England in the mid-1990s, because of crises in the system, Home Secretary Michael Howard, *inter alia*, ruled that greater use should be made of handcuffing. This, of course, affected men as much as women, but it was the latter who suffered the greatest distress because of this new humiliation. It had been common in the past for women prisoners to appear in public without restraints at the governor's discretion. Now there were no exceptions. The effect was, by agreement, unnecessary restriction on undue 'freedom', but on essential personal needs, including health. Pat Carlen reports staff and prisoner experience. A governor told her:

> One of the saddest things I heard was a woman saying: 'I am not going to the child custody hearing because if I have to go in handcuffs with two prison officers, the picture that I will present is not a picture I want to give to my children or to the panel'... [Previously] for child custody hearings I would send a prison officer but the prisoner would be licensed. The prison officer would only be there as emotional support, not to make sure

the prisoner didn't escape but to make sure that if the custody hearing was grueling or went wrong, there was someone there to pick up on the woman afterwards…and I have on occasion given a woman temporary release to take her child to school on its first day at school, because that's a milestone in a child's life…and I have to say that the number of times I have been let down by a woman is negligible. Even if they don't return, we know where they are; they're not going to be marauding around Woolworth's with bloody machetes or shotguns.[99]

Liz, a 19-year-old prisoner, told of a hospital visit:

I was handcuffed to my bed for three weeks for the abscess in my lung. Governor's orders they said. Now, I had a drip in my arm and I had a chest drain in my back – I don't know where they thought I was going to in that state! Every time I wanted to go to the toilet I was on them dog chains – feel like an animal on them. I'm sick, I'm very ill, I'm not feeling very well and I'm handcuffed to a bed.[100]

To add to all the usual humiliations, there were those associated with menstruation. Makhoere in South Africa mentions her difficulty when she is describing the uniform that is issued. She describes the 'baggy white shorts with no elastic where they ended, which was somewhere mid-thigh; they had elastic only at the waist'. She asks how women could be 'expected to use pads with that type of panties?'[101]

Beatrice Saubin gives an account of her utter distress in her prison:

In the royal prison of Penang, a woman's period was one more humiliation to bear. Tampons were unheard of, and sanitary pads were banned. Too many women would have thrown them down the three holes that served as our toilets, clogging the pipes.[102]

Even in British prisons there have been instances of distress caused by abusive treatment during menstruation. In Armagh Prison in Northern Ireland during the Republican uprising of the 1970s:

> If a woman had had her period on, say, the third of a month then she got her sanitary towels on the third of the following month, even though the period might have arrived earlier. There were also complaints that the supply of sanitary towels was inadequate.[103]

Immediately upon reception, this particular abuse was inflicted on Jenny Hicks, serving five years for fraud: 'I was in an awful state because the shock of my sentence had started off my period and although I asked for a Tampax I hadn't been given one.'[104]

In addition, some women from differing cultural backgrounds seem to have suffered special distress. In the Egyptian prison called The Barrages, Nawal El Sa'adawi gives an example of the hurt when there was cultural assault:

> One of the *munaqqabas* [munaqqabas are Muslim women who wear the face veil called the niqab] let out a scream – 'Infidels!' – when they uncovered her hair in front of the male prison administrators. They took her away to the disciplinary cell. From afar, we heard her screaming and we knew they had beaten her. We threatened to go on a hunger strike until she was returned to us, and as a sort of protest against her beating.
>
> Illness began to threaten the health of some of the cellmates One had a haemorhage; I demanded that a gynaecologist be brought from outside the prison. We discovered that the women's prison had no gynaecologist, male or female. Another cellmate was in the final stages of her pregnancy, and she began to get spells of fainting and weakness.[105]

Captives also commonly complain about being over-subscribed drugs. Jack Abbott complained that a member of staff had been threatening him. This was the response:

> A psychiatrist sees me in the hole. He tells me I am hallucinating. I am placed on injections of two hundred milligrams of Thorazine three times a day.
>
> At that time I was barely nineteen years old. I was one of the first prisoners in this country subjected to drug therapy in prison. Now it is common.
>
> I fought every time, until I could fight no more. (Five or six guards entered the cell and wrestled me to the floor three times a day and injected Thorazine into me.) I suffered severe physical side effects. At that time, there was not much known about the side effect called the 'Parkinson's reaction.' The prison doctor thought I was feigning. This gave me my first psychiatric record.
>
> This letter is about the instability 'crazies' have in prison. It is about how we who suffer from this prison-cultivated disease are dealt with.[106]

Eugene Delorme, a Santee Sioux Native American, who had been incarcerated most of his adult life, discusses the overuse of Thorazine in the Washington State Penitentiary:

> I'll tell you the big trick they had. They kept everybody on Thorazine, see. They give you Thorazine three, four times a day, and that was guaranteed to keep everybody quiet, in line and just kinda shuffling around like zombies, you know. I took my share of Thorazine, then after a week or so I started hiding it because I couldn't handle it any more. When you take Thorazine, well, you can't even think.[107]

Studies in the United States indicate that incarcerated women are more heavily medicated than incarcerated men: 'Many women become addicted to the medication, subsequently compounding their problems – especially if they came to prison with addiction problems.'[108]

Whether or not the drugs are prescribed to cure illness or to control captives is hotly debated in England as elsewhere. A woman prisoner, Josie O'Dwyer, writes that:

> Some women go in weighing eight stone and come out weighing thirteen stone. They take hundreds of Largactil and – Phew! – they go up like balloons in a very short time. Then you see them eighteen months after they've got out and they haven't shed a pound. Their pupils are massive, they're speeding out of their heads and they can't shift that weight. It's had a lasting effect on them. If you're really overweight you know you are; and every time you sit and look at yourself in the bath you know you are. You look and you think, 'That comes from prison.'[109]

She goes on to describe the effect of drugs prescribed for her in Holloway:

> I was put on a drug called Haloperidol and I lost all my co-ordination. The drugs didn't make me dopey but I couldn't lift my arm up and down to clean my teeth or brush my hair. I'd put food in my mouth and forget to chew it and then when I opened my mouth to speak the food fell out.[110]

Another aspect of the drug problem in England is the introduction of Mandatory Drug Testing in prisons in the 1990s. Against the background of increased drug use which is admitted by prisoners and staff, prisoners are routinely tested for drugs. The theory is that they would then receive 'treatment'. The policy was questioned in an article by Morag MacDonald as a result of research she carried out.[111] From this research it emerged that prisoners saw the process as 'degrading', staff were 'sceptical' of the results because prisoners were found 'negative' when they were known users, and because of the reduction in staff numbers, especially those who had been trained, the programme was erratic. But the most serious finding is a good example both of how theoretical ideas can flounder in practice and the skills of captives in beating systems. It was soon discovered by them that: 'hard drugs were less easily detectable than cannabis'.[112] The serious consequence was that prisoners were changing from soft to hard drugs, with the further result that:

> This is potentially dangerous for the community when prisoners are eventually released. If they have started a hard drug habit in prison, as a result of MDT, then they are likely to continue after their release, and worse, if they have shared needles, they risk spreading the HIV virus into the community.[113]

The ultimate cruelty is plain murder. Amongst the records of cruelty to captives, one of the worst concerns Northern soldiers captured and imprisoned by the Confederacy in the American Civil War. Especially notorious was the prison at Andersonville in Georgia, commanded by the notorious Wirz, discussed earlier, but there were others. One former prisoner, John McElroy, sums up that experience: 'No man was ever called upon to describe the spectacle and the process of seventy thousand young, strong, able-bodied men, starving and rotting to death. Such a gigantic tragedy as this stuns the mind and benumbs the imagination.'[114] The reputation of the prison is all the more remarkable because it only operated for nine months, from February 1864 until the end of the war.

The camp became notorious for the murder of prisoners. At the centre of the killing was something called the Dead Line. This was a mark some distance from the outer fence, the crossing of which meant certain death. But McElroy writes that a man did not have to cross the line to be shot:

> I can recall of my own seeing at least a dozen instances where men of the Fifty-Fifth Georgia killed prisoners under the pretense that they were across the Dead Line, when the victims were a

yard or more from the Dead Line, and had not the remotest idea of going any further.[115]

If they avoided being shot, the prisoners suffered such ill health, largely because of the atrocious weather and the starvation diet, that they perished in their thousands. In fact, it has been claimed that 45,000 men died, which represents 40 per cent of all the Union Soldiers who died in the South.

As might be expected, black prisoners were treated especially badly. McElroy tells of the fate of one amongst many:

> Major Albert Bogle, of the Eighth United States, (colored) had fallen into the hands of the rebels by reason of a severe wound in the leg…no surgeon would examine it or dress it… No opportunity to insult, 'the nigger officer' was neglected.[116]

A very authoritative account of events at Andersonville is provided by a doctor in the Confederate Army. Although a Confederate officer, Joseph Jones gave evidence effectively against Wirz. His evidence is reproduced by McElroy.[117] There is just a hint of the use made by Nazi doctors of the opportunities provided by the suffering of captives, when the doctor said:

> Smallpox had appeared among the prisoners, and I believed that this would provide an admirable field for the establishment of its characteristic lesions. The condition of Peyer's glands in this disease was considered as worthy of minute investigation. It was believed that a large body of men from the Northern portion of the United States, suddenly transported to a warm southern climate, and confined upon a small portion of land, would furnish an excellent field for the investigation of typhus, typhoid, and malarial fevers.[118]

This dismal recital of the depths to which people and the societies to which they belong will sink promises no end. Perhaps the only cause for optimism is that some, when freed, if they haven't been killed, manage some modicum of recovery, but we shall see that for many, if not most, the pain is ineradicable.

Notes

1. Nichols, J.G. (ed.) *Narratives of the Days of the Reformation* pp.132–154, quoted Thomas *House of Care.* p.14.
2. Lawrence *op. cit.* p.126.
3. Lawrence *op. cit.* p.95.
4. Deacon *op cit.* Dikgang Moseneke, interview, December 1987–February 1988.
5. *Ibid.* p.102.
6. Begin *op. cit.* p.154.
7. El Sa'adawi *op. cit.* p.183.
8. Lilje, Hans. 'The Final Act' in Moir. pp.48–49.
9. Rinser, Luise. *Prison Journal.* p.62.
10. Havers *op. cit.* p.44.
11. Applebaum *op. cit.* p.307.
12. Herling *op. cit.* p.207.
13. *Ibid.* p.306.
14. Shalamov *op. cit.* p.242.
15. Herling *op. cit.* p.103.
16. McElroy *op. cit.* pp.156–157.
17. Risner *op. cit.* p.101.
18. Bone *op. cit.* p.37.
19. Begin *op. cit.* pp.196–197.
20. *Ibid.* p.185.
21. Applebaum *op. cit.* p.195.
22. McElroy *op. cit.* p.483.
23. Mencía *op. cit.* p.68.
24. Hubbell *op. cit.* p.66.
25. Grünhut *op cit.* p.46.
26. Webbs *op. cit.* pp.117–118.
27. *Ibid.* p.183.
28. For a detailed discussion of the Gladstone Committee Report, see Thomas, J.E. *The English Prison Officer Since 1850: A Study in Conflict* passim.
29. Williams *et al. op. cit.* pp.51–55.
30. Mitford, Jessica. *The American Prison Business.* p.32.
31. *Ibid.* p.106.
32. Abbott *op. cit.* p.26.
33. *Ibid.* pp.48–49. Original emphasis.
34. McCain *et al. op. cit.* p.206.
35. *Ibid.* p.209.
36. Dodge *op. cit.* p.223.

37. *Ibid.*
38. Mitford *op. cit.* pp.262–263.
39. *Ibid.* pp.16–17.
40. Kropotkin *op. cit.* p.74.
41. Applebaum *op. cit.* p.473.
42. *Ibid.* pp.485–486.
43. Begin *op. cit.* p.125.
44. Duffy *op. cit.* p.43.
45. Chang *et al. op. cit.* p.158.
46. Deacon *op. cit.* pp.109–110.
47. Playfair, Giles. *The Punitive Obsession.* p.202.
48. Scheffler *op. cit.* p.21.
49. Herling *op. cit.* pp.105–106.
50. Lytton *op. cit.* pp.58–59.
51. Macartney *op. cit.* p.163.
52. Leopold *op. cit.* p.135.
53. Chekhov *op. cit.* pp.78–79.
54. Amnesty International Campaign on the United States. *'Not Part of My Sentence': Violation of the Human Rights of Women in Custody.* p.66.
55. Macartney *op. cit.* p.155.
56. Red Collar Man *op. cit.* pp.154–155.
57. Dostoevsky *op. cit.* p.216.
58. See Thomas, J.E. and Stewart, Alex. *Imprisonment in Western Australia: Evolution, Theory and Practice* for a detailed account of the whole of the report.
59. Slahi *op. cit.* p.259.
60. Albis, Wafa 'A Martyr' in Norma Hashim (ed.). *The Prisoners' Diaries: Palestinian Voices from the Israeli Gulag.* p.106.
61. *Ibid.* p.107.
62. Steiner *et al. op. cit.* p.6.
63. *Ibid.* p.4.
64. *Ibid.* p.79.
65. *Ibid.*
66. *Ibid.* p.85.
67. *Ibid.* p.89.
68. *Ibid.* p.97.
69. Scheffler *op. cit.* p.104.
70. Hubbell *op. cit.* p.98.
71. *Ibid.* p.156.
72. Red Collar Man *op. cit.* pp.81–82.
73. *Ibid.* pp.110–111.
74. Stratton *op. cit.* pp.16–17.
75. *Ibid.* p.21.
76. Macartney *op. cit.* p.111.
77. Behan *op. cit.* p.100.

78. *Ibid.* pp.66–67.
79. Musgrave *op. cit.* p.134.
80. Carlen *Criminal Women op.cit.* p.149.
81. Hutheesing *op. cit.* p.111.
82. Elstob *op. cit.* p.240.
83. *Ibid.* p.283.
84. Barker *op. cit.* p.169.
85. Applebaum *op. cit.* p.169.
86. Amnesty International Campaign on the United States *op. cit.* p.41.
87. Carlen *Sledgehammer op. cit.* p.104.
88. *Ibid.* p.104.
89. Slahi *op. cit.* pp.230–231.
90. *Ibid.* pp.225–226.
91. *Ibid.* p.226.
92. Scheffler *op. cit.* p.81.
93. *Ibid.* pp.75ff.
94. Lytton *op. cit.* pp.268–270.
95. Applebaum *op. cit.* p.296.
96. *Ibid.* pp.297ff.
97. Dodge *op. cit.* p.245.
98. *Ibid.*
99. Senior female governor quoted in Carlen *Sledghammer.* p.108.
100. *Ibid.* p.111.
101. Scheffler *op. cit.* pp.100–101.
102. *Ibid.*
103. Coogan *op. cit.* p.130.
104. Carlen *Criminal Women op. cit.* pp.130–131.
105. El Sa'adawi *op. cit.* pp.182–183.
106. Abbott *op. cit.* p.35.
107. Ross *op. cit.* p.118.
108. *Ibid.*
109. Carlen *Criminal Women op.cit.* p.166.
110. *Ibid.* p.167.
111. MacDonald, Morag. 'Mandatory Drug Testing in Prisons', p.23.
112. *Ibid.*
113. *Ibid.*
114. McElroy *op. cit.* p.3.
115. *Ibid.* p.66.
116. *Ibid.* p.69.
117. *Ibid.* pp.134ff.
118. *Ibid.* p.135.

— *9* —

Sex and the Captive

People in captivity, like people who are free, think about, talk about, and, if the opportunity arises will engage in, sexual activity. Historically in captivity the need for sex was recognised and easily met. In the long history of the Marshalsea, a London prison mainly for debtors, there was an acceptance, and exploitation, of sexual activity:

> We read in the City sessions papers in 1739 of Anne Minchen, who bigamously married two men, both makers of leather breeches; she was unfaithful to her second husband with the first, whom she comforted for a time during his confinement in the Marshalsea… Prostitutes confined there would need to bring money into their purses to survive, just as did tailors and engravers.[1]

Such freewheeling in respect of sex was to be one of the casualties of the reforming movement led by men such as John Howard at the end of the eighteenth century.

Captive writers naturally discuss sex life in prison, although they are sometimes more inhibited on this subject than on others. So what is to be done about this primal urge? Some who suffered explained the weird ways in which the desire was contained. Ian

Watt, a prisoner of war of the Japanese, describes how a change came over the men upon hearing about release:

> One of the things we had to think about now was women. I noticed that the topic asserted itself immediately, for the night the news of the coming of freedom came was the first time since captivity that – incidentally profanity apart – dirty stories came up continuously to the conversational surface. We had had three and a half years of sexual repression, and I can't help feeling that the way the sexual problem had been solved – or shelved – was the most surprising of the many adaptations we had made.
>
> Presumably the low diet helped: but there were also, undoubtedly, a very complete transformation of the sexual drive into other outlets.[2]

Wilfred Macartney recounts how he misses sex, but being an educated political man, nevertheless, oddly, compares it with the absence of newspapers: 'More than anything – yes, nearly as much as the sex deprivation – did this lack of news hit me.'[3] George Jackson recounts how he found a substitute:

> The cruelest aspect in the loss of one's freedom of movement is of course the necessity to repress the sex urge, but after ten years I have learned to control my response to that stimulus (one thousand fingertip push-ups a day).[4]

It would be remarkable if captives did not miss sexual relations, but there are situations in which, apparently, it is claimed, this can happen. T.E. Lawrence is one who claims that sheer exhaustion can cause loss of interest:

> By general rumour troops are accused of common lechery and much licence…some may make a boast of vice, to cover innocence. It has a doggy sound. Whereas in truth, with one and

another, games and work and hard living so nearly exhaust the body that few temptations remain to be conquered.[5]

In the hell of the prisoner of war camps in the Far East, such exhaustion and hunger had a similar effect. A prisoner in one of the camps wrote:

> The first thing to go was our sex urge. The craving for food was with us all the time…so low were we in vitality that had we seen a bowl of rice and a naked bird in a hut she would have got killed in the rush for the rice.[6]

Such experience has its echo in the accounts of prisoners in the People's Republic of China. Hunger there is only one of a number of causes of loss of libido:

> The problem of sexual dysfunction, particularly male impotence, has afflicted many inmates of the PRC laogai quite severely. This widespread impotence seems to have stemmed from a combination of chronic undernourishment, exhaustion from long hours of forced labour, puritanical Maoist ideology, and the physical debilitating round of mutual vilification and self-denunciation. Jean Pasqualini reckons that impotence had struck most of the laogai prisoners whom he knew very well enough to judge, himself included.[7]

Such problems of dealing with sexual urges are of course present in more civilised systems. Mark Benney, who was a 16-year-old Borstal boy in the 1920s, writes a very thoughtful account of the sexual feelings of young people, and how the institution creates a situation where they are dealt with:

> The institution provided for the free expression of every instinct but that most urgent in the adolescent youngsters who formed its population. The sexual impulse alone remained unsatisfied. The

consequence was pretty near disastrous… Freedom of contact among the inmates made for freedom of conduct. Only in their intercourse with each other had the lads an opportunity for the demephitisation their mental systems demanded. Inevitably, in these circumstances, vice flourished.[8]

Benney goes on to explain that at first, lads had limited privileges: they could not smoke, for example. Tobacco thus became, as we have seen, a form of currency. And the price to be paid was sex. If a lad was small and good-looking he would be approached. At first, he might resist:

But by talk with his fellow inmates he would become familiar with the idea of vice, and sedulous appeal to his vanity would gradually overcome his aversion. If he was timid, his new friend would promise protection; if he was lonely and unable to form satisfying friendships elsewhere, the undefined hope for an emotional attachment would weaken his resistance. By the very fact of his smallness and timidity it would be taken for granted among the other inmates that he was a 'queenie,' and the distress caused by such an undeserved reputation would suggest that if he were to have the odium he might as well enjoy the rewards of degradation. It required unusual integrity in a Borstal boy to withstand such influences.[9]

Benney goes on to deal with his personal problem, since he was young, small and seemingly effeminate in looks.

J. Davidson Ketchum describes how in the early stages of the imprisonment of internees in Ruhleben, when standards of behaviour of all classes of prisoners were chaotic, there was obscenity, 'and stories and jokes were predominantly sexual, smutty limericks and obscene photographs were produced with no trace of furtiveness'.[10] But he alleges – and this is a constant theme in his account – that as the camp settled in, 'normal' behaviour was resumed:

The later magazines are as pure as *Punch*. The same trend was apparent in the theatre, the frankly sexual appeal of the first 'girl' shows giving way to Gilbert and Sullivan and drawing-room comedy. Sex never became taboo except in certain puritanical circles, but the proprieties of 1914 were firmly established in public.[11]

Ketchum, though, never addresses the question as to just how sexual desire was handled by some 4000 men who had no contact with women.

The obvious outlet for sexual relief is masturbation. Sometimes the subject is treated with frankness. The upper-class Rupert Croft-Cooke is appalled by the openness with which sex is discussed amongst his fellow prisoners:

> Only one thing really shocked me at Wormwood Scrubs, it was to hear men of all ages openly boasting of their habits of masturbation. To anyone who has been in prison this will be commonplace, but to others it will seem almost incredible. Even schoolboy shame in this is forgotten, it is discussed as freely as any other topic of immediate interest.[12]

Such frankness is often attended by crude good humour, as common in the barrack room as it is on the prison landing. T.E. Lawrence seems to have no qualms about publishing such material, remarkable when it is remembered what elite company he kept in real life, outside of the Royal Air Force:

> Lofty, our six-foot two weed of a naval telegraphist, unfolded himself from the bed, and in his short shirt (the same size shirt as that which tightly fitted the trousers of little me) paraded with his sheet before each of us, triumphantly showing us its traces of his wet dreams... Sailor was curt with him. 'You should leave off pulling your plonk.' Lofty, the grinning chicken-hearted fool, protested with a break of feeble indignation in his throat.[13]

Brendan Behan writes that there were those, even in Borstal, who did not enjoy smutty talk. Once again, we see an example of the variation in the attitudes of 'captives', even though this absence of prurience is seemingly rare:

> 'Nothing wrong with that,' said Murray, 'I'd kip in the next bed to you, Harty. You know, Harty, I might even have you when we get to Drake House'… Harty's face twisted with disgust. 'Why does a grown-up bloke like you talk like that? Disgusting, the way you bleeders talk.' He looked round at everyone. 'Ow are you going to face your tart outside, talking like that?'[14]

> 'Well, during the silent hour, when I can't get a good library book, I try and get 'old of a picture book, and see if there's any girls, in swimming togs, like…and it 'elps me to plan my wank for the night. Don't you never do that, 'arty?'[15]

Zeno discusses the problem of sexual desire throughout his autobiography. He has a print of a woman he calls 'Elsie' hanging on his wall, given to him by a clearly understanding prison visitor:

> It shows the naked back and black-stockinged legs of a girl seated on the floor, her rounded, tantalising buttocks wrapped in a towel. I have spent hundreds of hours looking at her…her lips parted and pressing against the wet warmth of the hair, auburned by sweat… She wrinkles her nose and cat-slits her eyes at me. My loins move and my testicles press suddenly heavy against my thighs… Faustus sold his soul that he might see the face that launched a thousand ships. I would sell mine if this dead whore would come to life.[16]

Cohen and Taylor, in their study of very long-term prisoners in Durham Prison in England in the late 1960s and early1970s, discuss with the prisoners how they cope with the absence of normal sexual outlets. Their attitude to homosexual behaviour is complicated, but masturbation, even mutual masturbation, is acceptable:

> Moral indignation about the behavior was completely absent, but there was some indication that although there was little disapproval of mutual masturbation, the 'insertee', the passive partner in anal intercourse was still regarded as a subject for ridicule and patronage. The point was not, however, that homosexuality was immoral but only that its presence amongst some but not all on the wing was an additional source of tension. Masturbation caused less problems.[17]

An earlier, Victorian generation believed masturbation to be harmful and even dangerous. It was even believed that it could cause epilepsy. This belief in its danger is expressed both by captors and captives. In the 1860s, in Joliet Prison in Illinois, the prison doctor was quite sure:

> Proclaiming it his 'duty' to call the attention of the prison authorities to the 'prevailing habit of self-abuse (masturbation) among the convicts', he judged this habit to be the direct cause of 'five-sixths of the disease I have had under treatment' and of the male inmates purportedly low productivity at work.[18]

In tune with the belief that women were inherently wicked and directly responsible for any loss of control among men, he goes on to blame them because their very presence provokes the practice:

> Convicts are a class of men whose principles and tastes have been more or less formed from the course of life they have hitherto led…add to this the presence within the prison walls of a large number of depraved females, who, by secret contrivances, are in constant communication with the male convicts, and you will be at no loss to understand the temptations to this vice are irresistible to natures already fearfully depraved. *At any cost the female prison should be removed from the premises.*[19]

Stuart Wood, as a normal 16-year-old, masturbated, but as he was brought up in English Victorian society, his actions were attended by feelings of disgust, and he reflected the traditional concern that the practice is physically damaging. He even claimed that masturbation is a cause of crime:

> His mind becomes obsessed by sexual imagery and fantasies, and he enters upon practices which ease the pressure of his resistance to the conditions of his punishment at the cost of moral and physical health. Vicious habits are fatally easy to form in prison and are rarely, if ever, wholly eradicated; so easy indeed and so inevitable in most men and women, that punishment was awarded for such practices as for ordinary breaches of prison discipline…this gradual weakening of will power and loss of moral resistance due to vicious habits engendered and developed by imprisonment constitutes one of the most potent factors in producing recidivism.[20]

Serving a sentence later in another prison, Wood again is consumed with guilt:

> The habit of self-abuse got me into its fell grip and I became that pitiful thing – the habitual masturbate… At Reading I had fought against the habit of unclean thinking and the tendency to self-abuse, but now with the virility of young manhood, with its urgings and promptings, I took the line of least resistance and my mind became a festering sewer![21]

Oscar Wilde suffered, amongst all his other indignities, being reported for suspected masturbation. The deputy chaplain at Wandsworth Prison in London, W.D. Morrison – who was in fact a pioneer of prison reform, but, of course possessed of all the usual Victorian certainties about the deleterious effects of masturbation – alleged that Wilde's cell smelled of semen:

A prisoner who breaks down in one direction generally breaks down in several, and I fear from what I hear and see that perverse sexual practices are again getting the mastery over him. This is a common occurrence among the prisoners of his class and is of course favoured by constant cellular isolation. The odour of his cell is now so bad that the officer in charge of him has to use carbolic acid in it every day.[22]

The authorities 'indignantly' denied the charge.[23]

This very Victorian worry about masturbation even infects the thinking of such radicals as Stephen Hobhouse and Fenner Brockway. These two were amongst the most radical citizens of the day, in the early twentieth century. Yet, in their classic book on imprisonment, based upon their experience as conscientious objectors in prison, they discuss deterioration as a result of imprisonment and opine that: 'This process of deterioration among prisoners is not due directly to prison discipline, but to the practice of masturbation which has its origins in the earlier life of the prisoner.'[24]

Wilfred Macartney writes a very frank and sensitive analysis, so frank indeed that George Orwell, who reviewed the book, expressed some disgust, and when Compton Mackenzie, who wrote commentaries on each chapter, saw the section on sexual life in prisons, his 'first impulse was to gut it out of the book altogether', but then decided that it should stay in because it would show the public 'the true state of affairs'.[25]

Macartney describes how he enjoyed an ordinary sex life in his marriage before imprisonment, and had no experience of homosexuality or masturbation. But when he settled down and faced the monotony, boredom and isolation of a prisoner's life in the late 1920s, he began to change:

One was frequently left in a cell over the week-end for forty four hours without anything to read, and this was one of the main incitements to masturbation... Masturbation is general in prison, and it is referred to openly and indifferently.

But, like the others mentioned above, he felt guilty about it: 'I may state definitely that the post-masturbatory period was one of nausea and self-distaste, and that I never got over this. For a normal man it is a wretched substitute.'[26]

In the 1920s, Borstal boys in England were issued with two books: *The Narrow Way* and *The Pack of Lies*. These were intended, in the Victorian phrase, to be 'improving', since they 'discuss sex matters and the danger of self-abuse and other evils', but to the 16-year-old Jack Gordon they were counterproductive. Instead of putting boys off:

> We discuss these little books and laugh at the 'rude' passages, while one fellow named Chester, who knows all the bad parts off by heart, says he reads it every night in bed and admits openly that it feeds his mind with the food it likes and he gives way... [the books] sow evil seeds in soil that is ripe for rapid growth and encourage vice, and I cannot too strongly urge their complete removal from the Borstal boys' kit at Wandsworth.[27]

This is another example of how prisoners bring predominating culture into captivity with them, because this is exactly the reaction to an act, widely regarded as deplorable, indeed damaging, which someone with Victorian inhibitions would express. The fantasies about the harmful effects of masturbation are still alive. Even a sophisticated modern prisoner like Erwin James considers the physical effect. His summary shows the persistence of antique British beliefs:

> The landings of long-term prisons are littered with wan individuals, hollow eyed through years of unrestrained masturbation. Pathetic perhaps, but for those unable to master their instincts there are few options available through which to gain relief from the torment of Priapus.[28]

Jack Abbott is a relentless examiner of himself, and he applies this to masturbation. And at the same time he ascribes a different motivation to his action:

> I was so constantly and arbitrarily attacked in my cell there, after a while my desire for physical relief was so powerful and all-pervading that when the guards finally would leave off the attack and exit my cell, I would sometimes achieve an erection out of despair and pain.
>
> I have in those conditions had to masturbate to relieve myself, but not to masturbate with any vision in my mind, my imagination. The pure physical act of caressing the penis after numberless exposures to attack is enough. It is entirely a physical thing, entirely involuntary.[29]

In some institutions, this disapproval of masturbation is translated into an offence against prison rules, as is reflected in this verse by a female prisoner, Carolyn Baxter, on Riker's Island in New York State:

> *Ms. Goodall does not drink, swear or masturbate,*
> *'It's against God's will,' she says.*
> *Ms. Goodall does not gamble, gets paid to be slick*
> *an' creeps round after 1:00 AM to listen for*
> *creaking beds so she can give out incident reports*
> *To anyone she catches by the creaks*
> *of their bed 'Masturbating!'*
> *'It's against God's will,' she says.*
> *So I lay naked on the floor, along with cold*
> *tile, I feel like a private under the bunk*
> *hiding from the enemy.*
> */as her Sears/Roebuck crepe soles creep by the door –*
> *I wanted to ask, what's the difference between a*
> *creaking bed/a manic breathing heavy under the door.*[30]

In one Illinois prison every kind of sexual activity was regarded as perverse:

Homosexuality and sodomy are strictly forbidden and anyone caught indulging will be put in isolation and demoted in grade. Masturbation is as equally condemned but the punishment for doing so is not so severe. For this act one will possibly lose a few privileges and that is the end of it.[31]

This system added another, rather unusual deterrent: 'I forgot to mention that a letter of sexual deviant behavior will be sent to the relatives of any inmate or inmates caught in the former offenses.'[32]

Frank Norman mentions the subject of sex in his usual direct way:

I am often asked what one does for wemen. The answer, you don't. There is of course plenty of queers who are always willing to acomadate you, but this is a very dodgy bisiness indeed as if you get captured at it you can lose half a streatch remishion and no messing about. So it isn't worth the trouble, although quite a lot of that sort of thing goes on.[33]

If you have the money you would be surprised what you can get even in the nick!

I once knew a queer that had two sets of wemens underwear. Where did she get them from? I don't know but the fact remains she had them![34]

Here, Norman is discussing a most important element in sexual relationships in prison – homosexuality. Where conditions are reasonable, and the sexual urge remains or returns, the second principal outlet is homosexual practices. These sometimes go beyond mere physical satisfaction, and serious relationships can develop.

In his panegyric about Thomas Mott Osborne, the pioneering Warden of Sing Sing Prison in New York, Chamberlain refers briefly to homosexuality, largely because he wants to praise Osborne's efforts to minimise it:

Isolated from normal contacts with the opposite sex, the prisoner fills his long hours of confinement with brooding, and it is inevitable that at times his pent-up passions should induce voluptuous reveries which in turn demand gratification. The result is sodomy. No prison is free from it. It is the curse of the institutional system.[35]

Wilfred Macartney, at his most explicit, relates how he became involved in homosexual activity. His bravery in publicising this is remarkable, since not only was such behaviour regarded as reprehensible at the time, as can be seen from the curious language employed by Chamberlain in the extract above, but it was illegal, and, as we have seen, people were prosecuted for engaging in it. In addition, his revelations could have profoundly affected his personal relationships, not least with his wife. His honest perception is worth quoting at length:

When I went to prison, the idea of becoming even temporarily homosexual never entered my head. There are many homosexuals in gaol, and for at least four years I took no interest in them. The first knowledge that the mind was becoming perverted by the unnatural existence of gaol came to me through my dreams. The imagery began to change. The persistent, sharply accentuated image of womanhood became clouded after about three and a half years. Even when awake I began to find that fantastic images were pushing the original normal image out of the way. Gradually a homosexual shadow obscured the normal picture, and I began to have definitely homosexual dreams.[36]

Stuart Wood is even franker than Macartney on the subject of homosexuality, but is totally repelled by it. As a 16-year-old, he was of course vulnerable, especially because he was always hungry: 'Many a time have I gone down upon my knees and picked up the tiniest crumbs with my moistened finger.'[37] The landing cleaner, an elderly man, asked him if he was hungry. The cleaner had access to all the cells, and when drunks were jailed, since they could not face food, the cleaner would steal whatever was lying around, and trade it. Wood found two eight-ounce loaves hidden in his cell, an unimaginable amount:

> I mentally invoked blessings on his head and fell to. In my innocence I saw in that cleaner's offer just another instance of the sympathy and kindness prisoners often express and do for each other at considerable risk to themselves.[38]

Then the cleaner came into his cell, and said: 'You're going to be nice to Papa, ain't you':

> Even then I was too utterly green to take his meaning. But when he started pawing me about and used expressions which left no doubt of it, trying the while to induce me to indulge his homosexual emotions, I'm afraid my gratitude vanished!... He kept on trying to paw me about and didn't seem to be convinced that I was serious, I knocked him through the door with a crack on the jaw!... I felt physically sick to think I had eaten food provided by such a man.[39]

Jack Gordon, the Borstal boy mentioned earlier, expresses concern about putting homosexual boys in Borstal, and writes how surprised he is at the extent of homosexual behaviour at Feltham Borstal. He recalls a figure familiar to captives, and who is commonly called an 'arse bandit':

> His very presence and the general knowledge of his instincts were bad for Borstal. Some boys, who may never have given a thought to homosexual possibilities, and were lusty fellows, whose sex desires lay only like a smouldering fire waiting to blaze, were weakened by coming into contact with him. He would openly court an older boy for popularity or a cigarette, or himself would bribe with things like his food, cake, pudding and

little belongings as valuable to boys in Borstal as a pound note to those outside.[40]

Peter Wildeblood, as has been pointed out, was at the centre of a highly publicised prosecution for homosexual conduct in 1954. Such acts were illegal at the time, and he was sentenced to eighteen months. A fellow prisoner, who of course would have been aware that Wildeblood was a homosexual, gave him what his informant no doubt considered good advice:

> Oh, but the place is packed with gay people who are in for something else. Most of the screaming pansies are in for receiving, actually. Don't have anything to do with them, they're absolute hell, all having affairs with the Officers and bitching everybody like mad.[41]

Wildeblood writes about the several 'varieties' of homosexuals: 'There were three distinct types of homosexuals in the prison. First there were the genuine glandular cases, the men who were in fact women in everything but body.'[42] The second category, he explains, were those who had seduced small boys. These were not popular with the other prisoners – which prisoners would regard as a considerable understatement. Those in the third group, like the writer, were convicted of offences with men.[43]

Rupert Croft-Cooke, like Wildeblood, convicted of homosexual offences, draws the same picture of the blatantly effeminate prisoners:

> They kept together and by behaving far more outrageously than they would have done outside, they created some sort of defence against contempt and indifference. But not against ridicule. On ridicule they thrived, courting it from both fellow-prisoners and screws. They gave one another girls' names and insisted on using them.
>
> 'Come along, Smith,' shouted a particularly heavy and humourless screw one day. 'You're late.'

'Oh, don't keep calling me Smith,' was the hissed and mock-indignant reply. 'My name's Gladys.'

'You'll go up before the Assistant Governor if you talk like that.'

'I shouldn't mind. He's rather nice.' [44]

Wilfred Macartney too goes into some detail about the pattern of behaviour of the effeminate homosexuals: 'Three or four stand out – particularly Elsie and Nora.' [45]

Cosmetics were improvised but Nora was having an affair with a member of staff, and 'the real stuff was forthcoming, with scent and ribbons and silk underwear as well'. [46] This was:

> A long affair with a jailor known as S–, who was a very decent fellow...
>
> We looked after him, and took good care that he was never trapped while he was in Nora's cell. The affair became notorious throughout the prison, and many attempts were made to catch S–, but they were always foiled. There was a general conspiracy to defend S– and Nora from interference. That disaster overtook S– eventually was due to his getting away from our care. [47]

The 'disaster' arose, according to Macartney, because 'Nora' was released, and the relationship continued. Nora was a burglar, was arrested and found with letters from S–. The latter was dismissed. [48]

In an unnamed Illinois penitentiary, despite the threats of punishment, homosexuality was commonplace. Indeed, most of the prisoners writing about their experience there discuss it. Quite how much of it was consensual is not clear. One prisoner is quite frank about his behaviour:

> It was not long after this first incident with drugs that I developed a homosexual relationship with another inmate. As I said earlier, I lived in the hospital and had contacts with the patients in the hospital. Some of these patients faked illness in

order to have homosexual acts performed upon them. I know some of them did it out of fear, but the majority of them wanted to be willing partners.

I took this other inmate into an empty ward of the hospital and performed an act of sodomy on him. He was the passive partner in this act of anal intercourse. It was sexually satisfying and afterwards I felt no feelings of remorse or revulsion even though up until that time I had disliked even the mention of someone committing a homosexual act.[49]

Clinton Duffy was the Warden of San Quentin prison in California from 1940 to 1952. In his autobiography he notes the problem of sexual deprivation amongst both men and women prisoners. At one point there were about one hundred and fifty women prisoners, and before he became Warden, he would be sent to sort out problems in the women's wing. He had to:

Straighten out feuds, investigate escape plots, up break up 'romances' carried on through the medium of smuggled or planted notes. Some of the girls – most of them were actually quite young – showed amazing ingenuity and persistence in keeping these artificial love affairs alive, and many of them would have taken any risk necessary to get their hands on a man.[50]

When it came to homosexual men, Duffy had strong views and a determined solution:

There are other aspects to the sex-in-prison problem, of course, that are not quite so romantic, but they must be faced. Society cannot ignore the question of homosexuality, neither can a prison warden, and in San Quentin it was a nightmare for years. When I began my first term as warden, the bisexual inmates were allowed to work and mingle with the other men in the yard, and I knew very well that over the years they had fomented more violence, engaged in more feuds, and perhaps cost more lives than all the other prisoners put together.[51]

After the murder occasioned by a homosexual row, Duffy made his decision, as might be expected from such a strong character:

> We didn't want any more killings that could possibly be avoided, and no time was wasted in doing something about it. We cleaned out the old Spanish cell block, put up steel control fences around it, and the rounded up all the known aggressive homosexuals. There were about eighty men altogether, and we put each one into a single cell and assigned them to work in the prison laundry under special guard.[52]

In the enclosed and heated atmosphere of captivity, it is to be expected that it is persistently reported that stronger captives will force the weaker to engage in homosexual practices. In the case of the sexual drive and its satisfaction, race, normally one of the great dividers in captivity, seems not to have been as paramount as in other situations. It did not save the African American Donald Peck. He was convicted of rape in 1947:

> Not only because of his innocence, but also because of his youth, good looks, and timidity, he was made to order for the wolves. An old-timer, who was here when Peck came, said, 'they passed him around like a beach ball'.[53]

So homosexuality is not always consensual, and from prison there are many reports of physical pressure. The cultural dimension of racial friction, which is of course a signal feature of American society, is never far away. In prison there is a special opportunity for revenge on white people. Another prisoner – and he is not the only one – describes what happens. In this particular prison, the ratio of black to white was about 80 per cent to 20 per cent:

The blacks unmercifully pounce on the white 'fish' as they come in…The more slightly built are the prime targets to these blacks… You must make a decision quickly; either fight or submit to their requests for money, (money in the form of cigarettes or food). Supposing you take the lesser of two evils and pay the oppressor; after getting his foot in the door, so to speak the Negro would usually suggest the white submit to practicing homosexuality. The white acting as the woman of course.

Another method used by blacks to fulfil their homosexual needs, is simply ganging up on one inmate and beating him, either until he willingly submits, or until he is unconscious and sex relations can progress.[54]

Several prisoners answer the question as to why white prisoners do not intervene. The answer is that they are frightened to do so because they are outnumbered. And so sex becomes an element in the battle of race:

In the Indianapolis County Jail in 1961 a young man – unless he was extremely unattractive – had two choices: to ride or to be ridden. And during the months in jail, when he was shouting his innocence to anyone who would listen, he – along with others – was venting his anger and frustration through sexual advances on other less strong young men.[55]

Allegations by young captives against staff are commonplace. And so this statement by a teenage prisoner in Illinois is typical rather than exceptional: 'Two of them at the Andy Home were homosexual – trading cigarettes (which were forbidden) to the inmates for sexual privileges.'[56]

In prisoner of war camps too there was homosexuality: 'In some camps dressing up as a woman turned out to be a perilous pastime.'[57] This prisoner explains that in the camp productions:

The girls really looked like girls...dutiful swains would wait outside the theatre after the show. They couldn't take them to dinner so they took them, instead, to quiet places in the compound. The trouble was, though, that there was very little privacy for love affairs of this nature. The boy friends used to get very jealous if you so much as glanced at their girl friends. There was a corporal in the Military Police who was violently in love with one of the actresses called Jerry.[58]

The authorities, both guards and prisoner deputies, tried to stop such practices. What would happen is that they would tell everyone that two prisoners were behaving in that way and they would be tried, and perhaps 'sent to Coventry'. Barker describes the effect: 'Not being allowed to speak to anyone and to be spoken too by anyone is unpleasant enough anywhere; in a POW camp it is a dreadful sanction.'[59]

In Russia, like the abuse of women, male homosexual violence was rife and normal. Some of the criminal bosses had young men as sex partners and they benefitted materially from that relationship. And of course there were no inhibitions:

One of the kids had hung on to his bread ration until evening when he asked Mashka, who had had nothing to eat all day, 'Do you want a bite?'

'Yes,' Mashka replied.

'Then take your trousers down.'

It took place in a corner, into which it was difficult to see from the spyhole, but in full view of everybody in the cell. It surprised no one and I pretended not to be surprised by it.[60]

Currently in British prisons homosexual relationships present a novel problem, since same sex marriages are permitted and legal in the free society. A *Guardian* report of 21 February 2015 tells us that a 'Gay Couple Serving Life Sentences to Marry in Prison'. A 'source' said that the men 'managed to get on the same wing and had sex regularly'.[61] Even more bizarre is the fact that one had been convicted of the murder of a man he had met on a gay chat line, and the other for a 'gay-bashing' killing. This is an example of how the administration of English, and for that matter all, prison systems cope with legislation outside the walls, which must affect what is to be done inside. These problems have ranged from the ban on smoking in public places to much more serious matters, of which the above is an example.

There is, of course, homosexual behaviour in women's prisons too, and the 'problems' arising from this are as great as those in men's establishments. In Holloway, Jane Buxton soon became aware of its extent:

> Some more of my discoveries on the yards are lesbian love letters, written on lavatory paper and for some reason carelessly discarded and only half torn up. I've seen enough of them to realize what they are and they all seem to me to be rather sad. I have been surprised at the amount of open homosexuality there is here.[62]

In Ravensbrück Concentration Camp lesbianism was very common. In her magisterial account of the camp, Sarah Helm collected considerable amounts of evidence of this and other sexual practices from ex-inmates and from documents. Just one example is that of a French prisoner in Ravensbrück, who tells how her block was 'bedlam':

> The first time I was propositioned by a *Jules* she offered me a piece of chocolate. They had trousers and jackets and walked around with cigarettes in their mouths looking for a fight or for sex. Block 27 was impossible – *affreux*, dreadful.[63]

Even though life was punitive and dangerous, lesbianism seems to have been both common and for some a real problem. The overcrowding exacerbated its opportunities, and 'it was most prevalent in the "asocial" blocks'. Nanda Heberman was a political prisoner, but religious, and a *Blockova*:

> She watched in astonishment praying for these 'lost souls'. 'They performed the most depraved acts with each other.' Her explanation was that the women were so 'morally deprived' that 'sexuality was the only thing left for them'... The prisoner lesbianism took many forms. Some of the women who came here were openly gay. Although female homosexuality was not a ground for arrest, a handful were listed on the records as *lesbisch* and wore black triangles. Many confirmed lesbians made no attempt to hide their sexuality, some taking on men's names – Max, Charlie or Jules – and sometimes preying on others who were not gay but were easily drawn in. Other women offered sex in return for food.[64]

Rose Giallombardo looks in great detail at homosexual behaviour in her study of the federal women's prison in Alderson, West Virginia. What emerges from this study, which is substantially based on the experience of prisoners and staff, is that homosexual relationships seem to be the cement which binds the prison society together:

> The vast majority of inmates adjust to the prison world by establishing a homosexual alliance with a compatible partner as a marriage unit.[65]

> Anyone who does not engage in homosexual activities in one form or another is automatically labelled a square.[66]

To support such a remarkable assertion, Giallombardo produces figures based on estimates by staff and prisoners. Apparently, inmates who are 'very much involved...place the figure at 90 or 95 per cent'. Staff estimate 50 or 75 per cent 'which agrees with the usual estimates I obtained from squares'. But some staff set the figure at 100 per cent. Staff, it seems, tolerate homosexual behaviour unless it is blatant.[67]

In the same prison there was a subtle categorisation, any individual's place in it being dependent on their sexual/social behaviour. Giallombardo lists no fewer than eleven of these, of which the dominant groups are the 'femmes', who perform the female role and the 'stud broads' who act as men.[68]

In Alderson, the homosexual relationship was not confined to sexual activity: a point frequently made is that much sexual activity is carried on within the context of an affectionate, often loving relationship. Giallombardo notes that it is central to the creation of 'families', where women act in the roles of mother, father and children. When it comes to social behaviour, the 'wife' is expected to do the housework and look after her 'husband' as would happen in the free society. There is even the phenomenon of divorce.

Helen Bryan, a prisoner in Alderson, does not go into as much detail as Giallombardo, but she does recount that homosexuality 'is a fact for a small percentage of the girls'.[69] In any case, she claims, staff supervision was such that opportunities for sexual contact were few, although she would agree with Giallombardo that relationships were intense, and often very serious. They could lead 'to many of the fights, verbal and physical, which occurred'.[70]

From the evidence Giallombardo adduces from other studies, Alderson Prison does not seem to be exceptional in the United States, although not all outside observers agree with this picture of 'families' in American prisons. Luana Ross writes of her research that: 'I found little evidence of family-type relationships existing within the Women's Correctional Centre (Montana). The prison views this type of relationship as inappropriate and generally discourages such associations.'[71]

There are some very personal accounts of love affairs between women in captivity. Beatrice Saubin, in her Malaysian prison, leaves frank details of her homosexual liaison as she describes the intensity of her feelings: 'I'd learned that in prison, sexuality went haywire like everything else. Intimacy was impossible, and love was reduced to animal impulses.'[72] Then a prisoner called Noor arrived: 'When Noor looked me over from head to toe, it felt like an invitation.'[73]

> There was some foreplay and then: there we were, kissing feverishly on a bed as hard as a rock. It's hard to say which of us was more ardent. In a matter of seconds we were wild about each other.[74]

The relationship was not without the expected complications: 'Noor was jealous. We started having more and more fights, alternated with fiery reconciliations on our cement bed.'[75] After one especially violent attack, Noor was put in solitary confinement for a month: 'We never made love as furiously as we did when she got out.'[76]

Staff deal with lesbianism in a variety of ways. Sometimes they ignore it, or issue a warning. But there are rare accounts of absolute crusades against it. In the Illinois State Reformatory for Women at Dwight in the 1950s, the Superintendent was Ruth Biedermann. Her behaviour is often mentioned in this book. Under her, the prisoners were swamped with rules and violations of these rules, but her especial target was homosexuality, or more correctly the slightest hint of anything approaching it. Staff kept interminable watch on prisoners and there are accounts which show the lengths staff went to in their relentless attempt to predict any suspicious relationship. Biedermann's obsession with suspected homosexuality permeated all aspects of institutional life. Former teacher Edward Reis readily admitted:

> There was a tremendous obsession with homosexuality. The joke was that at any time two inmates looked at each other it was homosexuality. And if anything actually happened they threw them into the hole for months.[77]

Of course, in the long term (and probably in the short) such energy spent in trying to prevent sexual liaison was completely wasted. The United States penal system throughout much of its history has been plagued by the practice of using the treatment of prisoners as a political football, and a consequential policy of appointing political sympathisers to posts in the system. In 1926, there was an Inquiry into the Joliet-Stateville, Illinois, penitentiary complex. During the course of this, the 'matrons' of the women's prison (not for the first time or the last) displayed utter disloyalty to their reforming Superintendent Elinor C. Rulien. This caused the Inquiry to call for her dismissal, especially because they believed: 'There was a wealth of evidence…to show that immoral practices between inmates have become so common and open that it stands out as the most revolting and disgusting feature of this investigation.'[78]

In some situations male prisoners have access to female prisoners, which ostensibly seems unlikely. If there is an opportunity to engage in pseudo- or actual sexual behaviour, then of course people will take it. Phoebe Willetts describes such a situation when she was in Hill Hall, an open prison in England. She worked in the garden and in an adjoining part of it, divided only by a thin wire, was a party of male prisoners from London's Pentonville Prison:

> Of course the men and the women didn't take any notice of each other while the officers were looking, or on a walk with an officer watching us with an eagle eye at each end of the crocodile. But with only one gardening officer and a large piece of garden to work, much larger than the piece we were allowed to go in, it wasn't possible for her to keep her eye on absolutely every prisoner all the time, and the same applied to the men. So the result was rendezvous arranged behind any available form of cover. Women had been forcibly taken away from their homes and their menfolk, and equally forcibly placed in close proximity to men, who in their turn had been taken away from their womenfolk. Whether they liked it or not they must work within sight of each other and soon they found they were in reach of each other. For some in this life of strain this temptation was too much for them, while for those who wanted to remain faithful to

their husbands at home it was a constant embarrassment to have to work in such a compromising situation.[79]

Willetts explains that occasionally staff would swoop and 'try to stop the notes and illicit meetings':

> But it wasn't long before the whole thing would start again. Even the fact that a married woman with three children ran away with a man after making arrangements behind a haystack, while the families of both thought that they were safely locked up under the protection of Her Majesty's Government, didn't appear to shake the Home Office.[80]

In 1973, the Illinois Department of Corrections announced that the institution at Dwight, which previously held only women, would now hold prisoners of both sexes:

> In 1976 a legislative committee described Dwight's population of 105 women and 48 men as 'a rather strange mix of inmates'. The men were mostly non-violent offenders, typically fifty years of age or older. Many had serious medical problems. Despite this several female prisoners became pregnant each year.[81]

It is not clear though whether it was the male prisoners, or the staff or somebody else who were responsible for these pregnancies. It seems perfectly feasible that the classic results of a situation where men supervise women were in evidence. In an investigation of sexual abuse of women in US prisons: 'Illinois was one of five states singled out for an in-depth investigation.'[82] The report found that there was: 'A serious problem with sexual misconduct in Illinois correctional facilities for women, including frequent privacy violations and sexually explicit verbal degradation of female prisoners, inappropriate sexual contact, and, at times, rape and sexual assault.'[83] As is usually the case, protests from women were counter-productive: 'When female prisoners have attempted to report sexual misconduct, they

Sex and the Captive

have faced a biased grievance and investigatory procedure and often have suffered retaliation or even punishment by prison staff.'[84]

Women in the Gulag were exploited as much as anywhere else: by staff, by criminal prisoners and by inmates who exercised authority, whether formal or informal. As in the German camps, some women operated as prostitutes in a desperate attempt to stay alive. There was also an unusual motive for women to agree to sex. There was a deliberate attempt to become pregnant so as to be excused from hard work, to get better food and even so that advantage could be taken of the periodic amnesties given to women with babies.[85]

Some arrangements were tinged with a kind of normality. A female captive receives 'a standard love letter' from a prisoner who is a cobbler – a privileged job. He suggests they live together and when she declines he thrashes her with a metal rod. This makes her change her mind and 'thus began my family life…I got healthier, walked about in nice shoes, no longer wore the devil knows what kind of rags: I had a new jacket, new trousers…I even had a new hat.'[86] Her man was then transferred and the man responsible for his transfer took his place as her protector, and the usual benefits followed.[87]

Apart from these quasi-'normal' relationships, as might be expected there were levels of brutality to obtain sexual satisfaction which are about as extreme as any in captive society:

> Edward Buca was once working beside a women's brigade in a sawmill. A group of criminal prisoners arrived. They 'grabbed the women they wanted and laid them down in the snow, or had them up against a pile of logs. The women seemed used to it and offered no resistance. They had their own brigade-chief, but she didn't object to these interruptions, in fact they seemed to be just another part of the job.'[88]

Such corruption was not only to be found in the mayhem of the Gulag. In the chaotic Tsarist system women were fair game, and violence was commonplace:

The marching convoys reserve special torments for women. Despite the fact that most female convicts had no history of vice, the assumption of officials was that all female convicts were prostitutes even before they entered the marching convoys. In 1839, one Polish exile, Justynian Ruciński, observed first-hand how every female exile was obliged to take a lover in the marching convoy. The choice of partner was not her own, though, but that of the convicts, who auctioned the woman off to the highest bidder among her 'suitors'. If a woman rejected the proposed union 'she was subjected to terrible reprisals'. On several occasions, Ruciński 'witnessed horrible rapes in broad daylight'.[89]

Himmler, in his usual bizarre fashion, decided that prisoners in the Concentration Camps could be encouraged to work harder if they were given vouchers to use brothels, which he established. These were 'staffed' by the women prisoners from Ravensbrück. They were told that they would be freed after working for six months. They 'had to be pretty, with good teeth, and with no venereal infection or skin disease'.[90] At first, there were plenty of candidates with experience, since among the 'asocials' there were large numbers of prostitutes. As time went on, the health of such people who were taken off the streets deteriorated, and staffing the brothels became one of the many problems with which the regime had to deal.

In many European systems there are schemes where prisoners go out to work. This provides an opportunity for sexual encounters, including meetings with wives or partners. In some open prisons, it is no surprise to learn that prisoners manage to engage sexually with visitors in the much more relaxed regime.[91] The experience of prisoners of war in the twentieth century varies. In Britain, German and Italian prisoners were often given considerable freedom, mixing freely with the community, and were thus able to have relationships with local women, often to the disgust of many people in the community, especially those who had family members in the armed services. Yet, 'Even though German and Italian prisoners had access to local woman one official in charge reported that: "There was quite a lot of homosexuality – certain boys would be let off jobs.'" [92]

In the recent history of captivity, it is remarkable how German and Italian prisoners in the West seemed to have been so very favourably dealt with. Barker recounts a common phenomenon of wartime Britain: 'Local girls fell over them! One of the Austrian boys, it was said, increased the local population by twelve! Two POWs, saying they were Polish, played in local dance bands, making, stealing or borrowing their clothes.' [93]

Hans Joachim Thilo, a German officer who was captured in France in 1944 and imprisoned in Canada and England until 1947, expresses a common experience:

> In the meantime Christians in our village had made a habit of inviting us to their homes every weekend. All the lectures of the re-education officer taken together were not anywhere near as valuable for a P.O.W. as an hour spent in the home of an English family. [94]

There is no doubt that this freedom was used to have sex with local women.

Prisoners in German hands were warned that any illicit contact with German women carried the death penalty, although it seems unlikely that supervision could be so strict as to ensure that no such contacts could take place. The Germans appear to have tolerated liaisons between prisoners and foreign slave women. [95] Barker describes first-hand accounts of regular 'relationships' with other slave workers who 'came from every walk of life…after a week or so we all had a girl friend except the misogynist'. [96]

In 'ordinary' German prisons there seems to have been plenty of opportunities to engage in sexual activities. Luise Rinser, writing of her experience in 1944, is surprised that any sexual desire is left yet:

> At last Mariechen, who has now spent a week in the smiths' cell, told us what went on there. On evenings when they were bored

'a longing took hold of them', as Mariechen put it, that is to say they were hankering after love, or to be more precise sexual pleasure. They satisfied their needs without any embarrassment, each one on her own or else in couples, just depending. The girls who work in the smithy get two big slices of wurst every day at break, with a bottle of beer. Also, they work alongside men, civilian workers who put food their way but naturally expect some service in return, which is paid them – in spite of wicked Fräulein Sch.'s watchfulness – behind machines, piles of planks, in the coal cellar, or if there is no alternative hastily in the toilet. It seems they lead quite a merry life there. That is why they look far better, more looked-after, and less embittered than the rest of us, too. M said that one of them even got pregnant like that once, but the men gave her something to get rid of it.[97]

Even prisoners of war in Russia managed to find sexual outlets. It is claimed by Erwin Herman that when he and his colleagues became prisoners after Stalingrad, they were examined by a Russian nurse who selected those she 'fancied' and allocated them work in the nurses' quarters. He goes on to claim that when he escaped, he lived for a time with the wife of a Soviet officer.[98] Bearing in mind the background of German experience at Russian hands, this seems to have been unlikely, to say the least.

Allegations of homosexual affairs between staff and prisoners, such as those made by Wilfed Macartney, lead to the question of heterosexual relationships between staff and prisoners. Obviously, such relationships can only happen in those systems were staff of one sex are in charge of prisoners of another. Rules set out by the United Nations are clear that male staff should not work with female prisoners: 'Intrusive searches shall be conducted in private and by trained staff of the same sex as the prisoner.'[99] This critical rule was strictly adhered to, for example in England, for most of the twentieth century, finally, at last, codifying a key point of the reformers at the end of the eighteenth century. They had made a demand that prisoners of one sex should not be supervised by staff of the other sex.

The situation before this was reported in the English publication *The Gentleman's Magazine* in 1757. The reporter was greeted by the Keeper of a prison with an invitation: 'When you have a mind to have one of these girls that you fancy lie with you all night you may have her; the custom is to pay for her bed and to tip me a shilling.' This invitation was extended to the public and, in addition, keepers of brothels would select suitable prisoners, pay their fees and take them home. So the writer concludes: 'the place may be considered a great brothel'.[100]

The situation was at last brought under control when Sir Robert Peel, as Home Secretary, steered through a reforming Act in 1823. Amongst a gala of reforming measures was that which made it compulsory for female prisoners to be supervised by female staff. Until then there had been no female warders at all.[101] In England, a pioneer of the policy of separate supervision, a recent new policy, represents a reversion to earlier times. In 1988, there was promulgated by the Prison Service the 'Opposite Sex Posting Agreement'. It is now usual for prisons in England to use male and female staff to supervise male or female prisoners. This dangerous change has led to the inevitable result. Ministry of Justice figures produced in June 2012 showed that, during a 33-month period, 126 prison 'workers' had been caught (and often prosecuted and imprisoned) for being 'too close to prisoners'.[102] Predictably too there have been a plethora of complaints from women about the intrusion of men into their privacy, for example watching while women are using the toilet. There have been other adverse effects on female prisoners, apart from the complications of sexual behaviour, as a consequence of 'Opposite Sex Posting'. Central to this dogma about equal treatment is the experience that when gender is treated as something to be ignored, women suffer. This was summed up by an experienced female governor:

There was a time in the eighties when women became much more integrated with the male system, and we lost what was known as P4 which was the Headquarters organization that looked after women offenders. When they integrated the male and female systems they didn't look at what was working well in the female system and say, 'Let's adopt that for the males'. Instead they tended to overlay the male Service on to the female Service, and we lost some of the good stuff, like the particularly good relationship the prison officers had with the women.[103]

This simple policy has always been ignored in many of the prison systems of the United States. Any hope of implementing it has been undermined, seemingly permanently, by the demands of laws about gender equality, which insist that staff of one sex must be allowed to work with prisoners of the other. Courts in the US have ruled that anti-discrimination employment laws mean that prisons and jails cannot refuse to employ men to supervise female inmates, or women to supervise male inmates.[104]

Although some administrations place restrictions on this, for example by forbidding men to supervise women showering, an attempt to enforce complete separation in Nevada was challenged in the courts by male and female staff. They won, with the court deciding, unbelievably, that:

It was not against the law for male correctional officers to conduct clothed body searches of female inmates which included touching their breasts and genital areas, unless there was evidence (as had been presented in Washington) that the women would suffer severe distress. Even if there was such evidence, the court held, cross-gender searching would be legal if it could be shown to be necessary for security reasons because there were not (enough female staff).[105]

This practice, which is a source of complaint by women, is common. This abuse was reported in Michigan in 1995 by a US Department of Justice investigation: 'Officers abused women during pat-down searches by "routinely touching all parts of the woman's body, including fondling and squeezing their breasts, buttocks, and genital areas in ways not justified by legitimate security needs".'[106] The protection of women has been so disregarded in America that, for example, in Vermont a contractual labor law 'specifically forbids assignment on the basis of gender'.[107]

As a consequence of this policy, the situation of disregarding gender would appear to be even more serious in some other parts of the United States. It was reported in 1992 that in Arizona 'more than 60 people who worked with female inmates...have been dismissed, have resigned or have been disciplined as a result of sexual misconduct'.[108] Another example of this behaviour occurred when three women in a US federal prison complained that they had been sexually abused: 'One of the women, reported that she had been beaten, raped and sodomized by three men who in the course of the attack told her that they were attacking her in retaliation for providing a statement to investigators.'[109] In reality, the temptation facing staff and the vulnerability of captives overcome any legal or ethical scruples.

There are many other documented examples of sexual harassment by male staff:

> Women at the Women's Correctional Centre (Montana) claim that they are sexually intimidated by male guards. One form of intimidation is male guards on night duty 'peeking' at them in their cells when they are undressing for bed. Regular bed checks are part of prison policy and are to occur at scheduled times, but prisoners maintain that some guards arrive early and surprise the prisoners... Native prisoners are modest and have a particularly difficult time coping with this violation.[110]

Sexual misbehaviour by staff is sometimes defended on the grounds that the inmate has consented. In countries where such misbehaviour is not specifically illegal, it is, in theory at least, condoned. Thirteen of the American states 'do not have such laws',[111] which forbid sexual misbehaviour. Commonsense would indicate that it is not possible for an inmate to consent, in any real sense of the word, to sex with a member of staff, since the power wielded by staff is immense and the consequent pressure to agree is so considerable as to be irresistible. The International Criminal Court has ruled that in the 'custodial environment', consent is not a defence if the victim is 'threatened with or has reason to fear violence, duress, detention, or psychological oppression'.[112] After the abuse, the inmate, for obvious reasons, is likely to feel unable to complain for fear of reprisals.

In the nature of things where a prison has no ethical standards at all, as in the German Concentration Camps, there is no check on either consensual or abusive behaviour. As the war progressed such rare decency as did exist in the early days of the camps evaporated altogether. This was especially hastened by the conscription of female guards who were promiscuous, to put it mildly. Höss bore witness to this, writing of those who were sent to Auschwitz: 'after just a few weeks' training at Ravensbrück they were "let loose on the prisoners"'.[113] Before long, they were thieving, having sex with male prisoners, and '"an epidemic of lesbianism"' broke out.

When women were sent out to do factory work, one witness described the wretched state and the dissolute behaviour of the female guards:

> These recruits arrived with their clothes in a terrible state. They had to wait with us in the canteen while their new uniforms were fetched, and as they waited they often behaved worse than the worst street prostitute. I had to stand and watch while one of the new guards who was going to be in charge of us, lay on the table and was given the full treatment by an SS officer.[114]

Helm documents instances of sexual relationships between staff and prisoners. Rolf Rosenthal was a doctor at Ravensbrück, specialising in carrying out the interminable abortions on prisoners, which he did with great cruelty. He made a prisoner who worked with him pregnant 'at least twice', and aborted her on each occasion. At last, Rosenthal was sentenced to eight years in prison, reduced to six years by Himmler, who considered that 'there were mitigating factors'.[115]

Nanda Heberman points out that perhaps one of the reasons for the degree of lesbianism in Ravensbrück was that: 'There were no men around. The SS men reviled the women prisoners, and sexual contact meant dismissal.'[116] Such first-hand experience must of course be respected, but it seems unlikely that the kinds of individuals who were in the SS would be frightened away from the temptations presented by several thousand vulnerable women. And as Helm points out, when the standard of women selected for the brothels fell: 'Himmler ordered that the SS try them out before they were hired.'[117]

Sexual misbehaviour is often linked to torture and humiliation. For women, the possibility of rape is a constant fear. This political prisoner in El Salvador conveys this horror:

> In the case of women, sexual abuse, the constant pawing, and the threat of rape are amongst the repressive apparatus to demoralize. The mere fact of feeling an assassin's hands on your body causes revulsion and anguish. Even though I had known all this would happen, it was a brutal, horrible experience.[118]

An unusual, though unlikely to be unique, problem of sexual license amongst staff in England was reported in *The Guardian* in March 2002. Under the heading 'Prison Chief Acts Against Bullying Lesbian Officers', it emerged that nine female officers at Holloway 'ran a regime of sexual bullying and intimidation of younger staff':

> The inquiry found that the seven ringleaders would indulge in 'intrusive and offensive' sexual harassment of new female staff to make them adopt lesbian practices. The recruits would also be 'paired' with a girlfriend on the staff, although these relationships were not always consensual.

Those concerned 'have been transferred to other duties', and 'at least four of the nine face disciplinary charges'.[119]

These sanctions would appear to be light in the context, since they took no account of the fact that these officers were dealing with vulnerable prisoners, although: 'The inquiry found no evidence of similar treatment of inmates.'[120] It is likely against this background of ill-discipline that this finding is questionable.

In some penal systems at various times, including the present, there exist official opportunities for captives to engage in sexual activity with free people. The usual term applied to such arrangements is 'conjugal visits'. However, since such a term smacks of pretentiousness or can raise a smirk in some places, another expression is used. The American prison systems, expert as they are at euphemisms, describe them as 'extended family visits'. And yet this is not altogether untrue since in some jurisdictions entire families *can* visit and spend time together in private.

A surprising number of countries allow conjugal visits. They include – and these are just examples – Brazil, Denmark, Israel and Germany. Countries which aspire to Christian values generally will not subscribe to such a scheme. The United Kingdom, New Zealand and Ireland will not, variously for puritanical or punitive reasons. In some countries which have such values, but have jurisdiction by state, the position is variable. Thus in Australia the Australian Capital Territory and Victoria allow conjugal visits, as do five of the states of America: California, New York, Connecticut, New Mexico and Washington. No such visits are allowed in the US Federal Prisons. A very good example of the truism that captivity is set within the context of the broader society can be seen in the case of Saudi Arabia. There, if a man has, say, two wives, he may be allowed a visit with each. Almost everywhere, such visits are only allowed for prisoners convicted of minor offences, where there is no danger of violence and the participants are not infected with Aids or venereal disease.

There is a great deal of controversy about conjugal visits. Those who support the policy point out that the practice encourages good behaviour in prison, recognises the reality of sexual need and is an important element in the vital process of maintaining family cohesion. To that end, in some places there are private apartments, provided with normal domestic equipment which can be used so that entire families can visit. Opponents object to the cost, to the danger of violence (there have been notorious cases such as that where a prisoner murdered his visitor), and the possibility of pregnancy, which could lead to further problems for the family. There are also, for some, deeply moral and ethical problems. These include condoning the use of contraceptives (these are often issued by the institution), and whether unmarried or homosexual visitors should be admitted. At least one country, Mexico, allows married, unmarried women and homosexuals to have conjugal visits. But the overwhelming objection is to the 'mollycoddling' of people who are supposed to be undergoing punishment.

The captive will always find some way of relieving natural and understandable sexual frustration, ways which may be allowed or condoned, or more generally condemned, and sometimes punished. Where such activity is explicitly forbidden, the attempt to suppress it is surely the most notable failure of all the attempts to control the captive.

Notes

1. White *op. cit.* p.145.
2. Watt *op. cit.* p.151.
3. Macartney *op. cit.* p.90.
4. Jackson *op. cit.* p.108.
5. Lawrence *op. cit.* p.130.
6. Barker *op. cit.* p.132.
7. Williams *et al. op. cit.* pp.99–100.
8. Benney *op. cit.* pp.220–221.
9. *Ibid.* pp.221–222.
10. Ketchum *op. cit.* p.55.
11. *Ibid.*
12. Croft-Cooke *op. cit.* p.233.
13. Lawrence *op. cit.* p.115.
14. *Behan op cit.* p.158.
15. *Ibid.* p.164.

16. Zeno *op. cit.* pp.160–161.
17. Cohen and Taylor *op. cit.* p.92.
18. Dodge *op. cit.* p.40.
19. *Ibid.* p.41. Original emphasis.
20. Wood *op. cit.* p.32.
21. *Ibid.* pp.60–61.
22. Ellmann *op. cit.* p.464.
23. *Ibid.*
24. Hawkins, Gordon. *The Prison: Policy and Practice.* pp.59–60.
25. Macartney *op. cit.* p.428.
26. *Ibid.* pp.418–419.
27. Gordon *op. cit.* pp.62–63.
28. James *A Life Inside op. cit.* pp.5–6.
29. Abbott *op. cit.* p.55.
30. Scheffler *op. cit.* p.108.
31. Chang *et al. op. cit.* p.98.
32. *Ibid.*
33. Norman *op. cit.* p.32.
34. *Ibid.* p.103.
35. Chamberlain *op. cit.* p.327.
36. Macartney *op. cit.* pp.419–420.
37. Wood *op. cit.* p.64.
38. *Ibid.* pp.64–65.
39. *Ibid.* p.66.
40. Gordon *op. cit.* p.103.
41. Wildeblood *op. cit.* p.107.
42. *Ibid.* p.108.
43. *Ibid.*
44. Croft-Cooke *op. cit.* pp.142–143.
45. Macartney *op. cit.* p.420.
46. *Ibid.* p.421.
47. *Ibid.* p.421–422.
48. Macartney *op. cit.* pp.420–423.
49. Chang *et al. op. cit.* p.113.
50. Duffy *op. cit.* p.109.
51. *Ibid.* pp.112–113.
52. *Ibid.* pp.113–114.
53. Knight, Etheridge. *Black Voices from Prison.* p.106.
54. Chang *et al. op. cit.* p.227.
55. Knight *op. cit.* p.109.
56. Chang *et al. op. cit.* p.48.
57. Barker *op. cit.* p.132.
58. *Ibid.*
59. *Ibid.* p.133.

60. Applebaum *op. cit.* p.289.
61. Pidd, Helen and Allison, Eric. 'Gay Couple Serving Life Sentences to Marry'.
62. Buxton *et al. op. cit.* pp.115–116.
63. Helm *op. cit.* p.174.
64. *Ibid.* pp.92–93.
65. Giallombardo *op. cit.* p.136.
66. *Ibid.* p.116.
67. *Ibid.* p.151.
68. *Ibid.* p.123.
69. Bryan *op. cit.* p.251.
70. *Ibid.* p.252.
71. Ross *op. cit.* p.152.
72. Scheffler *op. cit.* p.159.
73. *Ibid.*
74. *Ibid.* p.160.
75. *Ibid.* p.161.
76. *Ibid.* p.162.
77. Dodge *op. cit.* p.236.
78. *Ibid.* p.146.
79. Willetts *op. cit.* p.15.
80. *Ibid.* p.16.
81. Dodge *op. cit.* p.254.
82. *Ibid.* p.256.
83. *Ibid.*
84. *Ibid.*
85. Applebaum *op. cit.* p.293.
86. *Ibid.* p.286.
87. *Ibid.*
88. *Ibid.* p.290.
89. Beer *op. cit.* p.42.
90. Helm *op. cit.* p.198.
91. Breed *op. cit.* p.107.
92. Barker *op. cit.* p.103.
93. *Ibid.*
94. Thilo *op. cit.* p.120.
95. Barker *op. cit.* p.123.
96. *Ibid.* p.133.
97. Rinser *op. cit.* pp.106–107.
98. Barker *op. cit.* p.134.
99. Standard Minimum Rules for the Treatment of Prisoners, Rule 52 (1).
100. Webb and Webb *op. cit.* p.23.
101. *Ibid.* p.74.
102. Alleyn, Richard. 'Prison Guards Caught Having "Inappropriate Relationships" with Inmates.'

103. Carlen *Sledgehammer op. cit.* p.135.
104. Amnesty International Campaign on the United States *op.cit.* p.52.
105. *Ibid.* p.54.
106. *Ibid.* p.43.
107. *Ibid.* p.53.
108. *Ibid.* pp.39–40.
109. *Ibid.* p.59.
110. Ross *op. cit.* p.167.
111. Amnesty International Campaign on the United States *op. cit.* p.50.
112. *Ibid.* p.49.
113. Helm *op. cit.* p.309.
114. *Ibid.*
115. *Ibid.* pp.353–354.
116. *Ibid.* p.93.
117. *Ibid.* p.353.
118. Scheffler *op. cit.* p.39.
119. Pallister, Davis. 'Prison Chief Acts against Bullying Lesbian Officers.'
120. *Ibid.*

— 10 —

The Political Captive

Political prisoners have abounded in the history of civilisation and their stories are an important guide to the horrors of being locked up. Every regime has locked up its opponents, and the victims are a gallery of heroes and villains: whether the one or the other will depend on an individual point of view. Amongst them are several English kings – Richard II, Henry VI, Edward V and Charles I – and politicians such as Adolf Hitler and Nelson Mandela. Then there are those who oppose such politicians: Dietrich Bonhoeffer, opponent of the Nazi government; and Menachem Begin, who allegedly tried to subvert the Soviet government and subsequently became Prime Minister of Israel. There are writers who protested politically and most dangerously in their writings, for example Fyodor Dostoevsky, imprisoned for allegedly trying to overthrow the Tsar. There were those motivated by political beliefs who were caught up in wars, such as Peter Elstob and Arthur Koestler, both victims of the Spanish Civil War in the 1930s. And there were people for whom death meant nothing, but the cause meant everything: for example, those who followed Fidel Castro in the Cuban Revolution. In this category too there are the victims of the foundation of the State of Israel, Palestinians, often subjected to very long sentences. And there were the seemingly less threatening, like those who protested in Britain against nuclear weapons in the mid-twentieth century. All were defined as committing crimes against the state. Unfortunately for those states, many of these prisoners were articulate and often left a record of their experience. In some cases, their suffering became an inspiration to succeeding generations.

Some of these we have already heard from. Some are not as well known as they deserve to be. Just one example is the Japanese activist Kaneko Fumiko. She was sentenced to death for allegedly plotting to kill the Emperor in March 1926. The sentence was commuted, but shown the commutation document, she tore it up. In July 1926, she hanged herself in prison. She was about 24.[1]

As well as the ever present phenomenon of incarcerated 'politicals', there is the interminable question as to who qualifies for the category. In the same way as there has been dispute about who is entitled to be defined as a political prisoner, so there has been argument about who is a prisoner of war, with the protection, in civilised societies, that status brings. American pilots captured during the war in Vietnam demanded, and supposed, that they would be treated as prisoners of war. But they were soon disabused of that expectation. One interrogator made that clear:

> 'You must understand,' he told Larry (Major Lawrence N Guarino) 'that your position here is and will always be that of a criminal. You are not now or ever going to be treated in accordance with the Geneva agreements, because this is an undeclared war. You have criminally attacked our people, and it has been decided that you are always to be treated as a criminal. You must cooperate and show repentance for your crimes to earn good treatment. Sooner or later, you are going to show repentance. You are going to admit you are a criminal. You are going to denounce your government. You are going to beg our government for forgiveness.'
>
> Thus, by mid-June, 1965, Hanoi had determined to treat its American prisoners as common criminals.[2]

Then there are people convicted of legally criminal offences, who protest that their convictions are based upon a wrong premise.

These include animal rights protestors, every persuasion of political 'offender' and even some bank robbers who will say society, and the share they have been given in it, is unjust and that their actions are designed to achieve some sort of balance. There are also some criminals who refuse to distinguish between the criminal and the political. Seán Bourke was serving a sentence of seven years in Wormwood Scrubs Prison in London for the attempted murder of a policeman when he met George Blake, whom we have already met in this book. This man, an officer of the British Secret Service, had been convicted of spying for the USSR, and given the longest fixed sentence in the history of British justice – 42 years – in 1961. In 1966, Bourke, by now free, engineered Blake's escape and his flight to Moscow. Bourke later ruminated on why he had helped Blake: 'The length of his sentence was a factor, certainly; and of course he was not an ordinary criminal but a prisoner of conscience.'[3] This, despite the fact that firm evidence showed that Blake had been responsible for the deaths of many people. This raises the central dispute: If actions cause the deaths, often of innocent people, should they be treated as political?

Bourke eventually returned to Ireland – he was an Irish subject – and, after a few days, was arrested because of an extradition request from Britain. The District Court ordered that he be handed over to British Special Branch, and an appeal was launched. The High Court heard the case and ruled that helping Blake to escape was 'an offence connected with a political offence'. The State appealed, but the Supreme Court upheld the High Court decision. This is of relevance to this discussion because it is an example of the tangled arguments about what comprises a political offence; Ireland has a long experience of this debate.

This confusion about what is meant by a political prisoner is exemplified, and it is not the only one, by the debates about the British suffragettes at the beginning of the twentieth century. Was, for example, the smashing of windows – such a seemingly non-dangerous act, unless one were standing behind the window – a criminal enterprise or a political one? Politicians wrestled with the question and Winston Churchill, in one of his moods of liberalism, a mood of great importance in the history of penal reform, introduced something called Rule 243a. This awarded certain privileges to second division prisoners, for example, visits and letters once a fortnight, the wearing of one's own clothes rather than uniforms, group exercise twice daily, first division food (in the form of food parcels from outside), books and the ability to do one's own work rather than prison labour.

The point to note here is that, although grand rules may be proclaimed from above, their application is dependent upon the mood, conviction and personality of the individual head of the institution – especially in England, the governor – and attitude of the basic grade members of staff: 'In practice, suffragettes benefitted from privileges even before they had been granted them formally, with prison treatment depending on the institution and individual officers.'[4]

The suffragettes would have expected special treatment since they did not regard themselves as criminals. Constance Lytton expresses a representative opinion. Reflecting on the fact that she had often seen the 'Black Maria' pass in the street, she wondered about the people inside:

Now I was myself one of the criminals. I should know the sensations from actual experience, literally from within. Of course I in no sense regarded myself as a criminal, and was aware of a detached spectator's commentary running through my mind all the while.[5]

In this debate about categorisation, Edith Bone, the Hungarian 'spy', offers a definition of the political prisoner:

The political prisoner is unique, not one of a herd – he has opinions, he pursues aims, and above all, he is a volunteer, arbiter of his own fate, risking captivity or death for some cause more important to him than life and liberty. The attitude of his captors is also different; there is none of the camaraderie often observed towards prisoners of war by their guards, who may think that their own preservation from a similar fate is merely a matter of luck.[6]

But is this definition accurate enough? And does it embrace the defence put forward by Nelson Mandela at his trial for sabotage in 1964? Here, his central point was that he and his fellow prisoners had no choice but to resort to violence. This was because the government made it illegal to engage in any peaceful attempts to change the civil restrictions under which non-Europeans suffered.

In some countries, at some times, the law stipulates that political prisoners are not to be treated as criminal prisoners. In Cuba, even under the Batista regime overthrown by Fidel Castro, there was such provision:

> Section A of Article 7 of Decree 3688, based on constitutional provisions 26 and 27, stated, 'Political detainees or prisoners will be held in areas separate from those provided for common criminals and will not be subjected to any kind of work or other penal regulations applied to common prisoners.'[7]

In addition, Section B of Article 7 of Decree 3688 'expressly prohibited the solitary confinement of any prisoner'.[8] The fact that such rules exist on paper does not mean that they were observed in practice, which they certainly were not in Batista's Cuba.

I have discussed in earlier chapters something of the lives of political prisoners and the context of their incarceration. I will now look at four examples which illustrate in rather more detail the issues surrounding political imprisonment, how such prisoners are treated, how they fit into the life of their prison and the means by which they adapt to what is, for most, a very alien environment. The examples I will use are taken from the United States, South Africa, Northern Ireland and Palestine.

In some countries, the link between race and political disaffection is pronounced, and the United States is a good example. There was a prison riot in Attica Prison in New York State in 1971, in which no fewer than 29 prisoners and 10 hostages died when the rioters were stormed. Some saw this as part of a big picture of revolt against the state:

> Attica before the massacre offered us a sleeping but graphic image of the monumental feats obtainable by men and women moving along a revolutionary course...in a figurative sense, it invoked visions of the Paris Communes, the liberated areas of pre-revolutionary Cuba, the free territories of Mozambique.[9]

This was written by Angela Davis, a black academic and a radical activist in the US, active especially during the 1960s and 1970s. The New York Commissioner of Corrections came to a similar conclusion. He wrote of:

> Leftist militants...who...seek to turn America's correctional system into a revolutionary battleground... On the eve of Attica, then, the disinherited and the villainous, the alienated and the pawns, the flotsam and jetsam of society, and a new generation of revolutionary leaders focused on the prisons as their point of leverage. Here was where the Establishment could be made to buckle and the class issue could be most clearly defined.[10]

It may be noteworthy that he saw this as a 'class' issue, not an issue of race, and the rioters, he seems to believe, were in any case abnormal. There is some evidence that the prisoners saw this as a 'war' too, with overtones of 'class'. Amongst their demands was one (rejected) that anyone who wanted should be given a safe passage to a 'non-imperialist country'.

In the case of Attica – and this may be said to be typical of the United States – 'the Attica officers were all white whereas nearly two thirds of the inmates were black or Puerto Rican'.[11] As the commission report puts it:

> Predominantly poor, urban, black and Spanish speaking inmates were placed under the supervision of white officers from rural areas…they began with little or nothing in common, and Attica was not a catalyst which made people want to learn about each other.[12]

When it comes to whether imprisonment is a political process, George Page describes what happened when he was serving in the US Army in Greenland. The political messages he received were the cause, or at least contributed to, his being eventually locked up:

> I began to listen to 'Moscow Molly' over Radio Moscow every evening at six o'clock. And for the first time in my life I saw the white man in a different light. I was aware of the white problem in America but in a very limited sense, having never taken the time to look into it properly. It was then, in Greenland, in 1952, that I first became consciously outraged and confused…now the confusion is gone – not only for myself, but for thousands like me. I will no longer accept a system which governs by sucking the blood of colored people.[13]

Such feeling spills over into violence, which the prisoners explain as the result of abuse which in turn arises from discrimination, caused by a supposed political reality, to which they do not subscribe. In September 1969, there was a protest in the Indiana State Reformatory, in which a prisoner was killed and 46 were wounded. A group of young black men were transferred to the Indiana State Prison, and Etheridge Knight, himself a black prisoner, carried out a clandestine exchange of letters with some of them, sent to 'The Rock' an isolated prison within the prison. These letters demonstrate their total rejection of the political status quo, and even the efforts of black 'Uncle Toms' to reform it. The tone of these may be seen from these extracts. The language is an interesting indicator of the distance between captive and captor and black and white:

> Look Knight, to be honest, I am shitty at you and the rest of these so call black brothers who know that I haven't did a dam thing to get lock up, but yet and still they fucking afraid of this punk ass honky until they just stand back and see a brother getting frame up and being victimized without opening up their mouth in attempt to stop these mad dog honkies from fucking over black people.[14]

Another prisoner, equally angry, wrote:

> I, beginning to wonder just how far submerged you are in this white wash…it is beginning to appear that you're a very gullible, unaware, potential Uncle Tom. Maybe if you would stop thinking the only thing that a nigger has to do in order to be black is to avow to hate whitey, look extremely hard, and never smile, you can wake up to the nature of the enemy. I would like to point out something to you (Tom), I hope you don't think I'm mad at you because I'm not, but it is getting sickening for these so called evangelists of blackness talking about their hunky friends, their trust in the swines will end up with some of my people tricked write into a gas chamber.[15]

These letters also demonstrate the tensions and differences among 'political' prisoners who ostensibly are on the same side. Knight, of course, with his political views, would not accept these attacks, and replied on the same day in December 1968:

> Peace. Look, I am going to ignore all of your wild rhetoric for the moment, but I have to say this: who the fuck are you to rave and rant and call anybody an Uncle Tom when you are supposed to have so much love for yourself, your family, and for black people, and yet you blow your chance to go home where you can really

do something – all because you can't keep your mouth shut up there. Even a Tom wouldn't do that.[16]

This mechanised fucking of humanity by perverted Europeans gave birth to the French penal colonies, the British convict ships, etc.; and these grotesque babies multiplied and spread all over the world. Everywhere the master went, his jails were sure to go.[17]

H. Rap Brown, 'a ghetto youth', wrote in the same vein from his prison, this time specifically advocating violence.

I am a political prisoner, jailed for my beliefs that black people must be free. The government has taken a position true to its fascist nature. Those who they cannot convert, they must silence. This government has become the enemy of mankind…to desire freedom is not enough. We must move from resistance to aggression, from revolt to revolution. For every black death, there must be ten dead racist cops…the laws to govern us must be made by us.[18]

Another fighter against what he saw as a rotten state was Eldridge Cleaver: 'Like many other youths of the "ghetto", Eldridge Cleaver followed an objective course of events that ended in a penitentiary… the first step for the ghetto youth is the pure and simple rejection of the law.'[19] To Cleaver, in this political whirlwind, even rape becomes a political act and instrument of freedom. It is a somewhat strange belief that violent sexual attack is admissible as social protest, but nevertheless Cleaver claims that it is:

I became a rapist. To refine my technique and *modus operandi*, I started out by practising on black girls in the ghetto – in the black ghetto where dark and vicious deeds appear not as aberrations or deviations from the norm, but as part of the sufficiency of the Evil of a day – and when I considered myself smooth enough, I crossed the tracks and sought out white prey. I did this consciously, deliberately, wilfully, methodically – though looking back I see that I was in a frantic, wild, and completely abandoned frame of mind.

Rape was an insurrectionary act. It delighted me that I was defying and trampling upon the white man's law, upon his system of values, and that I was defiling his women – and this point, I believe was the most satisfying to me because I was very resentful over the historical fact of how the white man has used the black woman. I felt I was getting revenge. From the site of the act of rape, consternation spreads outwardly in concentric circles. I wanted to send waves of consternation throughout the white race.[20]

Soon it was supposed in the United States that Islam held the answers to political repression. Charles Baker is an example. He was convicted for murder in the course of a robbery, and sentenced to a life sentence:

And my reasons for accepting the teachings of Islam are because I recognized from the teachings of Islam that this white man was the devil, I recognized from the teachings of Islam that this white man had deceived the black man, had indoctrinated the black man, had trained the black man to think – had conditioned his way of thinking… When I first heard the teachings of Islam – it was something new, it was something that I had never heard before and…it was something I wanted to think but didn't know how to think it.[21]

In South Africa under Apartheid, race and politics were of course inextricably linked. It is commonly said that political prisoners have always been especial targets for naked, inexcusable brutality, and the point may be exemplified here from this episode on Robben Island:

Mr. Mlambo, a twenty-year-stretch man, a short man, was made to dig a pit big enough to fit him. Unaware of what was to follow, he was still digging on when he was suddenly overwhelmed by a group of convicts. They shove him into the pit and started filling it up… When they had finished, only Mlambo's head appeared above the ground. A white warder who had directed the whole business, urinated into Mlambo's mouth. The convicts tried to open his tight-locked jaws, but could not…the warder pissed and pissed; it looked as though he had reserved gallons of urine for the purpose… When the warder had finished…vicious blows of fists and boots rained around the defenceless head sticking out of the ground.[22]

This Johnson Mlambo, a senior member of the Pan Africanist Congress – one of the major political groups at the time – seems to have suffered as much as any. At one time, political prisoners colluded with criminals in stealing food. This meant, of course, that others suffered. It was decided by the political hierarchy that this should stop, and since the Pan Africanist Congress were the main offenders, Mlambo took the lead. He tried to take away a dish from a thief, who then: 'put his finger into my eye socket and that is how I lost my eye'.[23]

On the island, the white warders were persuaded (if they needed persuading) that the political prisoners were terrorists. This was not a game on the part of the staff, but had a deadly purpose:

Criminal or non-political prisoners were also apparently used to brutalise and terrorise the political prisoners… (Prisoner) Moses Dlamini suggests the criminals were an essential part of the terror of the early years. They were members of vicious and notorious gangs, who were 'hand-picked by the enemy from the most notorious maximum (security) prisons of South Africa to come and demoralise and humiliate us with the assistance of the uncouth, uncivilised, raw Boer warders so that we would never again dare to challenge the system of apartheid colonialism'. According to Dlamini's account, the gang members were removed from the Island in 1965. When they left there was an immediate sense of space being opened up, which permitted a 'blossoming of cultural activities throughout all the cells in the Island'.[24]

It seems odd that the government should remove such a potent source of helping to control and punish 'politicals'. Some former prisoners thought there was a reason:

> The criminals were removed because the politicals had begun to politicise them and even recruit them into their organisations. According to Neville Alexander, the state also realised the non-political prisoners helped the political prisoners to get access to newspapers, and kept them up to date with the news, despite the fact that newspapers and radios were prohibited.[25]

Nelson Mandela discusses the practice of mixing the two categories, claiming that the gangsters were put there to 'inhibit any political discussion'. Nevertheless, he tried to reach out to them:

> To counterbalance the effect of these new political allies the authorities also put a handful of common-law prisoners in our section. These men were hardened criminals, convicted of murder, rape and armed robbery. They were members of the island's notorious criminal gangs, either the Big Fives or the Twenty Eights, which terrorized other prisoners. They were brawny and surly, and their faces bore the scars of the knife fights that were common amongst gang members. Their role was to act as *agents provocateurs*, and they would attempt to push us around, take our food and inhibit any political discussions we tried to have... I saw the gang members not as rivals, but as raw material to be converted.[26]

Mandela also represented such prisoners when they made complaints about beatings and other injustices.[27]

We have seen from the example of Mlambo being buried that criminal prisoners were happy to join in abusing 'politicals'. Yet, even within the political groups in South Africa there were divisions, as there are in all protest movements. In South Africa, these were compounded by differences of tribe, which, allegedly, the prison authorities exploited by putting members of different tribes in the same accommodation. This added to the complication that political affiliation was divided along tribal lines anyway. It is claimed that this policy of division failed:

> In this particular section, the relationships were just wonderful and I made a lot of friends with both groups. And you know, in fact, [we] spent a lot of time learning each other's languages, and didn't care much about their differences.[28]

Some were not so sure. Another prisoner, Saths Cooper, believes that:

> When the sordidness of prison behaviour is examined there is little difference between the common law and political prisoners generally. Where the former are often organised into deadly rival gangs, the latter are organised into often warring political groupings.[29]

In any case, it is improbable that people who were prepared to risk their lives for their political beliefs would easily submit to the ideology of others with which they disagreed. This was inherent in the situation and can be exemplified by the confrontation between two of the giants of the struggle:

> Mandela and Mbeki represented 'polar opposites in attitudes and opinions', according to the memorandum which was sent from Robben Island to the movement in exile. The personality clash and political impasse between them lasted for several years, 'at times reaching extreme tension and bitterness'. Allegations

abounded, including one that some members were abandoning the armed struggle and another that some were fomenting racial discrimination. Mandela's status as the most senior ANC leader on the island was also called into question.[30]

A very good example of the dispute over the definition of 'political prisoner' is the argument which has always raged about the members of the Irish Republican Army, usually, but not always, convicted of manifestly violent acts. Some of the most complicated examples of the consequences of the imprisonment of 'political' prisoners are found in the tangled and tragic history of the relationship between Britain and Ireland. The focus of that history was the historic demand of Ireland for independence from Britain and the refusal of the latter to grant it. After independence was finally taken by most of Ireland in 1921, the demand by Republicans – who were mostly Catholics – for the handing over of the remaining 'six counties' (Ulster) dominated the political relationships of Britain, especially the Ulster government, and Ireland.

For the whole of the history of these relationships, people were locked up, often for extremely violent offences. An early example was a hero of the Republicans, O'Donovan Rossa, sentenced to life imprisonment in 1865 for his part in a dynamite campaign. His behaviour in prison was a symbol of what was to come. In 1870, the Devon Commission noted that no amount of punishment for offences in prison, including 'the almost continuous employment of bread-water punishment diet…and handcuffing', deterred him. Edmund du Cane, the Director of Prisons, asked him to start again, and if he behaved, he would not be punished:

> The marked and immediate effect of the few well-chosen words of Captain du Cane, accompanied by a total remission of the punishments undoubtedly incurred by the prisoner's conduct, show in well-defined contrast the influence of moral agency as against the long continued measures of coercion accompanied

with a total of more than forty days of bread and water diet spread over the period from May 1 to October, 1868.[31]

The struggle, to the outsider and to those involved, seemed unending:

> After independence in the south of Ireland, the campaign in the north continued, with imprisonment, hunger strikes and deaths. By 1971 the situation was very serious, and the response of the Government was to introduce 'internment' in August 1971. The British government then introduced a Detention of Terrorists Order. (1972) Commissioners would 'hear the cases of detainees, but would sit in private and would not be bound by rules of evidence'.[32]

All of this led to enormous resentment on the part of Catholics in the north, and in the rest of Britain and in the United States, and as a result, and, in part because of the hunger strikes being carried out by prisoners, the policy changed. In 1972, 'Special Category' was granted to Republican prisoners, and later to 'Loyalist' Protestant prisoners who were imprisoned for retaliating against what they saw as a threat to their power. In 1972, after the interminable debates about the protection of the Protestant people in the North of Ireland, the Diplock Report concluded that:

> The only hope of restoring the efficiency of criminal courts of law in Northern Ireland to deal with terrorist crimes is by using an extra-judicial process to deprive them of their ability to operate in Northern Ireland... With an easily penetrable border to the south and west the only way of doing this is to put them in detention by an executive act and to keep them confined, until they can be released without danger to the public safety and to the administration of criminal justice.[33]

It also contained proposals amounting to major changes in the law. For example:

The onus of proof as to the possession of firearms and explosives should be altered so as to require a person found in certain circumstances to prove on the balance of probability that he did not know and had no reason to suspect that arms or explosives were where they were found.[34]

This shows that the British government was admitting its failure to subdue the IRA activists through due process of law.

One important result of the 'Special Category' was that the public was told of 'terrorists' acting like prisoners of war, holding parades and generally managing their own discipline in what was supposed to be a criminal prison. In the country at large there was still no sign of peace and there followed another report, this time by Lord Gardiner. This opined that 'the introduction of Special Category Status was a serious mistake' and that 'the earliest opportunity should be taken to end the Special Category'.[35]

In the negotiations which followed, the IRA made the claim which political prisoners have made everywhere: 'They are political prisoners and any other imaginary label tagged on to them by the British government will not make the slightest difference to that very basic fact.'[36] Nevertheless, the Home Secretary announced that after 1 March 1976, there would be no Special Category for new prisoners. The situation seemed to be straightforward and was set out in a statement by the Northern Ireland Office:

Each and every prisoner has been tried under the judicial system established in Northern Ireland by Parliament. Those found guilty, after due process of law, if they are sent to prison by the courts, serve their sentences for what they are – convicted criminals.

They are not political prisoners: more than eighty have been convicted of murder or attempted member and more than eighty of explosive offences. They are members of organizations responsible for the deaths of hundreds of innocent people, the maiming of thousands more and the torture by kneecapping, of more than 600 of their own people.[37]

This change of policy was described as 'Criminalisation'. This was repeated by many politicians, many times. The response by the prisoners was dramatic. It was a controversial response amongst prisoners and their families, attracted worldwide attention, and is amongst the most unusual of protests by captives.

The prisoners who were first involved in the protest were in a prison outside Belfast originally called Long Kesh, but, in an attempt to break with an ugly past, the name was changed to The Maze. In this prison there were 'H blocks', soon to acquire legendary status. They were so called because they were two parallel blocks of cells joined by an administrative block.

The central plank of the protest was the refusal to wear prison clothing; instead they wore only a blanket, hence the phrase, 'On the blanket'. From here, the situation escalated and soon chamber pots of faeces and urine were being thrown, it is said by prisoners *and* staff, at one another. There are claims and counter-claims as to who started this. What is certain is that soon excreta were being plastered on the walls of the cells. Visitors reported that, for example, the cell: 'Was covered in excrement almost to the ceiling on all four walls. In one corner there was a pile of rotting, blue molded food and excrement.'[38] One prisoner described the maggots which soon began to appear: 'You wake up with them in your hair and your nose and your ears. You lift up the mattress and they are crawling under it.'[39]

The way the staff dealt with this was to use firemen's hoses to wash down the walls, which involved the forcible removal of the prisoners, but this had little effect because the prisoners immediately began to smear the walls again.

Amongst the indignities about which prisoners complained was searching. It is alleged that a prisoner would be dragged along by the hair and arms, being pushed into iron bars on the way – a procedure called 'trailing'. Then, a prisoner would be held and his anus inspected, sometimes with a metal detector, followed by inspection of his mouth to see if he had any contraband: surely very unpleasant procedures. Yet as one prisoner admits:

> Everything goes up your bum. The lads are circling around so that the screws don't see the priest slipping us the cigarette box. We roll up the fags in our hands and cram the tobacco into a biro casting. Then one of your mates comes up behind you and you bend down and up it goes. The lads make sure it is well up so nothing will show when the screws search us after Mass. It's amazing what fits up there – one fellow brought out three pencils that way and another hid a pen, a comb and a lighter. You don't feel it unless the casing is too long, but you do bleed all the time and sometimes pieces of flesh come off. Everyone has piles.[40]

All of this was within the context of being kept in a cell for 24 hours a day.

At first, the Republican women in Armagh Prison did not join in, since the IRA Command felt it had enough to do managing the men's protest. But in 1980 the women began their protest. Loyalist, that is Protestant, prisoners also engaged in different kinds of protest, and in 1978 some began a blanket protest.[41]

One of the most controversial, and to some deplorable, reactions of the IRA to the abolition of the Special Category was the adoption of a policy, advocated by the prisoners, of murdering prison staff. By 1980, eighteen prison staff had been murdered, including a governor, an assistant governor and a woman. In addition, the wife of one of the officers was killed.

Throughout all this period, there were allegations of torture being inflicted both inside and outside the prisons. There were visits by prominent churchmen, commissions of enquiry by government agencies and international reports by organisations such as Amnesty. The allegations were firmly made, and as equally firmly denied. The situation remained deadlocked until towards the end of the 1970s there were a number of spectacular deaths as a result of hunger strikes. Eventually, at the end of 1981, Republican prisoners were allowed to wear their own clothes.

Even though, to put it mildly, the allegations of ill-treatment were probably grounded in truth, there is a particular difficulty in sorting out fact from fiction in the treatment of Irish political prisoners. This is not confined to the events of the 1970s, but goes back many years. After the 1916 Easter Rising, a man called Gerald Boland was imprisoned. He eventually became Minister of Justice in the independent Irish government. In later years, he told Coogan:

> We weren't badly treated really, we had enough to eat, we could get in parcels and there was liberty enough in the compounds. But we made out we were being given a dog's life. Every little thing we blew up for publicity. We'd do anything for a crack at the British. We had the whole country agog with our propaganda.[42]

In one of the paradoxes which punctuate Irish history, Boland became famous as a hard-line attacker of the IRA.

One complete expression of the subtleties of the division between political and criminal prisoners can be seen in the conflict between Israel and Palestine. Although many of the Palestinian prisoners have committed violent acts, they see their activities as political: 'Perhaps more than any other implication, the use of the term "political activity" indicates the ongoing colonial confrontation in the West Bank and Gaza Strip between the Palestinians and the Israelis since their occupation in 1967.'[43] Many thousands of Palestinians have been imprisoned. Figures of course vary from time to time, and from claim to claim: 'At the end of November 2017 there were 5881 Palestinian security detainees and prisoners being held in Israeli Prison Service (IPS) facilities… another 730 Palestinians…were in IPS prisons for being in Israel illegally. The IPS classifies these Palestinians – both detainees and prisoners – criminal offenders.'[44] Another source writes: 'Since the occupation of the West Bank and the Gaza Strip in 1967, more than a quarter of the Palestinians have been imprisoned by Israel on political grounds.'[45]

Of these, hundreds have been locked up under 'administrative detention', that is, without trial. This is the same procedure as we have seen in Northern Ireland. It happened too in Tsarist Russia, where people were detained indefinitely, removed from their home ground, and all without the remotest pretence of a hearing. Some Palestinians have been imprisoned for many years. The Israeli government refuses to treat these captives as prisoners of war, which they demand, and instead describes them as 'security prisoners'. It is worth noting that the demand for prisoner of war status is much debated by international bodies and that it is a most difficult question.

Generally, in many countries, political prisoners are better treated than criminals, but in Israel it appears that they are more disadvantaged than criminals. In a chapter which *inter alia* deplores the practice of classifying all 'security' prisoners as one entity, Alon Harel writes that:

> This classification has enormous importance for prisoners. Security prisoners are deprived of many of the rights granted to non-security prisoners. For instance, section 19a denies security prisoners the right to phone conversations. Section 18 of the regulations governing security denies them the right to conjugal visits, and they also do not benefit from early release, which is often granted to other prisoners.[46]

There is frequent worldwide condemnation of a range of features of the Israeli system, such as 'administrative detention', the use of torture and especially the breaking of a rule of the Geneva Convention (Article 49) that such prisoners should be imprisoned in their own country. That Article states that: 'Individual or mass forcible transfers, as well as deportations of protected persons from occupied territory to the territory of the Occupying Power or to that of any other country, occupied or not, are prohibited, regardless of their motive.' Incidentally, with respect to Guantánamo, the United States of America is arguably also breaking a rule. The deleterious effects of this policy in Palestine are set out by one critic, claiming a parallel with the French prison at Devil's Island:

> Transferring the detainees to incarceration facilities outside of the occupied territory severs, in one fell swoop, their contacts with their community, their lawyers and their families, and uproots them from their organic environment. Such forced transfer makes fundamental rights of prisoners and detainees impractical or turns them into privileges subject to the whim of the hosting state.[47]

Sfard goes on to give a specific practical example of what this means. He relates the case of a prisoner called Hamed, who hadn't seen his mother for four years and his brothers and sisters since his arrest and conviction for involvement in murder 24 years previously. His mother was 75 and ill:

> With all the checkpoints, the fences, the monstrous bureaucracy requiring three permits – a permit from the military to enter Israel, a permit from the Civil Administration to pass through the Seam Zone, a permit from the Israeli Prison Service (IPS) to hold the specific visit, and the involvement of the General Security Service (GSS) and the Israeli Police in the process of clarifying entitlement to all these permits – the chance of Hamed's mother ever being able to visit him again, in her medical state, is very slim… (It) is like Devil's Island for the residents of Paris. A penal colony somewhere across mountains and oceans: mountains of movement prohibitions and preventions and an ocean of walls, checkpoints and a bureaucracy of segregation.[48]

The Israeli answer to such allegations is variously that such things do not happen, or that it depends upon what you mean by torture, or that it has not signed up to a particular Geneva rule.

Political prisoners are notable for the way they used the opportunity to educate themselves, but this was always linked to the political movement outside, as one Palestinian prisoner explained:

> Before being in prison, I was connected emotionally to the national struggle, but in jail I became connected to it intellectually and ideologically. It was in prison that I read the theory. Love of the homeland became more rooted for two reasons: my discussions with other people and my reading pamphlets and books.[49]

The arrangements for education by Palestinians were elaborate, and carefully organised, as they usually are for such captives:

> Perhaps the most unique achievement, the 'flagship' of the prisoners' movement at the time, was in the sphere of education. Education programmes, including general studies (history, languages, sciences) and studies of political theory and ideology, were introduced in prison through the fostering, and indeed through the enforcement, of daily schedules that allocated special time-slots for individual studies, instructed reading, group discussions of study materials, political meetings for the discussion of study materials, political meetings, the discussion of current (external and internal) affairs, and so forth. Political meetings, as well as studies of political ideology were conducted separately on the basis of organisational (factional) affiliation, whereas participation in the study of general academic subjects was voluntary and open to all ('cross-factional') and organised on the level of the cell or section.[50]

Despite the existence of 'factions', such tightly controlled structures were designed to counter the damage being done to the Palestinian people through the use of mass imprisonment. A father of four sons, all of whom had been imprisoned, said to them: 'Just as it was clear to me that every living creature eventually dies, it became evident to me that every Palestinian man would eventually be taken to prison.'[51]

Baker and Matar sum up this process:

> The term 'security threat' combines two benefits for the Israeli authorities and public opinion: it enables Palestinian prisoners to be stripped of their basic rights as diverse individuals, as they all belong to this large collective of 'threats', and simultaneously it enables the depoliticisation of their acts and the blurring of their political aims. What is common to these benefits is the rejection of the prisoners' subjectivity, both as individuals who deserve personal treatment, and as rational and essentially free beings who aspire to realise their freedom.[52]

A prisoner who became librarian to the prisoners explains that prisoners understood perfectly well the intended consequences of their imprisonment, and how any damaging effects could be countered:

> The political prisoners, from the beginning, understood the importance of the cultural side, and they understood that the prison authorities were trying to empty the Palestinian prisoner or struggler of his content; and when you empty him of his cultural content, whether a prisoner or not a prisoner, it will be easy to make him docile, to break him. Then it will be easier to fill his mind with other ideas... The prison authorities wanted to turn the prison into a cultural wasteland for us.[53]

The organisation of the prison community went beyond 'education'. The latter was just a part of a broader system which enabled the prisoners to succeed: 'in organising themselves inside Israeli prison buildings what they referred to as an "internal order/organisation/ regime" (*nitham dakhili*), which countered the imposed prison order and challenged it'.[54]

Such education did not only happen in Palestine. Political prisoners often take advantage of their captivity to improve their education. We have seen how this was done in the Apartheid prisons of South Africa. This was also done in Cuba after a failed attempt to wrest power from Batista. Mario Mencía describes what happened, quoting from letters of prisoners:

> Friend Bilito, we have organised an academy for the purpose of raising our educational level. We have named it after Abel Santamaría, in honour of that late compañero. Our subjects are philosophy, world history, political economy, mathematics, geography and languages.
>
> We have also founded a modest library, which we have named in posthumous tribute to Compañero Raúl Gómez García. It is composed mainly of books generously and patriotically donated by numerous friends. Mainly they are on political, economic, and social subjects. It also contains classics of Spanish literature.
>
> We have a very rigid class schedule, and we are all really motivated to learn. We believe that we should make the best possible use of the time we have to spend here.[55]

Mencía goes on to say that: 'The weapons were the library-two wooden book cases filled with books in the collective dormitory. The fortress was the academy, a small blackboard and the wooden tables on which they ate under the ledge in the yard.'[56]

The quintessential experiences of the political prisoner though are the same as those of the criminal. In 1940, Helen Bryan was the Executive Secretary of the Joint Anti-Fascist Refuge Committee in the United States. In 1945, she was ordered to appear before the House Committee on Un-American Activities and it was demanded that she produce records of the organisation. She refused because she believed that such exposure would endanger people. She was cited for Contempt of Congress, and after several legal procedures was sent to prison for three months. In 1950, she began her sentence in the sole federal prison for Women in Anderson, Virginia, which has often been mentioned in this book. Her experiences were those of the criminal prisoners. The differences with her, and with most political prisoners' experience, are that she was middle class, had no experience of the Criminal Justice system, was fascinated by what she learned and reflected on it. Thus, like all newcomers, she took stock of her new surrounding:

> I sat down on the bed... The room was about nine feet long and six feet wide. At the right of the door was the basin, next to it, the toilet, then the bed which seemed quite comfortable. Underneath the window was the radiator and at the left of the window was one small straight-backed chair on which were magazines. Fresh towels hung over the basin, soap and a drinking cup were on it. This, then, constituted my home for the next two weeks.
>
> The key turned in the lock, and I jumped as though I had been shot.[57]

When a prison contains political prisoners, whether or not the law regards them as such or as 'prisoners of war', a complicated triangle exists. Political prisoners suffer at the hands of two opposing and contradictory forces in that triangle: the staff and the 'criminal' prisoners. It is only rarely that an effort is made by the authorities to separate the two categories of captive, since systems do not generally agree to such prisoners self-definition. This *can* happen, as in one Indian experience:

> Every effort was made to keep political prisoners and convicts apart. This was more easily done in the men's prisons as certain gaols were reserved only for politicals. But it was not so easy in the women's gaols as there were not such large numbers of us.[58]

This policy, no doubt based in this case upon the wish to prevent the spread of insidious ideas, is rare. This is partly because it is not very practical, but also because the authorities and the frontline staff believe that the politicals *are* criminals. The distaste on the part of gaolers for captive politicals is commonplace, as in this case from India, where Hutheesing observes that: 'The wardresses were of the very worst type and were generally rude and insulting to all the politicals.'[59] Or, as in this experience of Wafa Albis, a Palestinian prisoner in an Israeli gaol:

> One of the torture methods used against me was putting me in with criminal female Israeli prisoners. They were fat and had no manners. They tried to distress me by going half-naked. When one of them asked for a cigarette and didn't get it, she tried to commit suicide by cutting her vein. They always stayed up until dawn, disco dancing and watching pornographic channels…if I had slept, they might have attempted to kill me. I actually heard two of them planning to strangle me with a TV cable. Had I not stood up and attacked one of them harshly, I might be dead now. For that, I was sent to solitary confinement.[60]

The outside observer must be left wondering if there is any control at all in Israeli prisons.

Women, of course, as is well documented, are insulted and abused sexually in Israeli prisons: 'Physically, Palestinian female prisoners are also subject to all forms of torture during interrogation, including beating, shaking, suspension, segregation and forced nakedness.'[61]

Some had even worse experiences:

> Rasmiya Odeh's tale of rape was strongly documented by defence lawyer Felicia Langer and the London *Sunday Times* report of June 19, 1977 which concluded that 'torture of Arab prisoners is so widespread and systematic that it cannot be dismissed as "rough cops" exceeding orders. It appears to be sanctioned as deliberate policy.'
>
> In Rasmiya Odeh's case, her father was brought to prison and was ordered to rape his daughter. When he refused, prison officials forced a stick into Rasmiya's vagina and left her to bleed, while her father lay unconscious on the floor.[62]

So, one of the main divisions in captivity is between the political and the criminal prisoners. This, and the concomitant suffering by the former, is a constant theme in prison writing. The best, but by no means exclusive, examples can be seen in those regimes where there were legions of political prisoners: Nazi Germany and Soviet Russia. In the latter, under Stalin after the Second World War, Russian prisoners of war regarded by the regime as politically unsound because they had been captured: 'passed through the prisons of the Soviet Union in vast dense shoals like ocean herring'.[63]

In Buchenwald, where there were so many rivalries between prison groups, there was a classic division between the politicals and the criminals. The tolerant Pierre d'Harcourt found that he felt disgust about the behaviour of the criminals:

> I began to hate my fellow countrymen as a group almost more than I hated the SS...we saw so little of the SS... It so happened that the swindlers, thieves and traitors were on top, and spoke and acted for all the French in camp. They managed everything from the distribution of Red Cross parcels and mail to the rigging of transport rolls, and did so only out of self-interest. How many of the fine workers for the Resistance movement were sent off to be trodden to death in a cattle truck, so that some pimp from a Paris night-club might live?[64]

Dietrich Bonhoeffer, like d'Harcourt, was wary when it came to dealing with 'criminal' prisoners. During an air raid: 'one has to be cautious in opening the cell doors of the worst criminals, for you never know when they will hit you on the head with the leg of a chair and try to make a getaway'.[65]

Menachem Begin in the Russian Gulag was warned very early by a guard how he could expect to be treated by the *Urki*. The guard asked him what clothing he had brought with him. Begin lists the items of clothing, which were of good quality. The guard warned him: 'They'll take them away from you.'[66] Begin then tells how he was in a group of some eight hundred prisoners who were put on board a ship to be moved to a work station. They were a mixture of politicals and *Urki*. The journey was horrific, but:

The worst thing of all was the *Urki* domination in the floating communal dungeon. In the camp, too, the *Urki* had the upper hand… But, below deck in the *Etap* ship, the last barrier in the way of *Urki* domination fell away: rule by criminals without restraint, absolute rule.[67]

In modern China, the same dynamic appears, and, like so many aspects of life in China, is defended as a means of 'reformation':

PRC political prisoners have often been singled out for such physical abuse at the hands of ordinary criminal inmates. Regardless of the prohibitions that appear in camp cadre manuals and legal handbooks, orchestrated inmate violence has all too often been considered an acceptable and even lauded form of discipline. Activist prisoners' beating of another inmate at the behest of a cadre has often been taken as an expression of their 'good attitude' and 'positive acceptance of remoulding'.[68]

Solzhenitsyn describes the realisation, as generations of politicals have, that the criminals are the principal threat: you suppose that your 'oppressors' are on the other side of the bars. But:

Suddenly you lift your eyes to the square recess in the middle bunk, to that one and only heaven above you, and up there you see three or four – oh no, not faces! … You see cruel, loathsome snouts up there, wearing expressions of greed and mockery. Each of them looks at you like a spider gloating over a fly. Their web is that grating which imprisons you – and you have been had![69]

They are 'strange gorilloids'.[70]

If there are thieves in a cattle car…they take the best places, as is traditional – on the upper bunks by the window. That's in summer. So we can guess where their places are in winter. Next to the stove, of course, in a tight ring around the stove…the thieves not only took all the *suckers'* warm things away from them and put them on, but didn't even hesitate to take their *footcloths* out of their shoes and wind them around their own feet… It was somewhat worse with food – the thieves took charge of the whole ration for the car and then kept the best for themselves along with whatever else they needed.[71]

We have often seen that the wonder might be whether or not the staff have *any* control over what goes on. We have seen too that the staff usually have little sympathy with the politics of their captives, but in some cases the situation is, in any case, uncontrollable.

Every kind of justification is offered for the abrogation of care for political captives and their brutal treatment by criminals. In China, it helps 'remoulding'; in Russia, this 'policy' was explained by 'Soviet propagandists' as some kind of an exercise in democracy: 'Prisoners are given "internal economy" in the Soviet Union. They arrange their affairs amongst themselves. The authorities only supervise the process of their education towards lives of honest labour.'[72] This is just one example of the skill governments have in the use of words to conceal what is happening to captives.

However, as we have seen in our discussion about captives in authority, in the battle for power the politicals sometimes win. They did in Buchenwald, and they did when they were imprisoned in South Africa under the Apartheid regime. Even here, 'prisoner power' is not monolithic. There are hierarchies which, in the case of political prisoners, are formal. On Robben Island, those who were members of the African National Congress had different political beliefs from those who belonged to the Pan African Congress. The latter were, Mandela explains, for example, 'unashamedly anti-communist and anti-Indian'[73] and they believed that 'negotiations with the authorities were a betrayal'.[74] Mandela spent a lot of his time trying to handle the power struggle between these two and other political groups. There was, for example, argument about who should serve on a body called the 'High Organ', which 'made decisions about such matters as prisoners' complaints, strikes, mail, food – all the day-to-day concerns of prison life'.[75] But such organisations were not only divided along political lines, they were split over what is supreme in Africa: tribal loyalty. Thus, there was objection to the fact that the Xhosa tribe dominated the High Organ. Mandela, who was himself Xhosa, countered this by saying, "'How can you accuse me of discrimination? We are one people."They seemed satisfied by that.'[76]

If it were that simple, life in prison would be a good deal more placid, since, as we have seen, the people who are locked up for manifest, or what they believe to be manifest, political causes are the captives most likely to be recalcitrant because of the sacrifices they have made for their 'cause'. They know perfectly well what they were doing and where it might lead, and no amount of 're-education' is likely to change them. Because of what they are, they naturally present the staff with considerable problems of control and management.

Notes

1. For an account of her life based on her diaries see Kaneko, Fumiko *The Prison Memoirs of a Japanese Woman.*
2. Hubbell *op. cit.* p.54.
3. Bourke, Seán. *The Springing of George Blake.* p.18.
4. Schwan *op. cit.* p.153.
5. Lytton *op. cit.* p.61.
6. Bone *op. cit.* p.31.
7. Mencía *op. cit.* p.69.
8. *Ibid.*
9. Davis, Angela. 'Lessons from Attica to Soledad.' p.43.
10. Hawkins *op. cit.* p.75.
11. New York State Special Commission on Attica. *Attica: The Official Report of the New York State Special Commission on Attica.* p.80.
12. *Ibid.* p.93.
13. Knight *op. cit.* p.68.
14. *Ibid.* p.170.
15. *Ibid.* pp.171–172.
16. *Ibid.* p.172.
17. *Ibid.* p.6.
18. Giammanco, Introduction to Knight *op. cit.* pp.13–14 quoting H. Rap Brown.
19. *Ibid.* p.15.
20. Cleaver, Eldridge. *Soul on Ice.* pp.13–14, quoted Giammanco in Knight *op. cit.* p.19.

21. Charles W. Baker in Knight *op. cit.* pp.37–38.
22. Deacon *op. cit.* pp.105–106.
23. *Ibid.* pp.124–125.
24. *Ibid.* p.98.
25. *Ibid.* pp.100–101.
26. Mandela *op. cit.* p.483.
27. *Ibid.* pp.483ff.
28. *Ibid.* p.100.
29. *Ibid.* p.143.
30. *Ibid.* p.125.
31. Coogan *op. cit.* pp.29–30.
32. *Ibid.* p.56.
33. *Ibid.* p.67.
34. Quoted *ibid.* p.68.
35. *Ibid.* p.71.
36. *Ibid.* pp.173–174.
37. *Ibid.*
38. *Ibid.* p.223.
39. *Ibid.* p.19.
40. *Ibid.* p.15.
41. *Ibid.* p.195.
42. *Ibid.* p.33.
43. Nashif *op. cit.* p.19.
44. This information is supplied by the Israeli Information Center for Human Rights in the Occupied Territories. www.btselem.org/statistics/detainees_and_prisoners
45. Nashif *op. cit.* Introduction.
46. Alon, Harel. 'Who is a Security Prisoner and Why? An Examination of the Legality of Prison Regulations Governing Security Prisoners' in Abeer Baker and Anat Matar (eds) *Threat.* p.37.
47. Sfard, Michael. 'Devil's Island: The Transfer of Palestinian Detainees into Prisons within Israel' in Baker and Matar *op. cit.* p.189.
48. *Ibid.* p.188.
49. Rosenfeld, Maya. 'The Centrality of the Prisoners' Movement to the Palestinian Occupation: A Historical Perspective' in Baker and Matar *op. cit.* p.7.
50. *Ibid.* p.11.
51. *Ibid.* p.5.
52. Preface to Baker and Matar *op. cit.* p.ix.
53. Nashif *op. cit.* p.83.
54. Rosenfeld *op. cit.* p.7.
55. Mencía *op. cit.* p.37.
56. *Ibid.*
57. Bryan *op. cit.* p.12.
58. Hutheesing *op. cit.* p.112.

59. *Ibid.* p.117.
60. Albis, Wafa *op. cit.* pp.108–109.
61. Nahla, Abdo. 'Palestinian Women Political Prisoners and the Israeli State' in Baker and Matar *op. cit.* p.63.
62. *Ibid.* p.65.
63. Solzhenitsyn *op. cit.* p.237.
64. d'Harcourt *op. cit.* p.156.
65. Bonhoeffer *op. cit.* p.47.
66. Begin *op. cit.* pp.152.
67. *Ibid.* p.195.
68. Williams and Wu *op. cit.* pp.126–127.
69. Solzhenitsyn *op. cit.* p.501.
70. *Ibid.*
71. *Ibid.* p.571.
72. Begin *op. cit.* p.203.
73. Mandela *op. cit.* p.523.
74. *Ibid.* p.524.
75. *Ibid.* p.525.
76. *Ibid.* p.526.

— 11 —

On Freedom

There will come that moment, except rarely, when captivity must end. This may be at a point which the captive is able to anticipate or one which is sudden, as in release from a prisoner of war camp or discharge from a psychiatric hospital. By the time they are released, captives will have become accustomed to the culture of the institution, are not likely to have kept up with the 'feel' of society outside (although they may have kept abreast of the facts about what has been happening) and there is consequentially a major problem of trying, once again, to forget one culture and to learn, or more correctly, relearn, another.

Whatever the circumstances, the individual is faced with problems which many find as great as the experience of imprisonment itself. There is likely to be joy, of course. Helen Bryan, on the prospect of release from her United States federal prison was excited. Before her discharge she was handed her own clothes:

Carrying the plain brown carton that was full of magic for me, I hurried out of the building. How light the carton felt! How heavenly, how delicious, how utterly incredible it was to be carrying my own clothes. As I walked along the road, my heart was shouting, shouting to the dull grey skies, shouting to each building as I passed, shouting loud enough for the free world to hear, 'Two more weeks and I will be gone. Gone for ever and for ever.' And in that short five-minute walk from the building to our cottage those imaginary, but ever-present walls splintered into a thousand pieces.[1]

Even after, or perhaps because of, a very long sentence, a prisoner of the Israelis could still feel excited. As often happens, there is talk of prison being like a grave:

> I arrange my things. I touch my clothes and case, and I collect my remaining memories, which have become part of me and refuse to leave. Despite the breezes of freedom, I touch my face and count the wrinkles that increased every year in prison... I turn back to my case and recall the past, 25 years ago.[2] They are 25 years out of my life. Today I leave my grave and return to life. Prison was as bad as death,[3] ... Relief is finally in sight, Alaa'. Tomorrow, I will sit beside my parents' graves, complain of my pain, and share the happiness of freedom and victory.[4]

Captives express a number of worries about facing the world again. These include the sudden absence of control by others over almost every move, physical and mental, in what ways the world will have changed, and what the attitude of people outside will be to people who have disappeared and are now back. All of this is possibly preceded by that fairly recent phenomenon of mental torture: the parole system.

It is common now in many penal systems to operate a parole system. This means that if the authorities believe a prisoner has variously reformed, presents no likelihood of reoffending and is not a danger to the public, then that prisoner may be released early. This is subject to the condition that if any subsequent behaviour breaches the condition of release, then the prisoner can be recalled and must serve out any unexpired period of the sentence. In England, recall for a 'lifer' can be devastating and can mean another very long period behind bars.

It is a system which ostensibly has virtue. It means, obviously enough, that the pain of imprisonment is reduced, the state saves money and the individual can return to a normal life. Unfortunately, it is a system which creates enormous problems, notably for the prisoner. The main difficulty is the development of a coherent set of criteria for early release. Decisions are based on reports from a wide variety of people who have to make judgements about 'behaviour' which are coloured by views which can, in the nature of things, be idiosyncratic. This is true of any stages in the career of a prisoner. Erwin James discusses the case of a friend who was being considered:

> The recommendation after his last review, twenty months earlier, was that he should be transferred to an open prison. But before the transfer could take place he had received a visit from an outside probation officer. The visit lasted no more than fifteen minutes, but later the officer wrote a damning report based on the interview, using words and phrases which effectively branded Felix as an incurable criminal. This led to an intervention by the prison psychologist who ordered that Felix should partake in further offending-behaviour work 'just to be on the safe side'. Felix's lawyer then commissioned a counter report from an independent psychologist.[5]

This led to extensive arguments between the prisoner and the authorities, which was bound to create considerable and permanent ill will. Parole is a bureaucratic process, and naturally there are administrative mistakes. James recounts one episode in which a prisoner's:

> most important parole hearing so far was postponed. Two months, they said. 'There's a new system in place,' explained the governor. 'It's having teething troubles.' In May it was delayed again. 'Your file has been misplaced,' he was told, 'but it's been located. Your review will now take place in June.' The board should have sat a couple of days ago. Except a couple of days

earlier he received a memo, 'Due to unforeseen circumstances your parole hearing has been postponed for fourteen days.'[6]

Peter Thompson, before leaving Broadmoor, a famous British 'special' hospital for those convicted of crime and who are mentally ill, recounts his experience with the Mental Health Tribunal, which was an equivalent to the Parole Board. This was the body which could authorise a patient's release:

> At Broadmoor, a Tribunal would very rarely wish to discharge a patient against the opinion of the doctors concerned; but there are a fair number of cases where they would like to recommend a transfer, but are powerless to do this. The most they can do is unofficially to urge the responsible medical officer to consider a transfer in the near future. The purpose of the Tribunal is therefore largely defeated in such cases.[7]

Having experienced rejection of his own applications and those of other patients on several occasions, it is not surprising that Thompson's summary is that: 'It would not be exaggerating to say that the Tribunal system is apparently designed to create the maximum possible distress and sense of grievance on the part of the patient.'[8]

With or without the torment of parole hearings, anxiety is universal amongst those leaving captivity. And the fear of having to manage their own affairs strikes them some time before they leave. Early in her captivity, Phoebe Willetts observed it. Although she served only a short sentence, the prospect of release was of great concern. It began in Holloway early in her captivity. It was there:

> I had my first experience of gate fever. I had been queuing for a meal when I noticed someone crying to herself quietly in the corner. I asked the woman next to me if the weeper had had bad news from home.
>
> 'No,' was the reply, 'it is only that she is going home next week.'

'Oh,' I said innocently, 'that's all right if she is only crying for joy.'

'No,' said my informant in a hesitant voice, as if she found it difficult to explain. 'It isn't exactly joy, it's gate fever.'

As the conversation continued I gathered that the weeping woman had a good husband and children anxiously awaiting her return, and had looked forward for what had seemed so very long, to the day of return. Now that it was nearly upon her, she was frightened. Women who had been there long and had seen many people come and go, understood. Some people cried, some people behaved differently or oddly in their last week; everyone understood, it was just gate fever, that queer, inexplicable, indescribable disease that would hit all alike; that dread feeling that would come to all of us one day, the fear of life, like the fear of death; the fear of the unknown and the half-remembered world outside.[9]

Margaret Turner also notices how worried prisoners are as the time arrives to leave:

I have seen other prisoners just before their release get just as unhappy and it is very sad to think that they have got to such a stage that they don't want to face life outside. I suppose sometimes their tears are for the friends they are leaving behind, but the main trouble I think is that they feel unfit to cope with the problems waiting for them in ordinary life. In here they are looked after like very naughty children and never allowed to make any decisions for themselves and never allowed to go anywhere without an escort. Prisoners get to the state when they are really terrified of crossing the road by themselves and they become quite shy of mixing with ordinary company.[10]

Frank Norman, an entirely different kind of prisoner, echoes the concerns which are common but serious:

To tell the truth after the first year I didn't worry about it very much, in fact when it came near to the time I was to be let go I was a little sory and also scared. For as soon as I was free I had to find my own food, my own clothes and my own place to sleep and find my rent every week just as I had to before I went inside…[11]

I went through the first gate, this was the same gate I went through every morning but this time it was different this was the last time the very last time.

No more worries about getting nicked.

No more worries about rotten grub.

No more worries about being caged up.

All I had to worry about now was how I was going to stay out.

Where was I going to live?

Where was I going to sleep tonight?

Had I still got any friends?

Would I go screwing today the very first day that I got out?

What was I going to do, No where to go, and dead skint.[12]

Regaining control of your own movements is difficult and making even simple decisions after what may be years of captivity is a major challenge. In the especially controlling political situation in China:

Zhang has become so habituated to following the cadres' orders in his prison camp that he is subconsciously 'unaccustomed to the lack of control and berating by camp cadres following his release: I felt that I still needed to follow someone who controlled and led me'.[13]

Josie O'Dwyer, a female ex-prisoner in England, recognises just how dependent prisoners become:

Everybody talked big about 'when I get out of here' even though they knew damn well that they were going to come back because there was nothing for them out there anyway. But they had to talk like that; you had to give this sort of talk even though you knew that when it came to it you didn't actually want to go! You could never admit to *that*; that was the hardest thing to admit, that you had got to the stage where you actually like it there! What was the point of fighting, what was the point of fucking the system, singing anti-screw songs, stumping up and down glaring at them, using up all that energy...if you actually liked it there? No one could make sense of that, so no one ever admitted it.[14]

She goes on to say that she got a lodging near the prison, and she saw the prison officers all the time:

But I missed the attention. They were there but I had no claim on their attention any more. I couldn't handle that situation so I moved away. It was probably just as well that I did because I don't think I could have lasted much longer without doing something to get myself back in. I would have been back in Holloway, and with the total intent of being there.[15]

Across the other side of the world, a Gulag prisoner notes the same feeling: 'Knew a woman who actually did not want to leave her barracks: "The thing is that I – I can't face living outside. I want to stay in camp" she told her friends.'[16]

This feeling is expressed extremely well, with a Russian touch, that is to say the tradition of neighbourly spying, by Gustav Herling:

After many years of life in the camp the average prisoner becomes so unaccustomed to the idea of liberty that he begins to dread the prospect of having to live again – 'at liberty' – in a state of unceasing watchfulness, followed and spied on by friends, relatives and colleagues, exposed to suspicion by the very fact that he has just finished a prison sentence. The camp too, has to some extent become his second life; he is familiar with its laws and customs, he moves freely about the zone and knows how to avoid danger; the years behind barbed wire have blunted his imagination.[17]

The fear of change in the outside world is reinforced by the power of the institutional process. Despite the deprivation and the horror of being locked up, some people want to stay or go back. This is especially the case if the captive is mentally ill. The modern policy in Britain of releasing long-term psychiatric patients, often without proper support, is a cruelty derived from the failure to understand the ill effect of what should be a joyful experience: release. In an example of the parallels between prison and psychiatric hospital, Jeremy Bryan, a patient, is apprehensive:

So here, among the unstable, you feel safe: and your unaccustomed sense of safeness can easily induce an apathy, if not a hostility towards the idea of ever being discharged from it. Especially since cures seem to take so long; if, in fact they can be achieved at all. Why sweat out dozens of demoralising interviews with the psychiatrist in the dim hope of a discharge into an uncertain world of normalcy, when you can relax, drifting apathetically in the ward's soothing tide of fellow-sickness, and, forever undischarged, feel quite safe where you are?[18]

Peter Thompson was another psychiatric patient, in his case in Broadmoor, where he spent four years. He begins his account with his feelings on release:

The massive gates closed behind me, and I stood there in my ill-fitting suit, various bags, boxes and cases all around me, and more scared than I would have admitted by the sheer spaciousness of the outside world. I felt my inside pocket. The wallet was there, containing ten one pound notes provided by a thoughtful charity

– my total financial resources. After four years in Broadmoor I was free at last. I had fought and fought for my discharge, but now that it had actually happened I could hardly resist the urge to turn round and hammer on the gates to be let in again.

I had relied heavily on that strange institution that loomed behind me, and now, with what seemed indecent haste, the prop was about to disappear. Through years of mental strain and breakdown this community of the confused had shielded me from the harsh realities of a world which had broken me – or, perhaps, on which I had broken myself. Now that world lay before me again, and I was going to face the same sort of pressures and strains that had wrecked me before.[19]

He goes so far as to say that at one point he 'asked Broadmoor to take me back, but my request was turned down'.[20]

Then there is an overwhelming feeling that society has passed them by and forgotten them. In the nineteenth century, because of their opposition to the rule of the Tsars, many Poles were sent to Siberia. When they returned to Poland:

They often found themselves stranded and penniless in a land that had moved on and left them behind... Reaching home prematurely aged not only in body but in mind, former exiles would shuffle about their former towns and villages as representatives of a bygone era.[21]

Primo Levi describes the feelings he had when he was released from Auschwitz. He wonders what has been happening while he has been locked away. He has no idea about what might have happened in his home area:

Leonardo and I remained lost in a silence crowded with memories. Of 650, our number when we had left, three of us were returning. And how much had we lost in those twenty months? What should we find at home? How much of ourselves had been eroded, extinguished? Were we returning richer or poorer, stronger or emptier? We did not know; but we knew that on the thresholds of our homes, for good or evil, a trial awaited us, and we anticipated it with fear. We felt in our veins the poison of Auschwitz, flowing together with our thin blood; where should we find the strength to live our lives again, to break down the barriers, the brushwood which grows up spontaneously in all absences, around every deserted house, every empty refuge? Soon, tomorrow, we should have to give battle, against enemies still unknown, outside ourselves and inside; with what weapons, what energies, what willpower? We felt the weight of centuries on our shoulders, we felt oppressed by a year of ferocious memories; we felt emptied and defenceless.[22]

In the turmoil of post-war Europe after 1945, the world had certainly changed, and captives often had no idea what had been going on. Hanns Lilje gets the news that the Americans have arrived:

It is true, I am not glad. At least not in the obvious, almost simple way that my yelling and wildly gesticulating companion is. I immediately realise that for most of them a very toilsome way back to life is now beginning – wearisome formalities until we can really walk as free men again, the search for families, the question of where my home is now to be.[23]

Some, though, claim that there are advantages as well as manifest disadvantages in trying to integrate the experience of captivity with freedom. Braddon believes that a returning captive has definite advantages:

To the returning prisoner-of-war there must always be many advantages stemming from captivity as he starts civilian life again. For one thing he has criteria of black experiences compared with which the average hardship of normal life will seem trivial... For another, having experienced the nadir of personal freedom and his right to express himself, he will always be possessed of a tremendous incentive either to succeed in life or to enjoy as it is… He will return with a prison camp education behind him more valuable probably, and based on a curriculum infinitely wider certainly, than any University could give him… He will know himself as deeply and as pitilessly as could any psychiatrist or analyst… But he will find, to his consternation that the great and immutable laws of the code that protected and kept him alive in captivity no longer prevail in freedom.[24]

He goes on to say that the former prisoner will want to know why this code, which was so effective in the 'squalor and privation of the camp', cannot be applied outside. 'Free society will not answer him because it will not know what he is talking about':

He will not be able to solve the problem for himself because both the principles of his captivity and the blessed pre-war world he committed to memory as a captive are sacrosanct and not even to be criticised, still less modified.[25]

In his desperate attempts not to lose the memory of the freedom he once had, the prisoner-of-war who was captured in 1940, by 1945 had often sealed himself inescapably in a mental capsule of the thirties. For him, in 1945, the world was and would become again the world of the thirties: yet, lamentably for his peace of mind, to the rest of the world the thirties had been as transient as the twenties and all that mattered now was the latest life of 1945.[26]

Colin Franklin writes vividly about his stay in a tuberculosis hospital. While there, he met a man who had been in a Japanese prisoner of war camp. This man summed up his feeling of alienation: 'He said he had learnt to see what people were really like, and that the way they behaved in freedom no longer convinced him or appeared interesting.'[27]

The actual experience of dealing with society when the prisoner is released varies from miserable to the felicitous. Erwin James, a lifer, has been moved to minimum security and has begun work in the community:

> There have been days during my gradual reintroduction to society when I have found myself overwhelmed. The train journey which left me drenched in sweat after forty minutes of such intense self-consciousness that at one time I thought I was going to have an out-of-body experience; the time I hovered for half an hour outside a barber's shop desperate for my first civilised haircut in nearly eighteen years, but ultimately too nervous to enter for fear of being unable to manage friendly chit-chat convincingly.

Erwin James was exceptionally fortunate. Being employed outside the prison on a release preparation scheme was a pleasant experience:

> It helps that the office where I work as an information processor is staffed by people who have been prepared to welcome me as a colleague… Yet not a single day has passed when I have not been made to feel like a valuable member of the team.[28]

During his first appraisal at work, James tried to express his thanks, to which his manager replied simply: 'You work well and we're lucky to have you':

> There it was again: that total acceptance of me for who I am and what I can bring to the table – no more, no less… If anyone was ever to ask me, 'What aspect of your imprisonment has had the most influence on the way you developed while inside?,' my answer would be unequivocal. 'Acceptance.'[29]

Zeno, after a life sentence, is going out for the day for a job interview prior to release:

So the day has come at last...where is the wild excitement, the bursting chest, the feeling of exhilaration? Why does the realisation that I am to be free again for a few hours have no pronounced effect on me? ... Already I am beginning to wish myself back in Wormwood Scrubs.

He reflects on the first ten months of freedom and concludes that it:

is like facing a succession of Himalayan peaks. I don't know how to surmount them. Each one looms in front of me as did the years of my imprisonment, as some impossible, incalculable time.

There is something else which worries me desperately, but has little to do with my plans for the future. It is that if the Home Secretary were to recall me to prison tomorrow, I should feel no great sorrow or disappointment.[30]

Brian Stratton, leaving his English prison, was more phlegmatic: 'I smoked a roll-up and lay thinking: well, this is it. I'm out of this piss-hole today and the troubles are about to start.'[31] This last phrase shows that Stratton knew from experience that leaving prison would not be easy. It is above all an anxious time. Will things outside have changed much?

And when freedom happens, the shock is that the world has indeed changed:

With freedom, everything changes, and the ex-prisoner has to start growing up all over again. The world will have moved on in his absence. As Stavert found, even after 6 months, 'people' – meaning people who had not been in captivity – seemed to have changed. Some prisoners may even experience a feeling of reluctance when it comes to leaving their camp and returning to the world... Sidney Sheldrick was overcome with a feeling of sadness when he learned that the war was over and he would be going home.[32]

It really was very difficult to talk. We didn't know if we had changed, or how: we certainly didn't know how we seemed to others; and it would have been a poor response to the welcome we received to explain that we were subtly offended by it all, or at least made uneasy. The reason, I think, is that the welcome was – probably inevitably – directed to a stock notion of what a prisoner is; no one seemed to understand the real us. We weren't, as people thought, coming back from a long period of not-being, which was the usual mental picture of our lot that we met; actually, something important was ending for us, and until that happened, nothing else could begin: we were lost, because we had suddenly been deprived of the support of a society whose way of life was not less deeply imbedded in us because it had not initially been of our choosing, and into which we had for three and a half years put so much of ourselves that, for the time being, we didn't have much to spare for the society that had been restored to us.[33]

Ian Watt, another prisoner who survived the Burma Railway, was equally apprehensive.[34] As a result, Watt was oddly restrained upon hearing the news that Japan had surrendered: 'We were excited, sociable, but not, I think, really happy. Who knew what it would be like at home now? Would we be welcome? Had we changed? Did we smell?'[35]

Jim Quillen, having spent many years on Alcatraz, the island prison off California, agrees:

It is very difficult to describe the fear that lies hidden in the minds of those who have been in prison. It is an insidious threat that can suddenly rise to the surface and explode like an overlooked time bomb. It can be triggered by a word, a glance, a gesture, or just the close proximity of a stranger. This sudden eruption can toss you into a sea of self-doubt and uncertainty, and leave you struggling against the feeling of being somehow obviously marked out for the public to see as a criminal and an undesirable.

I knew this fear was just a figment of my imagination, yet it was real to me. The unfortunate part is that one cannot communicate these feeling to another, regardless of how close the relationship might be.[36]

Peter Wildeblood was somewhat bewildered, as well as apprehensive, in his first steps of freedom. His difficulties were compounded by the fact that his case had received national publicity, and his trial and that of the others involved attracted scorn and created a series of ribald jokes. His release was equally newsworthy:

> Then I walked out through the gate. I had never really believed that this would be the end, or even the beginning of a new chapter… For the first few days, I thought that people were looking at me; then I realised that I was flattering myself. I had forgotten that free men and women looked at each other in this way.[37]

A constant worry, especially for the 'criminal' prisoner, is possible hostility from former friends or colleagues. But Wildeblood's fears about how people would behave were not realised:

> When I went to the country to stay with my mother and father, I thought that meeting their friends was going to be the worst ordeal of all. There is probably no group of people more conservative, or less likely to understand a predicament like mine, than the middle-aged inhabitants of a small country town… I was surprised and moved to discover that I was quite wrong. Although most of them avoided any discussion of the case, they welcomed me back as though nothing had happened.[38]

Others were not so lucky. For many who have been released, these fears of rejection are not a fantasy. In the 1920s, there was much concern at the high rate of parole failure amongst women prisoners leaving Joliet Prison in the United States. The reforming Superintendent,

Elinor Rulien, observed correctly that: 'Public opinion is not kind to a woman who has made a mistake and been convicted.'[39] A former prisoner, Delores Sanders, went home to a small town, but after less than six months she had broken her parole: 'I went straight as long as I could but you know when you have a step-father and you are told you are an ex-convict, what's the use of trying to make good in a place like that'? She adds that 'she would rather be in prison than "go back as an ex-convict where everybody has known me since I was a young girl".'[40]

An English ex-prisoner, Jenny Hicks, is another who met the same kind of hostility:

> Yet despite my good fortune, my education and my will to continue with the creative reconstruction of my life along feminist and socialist lines, my life as an ex-prisoner has been one long obstacle race past prejudice, suspicion, bureaucratic indifference and condescension – often from those very organisations whose whole *raison d'etre* is supposed to be rooted in ex-prisoners' welfare.[41]

Another English prisoner in the last stages of his sentence, and under a scheme whereby he can go out to work in the community, tells how crudely he was treated. He is talking to a fellow prisoner about an application he has made for a job:

> 'Hello?' said a more formal voice moments later.
>
> 'Hello,' said Tam again. 'About the job…'
>
> 'OK, I'll just take some details.'
>
> 'I have to tell you first though,' said Tam, 'I'm still a serving prisoner. But I'm allowed to work outside. It's a resettlement prison…'
>
> 'That's not a problem,' said the formal voice. 'May I ask the date of your conviction?'
>
> But the question was asked too soon and Tam was obliged to answer.

'Erm…1979.'

After a pause, the formal voice said, 'Was that another sentence?'

'No,' said Tam, 'it's the same one.'

There was another pause, longer this time.

'Hello?' said Tam. Then again, 'Hello? Hello?'

Then he heard the gentle click of a handset being replaced. But it didn't put him off. He's had so many knock-backs during his epic prison sentence that the rebuff hardly registered on his personal scale of disappointments. And there were more to come.[42]

Such rejection is a common experience. In Norway, there is a prison sentence called 'preventive detention'. It is awarded to persistent offenders and is indeterminate. Prisoners believe that people in the free society regard those who have served such a sentence with trepidation:

The feeling of being 'looked at' after release is pronounced. There is a feeling that secrecy with regard to background is difficult to maintain in the long run. Furthermore, inmates frequently claim that members of law-abiding society invariably consider a sentence to preventive detention as a sign of the most serious criminal behaviour. The following excerpt from an interview is typical:

I'm leaving on Saturday. After the stay here I feel like giving up everything. I can't get further down after this. You can't get further down than being subjected to preventive detention… When they learn where you come from, they sort of avoid you and don't want to work with you, and that's a terrible pressure.[43]

A well-known New Zealand politician, John Alexander Lee, who as a young man had experience of reformatory life, expressed universal experience when he said to another former criminal, Ward McNally:

Men like you and me should never expect life to run smoothly. We are open targets for anyone who wants to shoot us down. My success in life has been built upon the fact that I have never worked for a boss. I'm too individualistic for one thing. For another, like you, I would have been too easily unseated. Prison backgrounds can never be lived down. People with axes to grind can defeat you because, as a former criminal, you're at a tremendous disadvantage. I realised that many years ago. But even knowing that I was still made to eat dirt.[44]

Perhaps it can be especially difficult for the well-known or famous person leaving captivity, as we saw in the case of Peter Wildeblood. The aristocratic Lord Nevill was conscious of this:

I was under no illusions when I came out of prison in November 1901. I knew that I had yet to bear what is by no means the lightest part of the punishment to a man having once been in the position that I had been in – the loss of friends, and the cold contempt of those who had once been among my most intimate acquaintances. I therefore made up my mind that the only thing to do was to face the world with eyes straight to the front, looking neither to the right nor to the left, but leaving it to everyone who might wish to recognise me to make the first advance.[45]

Another ex-prisoner from a stable background, Walter Musgrave, is equally worried about release. He is standing at Waterloo Station:

For several minutes I stood watching the crowds, the bookstalls, the tobacco kiosks, the fruit stalls, and the barrows of luggage labelled Cunard, Union Castle, Ellerman. I felt as though I had opened my own coffin and walked out to find the world not much changed. But I was alone, friendless. I wanted to talk to somebody.[46]

Taki, who was the son of a millionaire Greek, possessed of seemingly boundless self-confidence, though he had expected to encounter few problems, nevertheless shared some common emotions:

> An extremely restless night. By this time tomorrow, slopping out, prison food, life within a 13 foot by 7 foot cell, will be things of the past. And for some strange reason, I'm already feeling nostalgic.
>
> They tell me that my reaction is common. POWs suffer from a sense of guilt, of failure, long after they are liberated. Perhaps I'm going through something similar, but I doubt it. POWs are honourable men who think being taken prisoner is proof of some individual failure or cowardice on their part. Once free, their torment as prisoners is turned into guilt.
>
> This could hardly be the case with me. What is it, then? I could understand it if once outside I'd have had to worry about food and rent and heat. Not having to worry about money spoils many prisoners, giving them a security in jail they never had before.[47]

Occasionally, the discharged captive is helped by having powerful people who are prepared to help. Peter Thompson, leaving Broadmoor, was fortunate in having such friends:

> Nevill got me a senior management job in the City, arranging the 'decentralisation' of a merchant bank…few patients discharged from Broadmoor have had this priceless advantage of influential friends to get them work suited to their abilities. Without them, I should probably still be washing up in a transport café somewhere.[48]

Whatever the circumstances, the individual is faced with problems which many find as great as the experience of imprisonment itself.

Both during imprisonment and especially upon release, people worry about their appearance and the state of their bodies. American survivors of the Vietnamese prison camps had all of these fears. These are the feelings of John McCain, returning from Vietnam:

> Of course, we expected it would take much longer to shake off entirely the effects of our experiences in prison. Many of us were returning with injuries, and at best it would take some time for our physical rehabilitation to make satisfactory progress. I worried that my injuries might never heal properly, having been left untreated for so many years, and that I might never be allowed to fly again or perhaps even remain in the Navy. I faced a difficult period of rehabilitation, and I was for a long time uncertain that I would ever regain flight status. Although I never regained full mobility in my arms and leg, I did recover, thanks to my patient family and a remarkably determined physical therapist, and I eventually flew again.
>
> Neither did we expect to soon forget the long years of anguish we had suffered under our captors' 'humane and lenient' treatment. A few men never recovered. These were the last, tragic casualties in a long, bitter war. But most of us healed from our wounds, the physical and spiritual ones, and have lived happy and productive lives since.[49]

As may be expected, captives leaving the Gulag had additional problems. Anne Applebaum writes how prisoners were released in such numbers after the death of Stalin that there was not anything like enough transport to take them away from the camps. Furthermore, if they survived the experience of getting home, they found life impossible. They were still stigmatised, families had broken up and the process of formal 'rehabilitation' was labyrinthine, attended by stress, stolid bureaucracy and intolerable uncertainty about the result.[50]

In addition to such problems, those discharged from the Soviet Gulag must have found it especially difficult for another reason. They not only were to find themselves in a world of turmoil, but there was also a chance that they would be re-arrested. Their feeling was summed up by Gennady Andreev-Khomiakov, who was released in the 1930s:

> I imagined that I would be dancing instead of walking, that when I finally got my freedom I'd be drunk with it. But when I was actually released, I felt none of this. I walked through the gates and past the last guard, experiencing no happiness or sense of uplift.[51]

It may be noted that some prisoners' last experience of prison before they leave remind us, and them for the last time, of just how barbaric some systems are:

> 'The rivet, turn the rivet first...' ordered the senior smith. 'Hold it steady, that's right. Now hit it with the hammer...'
> The fetters fell to the ground. I picked them up. I wanted to hold them in my hand, to have a last look at them. Already I could hardly believe they had ever been on my legs at all.[52]

There is another seemingly strange difficulty facing the captive on release. During the time of being locked up, there may develop a feeling of worthlessness. But captivity also induces the contradictory notion, a sense of worth, excellence even, brought on by what is seen as the degenerate and seemingly inferior company around him. An American prisoner illustrates this. 'Bo Bo' had been convinced that he could make a living as a professional boxer on release:

> Bo Bo was released. He lasted exactly two months. Then he came back. It was the usual story. He couldn't find a job; he ran into his former delinquent companions; the squares wouldn't accept him; he was bored; the parole agent was hounding him; the police were dogging him because he had once pushed heroin – if there was an excuse for failing parole, Bo Bo had it. But what he didn't say, and what was probably closer to the truth, was that simply he had a good deal more status in the penitentiary

than he did outside. Inside everyone knew him; outside he was nobody. The Parole Board was right; Bo Bo had been living in a dream world.[53]

After interviewing 100 'white-collar' prisoners over a long period of time, Bryan Breed concludes that 'prison is the biggest dream factory in the world'. By this, he means that:

> Because of the enforced step back from society and the fact that the only realities are the fence around the prison, the warders who give orders minute by minute, there is no real sense of what it is like out there...this gives them an unreal expectation of what will happen to them when they leave the gates.[54]

Such fantasies include a belief that a job is waiting, which may or not be the case.

Mark Benney engaged in fantasy with his friend, Maurice. Just before his release from Borstal, he:

> painted a future for myself in Turneresque vagueness and colour. I would meet Maurice in London after I had returned from sea, and together we would steal thousands of pounds. We would share a luxurious flat, run our own Bentley, have women, actresses... I'd have my bedroom full of those Chinese jade things I had been so keen on as a kid, and I'd buy an expensive saxophone and play it at parties. We'd travel: stay in expensive Continental hotels.[55]

Later, in prison when he was older, he reflects again on release with a mixture of fantasy and realism:

> Discharge from prison is not always the lyrical experience which people unacquainted with prisons imagine it to be. Indeed for most prisoners it is not a transition from captivity to liberty so much as a transition from security to insecurity. Fear for the future dampens considerably the first transports of release.

Dreaming over many books in my cell, I had gradually lost touch with reality. The future, where I had thought about it, had been pictured in terms of the belle-lettrist. I would earn a modest living by writing essays and short stories, I would read, I would attend an occasional concert, theatre, ballet, I would enjoy the company of a small select circle of cultured men and women. My enthusiasm left no room for doubts; literature would solve all my difficulties.[56]

Some advanced penal systems have tried to establish a form of aftercare, based upon the commonplace recognition that the prisoner has to face often insuperable problems. Unfortunately, the recorded experience of such arrangements is not usually creditable.

Walter Musgrave speaks for the generality of British prisoners when he relates a vivid, convincing and depressing set of experiences at the then National Assistance Board, the government agency designed to alleviate poverty. He soon begins the depressing round of begging: 'I had been very slow to realise that my sentence did not begin when I was led in handcuffs from the Court to Wormwood Scrubs, but on my release.'[57]

This is a sample of the conversations which took place between Musgrave and the Board officials:

'Sit down, Mr. Musgrave. I understand from my colleague that you have taken accommodation at Five Guineas weekly for bed and breakfast. I must make it clear that such an exorbitant charge far exceeds the Board's scale.'

'I did NOT take this accommodation,' I retorted in a tone of exasperation, 'it was arranged for me by Mr. Gerrard who must surely know your regulations'.

'But you should have declined the offer, Mr. Musgrave. You should have declined it the moment you were informed of the heavy expense.'

'How could I on a Saturday?' I demanded, 'do you seriously expect me to sleep on the beach in mid-winter and to risk being picked up for vagrancy?'

'There is no advantage in being ridiculous, Mr. Musgrave. Quite apart from the de luxe area you have chosen we do not care to encourage prepared meals.'[58]

During the existence of the English Borstal system, there was an organisation called the Borstal Association or Borstal Aftercare. Jack Gordon was discharged from Feltham Borstal and expresses his profound gratitude to the system for helping him to gain the tools to stay out of trouble. But, when he reported to the Association, he found a gap between the stated aims and the practice of the organisation:

I had to see the chief official in charge of the Association and get introduced to my 'guardian'. I disliked the former on sight. His manner was all wrong. He seemed a snob doling out charity with an air of lofty superiority. I had learned at Borstal to respond to kindness, and here I sensed a feeling of hostility, mechanical advice, stock-phrased warnings, and lack of genuine interest. Red tape, a sickly handshake, and a cynical 'good-luck' all aroused in me a dislike of the very office building, and even of Borstal itself, and killed my happy thought of freedom... No boy with any spirit submits to what was doled out to me in that office, and I left it hoping never to see a sight of it or its officials again.[59]

His experience was not modified by later encounters.

Rupert Croft-Cooke is dismissive of the arrangement to help prisoners on release. He quotes from a government publication which mentions 'help and assistance': This finds expression in various ways – assistance towards securing employment; tools for the trade; rent for lodgings; clothing or financial aid towards immediate needs.

But, he goes on to claim:

The fact is that for a man leaving a prison like Wormwood Scrubs after a sentence of under three years, nothing whatever is done. If he can successfully argue the necessity for it he may be given his fare back to the town in which he was arrested and if he has a good story he might get fifteen shillings or a pound with which to re-establish his home, re-equip himself with clothes and tools and keep his wife and children until he can start earning again, since they will no longer be supported by Public Assistance.[60]

With his social background, Croft-Cooke simply moved back into the rather distinguished society which he had left. One of those who visited him in prison was Tom Driberg, at the time a very well-known Member of Parliament. On the night of his release, his friends held a party at which the actress Hermione Baddeley was present.[61]

D'Harcourt summarises all the several feelings and emotions of the released captive in this ultimate analysis of his experience after release. Like so many others, he cannot be excited by the end of a terrible experience:

> After five days I remember registering the thought that I should be making enquiries about being repatriated. With no enthusiasm whatsoever, no interest even, I got up and walked over to the main watchtower where the Americans had set up their H.Q.
> … As some degree of feeling had begun to flow again in my mind, I felt a kind of antagonism towards the world around me. It was as though I felt that I could never enter it or be part of it again, and the feeling made me resentful. Everybody and everything seemed to emphasise my 'differentness'. I almost wanted to be back in Buchenwald where I fitted in.[62]

D'Harcourt went to his sister's wedding, but could not join in: 'the life the ordinary Frenchman was living seemed sham, trivial, absurd, compared with life in the camp. The way of the normal world was an insult and a mockery to those who lived and died in Buchenwald.'[63]

As he recovered, he began a mad round of mindless pleasure seeking: 'It was not appetite, but a kind of obsessive greed.' He married a girl of 17 but 'there was no happiness in it and it inevitably failed'. His friends too went through the same experience: the drugs and drink killed many of them, 'as I suspect, many of them had hoped'. D'Harcourt concludes that it was: 'the first lesson of the camp – that it made beasts of some men and saints of others. And the second lesson of the camp is that it is hard to predict who will be the saint and who the beast when the time of trial comes.'[64] He wrote:

> The camp showed me that a man's real enemies are not ranged against him along the borders of a hostile company; they are often among his own people, indeed, within his own mind. The worst enemies are hate, and greed, and cruelty. The real enemy is within.[65]

Taki felt something of the same reluctance to socialise:

> That evening Bill Buckley and his son Christopher gave a large dinner party intended to welcome me back to the lawful world. At the last minute I got cold feet and phoned Christopher, who along with being one of my closest friends was also my best man when I married Alexandra. He dismissed my fears by reminding me that I would be among people who liked me.[66]

Eugene Heimler, a former Concentration Camp inmate, who worked as a psychiatric social worker after the Second World War, has a view, similar in one respect to d'Harcourt's and different in another. Both are concerned with sex and marriage. Both agree that after release, captives engage in frenetic sexual activity: Heimler uses the word 'promiscuity'. Where they differ is in behaviour about marriage. D'Harcourt talks about chronic breakdown, including his own, but in Heimler's experience: 'There are few broken marriages, though, because they are frightened to break up any relationship.'[67]

John Hoskison had to face the usual traumas upon release. He was surprised by the forgiveness he met from people he had known, but nothing surprised him more than the remarkable communication he had from the wife of the man he had killed:

> One day I received a letter. It had been sent from the wife of the man who had been killed in the accident. In the kindest words she suggested it might be a good idea to meet up – for both our sakes.
>
> Not long ago, on a sunny summer day, we met in the beautiful grounds of Wisley Gardens, near Guildford. At first we walked among the blossoming flowers but eventually we found a deserted wooden bench and sat down. It was so peaceful.
>
> I had already witnessed her compassion when she pleaded for leniency at my trial. But that afternoon she went a step further. In a voice that was so calm it took me aback, she explained that she and her family were now coping well. She said it was time to look to the future. Turning towards me, with a look of absolute sincerity, she asked me to do the same. The warmth and reassuring smile she bathed me with became the gateway to my future.
>
> For all the effort I had put in, over the long months, to get better, in the blink of an eye my life was given back to me. I was, and am truly humbled.
>
> I write these words as a free man.[68]

Nevertheless, like having to cope with being locked up in the first place, there is no avoiding the aftermath of release. The beginning of that last hurdle is summed up by Jeremy Bryan on his discharge from a psychiatric hospital:

> A last wave, and you will be at the front door. It will be unlocked and opened and you will pass through it. Then it will swing to and, audibly, be locked behind you.
>
> The locked door that stands between two worlds.
>
> And you know them both.[69]

Notes

1. Bryan *op. cit.* pp.262–263.
2. Albazyan, Alaa'. 'The Light of Freedom' in Hashim *op. cit.* pp.75–76.
3. *Ibid.* p.76.
4. *Ibid.*
5. James *The Home Stretch op. cit.* p.17.
6. *Ibid.* p.57.
7. Thompson, Peter. *Bound for Broadmoor*, quoting a Report of the Estimates Committee. p.113.
8. *Ibid.* pp.112–113.
9. Willetts *op. cit.* pp.6–7.
10. Buxton *et al. op. cit.* p.76.
11. Norman *op. cit.* p.81.
12. *Ibid.* p.191.
13. Williams *et al. op. cit.* p.108.
14. Carlen *Criminal Women op. cit.* p.169.
15. *Ibid.*
16. Applebaum *op. cit.* p.458.
17. Herling *op. cit.* pp.109–110.
18. Bryan *op. cit.* p.209.
19. Thompson *op. cit.* p.9.
20. *Ibid.* p.136.
21. Beer *op. cit.* pp.154–155.
22. Levi *op. cit.* p.378.
23. Lilje *op. cit.* p.50.
24. Braddon *op. cit.* p.65.
25. *Ibid. op. cit.* p.65.
26. *Ibid.* p.59.
27. Franklin, Colin. 'Hospital Sentence' in Mikes *op. cit.* p.190.
28. James *The Home Stretch op. cit.* pp.59–60.
29. *Ibid.* p.60.
30. Zeno *op. cit.* pp.186–205.
31. Stratton *op. cit.* p.131.
32. Barker *op. cit.* p.187.
33. *Ibid.* p.152.
34. Watt *op. cit.* p.141.
35. *Ibid.* p.151.
36. Quillen *op. cit.* p.333.
37. Wildeblood *op. cit.* p.172.
38. *Ibid.* p.176.
39. Dodge *op. cit.* p.142.
40. *Ibid.* pp.142–143.
41. Carlen *Criminal Women op. cit.* p.135.
42. James *The Home Stretch op. cit.* pp.177–178.

43. Mathiesen *op. cit.* p.73.

44. McNally, Ward. *Man from Zero.* p.158.

45. WBN *op. cit.* p.305.

46. Musgrave *op. cit.* p.136.

47. Taki *op. cit.* p.200.

48. Thompson *op. cit.* p.136.

49. McCain *op. cit.* p.345.

50. See Applebaum *op. cit.* chapter 25 for a full account.

51. *Ibid.* p.458.

52. Dostoevsky *op. cit.* p.356.

53. Manocchio *et al. op. cit.* p.150.

54. Breed *op. cit.* p.83.

55. Benney *op. cit.* p.243.

56. *Ibid.* pp.288–289.

57. Musgrave *op. cit.* p.145.

58. *Ibid.*

59. Gordon J.W. *op. cit.* pp.211–212.

60. Croft-Cooke *op. cit.* pp.238–239.

61. *Ibid.* p.250.

62. d'Harcourt *op. cit.* pp.181–183.

63. *Ibid.* pp.183–184.

64. *Ibid.* pp.184–185.

65. *Ibid.* p.186.

66. Taki *op. cit.* p.205.

67. Heimler *op. cit.* p.22.

68. Hoskison *op. cit.* pp.210–211.

69. Bryan *op. cit.* p.213.

Glossary

BOR British Other Ranks.

Cabsulih A system used by Palestinian prisoners for getting messages out of prison.

Cadre In China, a powerful public official.

Chokey In England, the punishment wing.

Coloured In the especial context of South Africa, the official term in Apartheid South Africa for a person of mixed race. In the especial of South Africa, context

CT (Corrective Training) A sentence introduced in England in 1948, now defunct.

ICRC International Committee of the Red Cross.

IRA Irish Republican Army.

Kempeitai Japanese Military Police.

Kite In American prisons, a clandestine letter.

Lag In British prison jargon, a prisoner.

Laogai Chinese euphemism meaning remoulding through labour brigades.

MO Medical Officer.

Nonce In British prisons, a child molester.

N'Yaarker In the Confederate Prisons in America, a term of abuse used by the Northern prisoners of those who were thieves and gangsters in the prison.

Peter In British prisons, a cell.

PRC People's Republic of China.

Red band In British prisons, a trusted prisoner.

***Schutzstaffel* (SS)** Extremely powerful organisation who, for most of the existence of the Nazi system, ran the Concentration Camps.

Screw British slang term for a prison officer.

Slopping out In British prisons, emptying a chamber pot.

Snout British slang for tobacco.

Stroke Trusted prisoner leader in English prisons.

***Sturm-Abteilungen* (SA)** Storm Divisions. Deadly rivals of the SS, they were involved in the initial stages of administration of the Concentration Camps.

Twirl In England, prison slang for a uniformed officer.

Urki (singular *Urka*) Term used to describe criminal (as opposed to political) prisoners in Russian prisons.

WRNS Women's Royal Naval Service.

Bibliography

Abbott, J.H. (1981) *In the Belly of the Beast*. New York: Random House.

Albazyan, Alaa' (2013) 'The Light of Freedom.' In Norma Hashim (ed.) *The Prisoners' Diaries: Palestinian Voices from the Israeli Gulag*. London: Islamic Rights Commission.

Albis, Wafa (2013) 'A Martyr.' In Norma Hashim (ed.) *The Prisoners' Diaries: Palestinian Voices from the Israeli Gulag*. London: Islamic Rights Commission.

Alleyn, Richard (2012) 'Prison Guards Caught Having "Inappropriate Relationships" with Inmates.' *The Daily Telegraph*, 8 June 2012.

Amnesty International Campaign on the United States (1999) *'Not Part of My Sentence': Violation of the Human Rights of Women in Custody*. Chicago, IL: Amnesty International.

Applebaum, Anne (2003) *Gulag: A History of the Soviet Camps*. London: Allen Lane.

Baker, Abeer and Matar, Anat (eds) (2011) *Threat: Palestinian Political Prisoners in Israel*. London: Pluto Press.

Baker, J.E. (1974) *The Right to Participate: Inmate Involvement in Prison Administration*. New Jersey: The Scarecrow Press.

Barker, A.J. (1974) *Behind Barbed Wire*. London: Batsford.

Beer, Daniel (2016) *The House of the Dead: Siberian Exile under the Tsars*. London: Allen Lane and Penguin.

Begin, Menachem (1977) *White Nights: The Story of a Prisoner in Russia*. New York: Harper and Row. (Original work published 1957.)

Behan, Brendan (1990) *Borstal Boy*. London: Arrow Books. (Original work published 1958.)

Benney, Mark (1936) *Low Company: Describing the Evolution of a Burglar*. London: Peter Davies.

Bone, Edith (1969) 'Solitary Confinement.' In Guthrie Moir (ed.) *Beyond Hatred*. Cambridge: Lutterworth.

Bonhoeffer, Dietrich (1970) *Letters and Papers from Prison.* London: Collins Fontana. (Original work published in English 1953).

Bourke, Seán (1971) *The Springing of George Blake.* London: Mayflower Books. (Original work published 1970).

Braddon, Russell (1963) 'Surrender, Like Marriage.' In George Mikes (ed.) *Prison: A Symposium.* London: Routledge and Kegan Paul.

Breed, Brian (1979) *White Collar Bird: The White Collar Man in Prison and His Problems.* London: John Clare Books.

Bryan, Helen (1953) *Inside.* Boston, MA: Houghton Mifflin Co.

Bryan, Jeremy (1963) 'True Madness.' In George Mikes (ed.) *Prison: A Symposium.* London: Routledge and Kegan Paul.

Burmeister, Werner (1969) 'Enemy Alien.' In Guthrie Moir (ed.) *Beyond Hatred.* Cambridge: Lutterworth.

Buxton, Jane and Turner, Margaret (1962) *Gate Fever.* London: The Cresset Press.

Carlen, Pat (1998) *Sledgehammer: Women's Imprisonment at the Millenium.* London: Macmillan.

Carlen, Pat (ed.) (1985) *Criminal Women: Autobiographical Accounts.* Cambridge: Polity Press.

Chamberlain, Rudolph W. (1936) *There is No Truce: A Life of Thomas Osborne.* London: George Routledge and Son.

Chang, Dae H. and Armstrong, Warren B. (1972) *The Prison: Voices from the Inside.* Cambridge, MA: Schenkman Publishing.

Charpentier, Armand (1935) *The Dreyfus Case* (translated by J. Lewis May). London: Geoffrey Bles.

Chekhov, Anton (1989) *The Island of Sakhalin.* London: The Folio Society. (Original work published 1895.)

Clarke, T.J. (1922) *Glimpses of an Irish Felon's Prison Life.* Dublin and London: Maunsel and Roberts Ltd.

Cohen, Stanley and Taylor, Laurie (1972) *Psychological Survival: The Experience of Long-Term Imprisonment.* London: Penguin.

Coogan, Tim Pat (2002) *On the Blanket: The Inside Story of the IRA Prisoners' 'Dirty Protest'.* London: Palgrave Macmillan.

Croft-Cooke, Rupert (1955) *The Verdict of You All.* London: Secker and Warburg.

Cronin, Harley (1967) *The Screw Turns.* London: John Long.

Davis, Angela (1971) 'Lessons from Attica to Soledad.' *New York Times,* 8 October 1971.

Deacon, Harriet (ed.) (1996) *The Island: A History of Robben Island 1488–1990.* University of the Western Cape, Bellville: Mayibuye Books.

Devlin, Angela and Devlin, Tim (1998) *Anybody's Nightmare.* London: Taverner Publications.

d'Harcourt, Pierre (1967) *The Real Enemy*. New York: Longmans.

Dodge, L. Mara (2006) *'Whores and Thieves of the Worst Kind': A Study of Women, Crime, and Prisons, 1835–2000*. Dekalb, IL: Northern Illinois University Press.

Dostoevsky, Fyodor (1985) *The House of the Dead* (translated with an introduction by David McDuff). London: Penguin. (Original work published in 1860–62.)

Duffy, Clinton (1958) *San Quentin: The Dramatic Story of an American Penitentiary*. London: Four Square Books. (Original work published in 1951.)

El Sa'adawi, Nawal (1986) *Memoirs from the Women's Prison* (translated by Marilyn Booth). London: The Women's Press.

Ellmann, Richard (1987) *Oscar Wilde*. London: Hamish Hamilton.

Elstob, Peter (1939) *Spanish Prisoner*. London: Macmillan.

Flanagan, Richard (2014) *The Narrow Road to the Deep North*. London: Chatto and Windus.

Fox, Sir Lionel (1952) *The English Prison and Borstal Systems*. London: Routledge and Kegan Paul.

Franklin, Colin (1963) 'Hospital Sentence.' In George Mikes (ed.) *Prison: A Symposium*. London: Routledge and Kegan.

Giallombardo, Rose (1966) *Society of Women: A Study of a Women's Prison*. New York: John Wiley and Sons.

Goffman, Erving (1961) *Asylums: Essays on the Social Situation of Mental Patients and Other Inmates*. New York: Anchor Books.

Gordon, Ernest (1969) 'No Hatred in My Heart.' In Guthrie Moir (ed.) *Beyond Hatred*. Cambridge: Lutterworth.

Gordon, J.W. (1932) *Borstalians*. London: Martin Hopkinson.

Goss, Warren Lee (1869) *The Soldier's Story of His Captivity at Andersonville, Belle Isle, and Other Rebel Prisons*. Boston, MA: Lee and Shepard. (This copy from the Internet Archive. The original is irreparably deteriorated.)

Grünhut, M. (1948) *Penal Reform*. Oxford: Clarendon Press.

Harel, Alon (2011) 'Who is a Security Prisoner and Why? An Examination of the Legality of Prison Regulations Governing Security Prisoners.' In Abeer Baker and Anat Matar (eds) *Threat: Palestinian Political Prisoners in Israel*. London: Pluto Press.

Hashim, Norma (2013) *The Prisoners' Diaries: Palestinian Voices from the Israeli Gulag*. London: Islamic Rights Commission.

Havers, R.P.W. (2003) *Reassessing the Japanese Prisoner of War Experience: The Changi POW Camp Singapore, 1942–5*. Abingdon: Routledge Curzon.

Hawkins, Gordon (1976) *The Prison: Policy and Practice*. Chicago, IL: University of Chicago Press.

Heimler, Eugene (1963) 'Children of Auschwitz.' In George Mikes (ed.) *Prison: A Symposium*. London: Routledge and Kegan Paul.

Helm, Sarah (2015) *If this is a Woman: Inside Ravensbrück: Hitler's Concentration Camp for Women*. London: Little, Brown.

Herling, Gustav (1952) *A World Apart*. New York: New American Library.

Hickman, Joseph (2015) *Murder at Camp Delta: A Staff Sergeant's Pursuit of the Truth about Guantánamo Bay*. London: Simon and Schuster.

Hood, Stuart (1969) 'The Narrow Grave.' In Guthrie Moir (ed.) *Beyond Hatred*. Cambridge: Lutterworth.

Hoskison, John (1988) *Inside: One Man's Experience of Prison*. London: John Murray.

Hubbell, John G. in association with Jones, Andrew and Tomlinson, Kenneth Y. (1976) *P.O.W: A Definitive History of the American Prisoner-of-War Experience in Vietnam, 1964–1973*. New York: Reader's Digest Press.

Hutheesing, Krishna Nehru (1963) 'In British Hands.' In George Mikes (ed.) *Prison: A Symposium*. London: Routledge and Kegan Paul.

Ignotus, Paul (1963) 'Assisted by Thugs.' In George Mikes (ed.) *Prison: A Symposium*. London: Routledge and Kegan Paul.

Israeli Information Center for Human Rights in the Occupied Territories (2018) 3 January. www.btselem.org/statistics/detainees_and_prisoners

Jackson, George (1970) *Soledad Brother: The Prison Letters of George Jackson*. Chicago, IL: Lawrence Hill Books.

James, Erwin (2003) *A Life Inside: A Prisoner's Notebook*. London: Atlantic Books.

James, Erwin (2005) *The Home Stretch: From Prison to Parole*. London: Atlantic Books.

Jeanty-Raven, M.H. (1969) 'Without Frontiers.' In Guthrie Moir (ed.) *Beyond Hatred*. Cambridge: Lutterworth.

Jessop, A. (ed.) (1879) *The Economy of the Fleete*. London: Camden Society.

Josey, Alex (1953) *Pulau Senang: The Experiment that Failed*. Singapore: Times Books International.

Kaneko, Fumiko (1991) *The Prison Memoirs of a Japanese Woman* (translated by Jean Inglis). New York and London: ME Sharpe.

Ketchum, J. Davidson (1965) *Ruhleben: A Prison Camp Society*. Toronto: University of Toronto Press.

Knight, Etheridge (1970) *Black Voices from Prison*. New York: Pathfinder Press.

Koestler, Arthur (1963) 'A Personal Affair.' In George Mikes (ed.) *Prison: A Symposium*. London: Routledge and Kegan Paul.

Krausnick, Helmut and Broszat, Martin (1970) *Anatomy of the SS State*. London: Paladin. (Original work published in English in 1968.)

Kropotkin, Peter (1971) *In Russian and French Prisons*. New York: Schoken Books. (Original work published 1887.)

Langer, Felicia (1975) *With My Own Eyes: Israel and the Occupied Territories 1967–1973.* London: Ithaca Press.

Lawrence, T.E. (1978) *The Mint.* London: Penguin Books. (Original work published 1955.)

Leopold, Nathan (1960) *Life+99 years.* London: Four Square Books. (Original work published 1958.)

Levi, Primo (1979) *If this is a Man* and *The Truce.* London: Penguin. (Combined volume.)

Lilje, Hanns (1963) 'The Final Act.' In Guthrie Moir (ed.) *Beyond Hatred.* Cambridge: Lutterworth.

Lytton, Constance (1988) *Prisons and Prisoners: The Stirring Testimony of a Suffragette.* London: Virago. (Original work published 1914.)

Macartney, Wilfred F.R. (1936) *Walls Have Mouths.* London: Victor Gollancz (Left Book Club).

MacDonald, Morag (1998) 'Mandatory Drug Testing in Prisons.' *Prison Service Journal 115, 22–25.*

MacKenzie, K.P. (1954) *Operation Rangoon Jail.* London: Christopher Johnson.

Maine, G.F. (ed.) (1948) *The Works of Oscar Wilde.* London: Collins.

Mandela, Nelson (1994) *Long Walk to Freedom.* London: Little Brown & Co.

Manocchio, Anthony J. and Dunn, Jimmy (1970) *The Time Game: Two Views of a Prison.* Thousand Oaks, CA: Sage Publications.

Mathiesen, Thomas (1965) *The Defences of the Weak: A Sociological Study of a Norwegian Correctional Institution.* London: Tavistock Publications.

McCain, John with Salter, Mark (1999) *Faith of My Fathers.* New York: Random House.

McElroy, John (2016) *Andersonville: A Story of Rebel Military Prisons.* Los Angeles, CA: Enhanced Media. (Original work published in 1879.)

McNally, Ward (1973) *Man from Zero.* Melbourne: Nelson.

Mencía, Mario (1993) *The Fertile Prison: Fidel Castro in Batista's Jails.* Melbourne: Ocean Press.

Mikes, George (ed.) (1963) *Prison: A Symposium.* London: Routledge and Kegan Paul.

Mitford, Jessica (1974) *The American Prison Business.* London: George Allen and Unwin. (Original work published 1971 under the title *Kind and Usual Punishment.*)

Moir, Guthrie (ed.) (1969) *Beyond Hatred.* Cambridge: Lutterworth.

Morrison, Leonard Haslett (1969) 'Reality Regained.' In Guthrie Moir (ed.) *Beyond Hatred.* Cambridge: Lutterworth.

Musgrave, Walter (1963) 'Warrant to Nowhere.' In George Mikes (ed.) *Prison: A Symposium.* London: Routledge and Kegan Paul.

Nahla, Abdo (2011) 'Palestinian Women Political Prisoners and the Israeli State.' In Abeer Baker and Anat Matar (eds) *Threat: Palestinian Political Prisoners in Israel.* London: Pluto Press.

Nashif, Esmail (2008) *Palestinian Political Prisoners: Identity and Community.* London: Routledge.

New York State Special Commission on Attica (1972) *Attica: The Official Report of the New York State Special Commission on Attica.* New York: Bantam Books.

Norman, Frank (1958) *Bang to Rights* London: Secker and Warburg.

Nunneley, John (ed.) (1998) *Tales from the Burma Campaign 1942–1945.* Petersham: Burma Campaign Fellowship Group.

Pallister, Davis (2002) 'Prison Chief Acts against Bullying Lesbian Officers.' *The Guardian,* 16 March 2002.

Pallot, Judith (2002) 'Forced Labour for Forestry: The Twentieth-Century History of Colonisation and Settlement in the North of Perm Oblast.' *Europe-Asia Studies 54,* 7, 1055–1083.

Paterson, Alexander (1911) *Our Prisons.* London: Hugh Rees.

Péan, Charles (1953) *The Conquest of Devil's Island.* London: Max Parrish.

Pidd, Helen and Allison, Eric (2015) 'Gay Couple Serving Life Sentences to Marry in Prison.' *The Guardian,* 21 February 2015.

Playfair, Giles (1971) *The Punitive Obsession.* London: Gollancz.

Quillen, Jim (1991) *Inside Alcatraz: My Time on the Rock.* London: Arrow Books.

Red Collar Man (1937) *Chokey.* London: Victor Gollancz.

Rinser, Luise (1987) *Prison Journal* (translated by Hulse). London: Michael Macmillan.

Risner, Robinson (1973) *The Passing of the Night: My Seven Years as a Prisoner of the North Vietnamese.* New York: Random House.

Rosenfeld, Maya (2011) 'The Centrality of the Prisoners' Movement to the Palestinian Occupation: A Historical Perspective.' In Abeer Baker and Anat Matar (eds) *Threat: Palestinian Political Prisoners in Israel.* London: Pluto Press.

Ross, Luana (1998) *Inventing the Savage: The Social Constructions of Native American Criminality.* Austin, TX: University of Texas Press.

Rossiter, Ray S. (1998) 'An Unforgettable Experience.' In John Nunneley (ed.) *Tales from the Burma Campaign 1942–1945.* Petersham: Burma Campaign Fellowship Group.

Rutledge, Dom Denys (1966) *The Complete Monk: Vocation of the Monastic Order.* London: Routledge and Kegan Paul.

Sandhu, S. (2016) 'HMP Ranby Prisoners "Muscle into" Office to Take Back Legal Highs, Report Finds'. *The Independent,* 25 February 2016.

Saro-Wiwa, Ken (1995) *A Month and a Day: A Detention Diary.* London: Penguin.

Scheffler, Judith A. (2002) *Wall Tappings: An International Anthology of Women's Prison Writings 200 to the Present.* New York: The Feminist Press at the City University of New York. (Original work published 1986.)

Schwan, Anne (2014) *Convict Voices: Women, Class, and Writing about Prison in Nineteenth-Century England.* Lebanon, NH: University of New Hampshire Press.

Sfard, Michael (2011) 'Devils' Island: The Transfer of Palestinian Detainees into Prisons within Israel.' In Abeer Baker and Anat Matar (eds) *Threat: Palestinian Political Prisoners in Israel*. London: Pluto Press.

Shalamov, Varlam (1990) *Kolyma Tales* (translated by John Glad). London: Penguin. (First published in English 1980.)

Shaw, A.G.L. (1966) *Convicts and the Colonies: A Study of Penal Transportation from Great Britain and Ireland to Australia and Other Parts of the British Empire*. London: Faber and Faber.

Slahi, Mohamedou Ould (2015) *Guantánamo Diary*. Edinburgh: Canongate.

Solzhenitsyn, Alexander (1974) *The Gulag Archipelago 1918–1956: An Experiment in Literary Investigation 1–11* (translated by Thomas P. Whitney). London: Book Club Associates. (Original work published 1973.)

Stanton, Alfred H. and Schwarz, Morris S. (1954) *The Mental Hospital: A Study of Institutional Participation in Psychiatric Illness and Treatment*. New York: New York Basic Books.

Steiner, Jesse F. and Brown, Roy M. (1970) *The North Carolina Chain Gang: A Study of County Convict Road Work*. Westport, CT: Negro Universities Press. (Original work published 1927.)

Stewart, Ian McD. G. (1969) 'What Sort of Charity?' In Guthrie Moir (ed.) *Beyond Hatred*. Cambridge: Lutterworth.

Stratton, Brian (1973) *Who Guards the Guards?* London: North London Group of PROP (Preservation of the Rights of Prisoners).

Taki, (Theodoracopulos) (1991) *Nothing to Declare: Prison Memoirs*. London: Viking.

Thilo, Hans-Joachim (1969) 'The Christian Church Comes to Life.' In Guthrie Moir (ed.) *Beyond Hatred*. Cambridge: Lutterworth.

Thomas, J.E. (1972) *The English Prison Officer Since 1850: A Study in Conflict*. London: Routledge and Kegan Paul.

Thomas, J.E. (1988) *House of Care: Prisons and Prisoners in England 1500–1800*. Nottingham: University of Nottingham.

Thomas, J.E. (2017) *The English Prison Officer 1850–1970: A Study in Conflict*. Stroud: Fonthill Media.

Thomas, J.E. and Stewart, Alex (1978) *Imprisonment in Western Australia: Evolution, Theory and Practice*. Perth: University of Western Australia Press.

Thompson, Peter (1972) *Bound for Broadmoor*. London: Hodder and Stoughton.

Watt, Ian (1969) 'The Liberty of the Prison.' In Guthrie Moir (ed.) *Beyond Hatred*. Cambridge: Lutterworth.

WBN, (Lord William Nevill) (1903) *Penal Servitude*. London: Heinemann.

Webb, Sidney and Webb, Beatrice (1963) *English Prisons under Local Government*. London: Frank Cass and Co. (Original work published 1922.)

White, Jerry (2016) *Mansions of Misery: A Biography of the Marshalsea Debtors' Prison.* London: The Bodley Head.

Wildeblood, Peter (1957) *Against the Law.* London: Penguin Books. (Original work published 1955.)

Willetts, Phoebe (1965) *Invisible Bars.* Peterborough: Epworth Press.

Williams, Philip F. and Wu, Yenna (2004) *The Great Wall of Confinement: The Chinese Prison Camp through Contemporary Fiction and Reportage.* Oakland, CA: University of California Press.

Wilson, A.N. (2002) *The Victorians.* London: Hutchinson.

Wood, Stuart (1932) *Shades of the Prison House: A Personal Memoir.* London: Williams and Norgate.

Zeno (1970) *Life.* London: Pan Books. (Original work published 1968.)

Subject Index

alcohol, uses of
  doctors selling to
    criminals in Russia
    161
  trafficking by powerful
    prisoners in the
    US 199
  used to build a power
    base in the US 119
  used to incriminate
    rivals in
    Concentration
    Camps 196
  women change partners
    for more vodka in
    Russia 84
aliens in Britain
  deported to Canada in
    World War 11, 35,
    185–186
Andersonville,
    Confederate POW
    camp
  abuse by prisoners of
    other prisoners
    189
  cruelty 146–147
  disease 307
  informers 125
  staff member Captain
    Wirz executed 147
  vermin 272
Attica Prison, New York
  riot 356–357

Auschwitz Concentration
    Camp
  'arbeit macht frei' 20
  extermination camp
    190
  Ravensbrück to provide
    kapos 195
  tobacco as currency 83

Bagne, French word for
    penal colony in
    Guiana 258
Bagram, American base in
    Afghanistan 235–236
Blake, George
  Russian spy 63–64, 353
  see also Wormwood
    Scrubs Prison
Boer Wars, Concentration
    Camps 238
boredom
  on combatting 65–70,
    72
Borstal Association/
    Aftercare 406
Borstal system 155–156
Broadmoor Special
    Hospital 386, 390,
    391, 401
Brockway, Z.R., prison
    reformer 201
  see also captives given
    authority as part of
    reform programme

Brown, H. Rap, American
    prisoner 359
Buchenwald
    Concentration Camp
  children 127
  'criminal' prisoners 377,
    379
  kapos 191ff.
  post-war use by
    Russians 253
  slave labour 190
Burma Railway
  adjustment by prisoners
    52, 63
  release 396
  description and
    numbers of
    prisoners 244
  futility of 52, 254
  kind treatment 63,
    166–167
  survival 63, 62

captives abusing their
    authority
  Andersonville
    executions ordered
    officially by
    prisoners 188–189
  Borstal 181, 183ff.
  Buchenwald kapos
    191ff.
  China 180
  Cuba 187

Names Index